LEAVING THE NORTH

Leaving the North

Migration and Memory, Northern Ireland 1921–2011

JOHANNE DEVLIN TREW

LIVERPOOL UNIVERSITY PRESS

First published in 2013 by
Liverpool University Press
4 Cambridge Street
Liverpool
L69 7ZU

This paperback version published 2016

British Library Cataloguing-in-Publication data
A British Library CIP record is available

ISBN 978-1-84631-940-2 cased
ISBN 978-1-78138-306-3 limp

Typeset in Garamond and Didot by Carnegie Book Production, Lancaster
Printed and bound by CPI Group (UK) Ltd, Croydon, CR0 4YY

Contents

For the migrant women in my maternal family line:

my grandmother, Roseena;

my mother, Margie;

and to my dear uncle,

John Devlin

who by staying at home

helped to anchor us all.

Abbreviations

BBC	British Broadcasting Corporation
CBC	Canadian Broadcasting Corporation
CRE	Commission for Racial Equality
CSO	Central Statistics Office (Dublin)
DELNI	Department of Employment and Learning Northern Ireland
DENI	Department of Education Northern Ireland
DETINI	Department of Enterprise, Trade and Investment Northern Ireland
DUP	Democratic Unionist Party
DWP	Department of Work and Pensions
ECNI	Equality Commission Northern Ireland
GAA	Gaelic Athletic Association
GB	Great Britain
HMSO	His/Her Majesty's Stationery Office
IPPR	Institute for Public Policy Research
ITV	Independent Television network
LFS	Labour Force Survey
MCMS	Mellon Centre for Migration Studies
NESC	National Economic and Social Council (Dublin)
NI	Northern Ireland
NILT	Northern Ireland Life and Times survey
NISRA	Northern Ireland Statistics and Research Agency
NINo	National Insurance Number
OFMDFM	Office of the First Minister and Deputy First Minister (Northern Ireland)
ONS	Office of National Statistics
PRONI	Public Record Office Northern Ireland
PSNI	Police Service of Northern Ireland
UCC	University College, Cork

QUB	Queen's University Belfast
RG	Registrar General (Northern Ireland)
RIC	Royal Irish Constabulary
ROI	Republic of Ireland
RUC	Royal Ulster Constabulary
SDLP	Social Democratic and Labour Party
UK	United Kingdom
VMR	Voices of Migration and Return
WRS	Worker Registration Scheme
YLT	Young Life and Times survey

List of Figures

Acknowledgements

T HIS BOOK has taken me on a very long journey, much longer than I
envisioned when starting out. Many people have helped me along and
I am particularly grateful to those who stood by me and always believed I'd
finish this book. My greatest debt is to the interviewees who contributed their
life stories to the *Voices of Migration & Return* oral archive held at the Mellon
Centre for Migration Studies. Without exception, the interviewees welcomed me
kindly and generously shared their stories, often through laughter and sometimes
through tears. It has been a joy and an enormous privilege to meet them all.
Though not all of their stories have made it into this book, each individual
contributed significantly to my knowledge about migration and I hope to
continue working with their narratives to produce further publications. Their
names or pseudonyms (to maintain confidentiality) and details of interviews are
listed with the bibliography.

I am very grateful to the funders of the research and publication. The Higher
Education Authority North South Programme for Collaborative Research, Strand
1, funded the initial research on return migration. This was followed by a
substantial research grant from the Arts & Humanities Research Council (UK)
to allow for interviewing emigrants living in Britain and Canada. I also wish
to acknowledge the very generous support of the Scotch-Irish Trust of Ulster
towards publication costs, without which it would not have been possible to
include coverage of the period from the founding of Northern Ireland in 1921
to 1945. Thanks to Alison Welsby at Liverpool University Press who has been
patient, kind and helpful, and to four anonymous reviewers who read the proposal
and manuscript at different stages and offered insightful comments that were
enormously helpful in shaping the book.

The Mellon Centre for Migration Studies in County Tyrone has been the
spiritual home of this project; my thanks above all to its staff team with whom
I have had the privilege to work as a research associate. To Dr Brian Lambkin,
Director of the Centre, my sincere gratitude for providing the humane environment
in which to learn, reflect and write about migration. To Dr Patrick Fitzgerald I
express my appreciation for the camaraderie and humour, and for being a walking
(and talking!) encyclopaedia of migration, Irish history, and many other things

besides. Brian and Paddy read each chapter, discussed ideas and generously shared their extensive knowledge. Libraries NI staff of the centre provided considerable assistance: Christine Johnston employed her in-depth knowledge of the centre's specialist migration library, alerting me to sources, obtaining items from other collections, and making helpful suggestions; Deirdre Nugent provided constant encouragement and friendship; Joe Mullan contributed his creative energy and good nature to work with me to develop the online VMR archive; Ian Nethery helped greatly in obtaining and editing the 'Bigger McDonald' photographs; librarian Chris McIvor (retired) assisted in many ways during the research stage, as did centre staff Sarah Cathers; Frank Collins; Nuala McSherry and Alastair Moran. Sincere appreciation must also go to our 'southern' partners on the *Narratives of Migration & Return* project: Dr Breda Gray; University of Limerick; Dr Piaras Mac Éinrí and Dr Caitríona Ní Laoire of University College Cork. I learned so much from you all.

The Mellon Centre for Migration Studies is located at the Ulster American Folk Park and I have had the privilege of participating with the park staff on many endeavours. Though there is not the space to mention everyone by name, I cite in particular John Gilmore; Dr Phil Mowat; Peter Kelly; Richard Hurst; John Bradley; Evelyn Cardwell; Pat O'Donnell; Liam Corry; Catherine McCullough; Fiona McClean and especially Briege McClean. Trevor Miskelly, park warden, deserves special mention for his 'daily' enquiries about my progress and for 'cheering' me on, and thanks also to Ken Boyd on security.

At Queen's University Belfast sincere appreciation is due my research supervisor, Professor Liam Kennedy, and to Professor Peter Gray for the work on the Dippam project. At the University of Ulster, Magee, I would like to acknowledge my colleagues at the School of History and the Institute of Ulster Scots Studies, in particular: Professor John Wilson; Professor Don MacRaild; Dr Frank Ferguson; Dr Billy Kelly; Dr Eamonn Ó Ciardha; Sinead Grant; Frank Carey; Dr Marie-Claire Peters; Dr Emmet O'Connor; Dr James Loughlin for advice and sources provided; and Andrew Maguire, whose PhD dissertation I've had the privilege to co-supervise. Special thanks to Magee colleagues and friends, Dr Andrea Redmond and especially Dr Philip McDermott in Sociology.

At the University of Ulster, Jordanstown, I thank *all* my colleagues in the School of Criminology, Politics and Social Policy. I particularly appreciate the support of Ruth Fee, head of school; Dr Cathy Gormley-Heenan, Director of the Institute for Research in the Social Sciences; school administrator Carol Morley; and Professor John Offer who has very tolerantly mentored me since I arrived at the school three years ago. Special mention must be made of my colleagues Dr Fiona Bloomer and Dr Jennifer Hamilton for their collegiality, support and help with juggling teaching loads. Thanks to Dr Wendy Saunderson for generously taking exam marking so I could meet my final deadline, and also to kindred spirit Dr Susan Hodgett in Sociology. Librarian Joanne Knox and library staff at Jordanstown and Magee were always helpful and obtained many vital publications for me.

Colleagues further afield have also contributed in many ways. Thanks to Patrick O'Sullivan who founded and managed the Irish Diaspora List. Special thanks to Professor Marianne Elliott, Institute of Irish Studies, University of Liverpool, for her friendship and encouragement. Ian McKeane, very sadly missed, of the Institute was enormously helpful in setting up interviews in Liverpool. Thanks also to Professor Bronwen Walter and Dr Dorothy Monekosso in England; Dr Lyndon Fraser in New Zealand; Professor Peter Toner and Denis Noel in New Brunswick; Prof. David Wilson, University of Toronto; Dr Lillis Ó Laoire of University College Galway; and filmmaker Mairead McClean in London, who has inspired me to 'visualise' my work in new ways. Every effort has been made to trace copyright for the historical images. Brian Mitchell of Derry Genealogy was instrumental in locating and dating the 'Bigger McDonald' photographs for this book which are reproduced courtesy of Libraries NI, and Deborah Harris, press officer, Belfast International Airport kindly helped locate photographs of Aldergrove. In California, thanks to Cynthia Miller of Coronado; Donna Goodner of Redlands; and Dr Nathan Gonzales of the AK Smiley Public Library in Redlands for tracking photographer Art Miller. David Shelton; GRO-Scotland and Geoff Peasah; ONS, scanned and emailed census tables; John Toogood, DENI, provided education data; and Dr David Marshall, NISRA, responded to several queries. Jonathan Collins of Collins Medals and Celia Green of the South Wales Borderers Museum (41st Regiment) in Brecon, Powys, provided valuable help tracing Captain Arthur Trew. Svend Robinson in British Columbia kindly provided confirmation about Canadian observers at the Drumcree protests.

I wish to remember my father, brothers and my great-aunt Lily Trew Edens, Trevor and Heather Edens, and Brad and Diane Trew for sharing family history research. My uncle John Devlin supplied constant practical and moral support. With her typically boundless generosity my dear friend Nancy Lokan provided me a home in Toronto while I conducted the Canadian research – thanks for that and so much more. Enormous appreciation to Roisín Keogh who I am truly blessed to know and also to Mairead and Mickey Keogh of Dungannon for their immeasurable kindness. To Kay O'Carroll in Cork; Ena McGurgan; Alison and Brian Vincent in Omagh; Anita Best and Kate Power in Newfoundland; Ron Zwierzchowsky in Ottawa; James Pettit and Marlene Bonneau in Montreal; and Oliver Ryan – my heartfelt gratitude. My mother Margie wanted so much to see this book finished but I had drafted only one chapter when she passed away with cancer. I like to think that her spirit continued to guide me throughout.

Introduction:
'The truth about stories':
Personal Perspectives
on Ulster Migration

*Telling the stories and the opportunity for victims and survivors from
every part of the island to tell their story is hugely important ... I
think it will take some considerable time before there is any sense of
agreement as to how those stories should be told.*

Rev Norman Hamilton, Presbyterian Moderator, media interview
following release of the Saville Inquiry Report, 16 June 2010.

'The truth about stories,' writes Native American author Thomas King, 'is that's
all we are' (2003: 2). From family stories, origin myths, fantastic fables or
historical tales; the human being is a 'story-telling animal ... a teller of stories
that aspire to truth' (MacIntyre, 1981: 201). It is in narrative form that we store
and retrieve our memories and transmit our histories, cultures and identities. As
individuals, we live by storying; repeatedly telling ourselves and others who we
are, what we do and where we belong. We think in story form, we remember
in story, we imagine the past and the future in story. From earliest childhood
we absorb stories from our parents, from our families, from the people around
us – for the most part, these stories teach us new things, keep us safe and help
us grow. Early – very early on – the stories begin to cohere and we each embark
on the process of making our own life story; one comprised of all the others.
As we journey through life we continually adjust, edit and expand our stories,
and wherever we go we bring them with us and add tales of new places and new
experiences. These stories and memories of our individual lives also offer insights
from social, psychological and geographical perspectives on larger historical
contexts by uncovering hidden histories or by supplementing the available

1

documentary evidence. In narrative our memories and histories intersect, develop from each other, become fixed and even sometimes entrenched. This, as King reminds us, is the power of stories:

> For once a story is told, it cannot be called back. Once told, it is loose in the world. So you have to be careful with the stories you tell. And you have to watch out for the stories that you are told (2003: 10).

This is a book about stories told by ordinary people from Northern Ireland and from the province of Ulster historically, all of whom have emigrated abroad, near and far, and some of whom have later returned. Their life stories, collected in interviews conducted from 2004 to 2010, are held in the Voices of Migration and Return (VMR) archive of the Mellon Centre for Migration Studies at the Ulster American Folk Park near Omagh, County Tyrone.[1] These migrant tales describe what it was like to leave Northern Ireland at various points in time over the twentieth century and offer us insights into life in very different places; societies with diverse histories, cultures and identities. Perhaps most powerfully, these stories of migrant lives provide critical and comparative perspectives on Northern Ireland; a place known for its 'difficult' or 'unusable' past so often defined by sectarian strife and violence.[2] How do the experiences of the people who left Ulster feed into this 'troubled' history? How do their stories narrate the past, 'difficult', 'unusable' or otherwise? Who left, who stayed, who returned and what were the personal, political and historical factors behind their decisions? What can we learn from their migrant perspectives on Northern Ireland that might provide alternative ways of imagining its future? What do we know of the scale, variety and composition of the constant population movement in and out of Northern Ireland over the last ninety years? As a means of illustrating the complexity or what has been called the 'throughotherness' (Fitzgerald and Lambkin, 2008: 255) of migration and how it is entwined with politics and history in Ulster, I begin with a migration story from my own family.

Arthur and Me

My great-grandfather, Arthur Trew (1866–1943), was an infamous character in the history of Belfast. Based in the Shankill–Springfield neighbourhood in the west of the city, Arthur was essentially a professional 'sectarianist' and a founding member and leader of the Belfast Protestant Association (BPA), a political organisation established in 1894.[3] The BPA purported to represent the cause of working-class Protestants within a framework based in fundamentalist Christian ideology. Unfortunately, these proletarian and Christian principles did not extend to the equitable treatment of Catholics and the BPA organised frequent sectarian protests, many of which descended into violence.

Figure 0.1: Arthur Trew,
c. 1901 (Trew family
collection)

Some heroic and humorous versions of Arthur's exploits had been passed down in my family, but there were few photographs of him and the chronology of these tales remained elusive. Seeking more concrete detail, I first asked my father what he remembered of his grandfather and sometime later, I interviewed Arthur's youngest child, my great-Aunt Lily, then aged ninety-one and still living in the Shankill. Perhaps the most notorious episode that came to light from my enquiries concerned Arthur's incarceration in the Crumlin Road Jail in 1901 'for his loyalty' as Lily expressed it and his triumphant release from jail a year later when hundreds turned out to cheer him as he was paraded through the streets of central Belfast.[4] Reports of the initial transgression and the subsequent coverage of the criminal trial in the *Belfast News Letter* revealed, however, that Arthur was convicted of inciting a riot against a Catholic Corpus Christi procession en route from St Malachy's College.[5] Stark differences in the oral and written accounts of the incident were a reminder, as Thomas King has warned above, about the need to be careful with stories. On the other hand, the published stories were almost entirely lacking in the fascinating personal detail transmitted in our family version.

Two curious facts emerged time and again in the fragmented tales I collected: that Arthur had been born in Barbados and that he had been named after an illustrious Captain Arthur Trew who had made a reputation for himself in the British Army in the Empire. Migration thus loomed large in Arthur's story and led to the awareness that my own childhood growing up in Canada in an Ulster immigrant family network was part of a much longer trajectory of migration in the Trew family. First of all, as immigrants, the Trews were part of the British colonial project in Ireland, appearing in Irish records of the late eighteenth century as being of Church of England denomination, likely from the north of England where the surname appears to derive.[6] They were evidently people of at least moderate means for on the 1st of July 1788, Andrew Trew, merchant of the townland of Derrycughan, County Armagh and his younger brother Thomas, signed a long-term lease at the yearly rent of £100 for just over seventy acres of land near the village of Markethill with the stated intention to grow flax.[7] Subsequently, Andrew's name appeared on the Flax Growers List (1796) and Thomas in the Freeholders records from 1815.[8] Other family members served in the imperial army 'migrating' around the Empire, such as Thomas Trew (son of Andrew?) who lost his left leg at the Siege of Bhurtpoor in India in 1805 and Markethill weaver James Trew, wounded at Badajoz, Spain in 1812 during the Napoleonic campaigns.[9] The illustrious Captain Arthur Trew, for whom all the subsequent Arthurs in the Trew family were apparently named, served in the imperial army from 1795 until his death in 1811.[10] Enlisting in Dublin and then stationed in Cork, he departed for the Canadas on 17th August 1799 with the 41st Regiment of Foot, never to return. Attaining the rank of captain in October 1804 evidently on merit; the recommendation from his commanding officer, Colonel Thomas Stirling, described him 'as a very deserving officer ... [who] has no powerful interests or connections to assist him'.[11] Captain Arthur subsequently took command duties in Upper Canada at Fort St Joseph (1805–1808) on Lake Huron and Fort Amherstburg (1808–1809) on the Niagara frontier; a strategically vital region in the defence of British North American interests in the ensuing war with the United States.[12]

The tradition of migration in the service of the Empire continued through subsequent generations of the Trew family and brings our story back to political activist Arthur whose father John also spent his career in the imperial army. John's record of 'exemplary' military service of over thirty-three years reveals that he served in the far reaches of the Empire – Malta, Gibraltar and the West Indies (Barbados) where he married Arthur's mother Elizabeth Newsam – Barbadian-born of English descent – and where their eldest child, political activist Arthur was born in Bridgetown in 1866.[13] Brought back to Ireland as a ten-year-old, I have often wondered if the key to Arthur's politics lay in his migrant past, influenced by his Barbados childhood. Was his outsider status as a child migrant a factor in the nonconformist stance he would staunchly maintain throughout his life? Was he appalled by the memory of the harsh working conditions of the West Indian plantation workers, many of whom were former slaves or did his experience of the Barbados-style apartheid of the day appear a suitable model for Ireland? Never one to join others, I wondered if Arthur's need to belong motivated him to form his own political organisations.[14] As Arthur continued his political activities in the early days of post-partition Northern Ireland, Empire migration continued among his siblings and later from the 1950s to the 1970s among his descendants, with them relocating to countries of the British Commonwealth – Canada, Australia, New Zealand, South Africa and Southern Rhodesia (now Zimbabwe) – prime destinations for Ulster Protestants.

The story of migration in the Trew family does not fit comfortably, however, with the predominant view of migration in Irish history – that of mass emigration and 'exile' associated with the Great Famine. This narrative of exile, however, has undoubtedly obscured a more complex picture of multidirectional movements of individuals and family groups over time. Certainly the multiple migration contexts evident in the Trew family story, including military service in the Empire, are probably more representative of the norm in Ulster, though almost certainly not uncommon in other parts of Ireland. Indeed, migration from the more industrialised and urbanised province of Ulster presents a scenario of multiple movements in many directions of people of all descriptions, with increasing urbanisation towards Belfast, individuals and families leaving and returning more often from towns and cities rather than farms, substantial Empire and Commonwealth emigration and immigration involving people of many ethnicities, and migrant motivations that have included adventure and opportunity as well as sectarian discrimination and poverty. Thus, the well-worn image of Northern Ireland or Ulster historically as 'such narrow ground', an inward-looking place, contrasts starkly with its rather dynamic migration history, demonstrating that its people have long been looking outward as well as inward, well connected with the wider world.[15]

The Trew family history also illustrates how political context, class and religious sectarianism are all factors which add to the complexity of migration histories in Ireland generally and most especially in Ulster. This is particularly true of the post-partition period and is reflected in the high rate of emigration from Northern Ireland in the decade immediately following partition and later during the worst years of the Troubles. Curiously, only a tiny literature exists to date which explores migration from Northern Ireland despite a considerable number of recent studies which treat migration in independent Ireland. Elsewhere (Trew, 2005a), I have noted that much of the literature on twentieth-century Irish migration does not even mention the North. While this conspicuous gap in Irish migration literature is no doubt due in large part to the complications that arise in dealing with data from two 'national' jurisdictions, generating a body of literature which does not include Northern Ireland has also served to perpetuate by default a 'partitionist' approach in thinking about Irish migration. This has somewhat contributed to the lack of discourse about Northern Ireland migration and enabled many Northern politicians to dismiss emigration as a southern phenomenon. It has also privileged recent historical perspectives seen through some ninety years of partition, ignoring the much lengthier trajectory of an Ireland undivided.[16] The legacy of religious sectarianism that is so much a part of Irish history is therefore embedded in Irish migration history.

An exception to this trend, and greatly to be admired, is recent work which has included stories of Ulster migrants within an all-Ireland context, without regard to national or denominational boundaries (Fitzpatrick, 1994; McCarthy, 2005, 2007; and Miller et al., 2003). The emphasis then, is on the commonality of the Irish migration experience, which in an ideal world is perhaps how it should be presented. But as well as commonality, there is difference and the daily negotiation of difference, of boundaries, of conflict, has long been a reality for the people of Ulster in particular. Thus, this book is necessarily an exploration of these boundaries, negotiations and mediations within a Northern Ireland frame, underpinned by the notion that all borders are to some extent fluid.[17] While in theory we speak of Ulster historically and of Northern Ireland in the present, in practice people's lives, memories and family histories straddle this border. Thus, differing spatial, historical and potential future constitutional constructs will be referenced throughout the book and terminology adjusted accordingly.

For clarity regarding nomenclature, usage in this book of the term Ulster, in spite of the current 'international' border that divides its territory, indicates the historical nine-county province that continues to exist in the present. The term Northern Ireland refers to the six-county area and its government that remained part of the United Kingdom after partition (1921). The terms Ireland, independent Ireland, Republic of Ireland (ROI) and the Irish Free State all refer to the twenty-six-county nation in different contexts.[18] Usage should not be interpreted as indicating any preference towards Irish unification, maintenance of the status quo or indeed any other potential resolution framework. It is ethically important, however, to acknowledge the aspiration of a considerable sector of the general public, and indeed of some of the interviewees who contributed to this book, to recover an Ulster and an Ireland undivided. Nevertheless, now some ninety years since partition, to deny the reality of Northern Ireland (e.g., by not using its nomenclature) is at best unhelpful and to my mind, positively obstructive; indeed, one goal of this book is to illuminate some of its intrinsic paradoxes. On the other hand, designations such as Northern Irish, Ulster-Scots, Scots-Irish, Nationalist, Republican, Loyalist, Unionist, confer national, ethnic or political belonging, and have therefore been confined to theoretical discussions of identity or employed only in the context of individuals interviewed during the research for this book who have self-identified in these terms.

In summary then, this book aims to give voice to the stories of ordinary individuals, all Ulster migrants, in which they remembered and reworked their pasts at home and abroad. Consequently, their narratives necessarily engage with the complexities of memory, geography, history and identity. Transcending borders and time, these multilayered memories and multigenerational stories shed new light on the history of this northern part of Ireland and its relations with the world beyond. Second, the book not only presents multidirectional perspectives on migration (e.g., immigration, emigration, return migration), but as the first comprehensive survey of the subject relating to Northern Ireland, it necessarily combines sociological, historical, qualitative and quantitative approaches. Perhaps most importantly, however, this book continues the project of 'putting migration back into history' to paraphrase Leslie Page Moch (2003: 1) – into the specific history of Northern Ireland, of Ulster and therefore of Ireland and the United Kingdom.[19] In so doing, the aim has been to recover a more multifaceted, nuanced and dynamic story of Northern Ireland that in taking account of the people 'leaving the North' has the potential to offer a more 'usable past' from where a better future might be envisioned.

This book is divided into two sections: Part I provides theoretical, historical and demographic analyses in Chapters 1 and 2 in order to contextualise the *Voices of Migration and Return* oral histories that follow in Part II. Readers preferring to engage immediately with the 'Voices' should advance to Part II directly, and refer to Part I as needed for context. Accordingly, theoretical perspectives concerning migration, memory and history are explored in Chapter 1 along with the methodological context that forms the basis of the research for this book. Historical and demographic perspectives in Chapter 2 include a comprehensive review of the statistical record and policy framework surrounding Northern Ireland migration since partition. In Part II, the theme of multigenerational migration in Ulster families is explored in Chapter 3. Migration is explored in Chapter 4 within the context of religion and identity. Chapters 5 and 6 consider and compare the experience of migration in the two principal host jurisdictions for migrants from Northern Ireland: Britain and Canada. Experiences of other destination countries are included in Chapters 3, 4 and 7. Finally, the multiple contexts of return migration are explored in Chapter 7. Due to concerns about length, it was not possible to include a chapter on child migration and the reader is therefore directed to a previous publication for this material (Trew, 2009a). Readers will note that I have taken an integrated approach to gender and have not dedicated a chapter to women's migration in this book. As just over half of the interviewees were women and their stories are well represented, I did not want to reify a gender hierarchy by setting apart women's experience against an implied male norm. Similarly, instead of separate chapters on Protestant and Catholic experiences of migration, discussion of this 'divide' has been integrated throughout the book. I have, where possible, tried to take account of class, which rather than gender or denomination, might arguably be a more relevant construct for the analysis of Northern Ireland, its migration, conflict and society.

PART I

Theory, History and Demography

Chapter 1

History, Memory, Migration

*My interest is not in a general recitation of historical times but
rather in those fragile intersections – the places where moments in an
individual's private life and personality resonate with and reflect a
larger, more universal story.*

Azar Nafisi, *Things I've been silent about.*[1]

Diaspora, Migration and Identity

'Whose diaspora, whose migration, whose identity?' (Mac Einrí and Lambkin,
2002) remain uncomfortable questions in post-partition Ireland. For although
the concept of diaspora has proliferated in academic discourses of migration
and identity since the 1990s, most often its application in the Irish context as a
'victim' diaspora (Cohen, 1997) has referred principally to the large number of
famine emigrants, mostly Catholics and successive chain migrations of that group,
primarily to the United States from 1845 to 1870.[2] The migration of Protestants
from Ireland has tended to be set apart in an often partisan and somewhat
marginalised literature on the Scotch-Irish that focuses on their eighteenth-
century emigrations from Ulster to North America, generally underplaying
the complexities of denomination, ethnicity and class composition of the
group.[3] However, recent scholarship on emigrant letters, family histories and
transnational 'Protestant' institutions, such as the Orange Order, has contributed
towards a better understanding of Protestant migration and a more inclusive
definition of diaspora in the Irish context from a denominational perspective.[4]
Of late, the term 'diaspora' has been applied specifically to Irish Protestants
(Jenkins, 2005; MacRaild, 2005b); Ulster migrants (Fitzgerald, 2006); Ulster-
Scots (Baraniuk and Hagan, 2007); and Northern Ireland (Cooper, 2009; Trew,
2010).[5]

It is perhaps worth noting at this juncture that it is the image of the Flight of
the Earls in 1607 – of people leaving *Ulster* – that is most often taken to symbolise

the beginning of the modern Irish diaspora.[6] Indeed, historical migration patterns for the province of Ulster are similar to general trends in the rest of Ireland; the principal difference owing to greater immigration in the seventeenth century due to the Ulster plantations. An examination of the numbers concerning emigration flows from Ulster is instructive. Historian Patrick Fitzgerald (2006) has presented a series of loose estimates (bringing together the estimates of several scholars) in roughly eighty-year periods spanning from 1607 until 1960 – from the beginning of the modern Irish diaspora to the time when air traffic took over from passenger shipping as the principal means of transatlantic travel. Fitzgerald's maximum estimates are employed in Figure 1.1, depicting that over the period North America was the dominant emigrant destination with some 65 per cent of all Ulster emigrants relocating there, especially after 1820. Approximately 30 per cent of Ulster emigrants chose Britain while less than 5 per cent chose British Empire destinations outside North America and only about 1.5 per cent relocated to Europe, most of that by 1750. Looking at this data another way, it becomes clear then that the period 1820–1960 accounts for around 90 per cent of Ulster emigration over almost four centuries (over 68 per cent in the period 1820–1890 and an additional 22 per cent from 1890 to 1960).[7] This runs counter to the popular perception of Ulster emigration as primarily an eighteenth-century phenomenon and draws attention to the relative paucity of migration analysis on the nineteenth and twentieth centuries, especially as it pertains to Protestants.

Figure 1.1: Ulster emigrants by destination, 1607–1960

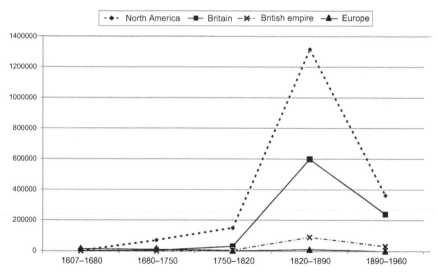

Data source: Fitzgerald (2006)

After partition, substantial migration between Northern Ireland and Empire/Commonwealth destinations in the interwar years continued to sustain expatriate communities abroad while bolstering burgeoning ideologies of statehood at home. The contribution of Northern Ireland to the war effort and the subsequent return of Commonwealth migration in the post-war years through the 1960s, prolonged this trend. Links established through migration were underpinned by official visits of Northern Ireland senior statesmen, such as Prime Ministers James Craig and Sir Basil Brooke, to destinations of the Commonwealth and the United States where they were enthusiastically welcomed by their expatriate countrymen and women.[8] Thus, we can observe early recognition by the Northern Ireland Government of its 'diaspora'; conscious of the importance of these connections in securing its own place within the greater imperial family.[9]

However, with the civil rights movement of the 1960s and the outbreak of conflict came international media exposure of the Northern Ireland Government's discriminatory policies and an increasing outflow of migrants dissatisfied with conditions at home – a 'reluctant diaspora' (Trew, 2010) that could no longer be relied upon to support the existence of the state.[10] Coupled with the imposition of direct rule in 1972, this contributed to the avoidance of discourse on migration and diaspora.[11] That there has been evident reluctance on the part of recent administrations in Northern Ireland to acknowledge the potential of migration to affect the welfare or the religious and ethnic composition of the resident population may be due to several reasons: 1) Northern Ireland does not control its own borders, migration or foreign policy so politicians and bureaucrats have been able, at least publicly, to maintain a 'hands off' stance; 2) since partition Catholics have represented the majority of emigrants (60%) due in large part to discriminatory policies in employment, education and housing, therefore any focus on migration would highlight institutional inequality and sectarianism;[12] 3) increasing Protestant 'brain drain' emigration since the 1970s and majority Catholic immigration since 2004 are contributory factors in shifting the majority/minority denominational balance and unwanted attention might destabilise the fragile peace and trigger sectarian incidents against minorities; and 4) the suspicion that emigrants, especially those that left during the 'Troubles', could not be relied upon 'in diaspora' to support the goals of a pro-union administration. Many of the emigrants interviewed for this book had a palpable sense of having been forgotten in the homeland, as in this example:

> I think people who've left have been completely abandoned. That's what I think. Nobody noticed us going, nobody's ever tried to look at us, why we might have gone, both Protestants and Catholics (Orla, interview, Liverpool, VMR–056).

Even in light of the recent wave of immigration since 2004, the prevailing view has been fixed firmly inward on the 'problem' of integrating incomers to local 'norms' rather than consideration of how they may connect Northern Ireland to the wider world (Chan, 2006; Chiba, 2010; Gilligan et al., 2011; Hickman et al., 2008; Jarman, 2006, etc.).[13] To date there has been no coherent approach to evaluating migration in view of the current and future economic development of Northern Ireland, nor planning for public expenditure (Jarman, 2005: 12, 2006: 58; Jarman and Martynowicz, 2009: 15).[14] Accordingly, two key arguments of this book are that relative silence about migration and diaspora in Northern Ireland has to date largely suited pro-union administrations and that public spending and policy development in Northern Ireland have, nonetheless, had a direct bearing on migration, especially emigration.

The study of migration and the relationship between homeland and diaspora is critical also to understanding the formation of the majority/minority dichotomy within Northern Ireland. To begin with, migration is often a fundamental cause of ethnonational conflict. 'Who was here first?' is the 'space-time' conundrum that often underlies conflict; 'the vertical and horizontal dimensions of being in the world' (Soja, 1989: 11).[15] Accordingly, the 'powerful sedentarism' of native/settler ideology comes into play, so often evident in the use of botanical metaphors (soil, roots, tree and branch) in national imagery and discourse that naturalises the link between people and place; 'a genealogical form of thought ... that is peculiarly arborescent' (Malkki, 1992: 28). Such metaphors reify social identities (usually majorities, but historically also ruling minorities) as 'the natural order of things'; ideology which can too easily mutate into the 'national order of things' (Malkki, 1992: 31). The examination of social or group identities in ethnonational conflicts as in Northern Ireland, therefore, requires investigation of issues relating to 'belonging', citizenship and the territoriality of 'home' in its many forms: from physical dwelling to imaginary paradise; a site of production or of leisure; a place of origin or destination; a place of security or a space of terror, abuse and oppression (Mallett, 2004; Rapport and Dawson, 1998). While the origin of ethnonational conflicts almost always involves migration, it is vital to recognise that the diaspora may play an important role in reigniting or perpetuating conflict or aiding conflict resolution.[16] Indeed, the existence of an expatriate population established around the world, especially throughout the British Commonwealth and in the United States has produced real benefits for Northern Ireland, evident in the contribution of the 'diaspora' to political and economic normalisation and even as demonstrated by recent passenger data, in the predominance of travellers whose reason for coming to Northern Ireland is 'visiting friends and relatives' (VFR).[17] Taking the year 2006 as an example shows that the VFR passenger flow was especially high among those travelling from Canada (over 75%); Australia (over 65%); South Africa (62%); and the United States (53%), while Western

Europeans featured most notably as business travellers. The prominence of Poland in the VFR flow indicates the recent significance of Northern Ireland as a site of the Polish diaspora.[18]

While the contribution of the Irish abroad to Irish culture and identity has been widely acknowledged south of the border, the question is why, in the substantial sociological literature on Northern Ireland identities, especially that concerning northern Protestants, has the influence of migration and diaspora been almost entirely ignored?[19] Indeed, the power and longevity of the Ulster-Scots[20] emigration story with its claim of numerous 'Ulster' American Presidents provides a striking example of how historical, familial and individual connections created through migration continue over many generations to contribute to the construction of social identities at home.[21] Back in 1996, James McAuley called for the need to examine the relationship of northern Protestant migrants to identity politics in Northern Ireland, 'if only to confirm … that the social and political identity of those from the Unionist tradition may not be as fixed as some would suggest' (1996: 63). Indeed, recent Northern Ireland migration research (Harbinson, 2010; Ní Laoire, 2002; Pooley, 2000; Trew, 2005a; 2007; 2009a; 2010) has noted the influence of migration on the construction of national identity and confirms that identity shifts can occur in a short period of time (Mitchell and Todd, 2007: 651).[22]

The evident uneasiness in Northern Ireland about the discourse of diaspora emanating from south of the border is also apparent in the lack of support on the part of the Northern Ireland Executive for recent Irish Government sponsored diaspora conferences and 'homecoming' initiatives.[23] For in spite of recent progress towards a more diverse and inclusive conceptualisation of the Irish diaspora little attention has been paid to its relation to the contested space of Northern Ireland (unresolved by the Belfast/Good Friday Agreement)[24] with very real disputed boundaries, political structures and identities.[25] Relative silence on northern Catholic disaffection and the lack of probing of key questions relating to the territory or 'homeland' of Ulster – 'north of the Black Pig's dyke' (Elliott, 2000: xxxviii)[26] – in official diaspora discourse have contributed to the occlusion of counter narratives of the Unionist and Nationalist North.[27] Indeed, several scholars have argued that Ireland's persistently monocultural image repeatedly invokes old boundaries and traditions – an Irish, Catholic, green and scenic island homeland – not inclusive of difference; political, ethnic, religious or other (Delaney et al., 2006, 45; Gray, 2000: 171–2, 2006a; Hickman, 2007: 17). Despite former President Mary Robinson 'cherishing' the 'Irish abroad' and advocating the de-territorialisation of Irishness outside national boundaries in the newly recast Article 2 of the Irish Constitution, the disputed border and territory of Northern Ireland remain 'the elephant in the room', so to speak. Emigrants and the 'discursively conceived diaspora' continue, nonetheless, to be 'official objects of governance' of the Republic of Ireland (ROI) which maintains consular services and support for emigrant agencies (Gray, 2006b: 361).[28]

Life Stories and Migration Research

Biographical methods are of value in capturing the lived experiences of migration and diaspora; the internal negotiations of belonging, exclusion, placement and displacement (Benmayor and Skotnes, 1994). 'Thinking of migration as a story' (Halfacree, 2004: 239) may also be helpful in getting beyond the economic discourse of migration to discover an alternative set of values, priorities and motivating factors. Migrant life histories can illuminate experiences of economic, social or cultural exclusion that can precipitate a decision to emigrate, as well as conditions of migrancy such as displacement, unfamiliarity and 'in-betweenness'. The theoretical and political potential of 'migrant ambivalence' expressed in life narratives may challenge dominant discourses of citizenship, equality, opportunity and modernisation (Lawson, 2000: 186).

Oral History and Irish Migration

The Voices of Migration and Return (VMR) oral archive, a collection of life narrative interviews conducted with ninety-three Ulster migrants from 2004 to 2010 and held at the Mellon Centre for Migration Studies forms the basis of the research for this book. The VMR collection draws on two migration studies, *Narratives of Migration and Return* (NMR) and *Northern Ireland Emigrant Narratives* (NIEN) which documented migration events occurring from the 1930s through the 2000s, with emphasis placed on the 1970s decade due to the high emigration rate from Northern Ireland and the outbreak of the conflict.[29] The use of digital recording, archiving and web dissemination technologies for the VMR corpus allows for 'non-synchronous telling and listening' (Gray, 2009: 114) and will make the material available into the future to audiences who will form their own questions and interpretations in relation to these narratives.

The focus on the individual lives of migrants represented in the VMR interviews has directly influenced the holistic perspective taken in this book to treating several types of migration together. Fundamental to this approach, recently championed in Irish migration studies by Fitzgerald and Lambkin (2008), is that migration is inherently multidirectional and that individuals may be involved in several processes of migration during their lives (immigration, internal migration, emigration, onward migration, return migration, re-emigration and re-immigration).[30] Life cycle and political and economic circumstances then provide other contexts for these migrations (e.g., childhood, retirement, forced or voluntary movements, labour conditions). The migration trajectories of the majority of the migrants interviewed for the present research did not generally conform to the older notion of a singular emigration event and subsequent permanent exile;

rather, they exhibited a tendency to multiple migrations suggesting that the issue of return usually remains unresolved until late in life (see Chapter 7). However, it also became clear through exploration of the family migration histories of the interviewees that multiple migrations were not purely a feature of modern life as this same tendency was evident among earlier generations (the subject of Chapter 3). The complexity of the multigenerational migration processes that were uncovered in the life stories demonstrates the value of biographical methods in migration research.

Several important studies have served as models for the present work, all of which have availed of interview methodology to investigate complex migration processes in British and Irish contexts. Breda Gray (2004) examined the experience of Irish female migrants in Britain as did Walter (2001) who also included the United States as destination, while Chamberlain (1997) and Hammerton and Thomson (2005) examined return migration (Caribbean and British–Australian respectively). Burrell (2006) interviewed members of three linguistically and ethnically distinct immigrant groups in Britain (Polish, Italian and Greek Cypriot) while McCarthy (2007), availing of pre-existing interview collections, compared the experience of Irish and Scots who migrated to English-speaking countries. The emphasis of much of this work is on the migration experience as situated in the host or destination country (indeed where most of the researchers themselves were located); illustrating a trend in the general migration literature for a 'bias towards receiving-country perspectives' (Castles, 2010: 1582). The present work departs from these examples somewhat in that it has been written 'from' the sending society and is based on multi-sited fieldwork at home and in several locations abroad as the research has necessitated my own travel or 'dislocation' to migrant destinations. In addition, my own background of being raised in a Northern Irish immigrant family in Quebec, returning eventually to the ROI and later back to Northern Ireland has prompted much personal reflection about dislocation, homeland, diaspora, borders and boundaries, identities and belonging. It has also led (following on from Chamberlain) to consider the 'ethos' that characterises Irish and Northern Irish migration and whether or not they differ in any respects. If the ethos of migration in pre-partition Ireland and indeed post-partition independent Ireland can be roughly summarised as migration equals opportunity versus migration equals exile, in Northern Ireland it must surely be that migration equals silence, fuelled by a sort of collective amnesia, what Chamberlain has called a 'motif of denial' (1997: 66).

Oral Narrative Research in the Context of Societal Conflict

The research strategy for the present work combined methodological approaches: life narrative interviewing (ethnography); statistical analyses (demography); and literature review (historiography). In Northern Ireland, it was especially critical as an ethnographer to be mindful of the sectarian nature of the conflict. Every aspect of the methodology, from the preparation of publicity outreach flyers, to the conduct of the interviews themselves, had to be passed through a sort of mental 'conflict filter' in order to lessen the potential for bias and to ensure sensitivity with the consciousness of the responsibility as researchers 'to contribute in positive ways to political progress and peace' (Morrissey and Smyth, 2002: 93). Sensitivity surrounding the terminology used to describe the NMR and NIEN projects in local media at home and abroad, for example, was essential to attracting potential participants for the studies. It was understood that some individuals would be reluctant to participate in an 'all-Ireland' all-island or cross-border project while others might not respond to advertisements which used the term 'Ireland' rather than 'Northern Ireland' or the reverse. Thus, advertisements were tailored (even in Britain and Canada) with these issues in mind.

Sensitivity in the research was required concerning the issue of victimhood, always contested but so central to the politics and society of Northern Ireland, which has generated a 'culture of suffering and grievance' (Morrissey and Smyth, 2002: 15); conditions which also reinforce traditional conservative gender roles (Fairweather et al., 1984). Bravery becomes equated with masculinity, women in active political ('warrior') roles are marginalised and the discourse of victimhood becomes feminised – the 'triumph of the weak' (Dowler, 1998: 165) – and appropriated to provide powerful iconic symbols of resistance. Images of women victims in particular (Derry Peace Women, the McCartney sisters, etc.) have been too easily appropriated by political factions in the race to win the propaganda war (Ashe, 2007; Callaghan, 2002). In *The Cost of the Troubles Study*, a survey of the impact of the conflict on ordinary people in the areas most affected, researchers Mike Morrissey and Marie Smyth (2002: 113) found that although men have been the primary casualties of the conflict (91.1% of deaths), 'the relative gender differences are much less stark when looking at the experiences of the living, as opposed to the statistics for those killed'. Their findings also show that women have been as likely as men to suffer from post-traumatic stress and that the reported impact of the conflict on their lives is roughly equal for both genders. Women are as likely, and sometimes even more likely, than men to have experienced the following: listening to their own tradition being abused; feeling blamed for the Troubles; the inability to talk publicly; having schooling disrupted; paramilitary punishments; and suffering bereavement. Morrissey and Smyth also reported how they uncovered two 'conflict' worlds: one inhabited by the media, researchers and those less affected, comprising the dominant discourse of the conflict where at least to some extent, thinking and knowing about the conflict is an option; and a second world inhabited primarily by victims and 'composed of many individual private spaces that are largely silent' (2002: 141). Several of the interviewees represented in the VMR corpus attempted to articulate such silent and gendered spaces of victimhood; spaces they carried with them even as emigrants abroad and which upon return, they were compelled to renegotiate.

Thus, during the course of the research it was vital to grasp how individuals inhabit different conflict worlds, not only by experience of their gender and relative victimhood but also in terms of class and geography. Place is important to people in Northern Ireland and daily conversations often centre on discussions of places. In view of the divided nature of Northern Ireland society, knowledge of territorial complexities 'on the ground' was vital during the interviewing stage as interviewees located the events of their lives in places having contested histories. The divided nature of the society was also revealed in the daily toing and froing of place – the institutional settings of individual lives (the school, church or social club one attended) – and in less obvious practices from the selection of an estate agent to the preference of local newspaper or radio station.

Having a mixed background myself as it is understood in Northern Ireland (one parent Catholic and one Protestant, mine both working class from Belfast) was an advantage in the research process, although clearly allowance had to be made for potential personal bias regarding aspects of the conflict, be they historical, cultural or territorial. Ethically, it was essential to be open with all study participants and community contacts about my background prior to conducting interviews. I believe this helped in creating an atmosphere of trust and openness – a 'safe space' not only for the interviewees but for me as well. During the interviews, I usually began by asking in detail about the interviewee's childhood, family background and community. In many cases, childhood memories were from the pre-Troubles era (before 1968) and described demographics and inter-cultural contact in communities that underwent great change subsequently. Each interview usually followed a more or less chronological sequence through the individual's life trajectory. Most of the interviewees embarked on the subject of the conflict without prompting. For those who did not, I was careful to wait for a natural opportunity to discuss it or, if that did not happen, brought it up at the end of the interview. While most people were quite willing, even eager, to air their views about the conflict, a few were quite reluctant and I did not pursue the subject beyond the apparent point of comfort.

Migration, Time and Generation

The VMR interviewees represent several generations (youngest aged thirty, eldest aged eighty-five at the time of the interview) and in addition, since they were all asked about migration histories in their families (the subject of Chapter 3), the consideration of generation is central to this enquiry. But how do we define generation? The 'problem' of generations and generational processes has been elucidated in the work of Karl Mannheim (1952 [1926]) who noted the tendency to think of generations in two ways: first, in the family sense of the link between children, parents and grandparents; and second, of a cohort of approximately the same age. The age cohort may exhibit a strong generational consciousness as a response to significant or traumatic events experienced at a formative stage in life, sometimes resulting in collective action (e.g., events of 1968). However, generations may also exhibit a lack of such consciousness; hence we may speak of 'invisible', 'silent' (Cavalli, 2004: 159) or 'passive' generations (Edmunds and Turner, 2005: 562). It has been suggested that 'active' generations are often followed by 'passive' ones; the former consume resources and opportunities at a high rate creating great social and cultural change which then leaves little for the next generation.[31] Thus, each generation must be considered within the context of greater world events and economies but also the local conditions which shape its opportunities or lack thereof (Loizos, 2007). For example, the generation of my parents – who were children during the Second World War – was faced with particular post-war economic challenges and opportunities in the United Kingdom that saw so many of their cohort become part of the great emigrant flow of the 1950s and early 1960s. Hence, as in this instance, examination of migration flows must take generation into account and thus the dimension of time; 'the crucial role of context' that links migration, geography and history (Castles, 2010: 1573).[32] But it is not only historical time that is important here. Time is embedded in migration-related concepts and processes in several ways: first, it is a fundamental determinant of immigration and citizenship procedures the world over; second, multigenerational time underlies the concept of diaspora (i.e., long-term settlement of immigrant groups linking generations); and third, immigrants as 'time pioneers' may introduce different conceptions and uses of time into the host society (Cwerner, 2001: 29).

In the current work, it is understood that each interviewee may have a specific generational 'value orientation' (Cavalli, 2004) that will undoubtedly have influenced their entire life experience, from individual migration trajectory, experience of sectarianism and conflict in Northern Ireland, to the conceptualisation and expression of identity. Thus, the interviewees have recounted their stories filtered through age, generational and historic effects, and what we have captured are stories told at one moment in time comprised of remembered episodes relating to other moments in time.

Memory and Emotion in Migration Research

History, Memory and Postmemory

The rise and increasing internationalisation of oral history in the post-war period and most especially since the 1970s, has no doubt influenced the growing interest in the relationship of history and memory (Thomson, 2007:

50). In fact, it is in studies of oral history that these two fields of scholarship may be brought closer together. Much memory scholarship is located in the field of psychology, employing scientific experimental methodology usually in institutional settings with select study groups to study cognitive processes, such as the mechanism of memory encoding and retrieval. In contrast, studies of memory based in the humanities and relating to history in particular, have tended to emphasise memory that is beyond the single lifespan, examining practices of commemoration, monuments and memorials, and their relationship to historical or national narratives (Hamilton and Shopes, 2008: x; Nora, 1984). Indeed, the development of the academic discipline of history in the nineteenth century with its emphasis on documentary and artefactual sources, and the creation of archives and museums led to less reliance on eyewitness testimony and indeed suspicion and even fear of oral sources, though some would argue that the divergence between fact and fiction, orality and literacy, actually dates back to ancient times (Ong, 1982: 16–30; Schole and Kellogg, 1966). Memory and history thus came to be placed in opposition; memory perceived as 'time-warped', while history was 'linear and progressive' (Samuel, 1994: ix).

Oral historians such as Alessandro Portelli have persistently argued, however, that with documentary sources we encounter the same issues of reliability and interpretation as with oral evidence since 'what is written is first experienced or seen, and is subject to distortions even before it is set down on paper' (1981: 101). Concern over temporal distance from an event applies as much to writing about it as it does to the oral recall of it, neither of which can be isolated from each other or from the wide influence of communications media. Portelli advocates that historians engage with subjectivity, which 'is as much the business of history as the more visible "facts"' (1981: 100). In so doing they must work not only 'on both the factual and narrative planes ... the past and the present' but most importantly 'on the space between all of them' (2003: 15).

However, Luisa Passerini has noted that in the case of fascist and communist regimes of the twentieth century 'where an atmosphere of lies and falsehood was perpetuated' in the bid to create utopian socialist societies, the lack of permissible subjectivity amounted to the 'cancellation of history' (1992: 8). With no room for dissidence, the past and its inherent diversity was expurgated in favour of the homogeneous present. But such 'public amnesia' – where memory turns into oblivion – also occurs in democratic societies in a process where one set of memories is replaced by another set, usually on purpose and sometimes by force (2003: 241). Such forgetting – what Paul Connerton has called 'repressive erasure' (2008: 60) – whether state-imposed, consumer-driven, socio-structural or traumatic, in some cases essential to survival and linked to forgiveness, is always related to power. Oral histories can help recover these suppressed histories – the silences, the forgetting – and moreover, reveal 'variations of subjectivity in history' (Passerini, 1992: 9).

Philosophers such as Primo Levi and Paul Ricoeur, however, remind us that the possibilities for historical representation (oral and written) may be limited. For Ricoeur the limitation is on the part of the audience – the capacity of either listeners or readers to take in the full scale of the horrors recounted, for example, in victim testimonies of the Holocaust or the Rwandan genocide, since 'the experience to be transmitted is that of inhumanity with no common measure with the experience of the average person' (2004: 175). For Primo Levi, it is the reliability of the testimonies of both victims and perpetrators that is in question: for the latter a 'convenient truth' is fabricated to alleviate guilt while for the former, excessively tortuous memories – or 'rememory' of trauma to employ Toni Morrison's concept (1987: 36)[33] – require that an alternate reality be constructed. Yet Levi defended the reliability of his own personal memories of the Holocaust, noting that 'time has somewhat faded them, but they are in good consonance ... and seem to me unaffected by the drifting' (1988: 21).

The oral testimonies in this book – some of which may be interpreted as 'victim' narratives – may complement or contest versions of events, truths or ideologies established within the wider frame of collective memory. However, the informants in the research carried not only their own memories but also those from previous generations (the subject of Chapter 3) whose recreated power may even have supplanted in some cases their first-hand experience. Marianne Hirsch (1997) coined the term 'postmemory' to describe this phenomenon in relation to children of Holocaust survivors, like herself, whose own lives were dominated by the memory baggage (including the gaps and silences) – the collective inheritance of trauma – that they carried from the previous generation. Other helpful concepts describing multigenerational memory have also come from Holocaust literature including 'remembering the unknown' (Fresco, 1984); 'mémoire trouée' (Raczymow, 1986); and 'absent memory' (Fine, 1988).[34]

As the conflicts of the twentieth century have receded into the distance and we have become embroiled in those of the present, there has been increasing interest in investigating multigenerational memories of trauma and violence in post-conflict societies with a view to demonstrating the long-term costs and effects of conflict. The particular power of this type of memory is 'mediated not through recollection but through an imaginative investment and creation' (Hirsch, 1997: 22). Recent oral history studies of Argentina's 'dirty war' (1976–1983), for example, have uncovered important findings concerning how memories of that conflict have been passed on, mediated, edited or even silenced in the bid to construct a past that the entire society can share (Kaiser, 2005). Several disturbing tendencies were observed in the way memories had been transmitted post-conflict to young people from their parents' 'witness' generation: a legacy of silences that was linked to a positive impression of the past; memories that tended to distort and simplify events of the conflict; denial of feelings of fear and terror; and generalised vague explanations of witness testimonies that were more or less accepted by the post-conflict generation without much questioning. In particular, there was found to be a strong inheritance of silence and denial in the postmemory generation, suggesting that this may be a 'process of self-deception ... to defend a positive self-image and cope with a difficult past' (Kaiser, 2005: 62). In this way, silence may also symbolise power especially when shared collectively and imposed on those who are therefore compelled to explain their resistance against a 'silent canonical background' (Fivush, 2010, 94; see also Alea, 2010; Cohen, 2002). Thus, how memory is transmitted between generations is crucial because of the way memory and forgetting can govern the present and shape the future (Passerini, 1992: 12).

The role of multigenerational memory and memory-based mythologising is particularly relevant in Northern Ireland as the first post-conflict and postmemory generation enters young adulthood and the government plans strategies for a 'shared future' (OFMDFM, 2006). Historian Marianne Elliott has articulated how young people in Northern Ireland carry two versions of history; one which is taught in school and another 'street history', its texts being the orally transmitted legends and iconic murals of conflict zones (2009: 16–17). There is some awareness on the ground of the need to address the concerns and beliefs of the postmemory generation, especially in ways that implicate young people themselves in the exploration of variant perspectives (Bell et al., 2010). In the autumn of 2009, for example, the play 'We Carried Your Secrets', a Theatre of Witness Production, described on its publicity flyer as 'original theatre performed by fathers who were on the front line during the Troubles and the next generation who have unanswered questions about the legacy', toured Northern Ireland and Donegal.[35] The paradoxical position of the postmemory generation came through clearly in the words of a daughter, 'I was taught not to lie, but we weren't supposed to tell anyone that Daddy was in the police.' Such endeavours which dissect the relationship between memory and conflict directly address the 'culture of re-enactment' and may be beneficial to processes of conflict resolution (Cairns and Roe, 2003: 4).

However, in Northern Ireland as elsewhere, behind the struggle for dominance of divergent collective memories and the historical narratives they construct in which 'memories of war tend to become weapons in a war over memory' (Dawson, 2007: 15) is the flawed notion that the public psychic space available for the representation of individual and collective memories and identities is somehow limited. This battle of 'competitive memory', as Michael Rothberg has recently articulated, produces a situation where there can only be winners and losers and consequently is unlikely to advance peaceful accommodation.

Rather than interpreting Unionist or Nationalist narratives in Northern Ireland as competitive or mutually exclusive, as bounded by limited public or psychic space where the struggle to forefront one version of collective memory necessarily impedes the view of the other, the way forward may well be 'multidirectional' where we might find the 'potential to create new forms of solidarity and new visions of justice' (2009: 5).

What migration can contribute to the study of history, memory and conflict is its inherent multidirectionality; specifically in the case of this book through examination of the personal memories of migrants that requires consideration of multiple perspectives, places, identities and collectivities, all within a comparative frame. For emigrants and their descendants living away from the homeland, 'diaspora memory', to borrow Mary Chamberlain's (2009) concept, is intrinsically multidirectional and provides the connectivity which links families, cultures and histories across oceans and down through the generations. By engaging migrant subjectivities, the goal here is to demonstrate not only the potential for multidirectional identities within Northern Ireland and out in the diaspora, but the extent to which they already exist. Writing in the early 1940s from her perspective as an 'Ulsterwoman' living in wartime England, Nesca Robb articulated the complexity of entangled Northern Irish identities and the difficult relationship to the past.

> We of the North clung passionately to the British side of our inheritance; we cherished loyalties which the extremists at least among our opponents were only anxious to sweep away. Yet, it would be an error to suppose that we had no love for Ireland and no sense of kinship with the rest of its inhabitants. The country had laid hold on us, as it does on those who live there. We are all alike the offspring of a community tragically at war with itself, forever united and divided by the tyranny of the past (1942: 4).

Thus, consideration of how history and memory operate together is fundamental to interpreting the life narratives of migrants represented in this book. On the other hand, theories and mechanisms of autobiographical memory also reveal important aspects of the processes of remembering and telling which are pertinent given the methodology employed in this migration study. A brief selective outline follows of some key concepts and related literature, some of which pertains specifically to migrants.

Mechanisms of Autobiographical Memory

There is an enormous range of scholarship investigating memory, but perhaps most relevant to the present discussion are studies which have examined the mechanics of autobiographical memory encoding and retrieval, and how individuals structure coherent life stories as a means of identity mediation and development.[36] Verbal narrative, imagery and emotion are all components of memory that are retrieved at the point of recall to construct autobiographical memories which are not filed away as wholly finished products, but are constructed in a cyclical retrieval process at the time of recall (Conway, 1996: 76; Rubin, 1996a, 1996b). 'Flashbulb memories' (Brown and Kulik, 1977) which are an especially vivid form of autobiographical memory with image-based representation, a high level of consistency and accuracy in memory recall, are said to form when an event causes four factors to overlap: surprise; importance; emotion; and consequentiality (Conway, 1995: 115). Remembering in almost videographic detail where you were when you heard about the 9/11 disaster is an example of this type of memory and links an individual's memory with the collective memory of the event in a way that is 'radically interactive' (Reese and Fivush, 2008: 202).[37] Flashbulb memories are also associated with first-time experience, evaluation of self and goal attainment or failure; all typically associated with migration (Conway and Pleydell-Pearce, 2000: 263). Thus, significant public events, personal trauma or new experiences may produce 'flashbulb memories' that contribute to the production of generational identity as these memories represent points 'at which we line up our personal history with the history of our times' (Conway, 1995: 123; following Neisser, 1982).

Reminiscence Bump

Another significant finding about the mechanics of autobiographical memory is that recall is particularly vivid in relation to certain periods in the lifespan and not to others (Fitzgerald, 1988). Essentially, the average person exhibits several memory stages over the lifespan: a period of childhood amnesia (birth to five years) with few isolated memories; a phase of high memory encoding known as the 'reminiscence bump' (RB), said to occur between the ages of ten and thirty years; and a 'period of recency' which in studies of older adults suggests that memories recede from the present (in the case of our informants at the time of their interview) back to the period of the RB (Rathbone et al., 2008: 1403).[38] This means that most people in later life will recall a much greater number of memories from the RB period than from other times in their lives.[39]

However, most significant for the subject of this book is the finding that the standard RB period may be altered by the experience of national conflict or periods of migration and settlement. A study of older Bangladeshis, for example, found that their RBs corresponded to the period of national conflict with Pakistan, especially the phase of armed conflict in and around 1971 when these individuals were aged between thirty-five and fifty-five years of age. Many of their most vivid memories also appeared to have the characteristics of flashbulb memories (Conway and Haque, 1999). In a series of studies investigating memory recall with migrants, it was found that the usual RB shifted to later for those individuals in the sample group who had experienced migration in their thirties (Schrauf and Hoffman, 2007; Schrauf and Rubin, 1998, 2001). Thus, these findings would suggest 'that critical, stressful, and potentially traumatic events do indeed affect the distribution of autobiographical memories by inducing secondary periods of enhanced encoding and subsequent retrieval' (Schrauf and Rubin, 2001: s77). Factors which are likely to enhance the recall of migration events are: longer migration durations in a location (five years or more); when the moves take place alongside another important life cycle event, such as marriage; and when the relocation also involves other family members (spouse and children), the implication being that a larger disruption is more easily remembered (Smith and Thomas, 2003: 47). The VMR interviewees had extraordinarily detailed recall of the period surrounding their migrations, no matter what their age at the time. In addition, those who had direct experience of violence exhibited 'flashbulb-style' recall, particularly clustered around the period of the 1970s and early 1980s, coinciding with the worst years of violence in Northern Ireland.

Structure of Life Stories

The study of life stories by social psychologists, in which narrative is understood as key to the development of identity (following from Erikson, 1959, 1963), is another area of scholarship that informs the present work. At its base, the life story model of identity considers that identity, which emerges in late adolescence and early adulthood, takes the form of a story; that is, with characters, plot, setting and themes (McAdams, 1985, 1993, 2001). The coherence of the life story is important to identity and is reworked throughout the lifespan in view of stages of life, goals and legacy, and individuals will fit their stories into a coherent narrative which best makes meaning for them (Staudinger, 2001). But just as there is an element of unpredictability in life, so too there is a teleological character to our life stories as we live with a future in mind imagining 'ends or goals ... towards which we are either moving or failing to move in the present' (MacIntyre, 1981: 201). For example, as people get older they often feel the desire to leave a positive legacy – to make a positive ending to their own life story (McAdams, 2001: 107). For the emigrant, the rupture with their previous life in the homeland – where they 'left their life story' (Grinberg and Grinberg, 1989: 133) – requires adaptive strategies (e.g., 'objects of memory' brought from home, maintaining contact with family and friends) to help bridge the transition to the new life in the starkly unfamiliar environment. Thus, memories will be remembered or forgotten, or adjusted over time to give the life story coherence. Life stories are also structured with component parts or building blocks and grouped into 'chapters'; extended temporal structures which may represent a period of months up to several years and may include several types of autobiographical memory (Conway and Pleydell-Pearce, 2000; Pillemer, 1998; Thomsen, 2009; Thomsen and Berntsen, 2008). 'Chapters' usually begin and end with a specific event memory and are often followed by an evaluative sequence in which the individual reflects on the event with comments on lessons learned or inferences about personality before the next 'chapter' begins (Thomsen, 2009).

Within this general frame, however, race, class, gender and other factors, such as life goals or external success, will influence how the story is told. Studies have shown that extraverted individuals tend to tell more personal stories; women's stories generally show more complexity and report more detail about emotions and personal relationships (McLean et al., 2007). Goal-oriented individuals may tell stories where their agency is forefronted, while the more socially conscious might tell stories that depict themselves as carers. Life stories tend to highlight the episodes considered most significant and although the recall of positive events may be generally more frequent among men (Alea, 2010: 154), writing or talking about negative, not positive, events is particularly associated with well-being (McLean et al. 2007: 267; Pasupathi et al., 2009: 116–17). Negative emotion from the original experience appears to be lessened in the retelling and through this process of storying the individual may gain important evaluative insights, thus turning a negative experience into a positive life lesson. However, socially negative stories may remain untold and may be harmful as they 'do not have the opportunity to be fully integrated into the self' (McLean et al., 2007: 274).

Life stories are also constructed within a larger cultural frame of collective historical narratives, as 'stories of a culture – stories of national identity, struggle and resilience – become the stories of an individual as he or she constructs his or her own personal narrative' (Hammack, 2008: 233). In the United States, for example, a national narrative of redemption, including a sense of being chosen by God combined with a high degree of purpose and agency, comes from the historical experience of European emigrants setting out for America in search of opportunity and religious freedom (McAdams, 2006). But how individual stories are set within master narratives has important implications for group conflict. Research with youths in Israel, Palestine and Northern Ireland has shown how individuals site their own stories within collective narratives incorporating historical persecution and insecurity, on the one hand, and unjust dispossession and loss, on the other. With each group portrayed in stereotypical character by the other, master narratives of identity are too easily reproduced that contribute to the reproduction of conflict (Bell et al., 2010; Hammack, 2008).

In summary, the individuals whose stories are represented in this book have all been subject to the mechanics of memory, the structuring of life stories, intergenerational memory transmission and the larger frame of collective historical narratives in the context of societal conflict. From the stories passed to them from previous generations, their own experiences recounted from early childhood through adulthood, and the untold stories and silences that remain in the spaces in-between, the challenge has been to assemble a coherent narrative within the larger frame of Irish and Northern Irish migration history and collective memory that goes some way beyond reductionist stereotypes and master narratives.

Chapter 2

Northern Ireland: Migration History and Demography

I believe that those who say Protestantism is prosperous even in this province are wilfully closing their eyes to realities. What an eye opener the next Census returns will produce![1]

Letter to the editor, Belfast News Letter, 15 July 1920

Significantly, on 21 July 1920, only six days following the publication of the letter above, the outbreak of sectarian violence, known as the Belfast pogroms, began which by 1922 resulted in a quarter of the city's Catholic population (some 23,000) having to flee their homes (Elliott, 2000: 374–5).[2] A few years later during the Boundary Commission hearings (1924–1925), it is evident how, in the absence of a plebiscite, outdated body counts based on 1911 census figures were bitterly disputed in border areas and used to argue for, or to contest, the redrawing of the boundary between the new Irish Free State and Northern Ireland.[3] More recently, an escalation of murders of Catholics followed the release of the 1991 census which recorded an increase in the Catholic population to 42.5 per cent (Elliott, 2009: 245). Clearly, demography has long been a source of anxiety in Northern Ireland; the main concern usually focused on the balance of Protestants and Catholics in the population and the repercussions of this majority/minority 'body count' for future governance. Migration affects this cohort balance and significantly it is *the* demographic factor – the others being birth, death and fertility – over which the government is perceived to exercise actual control. Although official migration policy is administered at the UK level, creation of a climate within Northern Ireland that may either encourage or discourage migration, especially emigration, consequently affects population balance. However, migration in

Ireland and Northern Ireland is influenced not only by local factors but by global economic conditions that generate the push and pull demands of labour and international markets. Geopolitical structures and networks are also instrumental in how, when and where migrants relocate. In the case of Northern Ireland, the British Empire/Commonwealth has been the most influential global system that has facilitated migration, first of all through mobility made possible by British nationality; second, by the provision of a travel and shipping infrastructure from British ports and airports; and third, by government assisted emigration schemes. Thus, this chapter provides a review of the important economic factors, relevant statistics, policy and political developments relating to Northern Ireland migration since partition, including consideration of British Empire migration as the primary context within which migration from Ulster and Northern Ireland occurred.[4] The chapter begins with a brief overview of population trends, followed by a detailed examination of the wider contexts of migration over time.

Demographic Summary

The first official census of Ireland was taken in 1821 and the total population recorded was 6,801,827 (Vaughan and Fitzpatrick, 1978: 3).[5] While the Ulster population amounted to 1,998,494, that of the six counties constituted as Northern Ireland (NI) since 1921 was at that time 1,380,451 or 69 per cent of the Ulster total. The highest population for the six counties recorded prior to the 2001 census was in 1841 at 1,648,945, after which due to high death and emigration rates during the great famine, its population declined sharply by 1851 to 1,442,517.[6] Like the rest of Ireland, population decline, due in large part to low marriage and fertility rates coupled with high emigration, continued in the six-county area until it reached a low point in 1891 at 1,236,056. Nevertheless, the fact that the six-county population by then comprised over 80 per cent of the total Ulster population demonstrates that from the mid-nineteenth century the six counties lost proportionately less population than the remaining three Ulster counties and indeed the rest of Ireland generally.[7] Between 1851 and 1920, emigration from all nine Ulster counties (largely to North America) numbering almost 1.25 million individuals comprised approximately 30 per cent of the total emigration from Ireland and the six counties that are now part of Northern Ireland accounted for just over 21 per cent of the total.[8]

Averaged per decade from 1921 to 2001, Northern Ireland had a greater outflow of people than inflow and it is estimated that over 500,000 people emigrated from Northern Ireland while some 1.5 million left independent Ireland (Delaney, 2002: 1). Figure 2.1 provides a comparison of net migration rates for both Irish jurisdictions since partition.[9] From the end of the Second World War, the total outflow from Northern Ireland has been estimated at 300,000 more than the inflow.[10] That the population has continued to grow (from 1.28 million in 1922 to 1.81 million in 2011) has been primarily due to birth rate.[11] For Northern Ireland, two decades stand out, the 1920s and the 1970s, as periods of intense political turmoil and dismal economic conditions locally, though the 1970s must be viewed in the context of the significant net immigration in the Republic of Ireland (ROI); the first time that the twenty-six-county area experienced a positive inflow since the British immigrations of the seventeenth century. The low out-migration in the 1930s and the high out-migration of the 1950s from both jurisdictions in Ireland reflect wider international conditions (the Great Depression and subsequent post-war boom) which affected British and European migration trends generally. By the turn of the twenty-first century, emigration slowed and immigration was on the rise, although a slight increase in outflow from Northern Ireland for the years 1998–2001 may indicate that economic recovery as experienced in the ROI from 1996 was somewhat delayed in the North.[12] Immigration became the dominant trend from 2004 coinciding with the accession into the European Union of eight countries of Eastern Europe, peaking in 2006–2007 with over 30,000 people arriving in each of those years and positive net-migration exceeding natural population growth in Northern Ireland for the first time in its history.[13] However, due to the economic downturn which began in 2008, immigration has declined substantially while emigration, especially of young people, has increased to the extent that concern has been expressed about a 'lost generation'.[14] This trend looks likely to continue into the near future as youth unemployment rises.

Nevertheless, the 2011 census recorded the highest population ever in Northern Ireland of 1,810,863, an increase of 7 per cent since 2001, with females accounting for 51 per cent.[15] Northern Ireland comprises 2.87 per cent of the United Kingdom (UK) population and accounts for around 2 per cent of total UK immigration and 3 per cent of total emigration.[16] Although the population is aging quickly, the median age having increased from thirty-four to thirty-seven since 2001, nevertheless, in the European context, Northern Ireland still has a young age profile with a relatively high proportion (20%) aged birth to fourteen, showing a 10 per cent increase in children aged birth to three years and a lower than average proportion (15%) aged sixty-five and over.[17] By the third quarter of 2011 (June–August) the Labour Force Survey reported that 799,000 people were in employment. Unemployment was 7.6 per cent, up 0.6 per cent since the previous year, but still lower than the overall UK rate of 8.1 per cent, the European Union rate of 9.5 per cent and the ROI rate of 14.5 per cent (July 2011).[18] The Northern Ireland workforce was largely dependent on public

Figure 2.1: Ireland net migration by decade (per 000)

Decade	Ireland	Northern Ireland
1921–31	–10.9	–8.0
1931–41	–3.1	–1.9
1941–51	–9.3	–3.6
1951–61	–14.1	–6.5
1961–71	–4.5	–4.5
1971–81	+3.2	–7.3
1981–91	–5.6	–4.4
1991–01	+3.3	–0.2
2001–11	+8.1	+2.2

sector employment, the main sectors listed as: public administration, education and health (33.4%); distribution, hotels and restaurants (20.6%); banking and finance (11.4%); manufacturing (11.8%); construction (8.1%); transport and communication (5.8%); energy and water (1.5%); agriculture, forestry and fishing (3%); and other services (4.4%).[19] While this summary lists the basic migration trends in Ireland and Northern Ireland, understanding the causes requires consideration of migration in wider contexts.

British Empire Migration

From 1815 to 1930, approximately 51.7 million people left Europe and of this, some 18.7 million left the British Isles (11.4 million from Britain and 7.3 million from Ireland) (Baines, 1995: 3).[20] While much of this emigration was destined for locations throughout the British Empire, the United States consistently remained the single largest recipient of people leaving the British Isles (62%) during the nineteenth century (Richards, 2004: 4). British migration to destinations within the Empire became more numerically significant from the turn of the twentieth century and surged in the years following international conflicts – the Boer War, and the First and Second World Wars – events which forged imperial unity and Commonwealth solidarity. Historian Stephen Constantine has suggested that British Empire migration in the long twentieth century is comprised of two ideologically distinctive eras: the first from the 1880s through to the early 1940s as the period of overseas settlement or population transfer to the British dominions; the second, 'diasporic' period beginning in the post-war era when the British arrived as 'preferred' foreign nationals in independent Commonwealth nations by then equipped with their own citizenship legislation (2003: 19).

The period of overseas settlement witnessed the increasing focus of British migration towards the British overseas dominions.[21] While only approximately one-third of British emigrants during the 1880s and 1890s left for Empire destinations, the outflow shifted markedly to over one-half from 1900 to 1914, increasing to over 70 per cent for the interwar years (Constantine, 2003: 20; Plant, 1951: 174–6).[22] Total numbers of British emigrants over this period were also considerable with 1.64 million departing in the 1880s increasing to 1.67 million in the first decade of the twentieth century and over 1.81 million during the 1920s.[23] However, due to the worldwide depression in the 1930s, the UK actually experienced a net immigration (164,605) and the outflow of British emigrants was drastically diminished (334,467). Overseas settlement was fuelled by the ideology of imperial unity that portrayed the interests of Britain and the dominions in 'natural harmony' (Constantine, 1990: 7). 'Men, money and markets' (Hancock, 1942: xiii) was the foundation of the imperial system; a strategic defence network in which the redistribution of the British population to the dominions through emigration facilitated the transfer of capital and the development of trade thus guaranteeing self-sufficiency and security in the event of conflict.[24] The imperial system was also bolstered by religion, not only by the missionary projects of the British Christian Churches, but by the concept that it was a moral Empire governed according to ethical principles that justified the 'rightness' of imperial expansion (Carey, 2011: 14). The extension of the Empire provided an opportune response to social Darwinist concerns about the perils of overpopulation and urbanisation in Britain: hence emigration was mooted as one strategy within a developing framework of social reform that sought to alleviate such social ills as unemployment, poverty and overcrowded housing conditions (Constantine, 1991).[25] The surplus population could simply be redistributed within the British family to the empty land and wide-open spaces of the dominions in a manner that would optimise trade and security. Significantly, the government body established in 1919 to oversee emigration policy was named the Oversea Settlement Committee (OSC), thus avoiding the term 'emigration' and any negative connotations of 'exile'.[26] Though dressed in the rhetoric of twentieth-century social reform, the rationale which underpinned the British emigration agenda in the interwar period was actually little changed since the era of the colonisation schemes of the early nineteenth century (arguably dating even further back to the seventeenth century); a perspective that was not lost on the dominion governments.

Migration within the British Empire was greatly facilitated by common nationality; the status of 'British National' applied to jurisdictions of the Empire and Commonwealth until shortly after the Second World War (1947–1950) when evolving independence of the dominions was fully codified in citizenship legislation.[27] Citizens of Ireland were an anomaly in this regard as from the 1935 Irish Nationality Act they ceased to be British subjects in Irish law, though not in the British dominions until Ireland ceded from the Commonwealth in 1949 (Heuston, 1950: 85, 89). Even then, Irish citizens who wished themselves or their children to remain British subjects could make the claim to do so and both governments agreed in any event that their respective citizens would be exempt from alien status in the other's jurisdiction.[28] Thus, it is important to consider that until the end of the Second World War, the dominions (including Ireland) were part of a larger British world 'abounding in diasporas' (Hyam, 2006: 8) in which conceptions of nationality were quite fluid and mobility within the Empire and Commonwealth was less restricted than is currently the case.

The 'diasporic' phase of post-war Empire migration saw the transfer of British migrants to 'friendly' independent Commonwealth nations where they were generally the most privileged of ethnic groups (English, Scottish, Irish and Welsh). In these post-war years, 1946–1963, five out of six British emigrants relocated to the 'Old Dominions' (Bridge and Fedorowich, 2003: 5); and of the 1,327,000 British emigrants in the high emigration decade of the 1950s, approximately 80 per cent went to Commonwealth jurisdictions (Constantine, 2003: 25). Preferential immigration policies for Commonwealth citizens in the dominions continued in spite of new citizenship legislation, however, 'preferred status' was gradually eliminated during the 1960s and 1970s.[29] Nevertheless, from 1964 to 1980, just over 3 million UK citizens emigrated with approximately three-quarters going to Commonwealth countries; 1.26 million (almost 41%) to Australia and New Zealand, and over 535,000 (17.3%) to Canada; while a significant 506,000 (16%) went to European countries and 412,000 (13.3%) to the USA (calculated from Mitchell, 1988: 84).[30] In recent years, from 2006 to 2010, the principal motivating factor for the emigration of British citizens was work-related reasons (over 50%) and still one-third of British emigrants relocated to the 'old dominions' with the five top destination countries being roughly in order of preference: Australia; the United States; France; Spain; and Canada. By 2006, there were 592,355 UK-born living in Canada; 1,038,156 in Australia; 244,803 in New Zealand including 4,779 Northern Ireland-born (hereafter NI-born).[31] The British diaspora was estimated at 56.9 million in 2006, with 7.9 million people claiming British ancestry in Australia; 12.1 million in Canada; and 28.6 million in the United States (Finch et al., 2010: 27–9). Data on pensions paid to overseas residents (only available on a UK-wide basis) indicates the prevalence of UK citizens living in Commonwealth countries as well as the significant number of Irish returnees from the UK to the ROI (Figure 2.2).[32] The dramatic increase evident in pensions paid to residents of France and Spain between 2002 and 2008 reveals the recent tendency of more affluent UK citizens to retire abroad to warmer climes. This may also account in part for the large number of pensions paid to residents of Australia.

Signs of the shifting attitudes and perceptions of the home and dominion governments can be observed in the census and immigration data of the individual jurisdictions as definitions of citizenship evolved over time. For example, who was classified as 'foreign' in the census? What racial categories were used to describe immigrants? Which countries were recognised in 'country of birth' data? When was Irish distinguished from British nationality in the census and immigration data of other countries?[33] When were Northern Ireland and independent Ireland recognised as distinct entities? Clearly, the perspective from the dominions differed substantially on these issues from the UK. Like the parent–child relationship, each was at once familiar and yet ignorant of the other as through time they gradually developed distinct identities, though these did not necessarily 'contradict or undermine Imperial Britishness' (Bridge and Fedorowich, 2003: 6). The processes of colonisation and migration shared by home and host jurisdictions sometimes served to exacerbate the tensions of their relationship, but also exposed intriguing aspects of emerging national identities and the conceptions each society had of the other, of their own respective place within the Empire and the greater world. One must also take special note here of Ireland's (and Ulster's) own history of colonisation and that, in a sense, the

Figure 2.2: UK pensions paid abroad (000s)

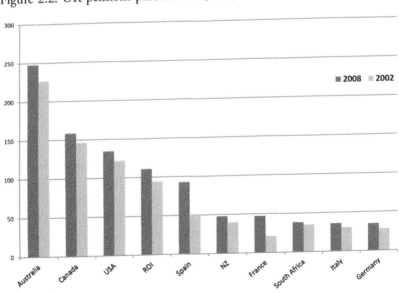

Source data: Dept. of Work and Pensions

large outflow from its shores overseas, especially to other regions of the Empire, was a further stage in this process. That Northern Ireland continued to recognise 'Commonwealth citizens' as distinct from 'foreign-born' in its own census as late as 1991 is indicative of its sense of itself within a larger imperial system; in the 2001 census these categories were combined as 'born abroad'. Thus, the individual jurisdictions of the UK and each dominion held their own evolving interpretations of belonging and not belonging, of citizen and foreigner, of the definition of British, Irish, Australian, Canadian, etc.

Assisted Emigration Schemes

The British Empire consisted of a 'plethora of networks' (Bridge and Fedorowich, 2003: 6) – kin, commercial and institutional linkages – that greatly facilitated migration. While many British Empire migrants availed of some form of government or charitable assistance, it is important to remember that the overwhelming majority of emigrants were self or family financed and that kinship networks were the principal source of emigration and settlement assistance in the dominions. Nevertheless, assisted emigration schemes, some sponsored by government and aided by charitable organisations, such as the Salvation Army which by 1930 had assisted approximately 200,000 British migrants mostly to Canada, were an important facet of Empire migration (Harper, 2008: 171). Throughout the nineteenth century, the British Government appointed numerous committees and commissions to examine migration and colonisation policies and several attempts at assisted settlement for British and Irish migrants within the Empire met with limited success (Snow, 1931).[34] Some early schemes earned the dubious reputation of 'shovelling out paupers'; a convenient means of clearing the overcrowded estates of the landed gentry (Johnston, 1972). Much nineteenth-century assisted emigration took the form of land schemes, a combination of reduced or free passage and land available at little or no cost to intending immigrants, requiring in return proof of settlement activities such as house building and crop production within a specified time period.

Towards the end of the First World War, assisted settlement was proposed by the Dominions Royal Commission (1912–1917) to aid the demobilisation of soldiers, reviving a tradition of assisted military migration that dated back to the era of the Napoleonic wars. The Soldier Settlement Scheme operated from 1919 to 1924 with over 86,000 military personnel and their dependents settling in the dominions, most to Canada and Australia (Fedorowich, 1995; Roche, 2011).[35] Persistent high unemployment in the United Kingdom throughout the 1920s, which seldom dipped below 10 per cent, was a strong factor motivating the development of further assisted settlement schemes and even trade unions were broadly supportive in order to avoid reductions in British wages (Garside, 1990: 184).[36]

The passage of the Empire Settlement Act (ESA) in 1922, financed in large part by Britain with subsequent assistance agreed with the dominion governments, led to the emigration from 1923 to 1936 of 405,230 assisted British migrants, representing 36 per cent of total British Empire migration over the period. Of these, 186,524 went to Canada (46%); 172,735 (42.3%) to Australia; 44,745 (11%) to New Zealand; and only 1,226 (0.3%) to South Africa (Constantine, 1990: 16). The ESA programme initially consisted of a variety of schemes, which included a combination of reduced passage and land schemes aimed at adult males and families while single females were much sought after for domestic work and to correct the significant imbalance in the gender ratio of the dominions by serving as 'future mothers of the Empire' (Gothard, 1990: 78).[37] However, there were reservations about sending young single women across the world on their own, thus the need for women's emigration organisations in the UK and in the dominions which made travel and reception arrangements for female emigrants.[38] Indeed, one proposed solution was that each emigrating family 'should be encouraged to take an unmarried sister' to be a 'comfort and help to the wife' and who 'before long ... would be established in a home of her own' (Fisher, 1925: 605).[39] Children were also assisted to migrate to the dominions on schemes coordinated primarily by voluntary, church and child welfare organisations, such as Fairbridge and Barnardos, though many children were then placed in family homes and farms where they were expected to work. From 1888 to 1923, approximately 78,000 British children were sent to Canada, though by the mid-1920s, the delegation that travelled to Canada to inspect the system of child migration was encouraging legal adoption.[40] However, as G. F. Plant, member of the delegation and Secretary of the Oversea Settlement Committee later recalled, 'Canadians, it was said, could not risk adopting a child direct from the United Kingdom'! (1951: 134).

In the dominions, suspicion of assisted immigrants – perhaps the legacy of the 'paupers' schemes of the previous century – centred on the question of the employability of primarily urban working-class migrants in agriculture and fear that they would become a burden to the state. There was also the perception of unfairness regarding the subsidising of new immigrants while the native-born were not given the same opportunities and in Canada, the particular fear that the Canadian-born might consequently be driven out as emigrants to the United States (Schultz, 1990: 152). However, many who voiced opposition to assisted immigration were also opposed to social reform. Since Britain had more advanced social legislation, there was genuine anxiety that British immigrants to the dominions might demand similar services. Dominion governments tended to resist state intervention leading to social reform, as they wrestled with modelling their developing societies on 'old world' British/European nanny states or 'new world' (i.e., American) market economies. Reformers, however, were quick to defend new immigrants by pointing out that previous generations had received substantial settlement assistance during better economic times, especially in the form of free land (Cavell, 2006: 348–9).

Because the majority of British migrants after the First World War were from urban areas, the need was identified for agricultural and domestic training geared to the specific conditions of the dominions. Training hostels for women were established to equip them with domestic skills appropriate to employment abroad and several training farms were established in the United Kingdom to train male agricultural workers, including the Richhill Farm in County Armagh, Northern Ireland. Agricultural equipment and modern household appliances were supplied by the dominion governments and the staff hired was familiar with conditions overseas. The Canadian Ministry of Immigration and Colonisation also created a women's division and based recruiting officers in Britain, but also in Dublin and Belfast (Mancuso, 2010: 605). Although 80 per cent of assisted women migrants under Empire Settlement schemes went to Canada (Gothard, 1990: 89), with the Glasgow office issuing the most warrants for the senior dominion (Barber, 2005: 70), Canada accepted only 506 of the domestic trainees, most of whom did not fulfil the one-year requirement to remain in service (Mancuso, 2010: 600).[41] The modern aspirations of many British female immigrants frequently did not match the expectations of their dominion employers who wanted submissive, hard-working and house-bound servants. Thus, attitudes towards female British immigrants were mixed. As a letter from a patron in Toronto that appeared in the *Imperial Colonist* attests, Canadians were particularly sensitive to English 'superiority', suggesting that only 'sensible' English girls be sent out and that, 'The Scotch and North Irish get on much better and are both loved and respected' (quoted in Chilton, 2007: 79).[42] Overall, Canadian employers considered Scottish women the most reliable and Irish Roman Catholics were the least preferred, though rural women were favoured over women from large urban centres (Chilton, 2007: 72; Mancuso, 2010: 606).

By the onset of the Second World War, the 'men, money and markets' imperial strategy was clearly in decline. The combination of assisted and independent emigration in the interwar period had not achieved desired Empire migration targets, nor had Empire trade reached anticipated levels. For in spite of the imposition of a variety of protectionist measures agreed at the 1932 Imperial Economic Conference to stimulate trade and develop markets within the Empire, by 1936 a full 60 per cent of imports to Britain originated from outside the Empire and only 29.2 per cent from the overseas dominions (excluding the Irish Free State, but including India and Southern Rhodesia). Britain exported 49.2 per cent of her goods to the Empire (including Ireland), but only one-third to the overseas dominions. Indeed, British trade was increasing more rapidly with Scandinavian and Baltic countries than with Empire countries (Hancock, 1942:

231). High levels of unemployment in the dominions and the falling birth rate in Britain during the 1930s severely restricted British emigration.[43] The Oversea Settlement Board recognised that the industrialising dominions required skilled workers for manufacturing rather than agricultural labour; consequently, it recommended that assisted emigration based on land schemes should be discontinued. In addition, the development of social welfare programmes would be required in the dominions to equal those available in Britain if 'migration-mindedness' (i.e., the desire to emigrate) was to be maintained in the British population (Oversea Settlement Board, 1938: 29).

Although assisted emigration schemes were greatly reduced after 1930, they were revived again in the post-war period, but by this time they were geared almost exclusively to defraying the costs of travel as with the 'ten-pound passage'. The ESA was renewed in 1937 for fifteen years on half its previous budget, and from 1952 renewed at five-year intervals applicable only to Australia until lapsing in 1972 (Constantine, 1998).[44] Canada (from 1951) and New Zealand (from 1947) opted to finance their own assisted passage schemes in order to maintain control over the selection of immigrants.[45] The Ontario Government operated the short-lived Ontario Airborne Immigration Scheme from 1947 until spring 1948 when over 7,000 British immigrants were landed at Malton Airport near Toronto (Swaffer, 1947: 532).[46]

Northern Ireland: Migration and Empire

Interwar Migration, 1920s–1930s

It has been suggested that Ulster's commitment to the Empire was lukewarm until a surge of imperial feeling inspired by the Boer War saw Ulster's first 'blood sacrifice to the cause for Empire' (Jackson, 1996: 136). However, at this time a series of landmark royal events (1897–1902) – Queen Victoria's diamond jubilee, her death and the coronation of Edward VII – also served to strengthen imperial feeling. The link between Unionism, Protestantism and Empire in Ulster, however, was strongest when under apparent threat by Catholic nationalism, most particularly at the time of the third Home Rule Campaign (1911–1914) and again in the early years of the new Northern Ireland. These periods of Unionist insecurity were also characterised by relatively high levels of emigration to the dominions. The birth of Northern Ireland into the Greater British world in the aftermath of the First World War coincided with a significant shift in Empire relations as the dominions, led by Canada, were actively seeking equality of status in their relationship with the UK; a demand to which Britain acceded in the Balfour Declaration of 1926 and legislated in the Statute of Westminster, December 1931. Northern Ireland aped the increasingly assertive dominions with 'a Parliament and Government of its own'[47] and was empowered to make its own legislation, none of which was ever overturned by the Westminster Parliament (Fitzpatrick, 1998: 144).[48] Though it suffered from the lack of financial autonomy and politicians were always keen to stress its pride of place as integral to the UK, it nonetheless occupied 'a position somewhat unique within the British Empire' as 'a quasi-unit' (Harrison, 1939: 64) of the United Kingdom.[49] The key point here, however, is that Northern Ireland in the 1920s was trying to establish its own identity within the Empire just as dominion status was being radically redefined.[50]

That Northern Ireland was sensitive to its position within the Empire is clear from political and commercial connections fostered with the dominions, most especially Canada and New Zealand which were perceived to have populations of sympathetic Unionists. These connections were bolstered after partition by official state visits of leading politicians.[51] When Northern Ireland Prime Minister, James Craig, toured Canada with his wife and two children in 1926, for example, they were greeted by large crowds of their fellow countrymen and women wherever they went (Fedorowich, 1999: 1174). Craig also made official visits to Australia and New Zealand in 1929–1930 and several dominion prime ministers, some of whom had Ulster connections, made visits to Northern Ireland while they were in the UK to attend imperial conferences (Jeffery, 2008).[52] During the 1920s and 1930s, the imperial conferences also provided opportunities for Northern Ireland to establish its own identity within the Empire, employing 'personal economic diplomacy' to market its products to the dominions while seeking preference against foreign competition (Ollerenshaw, 1996: 177). For the 1923 Imperial Economic Conference in London, for example, a Northern Ireland Ministry of Commerce sub-committee, which included several influential Ulster businessmen, prepared an assessment of Empire markets for Northern Ireland products and Canada was deemed to be a particularly important market for linen, rope and binder twine. By the time of the 1932 Imperial Economic Conference, Canada and Australia were seen as important markets for Northern Irish exports, especially in view of the negative impact caused by the imposition of 'vindictive tariffs' on Northern Irish and British goods by the Irish Free State.[53] In that year, Northern Ireland linen, 'the centre of gravity of the British linen industry', employed a workforce of 90,000.[54] Thus, the rather shaky 'political independence' of Northern Ireland was considerably bolstered by establishing relations – political, commercial and human – with the dominions, and greatly facilitated by Empire migration policy.

From 1922 to 1937, over 94,000 emigrants left Northern Ireland for destinations overseas:[55] approximately 50 per cent to Canada; 30 per cent to the United States; and 16 per cent to Australasia.[56] There was also a substantial inflow or return flow from overseas amounting to 31 per cent of the outflow overall (1924–1937) (see Figure 2.3).[57] However, distribution of the outflow and inflow over the period was not at all even, with outflow greatly diminishing after 1930 and a doubling of inflow from overseas in the years 1930–1933; a sign of the Great Depression.[58] While data on migration between Northern Ireland and Britain is not available for much of the interwar period, movement in the years before and after partition was evidently significant as by 1931, there were 137,961 people resident in Britain who had been born in the six counties and by 1951 their number had increased to 178,319.[59] The 1937 census for Northern Ireland reported that about 34 per cent of the net outflow since 1926 had been destined for 'countries within Europe' (i.e., mainly Britain). Indeed in 1932, the Northern Ireland Government contacted authorities in London about the need for a 'reliable indication of the net movement between Northern Ireland and Great Britain – a movement which, in view of the almost complete cessation of migration to other countries, may become considerable'.[60] Their supposition proved true and for the remainder of the century Britain became the principal destination for Irish migrants from the North and South.[61]

Immigration was also of considerable importance to Northern Ireland during the interwar period (Figure 2.4 shows the distribution of immigrants to Northern Ireland as listed in each full census from 1926 to 2011).[62] The 1926 census provides a fascinating picture of the immigrant or 'foreign-born' population resident in Northern Ireland, revealing that the vast majority were either British subjects by parentage (39%) or by marriage (23.6%). Thus, only 0.13 per cent of the total population of Northern Ireland in 1926, were neither British nationals nor British subjects. Although Americans comprised almost 67 per cent of the 'foreign-born' category, two-thirds were actually British subjects by marriage or parentage, reflecting the return migration of families from the United States. The particularly high figure of those born in independent Ireland but resident in Northern Ireland in the interwar years, suggests significant movement from south to north during the years immediately before and after partition. It is estimated that approximately 24,000 persons, mainly Protestants, came north to live in Northern Ireland at this time, many of them purchasing farms and businesses intending permanent settlement (Dooley, 1996).[63] The Protestant population of the twenty-six counties had certainly declined significantly between 1911 and 1926 (from 10 per cent to 7 per cent of the population), with at least 60,000 departing though the majority left for destinations outside Ireland (Delaney, 2000: 71–2).[64] However, population movements in the years following partition – a sectarian sorting out – included Catholics as well as Protestants. By the spring of 1923 it was estimated that 20,000 southern Loyalist refugees had arrived in Britain while 1,650 northern Catholics had fled south of the border. Applications for assistance grants in the first two years following partition – the majority of which went to displaced persons – show that at least half of those

Figure 2.3: Destination countries overseas for 'British' migrants leaving from and returning to Northern Ireland, 1920s–1930s

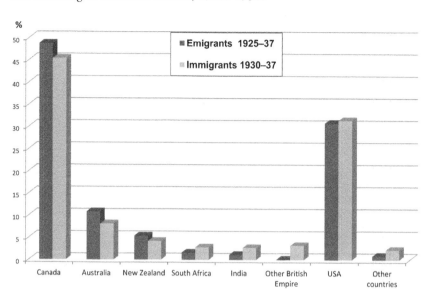

Source data: Board of Trade as reported in the *Ulster Year Book*.

assisted were Catholics, countering the notion that all southern Loyalists were Protestants (Brennan, 1997: 406–8). At the same time, the Northern Ireland Government turned a blind eye to over 3,000 men, presumably Catholics, who from April 1922 to March 1923 journeyed south to Dublin in the hope of joining the Provisional Government Army, though many later returned or left Ireland altogether when employment south of the border failed to materialise (Lynch, 2003: 318–19).[65]

Although political insecurity and incidents of violence no doubt influenced the high level of emigration from Northern Ireland in the years following partition, the lack of a stable economy was another vital factor in the outflow. While the United Kingdom as a whole was in recession throughout much of the 1920s with unemployment averaging around 10.5 per cent, it was Northern Ireland that experienced the most devastating levels of unemployment. In 1922, the jobless rate in Northern Ireland was at 22.9 per cent, by 1925 at 24.2 per cent and remaining high at 23.3 per cent in 1926, the year of the General Strike. Although unemployment declined sharply in 1927 to 13.1 per cent, its lowest rate in the decade, by the early 1930s it had climbed to unprecedented heights peaking in 1931 at 28.1 per cent with an average of 25 per cent over the decade.[66] In comparison, British unemployment reached a high in 1932 at 22.1

Figure 2.4: Resident population born outside of Northern Ireland, 1926–2011

Country of Birth	1926	1937	1951	1961	1971	**1981	**1991	2001	2011
NI total population	1256561	1279745	1370921	1425042	1536065	1490493	1588794	1685274	1810863
GB Total †	53207	48905	62046	63196	76575	65077	64734	*82068	*83517
England	28128	25263	38457	41200	GB	GB	GB	61609	64717
Wales	682	1589	1945	2215	GB	GB	GB	3008	2552
Scotland	24165	21829	21371	19487	GB	GB	GB	16772	15455
Man & Channel	232	224	273	294	GB	GB	GB	567	693
Ireland	63919	59329	61056	53124	46402	35604	35380	39051	37872
Commonwealth	3144	4109	4401	5744	7383	7855	8427	‡10905	‡16434
Foreign	4516	5073	5468	6032	7665	8460	8872	‡15761	‡64187
Adjustment for Visitors		-3405	-6104						
Total non–NI–born	124786	114011	126867	128096	138025	116996	117413	147785	202010
% non–NI–born	7.40%	7.18%	8.51%	8.34%	9.69%	7.85%	7.39%	8.77%	11.16%

Source: Census for Northern Ireland, 1926–2011: † Includes Isle of Man & Channel Islands; * includes UK not specified = 112 (2001) and 100 (2011); ‡ author's calculation from census data; GB = figure only available for GB; ** original census totals[i]

---

[i] NISRA now generally employs the mid–year population estimates for 1981 (1,543,000) and 1991 (1,607,300) because the original enumerations were problematic due to non–response (see chapter 4). However, I maintain the original totals in this table for the purposes of showing the proportionality of the non–NI–born who were arguably less likely to be non–responders and which the newer estimates affect only slightly.

per cent and averaged at just over 16 per cent for the decade. Employment in the Belfast shipyards fell from 24,000 in 1923 to only 8,000 by 1934 and Workman Clark shipbuilders closed down for good in 1935 (O'Grada, 1997: 131). Since Northern Ireland had after partition become liable for unemployment insurance and the Unionist Government had committed to parity with Britain, conditions would have been dire indeed had it not been for the grants that the British Government provided during the 1920s for the provision of relief schemes which put the unemployed to work on public infrastructure improvement projects.[67] To save the Unionist Government from bankruptcy, several other measures were attempted, such as: partial re-integration of unemployment insurance with Britain including new regulations that made large numbers of the unemployed ineligible for benefits; reduction of Northern Ireland's imperial contribution; and the provision of business loan schemes to stimulate enterprise, especially in the shipyards (Norton, 2001). The Unionist Government was particularly concerned about the disaffection of the Protestant working class, but conditions continued to be so poor that in 1932 riots erupted on the streets of Belfast. The Northern Ireland Government attempted to stimulate the economy with the New Industrial Development Acts of 1932 and 1937, which provided interest-free loans and grants to entrepreneurs, but the only lasting result was the establishment in 1937 of Short Brothers and Harland aircraft manufacturing in Belfast (Munck, 1993: 53). Ironically, the strength of the northern manufacturing industries – mainly shipbuilding and textiles production – on which the economic rationale for partition was largely based, declined steadily afterwards, only to revive by the outbreak of the Second World War (Bradley, 1999: 39). Between 1935 and 1949 net industrial production expanded by 62 per cent and the industrial workforce increased by 46 per cent (Johnson and Kennedy, 2003: 475). The steady movement of the population within Northern Ireland from rural areas into the greater Belfast industrial zone – a rural to urban internal migration that had been steadily increasing since the mid-nineteenth century – provided much of the growing workforce for industry. Even though by 1926, over 50 per cent of the Northern Ireland population was already resident in urban areas, this had increased to 53 per cent by 1937 despite the years of economic depression. In comparison, the population balance in independent Ireland remained in favour of rural settlement until the 1960s (Fitzgerald and Lambkin, 2008: 233); the urban majority evident in the census of the ROI of 1971.

Although migration policy remained under the control of the UK Government so that Northern Ireland was automatically party to Empire migration agreements with the dominions, Northern Ireland, nevertheless, exerted control over local policy and funding allocation through its own power to legislate and thus maintained influence on the implementation of such policies.[68] Close examination of the Stormont Papers in the interwar period reveals considerable discussion of emigration though usually somewhat camouflaged in the context of the debates on unemployment, agriculture or other economic matters. As the fledgling state sought to position itself within the Empire to economic advantage, criticism of migration by the Unionist Government was muted since it was a key aspect of imperial policy. However, the atmosphere of insecurity in Northern Ireland in the years immediately following partition was partly fuelled by the decline of Protestants in Ireland generally, and within Unionist ranks, concern was expressed about the numbers, especially of Protestants, that were at that time leaving Northern Ireland.[69] In 1924, for example, John Martin Mark, Unionist MP for Londonderry, speaking in the Northern Ireland Parliament noted that, '*of a certain religious persuasion* over 2,000 had emigrated during the last three months … a very large proportion of these were young men of the farming industry – farmers' sons who are the very backbone of our country'.[70] Subsequently, James Craig's 1926 holiday tour to Canada caused rumours to circulate at home that he might be encouraging Protestant emigration and he had to have his Belfast office issue a statement to quickly dispel this notion (Fedorowich, 1999: 1174–5).

In the Northern Ireland Parliament, much concern about emigration was repeatedly raised regarding the establishment of the agricultural training farm in the predominantly Protestant area of Richhill, County Armagh. This was an initiative under the Empire Settlement Act, the purpose of which was to train young men for agricultural work in the dominions, particularly Canada. The Richhill Castle estate had been purchased by the Northern Ireland Government in September 1926 at a cost of £10,500 with another couple of thousand allocated for refurbishment. Named the Richhill Centre for Overseas Settlement, thus sidestepping the term 'emigration', it boasted a farm of 192 acres equipped with sleeping and dining huts for the trainees and farm machinery provided by the Canadian Government.[71] Young men admitted to the programme received train fares to and from the centre, were housed on site and were provided with suitable clothing while undergoing the three-month course. In addition, the Northern Ireland Government agreed to pay the assisted passage for the trainees heading to Canada.[72]

Support for emigration in the fledgling Northern Ireland Parliament was divided along class lines. Unionist MPs were in favour of emigration and their support was often expressed in imperial terms. 'It is altogether to our advantage that we should have a large population, an outpost population, in Canada and the other great dependencies of the Empire' were the words of Sir Robert J. Johnstone, Unionist MP for Queen's University, in a parliamentary debate about unemployment in October 1926.[73] However, Labour, Nationalist and Independent Unionist MPs generally opposed the Richhill scheme on the grounds that Northern Ireland should not be bearing the costs of training young men for the dominions and that the funds would be better spent to keep people on the land at home by expanding agriculture if possible. Concern was also expressed about the hardship of life in Canada, that there was no unemployment insurance in that dominion if the emigrants were thrown upon hard times and that many of the emigrants over there were subsequently desirous of coming home.[74] Thomas Henderson, Independent Unionist MP for Belfast North, painted a dire picture of the situation with some resonance of famine times:

> Thousands of young men who went out from Ulster ... are now derelicts in the industrial cities of Canada and they cannot even get home. In the parks of Canada there are large numbers of young men lying at nights in utter starvation.[75]

When the matter of Richhill was raised again in Parliament on 4 May 1927, Nationalist MP, Joseph Devlin, vehemently objected to emigration being discussed yet again under the heading of 'unemployment'. While acknowledging that Northern Ireland had no jurisdiction for direct involvement in foreign affairs, he suggested nonetheless that the debate should take place under the heading 'Our foreign policy in regard to the emigration of the youth from Northern Ireland into another Country', and then declared 'I have never heard of so monstrous a transaction in my life than to give this valuable asset to a great rich country like Canada.'[76] Northern Ireland Labour MPs, Jack Beattie and William McMullen, were careful to tow the imperial line by supporting Empire Settlement on principle but, nevertheless, voiced opposition to emigration with the warning, 'do not be draining Ulster of its young men and leave her only with the old men'.[77] During the 'emigration' debate that continued the following day, Devlin in exasperation attacked the Empire aspirations of the Northern Ireland Government, 'My objection to this government is that they are always trying to fashion themselves in picturesque form: – "We are doing something great for the Empire, we are serving some great purpose."' To this, however, Unionist MP for Londonderry Dehra Chichester, herself a child of the Empire, replied describing emigration as 'the benefit we confer on a portion of the great Empire of which we are a part'. She rejected Devlin's notion of 'Canada as a foreign land' and spoke of the returnees being 'better citizens of *our State*' because of the experience they had gained abroad.[78] By the time the Richhill Centre closed in 1930, it had trained 767 workers of whom 505 went to Canada and 176 to Australia, although ninety-eight of them had by then already returned to Northern Ireland (ninety-three from Canada and five from Australia).[79]

Post-War Migration, 1940s–1960s

With the onset of war, overseas emigration from Britain and Northern Ireland slowed to a trickle, however, because the Board of Trade data gathering between 1939 and 1945 was interrupted and only resumed in 1946, migration data for the 1940s is patchy at best.[80] Canadian immigration data, however, provides a clue as to the scale of the decline as for the 1940–1944 years, there were only on average about sixty immigrants from Northern Ireland arriving annually in the country compared to the several thousand arriving each year during the 1920s and indeed around 1,400 annually for the 1947–1949 period when overseas migration resumed.[81] The 1951 census clearly shows that most movement (about 85%) out of Northern Ireland in the inter-censal period since 1937 was heading to Britain and that about 60 per cent of the emigrants were male.[82]

Because of the lack of Board of Trade data during the war years, Isles and Cuthbert employed other data sources in their economic survey of Northern Ireland to estimate migration flows for the wartime period (Isles and Cuthbert, 1957). By counting British residence permits for Northern Ireland migrants issued by the Ministry of Home Affairs, which to the end of December 1945 amounted to some 33,500, and combining this figure with ration card data, they estimated that the total number of wartime emigrants still absent from Northern Ireland by the end of 1945 was approximately 75,000. The emigrants fell into three categories: service personnel (approximately 35,000); workers placed by the Ministry of Labour into employment in Great Britain (from 25,000–30,000); and other emigrants who went to Britain independently (10,000–15,000) (Isles and Cuthbert, 1957: 241–2; Ollerenshaw, 2007: 192–4). In comparison, over 100,000 left independent Ireland during the war years for civilian employment in Britain (Delaney, 2000: 130)[83] while some 37,440 Irish men and 4,510 women served in the British forces (Connolly, 2000: 52).[84] From 1943 to 1946, Stormont issued 1,680 permits to citizens of Ireland for residence in Northern Ireland, though it is impossible to be sure that all were used (Delaney, 2000: 128–9). During the immediate post-war years (1946–1950) Northern Ireland net migration amounted to minus 22,000 overall (Isles and Cuthbert, 1957: 242), suggesting an annual outflow of approximately 4,500 per year with some 10,000 individuals emigrating overseas while 12,000 went to Britain/Europe.[85] Return from Britain during the same period was minimal probably due to the relatively full employment available, in comparison to the rising jobless rates in Northern Ireland.

The 1950s was the decade of highest Irish emigration in the twentieth century, particularly in the ROI which saw an average annual outflow of over 40,000 (minus 14.1 per 1000), with almost 60,000 individuals leaving during the peak year of 1957. The beginning of the boom in emigration already evident in the immediate post-war years prompted the establishment by the Irish Government of the *Commission on Emigration and other Population Problems* (1948–1954) in response to the issue. The outward movement from Northern Ireland was also substantial during the 1950s and amounted to a net loss of 92,228 (53% male and 47% female) for the decade, with an annual average of 9,185 (minus 6.5 per 1000) and some 68 per cent of the flow going to Britain.[86] In contrast, the proportion of emigration from the ROI destined for Britain in this period has been estimated at 80 per cent (Walsh, 1974: 108).[87] The difference in the proportion of emigrants choosing Britain in the two Irish jurisdictions is puzzling but may suggest the popularity among the Northern Ireland cohort to exploit the readily available assisted emigration schemes that operated to Commonwealth destinations during the 1950s and 1960s. For example, Canada received almost 25,000 immigrants from Northern Ireland during the 1950s, over 5,300 arriving in the peak year of 1957 alone.

Economic decline especially in manufacturing was a factor in the post-war outflow from Northern Ireland as jobless rates increased at home. While Britain's average unemployment was only about 1.5 per cent for the 1950s, nearing 2 per cent for the 1960s, the comparative averages in Northern Ireland were 7.5 per cent and 7 per cent, respectively, though in some years during the 1950s it was closer to 10 per cent.[88] The collapse of the linen textiles industry in the early 1950s was a precursor of the decline in other traditional industries, such as shipbuilding, in the following decade leading to the gradual shift to employment in foreign-owned companies that had started to establish in Northern Ireland (Johnson and Kennedy, 2003: 477). Signs of the economic downturn and the general shortage of housing in Northern Ireland compared to the easy availability of relatively low-cost emigration with the promise of full employment abroad were no doubt persuasive in leading many young people to emigrate.

Despite very significant emigration during the 1950s, the population of Northern Ireland continued to grow primarily due to an increase in the birth rate evident since the end of the Second World War, and most especially from 1956 onwards with 1960 achieving the highest birth rate in forty years.[89] Nevertheless, the 1961 census results caused enough consternation that emigration, which was especially notable among Catholics, was raised in Stormont. Increasing unemployment, poor availability of housing and rural depopulation, especially of Western counties, were the main concerns. Terence O'Neill, then Minister of Finance, blamed rural depopulation in part on the attractive portrayal of urban life on television and cheerfully noted that in spite of emigration, the population of Northern Ireland had nevertheless increased while that of the South had decreased by approximately 5 per cent.[90] Labour Party MP, David Bleakley, noting the preponderance for skilled leavers, suggested that a 'registrar for emigration' be set up to take account of who was leaving and where they were going and 'to ask that the Commonwealth countries should take a balanced proportion of our population instead of a selective proportion'.[91]

Immigration in the post-war period remained steady but on a small scale that did little to offset emigration. The number of those born in England, Wales and the offshore islands (40,675) made up almost 3 per cent of the total Northern Ireland population in 1951 – the highest number recorded in the ninety years since 1861 – while the percentage of Scottish-born decreased from a high of almost 2 per cent in 1926 to 1.56 per cent by 1951. The percentage of Northern Ireland residents born in independent Ireland remained high at 4.45 per cent (61,056) of the population in 1951 but ten years later in 1961, it had declined by 13 per cent (53,124 or 3.73%). While migrants from the USA and Canada formed the largest non-'British' immigrant groups in Northern Ireland, a steady post-war influx of migrants from European countries, especially Italy, Germany and France was also noteworthy. The third largest group of immigrants came in from the Indian subcontinent and the growing Chinese community, composed largely of immigrants from the territories of Hong Kong and Singapore was evident by the 1960s (Fitzgerald and Lambkin, 2008: 226).[92]

The 1951 and 1961 census counts show that immigration did not change the religious cohort balance in Northern Ireland overall; the Protestant/Catholic proportions of the immigrants differing only slightly from the native-born (approximately sixty/thirty-four). Differences between native and immigrant groups in 1951 were, however, more noticeable within Protestant denominations as Presbyterians represented a lower proportion among the immigrant group (21.7% of immigrants versus 29.9% resident population) while immigrant Anglicans were proportionately higher (33.3% versus 25.8%) reflecting the larger number of English-born in the inflow.[93] In 1961, the cross-tabulation of denomination by immigrant's country of birth revealed somewhat surprising results. For example, of the Scottish-born immigrant group, over a quarter were Roman Catholic and over 30 per cent were non-Presbyterian Protestant including 17.4 per cent Anglican, thus challenging the general assumption that most Scottish immigrants to Ulster were Presbyterians. The English-born immigrant group was 49 per cent Anglican and 20 per cent Roman Catholic, the rest comprised mostly of other Protestant denominations with Presbyterians amounting to over 14 per cent. Reflecting the movement of southern Irish Protestants to the North, 50 per cent of northern residents born in independent Ireland were Protestants: 18.5 per cent (9,808) Presbyterian; 28 per cent (14,879) Anglican; over 4 per cent (2,196) Methodist; and over 5 per cent were other denominations, comprised mostly of other Protestant sects.[94]

While Ireland had begun to look toward economic recovery based on its *Programme for Economic Expansion* (1958), in the North, cracks were showing in the industrial base with a downturn in shipbuilding and textiles during the 1960s (Ó Murchú, 2005). With emigration declining in the South and rising in Northern Ireland from the late 1950s, by 1961–1962 emigration rates were approximately equal for both jurisdictions (Daly, 2006: 219). Thus, from 1961 to 1971, the total net movement outward remained significant for Northern Ireland at 69,222 (minus 4.5 per 1000) with at least 70 per cent destined for Britain. However, this was also the time that change from sea to air travel as the principal mode of transport for migrants was underway and the Board of Trade from 1964 discontinued the use of 'sea registration cards' for shipboard passengers which hitherto had provided detailed information on migrants.[95] Thereafter, information on Northern Ireland migration was available only in the form of net migration estimates in annual population data and in the census tally.[96]

In Britain, return migration became a concern from the mid-1950s to the mid-1960s. The Board of Trade data on overseas Northern Ireland migrants available from 1961 to 1963 recorded 8,072 emigrants and 3,326 'British' immigrants, implying a potentially high rate of return of 41 per cent which would tally with high return rates to Britain that were at that time causing concern in view of the funding spent on assisted emigration schemes (see Chapter 7). Overall, from the 1920s through the early 1960s, the Board of Trade figures on overseas migration for Northern Ireland would suggest a return rate of around 30 per cent. There is no reliable data on the rates of migrants returning from Britain. Would they have likely been lower or higher than rates for overseas return? Large numbers of NI-born (all age groups) recorded in every census of England, Wales and Scotland throughout the twentieth century might be suggestive of a low return rate but proximity and common citizenship would favour the opposite. To provide a recent comparison, migrants arriving to Northern Ireland from Britain in the year prior to the 2001 census represented almost 37 per cent (4,410) of the outflow to Britain (approximately 12,000).[97]

Characteristics of Migrants, 1920s–1960s

Who were the individuals leaving Northern Ireland from the 1920s to the 1960s? Data concerning overseas migrants provides an intriguing comparison of the interwar and post-war eras (see Figure 2.5).[98] Male migrants comprised about 55 per cent of outgoing and incoming flows to and from Northern Ireland in movements overseas and with Britain over the entire period.[99] The significant proportion of housewives among emigrant females (one-third) and the even higher proportion in the return cohort (54%) indicate the importance of family groups in the interwar migration flows and may also suggest a tendency for women to marry while abroad. By the 1960s, an even larger number of married housewives in the outflow showed an increasing tendency towards emigration in family groups during the post-war years.[100] Children and youth generally comprised between a quarter and a third of the overseas emigrant and returning cohorts, again indicating a strong tendency towards migration in family groups; a pattern also characteristic of nineteenth-century Ulster migration.[101] The higher proportion of younger-aged children in the return cohort would suggest a tendency for families to return at an early stage of family development for reasons perhaps relating to the children (e.g., education or the lack of extended family contact and support abroad).

49

During the interwar years, the predominant occupations listed were farming for male emigrants and domestic labour for female emigrants; however, caution with the data is warranted here as these employment categories were eligible for assisted passage schemes. Many emigrants had no actual intention of pursuing such work upon arrival at their destination; indeed, as mentioned earlier in this chapter, their failure to do so in large numbers was a cause of concern in the host countries (e.g., see stories of Roseena in Chapter 3 and Leo in Chapter 6). With the onset of the Great Depression in the 1930s, a notable return flow of labourers and tradesmen may reflect the downturn in the construction industry in North America. By the 1960s, a marked increase in professional or clerical occupations and skilled trades (52–59%) among male migrants and a low percentage of agricultural, domestic and general labourers (11–14%) reflects the change since the 1930s in educational levels at home and the influence of new immigration selection policies in the destination countries. Similarly, the marked increase of

Figure 2.5: Occupations of Northern Ireland overseas migrants, 1920s–1960s

Males	*% Emigrants*		*% Immigrants*	
	1925–37	*1961–63*	*1930–37*	*1961–63*
Agriculture	39	5	16	3
Labourers	20	9	27	8
Trades	16	31	24	22
Clerical/sales	12	11	14	12
Professional	2	17	4	18
Transport	3	4	3	4
Other	7	17	12	22
Students/retired	–	6	–	11

Females	*% Emigrants*		*% Immigrants*	
	1925–37	*1961–63*	*1930–37*	*1961–63*
Domestic	45	6	23	4
Housewife	32	45	54	47
Clerical/sales	7	19	6	15
Clothing trades	3	6	2	2
Professional	3	14	6	17
Other	10	8	9	10
Students/retired	–	2	–	5

Source: Board of Trade data as reported in the *Ulster Year Book*.

female professionals and skilled workers (34–39%) is notable: almost half of the professionals were nurses, and teachers comprised another quarter. Accordingly, the oft-portrayed stereotype of Irish post-war migrants as poorly educated and largely unskilled would not appear to apply to overseas migrants from Northern Ireland (Compton, 1991a: 165; O'Grada, 1997: 214). This prompts several questions. Were Northern Ireland migrants of the post-war era generally better educated than the Southern Irish cohort?[102] Or can we assume that the emigrants leaving Northern Ireland for Britain – the principal destination of 1950s Irish emigrants, North and South – were largely unskilled and thus differed markedly from the cohort emigrating overseas that was subject to selective immigration policies?

Migration, 1970s–2000

From the 1970s until 2008, three phases of population movement characterised Northern Ireland migration (Fegan and Marshall, 2008: 7). From 1973 through the 1980s, there was significant population decline due to out-migration which in some years amounted to over 10,000 individuals, with the conflict evidently having a significant impact. During the second phase from the early 1990s until 2004, approximately 20,000 people were moving annually in and out of Northern Ireland. From 2004 to 2008, a marked increase in immigration was notable due primarily to EU expansion, with over 32,000 incoming by mid-2007 and with approximately 22,000 departing annually.[103] However, the economic downturn in the autumn of 2008 marked a new phase in the migration pattern with a decline in immigration and a 14 percent increase in emigration by 2011–2012, with almost 25,000 people departing.[104]

The 1970s witnessed the highest outward movement of population from Northern Ireland (net outflow = 111,423 or minus 7.3 per 1000) since the years immediately following partition; the loss essentially cancelling out natural population increase, despite the relatively high birth rate. It is assumed that around 70 per cent crossed the Irish Sea to Britain and that 19,000–25,000 took up residence in the ROI, no doubt attracted by its economic boom in the early to mid-1970s (Compton, 1985: 215; NESC, 1991: 282). Several reasons have been suggested for the significant outflow but problems with the reliability of the 1981 census count inevitably resulted in rough estimates of net migration that could be misleading; indeed, the original low population count initially served to mask the high outward movement of the 1970s.[105] The political implications of such a significant migratory movement in view of the conflict raging during the decade make it therefore remarkable that the influence of sectarianism and violence on the rate of emigration has received so little attention (although its role in internal migration has been widely acknowledged).[106] Indeed, in the general academic literature on Northern Ireland, the rare and brief discussions of emigration tend to link the outflow with economic factors, rather than politics.[107] Thus, the relationship between migration and the Northern Ireland conflict has remained largely unexplored; indeed, an aim of this book is to address this gap (see also Chapter 4). However, studies of the Northern Ireland economy have also articulated divergent views on the impact of the conflict; positions varying from highly critical ('Nationalist') accounts to rather uncritical ('Unionist') versions.[108] Factors such as de-industrialisation, excess labour supply due to the high birth rate or global circumstances have been cited as the most important elements influencing local economic conditions and hence out-migration. However, the conflict undoubtedly had an impact on economic trends. First, employment in foreign-owned enterprises dropped by half between 1973 and 1990 (O'Grada, 1997: 134).[109] Second, severe de-industrialisation occurred in the decade 1973–1983 with manufacturing output declining by one-third and net industrial output by 25 per cent (Johnson and Kennedy, 2003: 478). Third, in the face of de-industrialisation and a withdrawing private sector, the drastic increase in the UK subvention to Northern Ireland after 1970 led it to become 'dependant on a bloated public sector to save it from the abyss' (Bew et al., 1997: 118). The lack of economic development was particularly felt in Belfast and is reflected in the city's considerable population loss with an estimated annual outflow from the core city of 10,700 during the period of 1971 to 1991 (Boal, 2006: 78).[110]

The 1980s saw a resurgence in emigration from the ROI due to widespread economic recession with some 200,000 (5.6 per 1000) people departing mostly for Britain, three-quarters of them in the second half of the decade (Lee, 1990: 33).[111] The recession also hit strongly in Northern Ireland. In the decade to 1988, male unemployment more than doubled and female unemployment doubled; by the end of the 1980s, those unemployed represented over 15 per cent of the workforce, more than twice the UK average of 6.3 per cent (Gaffikin and Morrissey, 1990: 77). For Northern Ireland, the net loss of population, though less than the 1970s, remained substantial at 69,420 (minus 4.4 per 1000), with over 70 per cent heading to Britain. Examination of these figures year by year, however, shows that there was actually significant fluctuation over the decade: outward migration was highest in 1981, coinciding that year with enormous political unrest surrounding the hunger strikes.[112] Thereafter, emigration declined in the short term but increased dramatically again in the years 1986–1988, eventually tailing off and reversing to a small positive inward flow during the early 1990s.

A study of migration flows in the period 1975–1990 has explained the fluctuations in migration by consideration of Britain and Northern Ireland as part of a single national economy: that is, when Britain is in recession Northern Ireland is also in recession, when Britain is in recovery so too is Northern Ireland (Compton, 1992). Thus, the implications for employment opportunities are that when jobs are plentiful in Britain, increased emigration from Northern Ireland will take place to help fill them and conversely when Britain is in recession; return migration to Northern Ireland will increase. Accordingly, the early 1980s recession resulted in less outward movement from Northern Ireland, increasing sharply after 1985 due to the short-term economic recovery, with the flow reversing again during the early 1990s downturn. But paradoxically and in line with Ravenstein's law that any migration stream will generate a counter-stream (Fitzgerald and Lambkin, 2008: 301; and Ravenstein, 1885, 1889), increased outflow to Britain will also result in increased inward migration to Northern Ireland. Indeed, during this period, inward migration to Northern Ireland was in the range of 65 to 70 per cent of the outflow, most of this coming from Britain and consisting of those who had family connections with Northern Ireland, not 'primary movers' (Compton, 1992: 85–6). Northern Ireland contributed over 5 per cent of Britain's population growth (Compton, 1992: 81), demonstrating that due to its relatively high birth rate, it remained an important source of skilled workers for the UK labour market throughout the 1980s and 1990s (Compton, 1995: 95).[113] In terms of preferred destinations within Britain, a shift slightly away from the northwest of England towards Greater London was observed from the early 1980s, particularly for young adults (Compton, 1992: 94–9). This was no doubt part of the general shift in internal migration trends within Britain from north to south during the period (Stillwell et al., 1992).

The profile of 1980s migrants from Northern Ireland differed somewhat from those of earlier generations, generalised as interwar labourers and post-war skilled workers. In a study of Northern Ireland migration to Britain based on Labour Force Survey data for 1986–1988, it was found that emigrants tended to fall into two categories: well-educated, skilled individuals; and the low skilled (30–35%) who had tended to be unemployed in Northern Ireland prior to their departure. An immigration counter-stream from Britain (mostly returnees) was also noted of the unemployed who were liable to remain unemployed once resettled in Northern Ireland (Forsythe and Borooah, 1992: 117, 125).[114] Since a higher proportion of the 1980s emigrants, North and South, was university educated (mirroring the resident population), migration in this decade has often been characterised as a 'brain drain' (see the detailed discussion of 'brain drain' in Chapter 4). Indeed, growth in the student population in Northern Ireland during the 1980s (reflecting the 1960s baby boom) and the lack of sufficient third-level places contributed to a student outflow of some 2,000 per year to Britain; a significant proportion of the large overall movement of those in the fifteen to twenty-nine year age group that was especially marked among young women. Conversely young women also featured very significantly in the inflow to Northern Ireland, suggesting that females may have a propensity to return while males may tend towards permanent settlement abroad (Compton, 1992: 91–2). The 1980s also witnessed an increase in the return migration of retirees, many of whom had been 1950s emigrants.

Due to the lack of qualitative research on Northern Ireland migration, little is known about the motivations of migrants; however, a 1988 survey found that most of the emigrants surveyed had left for work-related reasons or to pursue further education while only 2.2 per cent claimed to have left because of the conflict. Fewer than 20 per cent of the migrants sampled declared an intention to return to Northern Ireland, however most interesting was how this differed by denomination (Protestants 16.5% and Catholics 25%). Reasons for not returning centred on career prospects such as the lack of good jobs available in Northern Ireland, while only 4 per cent cited the conflict (Compton and Power, 1991).[115]

Emigration from Northern Ireland throughout the 1990s and into the early 2000s continued apace although the extent of the migratory movement outward averaging 20,000 annually was somewhat masked by an almost equivalent inflow (net migration = minus 3,914 for the decade). Like the decade before, approximately 70 per cent of the outflow was to Britain and consisted increasingly of skilled workers, third-level students and graduates. Indeed, Northern Ireland continued to be a significant loser of graduate labour to Britain, in particular to Greater London, especially graduates with strong results (Hoare and Corver, 2010: 485–6).[116] While a return flow already mentioned for the early 1990s was largely due to the recession in Britain, by 1993 emigration from Northern Ireland had picked up again. The dramatically increased inflow to Northern Ireland evident in 1995 (4,700) may have been a direct result of the ceasefires of 1994 and perhaps a general impression at the time that 'the war was over'.[117] However, the improving Northern Ireland economy that outperformed other regions of the UK during much of the decade was no doubt a factor in the gradually increasing inflow (Johnson and Kennedy, 2003: 486). In comparison, emigration from the ROI to the UK decreased steadily during the 1990s and into the 2000s, and by 2008 represented only 15 per cent of the outward movement, thus breaking the traditional relationship between the Irish immigrant workforce and the demand for labour in Britain (Walter, 2008a: 182–3). However, since 2009 a steadily increasing outflow (not necessarily comprised entirely of Irish nationals) from the ROI to Britain had by 2011 reached 20,000 or almost 25 per cent of emigrants with almost 40 per cent heading to countries such as Canada and Australia, while only 6 per cent went to the USA.[118]

Migration Since 2001

From 2001 until 2008, immigration predominated in Northern Ireland, but by 2010 emigration was once again on the rise accelerating by mid-2011 to a level not seen since the 1990s (net migration = minus 1,500), with a significant outflow noted among the eighteen to forty-four age group.[119] The marked population increase in Northern Ireland since 2004 coincided with the accession of the EU8 countries of Central and Eastern Europe into the European Economic Area and the arrival of many of their citizens to work in the UK and Ireland; the single largest group from Poland whose UK-resident population grew from 75,000 in 2003 to 643,000 in 2011.[120] Despite the economic downturn in 2008, UK immigration has remained fairly stable since 2004, with some 566,000 long-term immigrants arriving in 2011, approximately one-quarter destined for London alone. Of these, 86 per cent (487,000) were non-British citizens, though 31 per cent (174,000) were EU nationals with 232,000 arriving for further education. The proportion of British nationals in the immigrant stream has steadily decreased since 1998 when they comprised 26 per cent of immigrants, amounting to only 13.8 per cent in 2011 (78,000).[121]

Immigration into the UK of citizens from Old Commonwealth countries (including Australia, Canada, New Zealand and South Africa) has also been declining in recent years and fell from 62,000 in 2006 to 45,000 in 2007 while immigration of EU8 nationals peaked in 2007 at 112,000, dropping to 68,000 by 2009 and rebounding somewhat in 2011 to 77,000.[122] Outflow from the UK since 2000 has consistently been over 300,000 per year, peaking in 2008 at 427,000 and amounting to 350,000 in 2011. Emigration of British citizens leaving the UK during this period showed a marked increase over the 1990s, peaking at 207,000 in 2006 and comprising just over 50 per cent of the total emigrant stream, however, with the economic downturn, by 2011 it had dropped to 149,000 or 43 per cent of total emigration.[123]

It is estimated that the rate of remigration of non-British nationals leaving the UK to return to their countries of origin or to move onward to other countries amounted to about half of the immigration flow over the last thirty years (3,186,200 outward versus 6,189,900 inward). At least 61,000 non-nationals have left every year since 1975, but recent rates have increased dramatically to well over 200,000.[124] Short-term immigration to the UK approximately doubled in the decade between 1996 and 2007 with many immigrants remaining less than four years. Thus, only about 25 per cent of those who arrived in 1998 were still resident in the UK in 2008 (Finch et al., 2009: 3). Most immigrants and emigrants were in the twenty-five to forty-four age category and many of the shorter term migrants have been students and temporary migrant workers, though a significant number have been highly skilled younger migrants coming from developed countries who had no intention of settling permanently. This type of transnational migrant tends to be 'super mobile', relocating several times between home country and other developed countries. Consequently, this has implications for the development of migration policies as competition for these highly qualified mobile migrants becomes increasingly fierce.

Because Northern Ireland is part of the UK migration system, data specifically on population movements to and from Northern Ireland tends to be patchy and estimates from several data sources are required to develop a detailed picture, especially of immigration.[125] Health registration data is the principal means of tracking annual migration flows in the UK because it covers the widest number of individuals. Employment data (national insurance, work permits) also provides an indicator for immigration, however, it accounts only for adults who apply for work permits and benefits. Children and adults who accompany workers and indeed undocumented migrant workers, refugees and asylum seekers are not represented. Employment data also measures inflow only; it does not tell us how long a worker intends to stay nor when they depart. The Northern Ireland census since 1971 has provided at ten-year intervals a profile of immigrants, including returnees, who moved into the region in the year prior to the census count (see Figure 2.6).[126] For example, in the year to 2001, 18.5 per cent of the migrant inflow (18,974) was under sixteen while 3.3 per cent were retirement age with the gender balance tipped slightly in favour of males overall. Roman Catholics comprised 38 per cent of the inflow; 47 per cent was Protestant; 3.2 per cent other religions; and 12 per cent claimed no religion.[127]

Figure 2.6: Immigrants to Northern Ireland within the year prior to the census 1971–2001, by country of last residence

Last residence	1971	%	1981*	%	1991	%	2001	%
GB Total	11144	65.8	7637	56.2	10282	65.7	11695	61.6
England	9627	56.8	5479	40.3	8675	55.5	8548	45.1
Wales	254	1.5	204	1.5	269	1.7	317	1.7
Scotland	1147	6.8	1646	12.1	1081	6.9	2668	14.1
GB not specified	0	0.0	246	1.8	102	0.7	0	0.0
Man & Channel	116	0.7	62	0.5	155	1.0	162	0.9
Ireland	1337	7.9	943	6.9	1458	9.3	2321	12.2
Abroad	4465	26.3	5018	36.9	3903	25.0	4954	26.1
Total	16946	100	13598	100	15643	100	18970	100

* Low figures for 1981 are likely due to under-enumeration in the census.

Taking immigrant inflow data from the 2001 census as an example and further breaking it down reveals the complexity of the composition of the movement inward. The principal regions of inflow were from Britain (61.6%); Ireland (12.2%); Europe (9.3%); North America (6.3%); and Oceania (3.2%). Further breaking down the inflow data by country of birth provides a much better

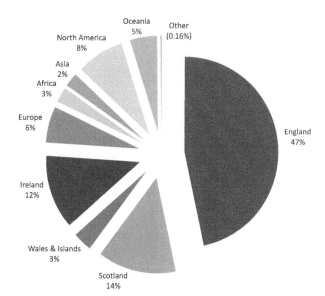

Figure 2.7:
Northern
Ireland-born
returnees 2001
by place of last
residence

Source: Census
2001, Table
EXT20040628A

picture of its composition. Notably, almost 37 per cent of the immigrant flow was in fact the returning NI-born cohort (6,935) and significant cohorts of English, Scottish and ROI-born migrants (25.3%, 10.5% and 7.9% respectively) came in from several jurisdictions. For example, 183 English-born came to Northern Ireland from the ROI, conversely 207 ROI-born came directly from England, fifty-seven from North America and twenty-three from Oceania. Almost 600 Scottish-born came to Northern Ireland directly from England while 272 English-born came in from Scotland. From the same data set, examining only the NI-born returnees by country of last residence provides a fascinating perspective on their migrations (Figure 2.7), not least that they form significant proportions of the total inflow arriving from England (38%), from Scotland (36%) and of those crossing the border from the ROI (37%).[128]

Annual out-migration figures to Britain from Northern Ireland estimated from the transfer of NHS registrations have remained fairly consistent since the last census with only slight fluctuations year to year (e.g., year ending June 2002 = 11,598; year ending June 2011 = 11,121; a rate of approximately 0.7% of total Northern Ireland population). Inflow to Northern Ireland from Britain averaged slightly higher (e.g., year ending June 2002 = 12,505; though this has also recently declined for 2011 = 10,323).[129] Of this, around 2,000 people each year leave Northern Ireland for Scotland and slightly more arrive from Scotland, which along with London, the northwest and southeast of England have been the most popular British destinations and source regions for outgoing and incoming migrants for Northern Ireland.[130] The majority of these NHS transfers likely represent the NI-born and their families.

Figure 2.8: Migration outflow from Northern Ireland to the ROI in the year prior to the ROI census, 1996–2011

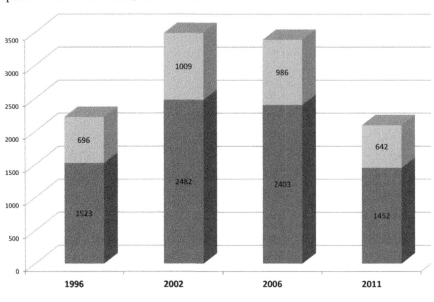

■ Rest of outflow   ▨ ROI-born in outflow

From 1996 to 2011, the ROI census recorded an increasing number of NI-born residents (1996 = 39,567; 2002 = 49,928; 2006 = 50,172; and 2011 = 58,470).[131] Figure 2.8 shows the cross-border outflow from Northern Ireland to the ROI in the year prior to the census; notably from 29 to 31 per cent actually represents ROI-born migrants returning from Northern Ireland.[132] The annual flow in the reverse direction from the ROI to Northern Ireland is estimated at approximately 2,000 persons per year (NISRA 2005: 5), however, 2010 showed a relatively average inflow (1,912) but a much reduced outflow to the ROI (678) because of severe recession in the South.[133]

Since 2001, there was also a consistently steady flow of population (7–8,000 annually) between Northern Ireland and countries outside the British Isles until the international inflow jumped to over 13,000 in 2005; followed by 18,000; and 19,000 in 2006–2007, when immigration surpassed natural increase as the principal factor in Northern Ireland's population growth. The figures showed a marked decline by 2010–2011 with outflow (14,100) surpassing inflow (13,400).[134] Figure 2.9 shows the top source countries for recent immigrants to Northern Ireland from outside the UK as indicated by new NHS registrations, employment (NINo, WRS, WP) and education data, all of which showed a marked increase from 2004 due to the influx from new EU8 accession countries.[135]

The new immigration is also evident in the school system. By 2011, the

Figure 2.9: Top source countries for recently arrived immigrants to Northern Ireland as indicated by health, employment and education data, 2004–2011[136]

Non–UK born resident NI pop 2011 (est.)	NHS reg Jan 05–Dec 11	NINo Apr 04– Mar 11	WRS May 04–Mar 11 (EU 8)	WP (2004–2009) (non–EU)	School Census 2005–11 Principal additional languages
Total	101,948	88,310	42,525	12,405	–
ROI 25,000	Poland 26,943	Poland 31,162	Poland 23,465	India 2,855	Polish
Poland 15,000	ROI 11,383	Lithuania 10,474	Lithuania 7,990	Philippines 1,910	Lithuanian
Lithuania 13,000	Lithuania 10,184	Slovakia 6,923	Slovakia 5,660	Ukraine 1,155	Portuguese
India 9,000	Slovakia 4,965	ROI 6,758	Latvia 2,480	–	Chinese (Cantonese & Mandarin)
Zimbabwe[a] 4,000	India 4,527	India 3,540	Czech Republic 1,630	–	Tagalog / Filipino

[a] Although the Zimbabwean-born immigrants are evident in small numbers in the health registration data (240 from Jan. 05 to Dec. 11), they do not feature largely in the employment data which may imply that many may be already be eligible British nationals and their dependents, reflecting the significant migrations of British citizens in the interwar and post-war eras to the region of former Southern and Northern Rhodesia and Nyasaland; now named Zambia, Zimbabwe and Malawi. The 'ancestral return' of these British nationals from Zimbabwe may have been motivated in recent years by the harsh policies of the Robert Mugabe regime against white property owners (NISRA, International Migration Tables: Table 1.36: NI Health Card Registrations from Non-UK Nationals by Country of Last Residence, January 2005–December 2011).

Department of Education's School Census recorded that about 3 per cent (5,100) of primary and 2 per cent (2,500) of secondary school students had a language other than English as their 'mother tongue'; in Dungannon this amounted to 13 per cent of pupils. Languages of the EU8 countries (with Polish predominating) represented over half of the foreign language group. In 2011, one in ten births (2,477) were to mothers born outside the UK and Ireland (1,210 of them from EU8 countries); amounting to approximately 21 per cent of births in the Dungannon area.[137] These birth statistics and the considerable proportion of children and youth under eighteen in the inflow indicate that there will be a demand for health, educational and social service provision that supports families into the future (Jarman and Byrne, 2007: 6). Thus, it is imperative to eliminate barriers that new immigrants face in accessing social, health and financial services

(Gibbs, 2010) and in obtaining recognition of their foreign credentials and work experience that results in so many immigrants being underemployed (Bell et al., 2009: 32–6; Devine et al., 2007: 347).

Overall, the five local areas in Northern Ireland which have experienced the highest percentage of population change due to international immigration since 2001 are Dungannon, Craigavon, Newry and Mourne, Magherafelt, and Cookstown; the majority of immigrants coming from EU8 countries especially Poland, Lithuania, Slovakia, with lesser but significant flows from India, the Philippines, China, Portugal and East Timor, and steady smaller numbers of other Western European nationals, Americans and citizens from Commonwealth countries.[138] Nevertheless, in spite of the focus on 'foreign' immigration, it is worth bearing in mind that even during the peak years of the inflow (2004–2007), immigration to Northern Ireland was predominantly from Britain and Ireland (49%) including Northern Ireland returnees, with new EU accession countries also showing strong representation (28%).

Over 50 per cent of international immigrants to Northern Ireland claim to have come to the UK for work, around 20 per cent for family reasons and less than 10 per cent for education.[139] In a recent survey, although new immigrants generally expressed satisfaction with life in Northern Ireland, especially that they enjoyed a good standard of living and found most of the locals friendly, nevertheless, a quarter of them had experienced some form of discrimination or verbal abuse (Bell et al., 2009: 129–32).[140] Certainly Northern Ireland's image did not appear to be very welcoming when in June 2009, Belfast hit the international media headlines with news that a group of over one hundred Romanian Roma had been forced from their homes in the Village neighbourhood of the city due to racist attacks and then had to be emergency housed in the local church and leisure centre.[141] Later that year, opposition to immigration emerged as an issue of the recession, as espoused by DUP MLA Tom Buchanan who stated, 'While we are aware of the immense contribution made by migrant workers, nevertheless, in the economic downturn, in the middle of recession with increased unemployment we must get our priorities right in saving employment for local people.'[142] Later that year, a newspaper article headlined 'Ethnic minorities "new victims in the Troubles-free Northern Ireland"' noted that in the previous year there had been 771 racist attacks against ethnic minorities, though this was still fewer than the number of sectarian incidents.[143] The focus of much of the immigration-related news since then has concerned illegal workers (usually in restaurants) and sham marriages. In one case, the legal wedding of a NI-born groom and his Chinese bride was disrupted 'moments before their wedding ceremony was due to start at Derry's Guildhall' when the couple were arrested by the PSNI, who were later forced to issue an apology.[144] Concerns about racial harassment have led to the adoption of 'anti-racist' strategies in the Northern Ireland Government and its agencies (Heenan and Birrell, 2011: 34).[145]

Refugees and Asylum Seekers

There has always been a small inflow of refugees and asylum seekers to Northern Ireland but until recent times, there has been little documentation of this migratory movement and even now, numbers are unreliable. Since April 2013, the Home Office has taken over responsibility from the UK Border Agency for the control, investigation and detention of undocumented migrants.[146] In Northern Ireland, these activities are conducted under the name Operation Gull. Immigration officers are stationed at Belfast City Airport; Belfast International Airport; Belfast City Docks; and Larne Docks, and may question incoming travellers with regard to identity and immigration status. They also operate an enquiry office adjacent to the Forestside Shopping Complex in Belfast. Since many undocumented individuals enter Northern Ireland over the land border with the ROI, immigration officers also cooperate with the police (PSNI) to act on intelligence concerning undocumented individuals who may be entering or residing in Northern Ireland (Latif and Martynowicz, 2009).

The first 'immigration removal centre' in Northern Ireland, Larne House, a nineteen-bed facility that opened in July 2011, may house individuals for a maximum stay of seven days only.[147] It opened with little fuss, although news of the proposed centre had caused considerable consternation in October 2010 when the British National Party (BNP) distributed anti-immigration leaflets in the local community that bore the heading, 'Are you ready for the benefits that a refugee/asylum centre will bring to your town?' and featured a faked photograph of two women wearing burkas walking down the Glenarm Road.[148] Between 2006 until the opening of the new centre, most asylum seekers were sent for detention to Dungavel Immigration Removal Centre in Lanarkshire, Scotland. Prior to this, those who became known to the authorities had been incarcerated in the Northern Ireland penal system; a breach of their basic human rights under the European Convention on Human Rights, Article 3, which guarantees freedom from inhuman or degrading treatment, or punishment (Latif and Martynowicz, 2009: 1). In the late 1990s, condemnation of this practice prompted investigations by the then newly established Northern Ireland Human Rights Commission (est. 1998) (Tennant, 2000).[149]

Many asylum seekers currently live in the community but they qualify for health and social services in Northern Ireland only if they are destitute and make themselves known to the authorities with the risk of being sent to a detention centre. According to a 2007 Report of the Refugee Action Group, there were 2000 refugees resident in Northern Ireland (RAG, 2007: 4) and since then the Belfast-based Bryson One Stop Service for Asylum Seekers has processed in the range of 200 main applications annually, with the principal countries represented being Somalia, Sudan, China, Iran, Nigeria and Zimbabwe (McNulty, 2012: 29).[150]

Conclusion: An All-Ulster Perspective

The demographic and statistical review of Northern Ireland migration provided in this chapter is in many respects incomplete, not least because of the partition of the province of Ulster, a condition not accepted by a large section of the population. Therefore, I conclude this chapter with consideration of Ulster as a nine-county entity and present the net migration data over the last century on an all-Ulster basis (see Figure 2.10).[151] For despite political accommodations past and present, borders – whether on the ground, inscribed on maps, described in books or imagined – remain fluid in time and space, ever changing, always imbued with power. In the act of telling their stories, however, migrants renegotiated these borders as their narratives crossed generations and geographies. These stories are the focus of the chapters that follow in Part II of this book.

Figure 2.10: Ulster (9-county) population and net migration

	NI pop. (end of period)	NI net migration	Ireland. 3 Ulster counties pop.	Ireland: 3 Ulster counties net mig.	Ulster total pop.	Ulster total net mig.	net mig (per 000)
1926–37*	1279745	–57651	280269	–29622	1560014	–87273	–5.6
1937–51*	1370921	–67267	253252	–45043	1624173	–112310	–7.0
1951–61	1425042	–92228	217524	–47407	1642566	–139635	–8.5
1961–71	1536015	–69222	207204	–22041	1743219	–91263	–5.4
1971–81	1532600†	–111423	230159	6191	1762759	–105232	–6.0
1981–91	1588794	–69420	232206	–13638	1821000	–83058	–4.6
1991–01*	1685274	–3914	246714	4946	1931988	1032	0.05
2001–11*	1810863	38400	294296	31258	2105159	68658	3.5

* Ireland's census years differ slightly: 1936, 2002.
† Revised census total.

PART II

Voices of Migration and Return

Chapter 3

'They were always missed, they were always mentioned': Migration, Generation and Family History

Memory, Generation and Emigration: Roseena's story

Montreal, Quebec. It is a sunny, warm July morning. I am a dark-haired, skinny child considered small for my six years, standing with my grandmother Roseena on the sidewalk of the Rue Sainte-Catherine – Montreal's busy main shopping artery. We are alone she and I, my tiny left-hand firmly in her grasp, unnoticed by the many people walking by. Roseena, a small plump woman then in her seventies, gazes dreamily up at the Hudson's Bay Company storefront across the street. Something in her mood causes me to look up at her. She sighs then and without altering her gaze, half whispers, 'I used to work here.' These words send my young mind into overdrive but I am unable to articulate my confusion. We cross the street and enter the store where she buys me a pink yo-yo in the toy department. In the years that follow, this scene, crystallised in my memory, continues to play over and over again in my mind. I still have the pink yo-yo. My confusion of that day stemmed from the fact that my maternal grandmother Roseena McParland, was in Montreal on a visit from Belfast. She lived in Ireland. How could she possibly have worked in this Canadian department store, which in her day had operated as the flagship store of Henry Morgan and Company? It was only several years later at the age of eleven when we were back in Ireland that Roseena told me the whole story.

Roseena was born in Newry, County Down at the turn of the last century, eldest child of John McParland, who worked as a delivery man for a local bakery and Catherine Kellett from the townland of Drumacarrow outside Bailieborough, County Cavan.[1] Catherine subsequently died of pneumonia at the age of thirty-two when Roseena was only six, leaving behind two other young children, four-year-old John Joe and infant James. As the eldest child and only daughter, Roseena with the help of a neighbour, minded her younger brothers, continuing to protect them from a spiteful stepmother once her father remarried. As they became young adults the children left home, Roseena to work as a domestic in the big houses of Belfast, John Joe to factory work in Birmingham and James to America in the early 1920s where he enlisted in the United States Army after working in a series of labouring jobs.

Not a lot is known of James' life in America except that he didn't like the army and after a couple of years he deserted; an offence punishable by death during wartime and by lengthy imprisonment during peacetime. In our family, the story is told that as a deserter, James changed his identity in order to evade capture and imprisonment. By erasing the curve of the P in McParland on official documents, he thus became James McFarland, a much more common name which made him harder to trace. Along with the change of name came an apparently transient lifestyle as James changed jobs and residences frequently, moving all around the United States. James' whereabouts were thus unknown for periods of time, but he always eventually got back in touch with Roseena by letter and he frequently sent packages which contained money and gifts, including a white gold watch Roseena always treasured.

Sometime during the early 1930s James married and settled in the town of Oxnard, California where he worked for the railway. He sent a few photographs back to Ireland of himself and his young daughter, Mary Pamela McFarland; one of these shows a prosperous looking James standing beside a 1930s-era automobile, another shows three-year-old Mary Pamela on her tricycle. As Roseena only corresponded with her brother via his place of employment, however, she always believed that James' wife was unaware of his Irish family and indeed of his original identity. Thus, when James ceased to make contact around 1940, Roseena made enquiries of his employer only to receive the reply that James had left his job some six months previously and the employer did not know of his whereabouts.

Ironically, in the mid-1920s Roseena had concocted a plan to try to meet up with James in America but due to the 1924 United States Immigration Act limiting quotas of Irish immigrants, she had decided that as a British subject and an experienced domestic who qualified for assisted emigration under Empire Settlement, it would be easier to go to Canada and enter the United States overland.[2] On 19 March 1927, Roseena left Belfast aboard the ship *Montrose II* of the Canadian Pacific Line, arriving at the Port of Saint John, New Brunswick on the 27th; a dangerous time to be crossing the North Atlantic due to the likelihood of icebergs.[3] Roseena, like most of the other young women on board, was listed on the passenger manifest as a domestic in third-class quarters. Upon arrival in Canada, however, as with so many 'domestics' who availed of assisted passage schemes, Roseena did not stay long if at all in domestic service – she certainly never mentioned it – preferring the glamorous retail world of the Henry Morgan and Company department store which had branches across the country. Not much is known of her stay in Canada which lasted about eighteen months, except that she worked her way from Saint John to Regina, Saskatchewan, stopping for periods in places like Montreal and Winnipeg, while she earned enough money to continue on. The purpose of Roseena's westward travel through Canada was to gain access to the United States, which she attempted without success at several crossing points along the border. Eventually she returned to Ireland without seeing James and married my grandfather in October 1928. The only visible remnants of her Canadian adventure were the few knickknacks she brought back with her – a tiny birch-bark canoe and a small Inuit soapstone carving – which were proudly displayed on the front windowsill until her death.

James' disappearance in America caused Roseena considerable distress

Figure 3.1: Portrait of James McParland sent to his sister Roseena in Northern Ireland, taken by Art Miller, Redlands, California, c. 1928 (courtesy of Cynthia Miller, Coronado, California)

throughout her life. My mother and uncle have recalled how the photographic portrait of James sent from America always hung like a beacon in the front hallway of their house and that Roseena often spoke wistfully of him (Figure 3.1). Early on she had even employed a private detective in the United States to try to find him and two decades later she contacted the Salvation Army Missing Persons service in Wales which handled queries for Northern Ireland; all to no avail. As an elderly woman, she passed the story and her grief to me and now, over thirty years later, it haunts me still.

Understanding Migration and Generation

The story of James' disappearance is my own postmemory; part of my 'narrative inheritance', to employ the concept by Howard Goodall (2005) who has suggested that such stories passed down the generations provide us with a framework through which we come to understand our own identities in the present. When the story is incomplete or unfinished, we may feel the need to complete it. As Goodall has suggested, narrative inheritance may foster attitudes and behaviours, and impel us to action, thus, 'there are narrative reasons for what we do and narrative motives locked into who we are. Identities are indeed the stuff such stories, such life sentences, are made of' (2005: 504). The legacy of James' emigration and eventual disappearance heightened my own awareness of the potential multigenerational impact that migration may have on families and individuals; the effects of which can be positive or negative, empowering or disabling. In Ireland as elsewhere, family migration narratives have been instrumental in creating and even perpetuating a collective consciousness of migration; often misleadingly represented in the Irish case as a culture purely of emigration. However, as many Irish families continued to produce great numbers of migrants over generations, a migration ethos developed which, as Mary Chamberlain has articulated in the Caribbean context, became 'a powerful dynamic in determining who migrates and why and with what effect, which in turn engaged with other family dynamics of colour, class, mobility or adventure' (1997: 93). Once a family migration history has been established, migration may sometimes be a strategy chosen, consciously or unconsciously, to consolidate an individual's identity, 'through direct contact with places one's ancestors hailed from, places that because of family stories, reading or tradition have acquired deep emotional significance and represent one's long-lost and devoutly desired roots' (Grinberg and Grinberg, 1989: 134).

Considering the growing interest in family history, it is perhaps surprising that to date few scholars have taken a truly multigenerational approach in Irish migration studies; a dimension thus far most often confined to works of Irish memoir, letters and autobiography. Historian Richard White's *Remembering*

Ahanagran – which he calls an 'anti-memoir' – is a striking example of how family stories, memory and the historical record intersect, reminding us that 'idiot simplicities about memory, identity and history can do so much damage' (1998: 5–6). Perhaps as White suggests, family stories still have much to contribute to national contests over identity and historical narratives. The benefit of employing a multigenerational approach is evident in John Herson's work on the Irish in Stafford for which he interviewed descendants of nineteenth-century Irish migrants in an attempt to trace trajectories from the present back to the past.

> It is feasible to explore whether faint echoes from the past are present in the communicated memories and legends current in the families of modern-day descendants of nineteenth-century immigrant Irish. This might reveal evidence about the trauma of emigration and the strength of the exile motif in the immigrant generation and their communication to descendants. It could also reveal attitudes and identities in Irish immigrant families from the nineteenth century to the present day, and the extent to which these were affected by the environment and institutions surrounding them (2006: 213).

Herson's study revealed that knowledge of family history decays substantially after the third generation, in other words once the likelihood of direct contact between generations (e.g., grandparent to grandchild) is no longer possible. But perhaps most importantly, his research has shown the extent to which the Stafford Irish married outside their group (mostly with the local English) and the impact this hybridity has had on identities of later generations. Herson also noted that there appeared to be little impact of Ireland's collective popular memories of trauma and exile, and concluded that there had been essentially no advantage for that group in maintaining an Irish identity in Britain.

During the interviewing process for our studies, interviewees were asked what they knew of migration in their families and their communities going back two generations – representing memories directly transmitted from one living generation to another, consequently spanning a total of three generations (i.e., grandparents, parents and children). What became clear during this process was the extent to which not only the known 'facts' of the migration events were passed down, but most emphatically their emotional impact. As with any good story, fact or fiction, it is the case that the more dramatic and emotionally arresting narrative will be the one that is remembered. This is also true of migration narratives and it perhaps explains in part why the subject of migration tends to provoke a strong emotional response in people generally. For in life histories, whether one's own or those of family members past and present, it is the emotional impact, to quote Sara Ahmed, 'of what sticks, of what connections are lived as the most intense or intimate, as being closer to the skin' (2004: 54), that will survive in narrative form to be passed down through the generations. Indeed, migration offers a plethora of intensely lived experiences provoking emotions from fear, sorrow and melancholy to excitement, joy and euphoria. In short, migration and emotion go together.

And while taking a multigenerational approach in our studies proved constructive for examining the emotional impact of migration, it also offered additional insights which emerged during the research process: 1) the extent to which Irish migration has long been and continues to be a dynamic, multidirectional process over time; 2) the importance of immigration to the ethnic and religious diversity of the Irish population, which has too often been portrayed as a 'two traditions' culture; 3) that Irish, Ulster and British identities at home and in the diaspora have always been multiple and hybrid, continually in flux over many generations; and 4) that transnationalism in the Irish case is certainly not new.

Families, Histories, Emotions

As mentioned above, successful family history narratives – those that survive to be passed down through successive generations – feature all the same dramatic elements of any good story: namely comedy; suspense; and tragedy. Partly, this is due to the performance context of oral narrative (Bauman, 1984), the usual mode of transmission for family stories. A pleasant uneventful story does not usually contain enough drama for the teller to craft a good performance and is therefore unlikely to find an attentive audience. In a heart-wrenching tale, however, dramatic elements abound enabling the teller to keep the audience spellbound. So it is that in the migration context, the uneventful ocean crossing is lost to memory while the stormy passage, when the ship was in danger of sinking, is long remembered. Family stories also serve to pass on the accumulated wisdom and value system of the family and its culture, and may thus provide continuity and unite succeeding generations as the family itself 'becomes a site of belonging' (Chamberlain and Leydesdorff, 2004: 233). This may include tales whose purpose is specifically instructive as for example, 'He did this and consequently a terrible thing happened, so best not to do that in future'. Again, elements of drama in the tale serve to provoke emotional responses which enhance the likelihood that the story and its instructive message will be remembered.

Della Pollock has suggested that oral history is an active process of 'making history in dialogue'. It is a transformational act 'moving memory into remembering' necessarily introducing change by translating 'subjectively remembered events into embodied memory acts' (2005: 2) during the telling process. The performance perspective emphasises this process as both subjective and creative, but one which, especially in an interview context, affirms the competency of the teller as the history 'made' is endowed with the sanction of the academy. In this sense both storyteller and interviewer/listener are implicated in the creation of history – both are witnesses to history.

The narratives which follow relate the migration experiences of individuals belonging to previous generations of the interviewees' families. In most cases, these were elicited during the early part of the interview following a more or less temporal progression through the life story. But these stories differed from the other parts of the life narrative in that they represent experiences of experiences, in other words, experiences at a remove. What interviewees recounted were not events they themselves had experienced first-hand, but rather postmemories – the experiences of others as told to them at a temporal (and often geographical) distance from the original events. Thus what the tellers reconstruct from their postmemories is imbued with the impact of those tales viewed through the prism of their own life experience. This is not to say that the emotional impact on the individual of the story passed down is less than if it were their own first-hand experience as hearing experiences of others may also alter our perspectives of self. A recent study observed the important role of family stories in child development.

> What is remarkable is that these family stories become part of our own personal self-definition. How we take on the stories of others and use them to create our own sense of self is an astonishing phenomenon still in need of a great deal of explication. Children who know their family history, who have shared in these stories, develop a sense of self – embedded in a larger familial and intergenerational context, and this sense of self provides strength and security (Fivush et al., 2008: 141).

In my own family, the disappearance of my grandmother's brother James in America, recounted above, has had an enormous impact although some family members have been affected more than others. However, my own sense of that impact on the family and its most particular effect on me personally has far outweighed the significance of several first-hand experiences in my own life.

'She grieved him all her life': Narrating Migration and Loss

When I interviewed Barry, an athletic man in his mid-forties who lives in Liverpool, I was struck by the story he told about his uncle's emigration and disappearance which was strangely similar to the story of James in my own family. Barry saw a parallel with his father's brother Jim, who like Barry was also the eldest of a family of nine. As Barry recounted, his Uncle Jim was only seventeen years old when, without a word to anyone, he departed the family home in south County Down after a dispute with his father – Barry's grandfather – and disappeared. Barry felt that this had been particularly hard for his own father as the second son who then shouldered the burden of the family because Barry's grandfather was prone to frequent drinking binges. The family did everything to try to find Jim, and like my family, even hired a private detective to search for him without success. A few years ago a local priest discovered through acquaintances abroad that Barry's uncle had gone to New Zealand and contact was re-established. After over sixty years away and having raised a family in New Zealand, Barry's Uncle Jim returned to Northern Ireland with one of his adult children for a visit. 'Now he's probably about eighty and he left when he was seventeen, so sixty-five years first time coming home. He met all the rest of his family for the first time in that amount of time' (interview, Liverpool, VMR–047)

Despite this recent happy turn of events, the language Barry employed, nonetheless, shows the continuing ambiguity of his own feelings on the matter and his sense of the impact of the disappearance on the family. Although he mentioned that his uncle's disappearance 'wasn't spoken about an awful lot really' he also referred to 'always hearing about Uncle Jim having gone'. He pointed to the dreadful impact of the lack of closure. 'It's almost worse than a death, because you don't know. You can't get over the process of mourning because you don't know if the person's alive or dead'. But it was as a devoted father of two teenagers that the story resonated most with Barry who spoke most poignantly of the effect of the disappearance of her eldest son on his grandmother:

My granny never spoke to him again after that. She didn't know where he went to. She died. She died before finding out where he was. And I think as far as I know, my granny grieved that all her life really, you know, the fact that she never saw or heard from him since.

Although Barry and his children live in Liverpool, he felt that it was very important for them to maintain close contact with Barry's network of family and friends in County Down. They make regular visits to Ireland often with extended stays in the summer.

The theme of loss predominated among the stories of migrants of previous generations, perhaps as Kerby Miller has noted of Irish Gaelic culture, because 'the very act of leaving Ireland, for any reason, was perceived sorrowfully' (1985: 105). However, as in Barry's narrative above, there was often a lost and found aspect – a notion of redemption – to the tales of loss reminiscent of the 'prodigal son' narrative in Christian tradition, although the 'prodigal return' sometimes occurred in a later generation.[4] Liz from East Belfast, remembered vividly the events leading up to the departure of her cousin for Australia in the early 1950s when she was only about seven or eight years old. An only child, she, her parents, grandmother and her mother's brother shared one house and formed a close family unit with her mother's sister, husband and their six children who lived in another house on the same street. When her aunt's oldest child, Hamilton, decided to migrate to Australia, the entire family was deeply affected:

> So it was a very emotional time when Hamilton left because we were all one extended family. I mean there would have been a dozen of us all living in those two houses. And I remember that quite clearly as a young child. Oh dreadful! It was almost like somebody dying. I mean you waved goodbye to somebody in those days when they were going as far away as that, there was very little chance of ever seeing them again (interview, Belfast, VMR–057).

Just as they feared, they never saw Hamilton again. Though he kept in touch initially by letter he died in Australia as a fairly young man. What was not known to his family was that Hamilton had married in Australia and his wife had also died young, leaving two young children that the family in Ireland knew nothing about:

> [Hamilton] never came back. He died there as a young man and in later years, children that no one knew he had have surfaced and have made contact with the family and have been over to visit here. And my family from here have gone to Australia twice now to visit them. They were left as orphans at a very young age out there.

Despite the happy ending of this story, a strong sense of loss and tragedy pervades Liz's narrative. One gets the sense of deep tragedy not only due to the premature death of her cousin, but of lost years, of children reared in an orphanage in Australia not knowing they had any family:

> My cousins who live in Bangor now, they got the call to say that these children were looking. And that was only in the last five years. So like fifty years have gone by.

Niall, born in England to a family from the Mournes area around Newcastle, County Down, recounted the story of his father's three brothers – Dan, John and Hugh – who had migrated to the United States prior to the First World War where their uncle, Father Dan, was a priest in Iowa. Brother Dan ended up in France where it turned out the family had a longer association:

> The O'Keenan's, who was my great-great-grandmother, started a lace business in Paris and they helped start the linen business here in Clanawillan where there was a mill … There's a letter in my grandfather's diary which I have – I gave it to the Public Record Office in Northern Ireland – and

there's a letter in it that's from O'Keenan and he was in Paris in the 1820s. And I noticed that in Clanawillan, the old mill wheel was all rusted over but it had on it some reference to France – I'm not sure, I'd need to check – but I thought it was 1816 and they brought that mill wheel over and helped them start that (interview, Newcastle, County Down, VMR–027).

Niall described how his Uncle Dan had gone to France during the First World War with the United States Army as part of General Pershing's group. After the war, Dan stayed in France, married and had one daughter. During the Second World War, Dan worked with the French underground and was afterwards awarded a military honour by the French Government. The two brothers John and Hugh did not live long. John apparently went up to The Klondike gold rush and soon after came back down to Omaha, Nebraska where he died of appendicitis, not yet aged twenty. Hugh joined the United States Army and was stationed in San Angelo, Texas where he died of the Spanish influenza at the end of the First World War aged only twenty-three. The sense of the tragedy in Niall's narrative emerged most strongly, however, when he described how his father had gone out to America many years later and arranged to have Hugh's body moved so that the brothers would be buried together:

My dad went over and brought Hugh's body from San Angelo, Texas, I think it was, to Omaha, Nebraska and they're both buried in the same graveyard in Omaha, Nebraska.

Mary, from south Armagh reported the story of her father's brother from Sligo who migrated to England to work for his uncle, who was already established there. He joined the British Army at the beginning of the Second World War and survived the Dunkirk campaign of 1940. The family only later found out that he was then sent on the Italian campaign and participated in the invasion of Sicily known as Operation Husky in July 1943 when he 'disappeared'.

And that was quite a fascinating story because he had come to England to work for an uncle as a young man and he was very headstrong, apparently, and not that easy to get on with and he fell out with the uncle and said, 'Right I'm going to join the army.' And so he joined the British Army but went missing in 1943. When you look back now as an adult, we grew up with this history, if you like, they didn't know he was dead for sure until 1945 till the war ended. And we've only recently, after my father died, we went on the website and found out where he was. And you get the grave number and everything so one of us, probably my younger brother who loves travelling, will definitely go at some stage to see that grave. He's buried in Syracuse (interview, West Sussex, VMR–083).

Mary reported that compounding this tragedy was that her grandmother who lived in Sligo received little sympathy or compassion from her community when her son was first listed as missing and two years later confirmed dead:

> My grandmother was ostracised by the neighbours because she had a son who had joined the British Army and that was also very common. I mean it's only very, very recently in the last couple of years, as far as I know, that the Eire Government has acknowledged the soldiers who died in the war; because it was not a popular thing to do at all.

So ironically while thousands of Irish from independent Ireland left of necessity to find work in England during the 1930s and 1940s sending money to support families at home, joining the British Army was often viewed as a step too far and many soldiers' families suffered considerably as a result.

A few of the interviewees reported the loss of family members abroad due to suspected foul play. David, originally from the Shankill in Belfast, mentioned that his great-uncle, who had migrated to New York City in the 1930s, was murdered on the street in a mugging incident during the 1960s. Eileen who grew up in West Belfast spent most of her summers at her mother's family farm in Donegal. As is fairly typical of rural Donegal families, there was a long tradition of emigration over several generations but the family farm, still in the possession of Eileen's uncle, served as a base for the visiting family members; most of whom had relocated to northern England, especially Bradford and Leeds. Eileen spoke, however, of one great-uncle who had gone out to the gold rush in America:

> There was one story about an uncle of my mother's – that would have been my grandfather's brother – he went out to follow the gold rush and he died out there and they got word back that he died. And my grandfather was always very sad about it … They think he was robbed and killed, him and a friend. Because I think they got a telegram back saying he had died but the circumstances were all a bit vague. It was all very sad. But I think in those days when people went away it was almost like a wake, wasn't it, people were going away and probably never to be seen again (interview, London, VMR–079).

Eileen also mentioned how her paternal grandmother's brother had migrated to America and lost touch with the family back in Belfast, something her grandmother always regretted. 'She lost touch and she always mourned him.' One gets the sense in these postmemories of loss, to paraphrase Simon Schama of how an absence may become a presence (1995: 25); that as Eileen described, 'You can remember stories of people going off and you know, *they were always missed, they were always mentioned*.' The lack of closure about the murdered and missing great-uncles in her family has been passed to Eileen's generation.

I suppose if you don't know what happened you'll never get it out of your system, you know, you're always wondering what happened and thinking about them and stuff. I still often wonder about my grandmother's brother that went off to America. Have I got cousins somewhere? You know we all think about it because we talk about it and stuff, my brothers and sisters and me. And you do wonder.

It is my belief that stories of 'the disappeared', as in the case of Eileen's family and of several others documented here, are so often handed down the generations precisely because they are unresolved. In his Irish Roots column in the *Irish Times*, John Grenham poignantly described the story of an Irish emigrant family who in the mid-1850s had become separated from one of their children at the Port of Liverpool as they were about to embark ship for America. The boy was never found and the family in the United States for over 150 years have never stopped looking, the agony of the loss 'embedded in the family's story of itself, generation after generation'.[5] In the sense that the larger family story is part of each individual family member's life story, the drive to produce a coherent family story (McAdams, 1985) may thus fall to future generations who can take on the task of resolving the mystery.

Roy, whose family is originally from an area known as The Birches near Portadown, County Armagh, recounted a classic story of multigenerational chain migration in his family to New Zealand. There were eleven children in his grandfather's farming family and as the farm could support few, seven of his grandfather's siblings migrated to New Zealand. The emigration began in late 1864 when the eldest child, Roy's great-Aunt Sarah emigrated with her husband, two young daughters and one of her younger brothers on board the ship *Ganges* bound for settlement in the Waikato Valley. Roy described the journey which took 102 days from Queenstown, County Cork to Auckland:

It was the last of the sailing ships. There were 400 passengers on board ship and 52 children died because they had an outbreak of whooping cough … including my great-aunt's older girl, the three-year-old girl, she died on the ship. The third – another girl – was born on the ship (interview, Belfast, VMR–018).[6]

Shortly after arrival, great-Aunt Sarah's second child died and her husband was killed a few years later when a tree fell on him. Nevertheless, Sarah stayed and remarried, and she and her brother were eventually joined by five of their siblings. In the next generation, however, the cycle of emigration and loss continued:

And then my aunt – my father's sister – she suffered from asthma and they thought that maybe if she went out to New Zealand to be with her aunts and uncles that it would be good for her asthma. I understand that's not the case but it seemed quite a good idea to them. So she went out to New Zealand around 1912 and on the way to New Zealand she met her husband.

As Roy reported, his Aunt Ruby and her fiancé, Jack Hamilton who was himself from Newtownstewart, County Tyrone, returned the next year all the way back to be married in Portadown at the insistence of Roy's grandfather. They brought one of the New Zealand cousins, Jennie Johnston, with them and she wrote a diary – which was in Roy's possession – detailing the events of the trip and the extended visit which lasted almost a year.[7] After the First World War, Ruby's unmarried sister Grace persuaded her father to allow her to go to Ruby in New Zealand, initially for a visit, but with the possibility of staying longer:

> So she [Grace] went out to New Zealand in around about 1920–1921. She then stayed – not quite sure how long she stayed – but she died in New Zealand … But she died just before she was due to come back … So my grandmother and my grandfather in 1922 they set out for New Zealand to visit their daughter and to see the other daughter's grave. So they spent about six months in New Zealand and then they came back.

Roy maintained regular contact with his relations in New Zealand; he visited them and they visited him in Ireland. After his retirement, Roy who spent much of his own life away working in Scotland embarked on researching and writing his family's migration story.

Another type of loss occurred when the person who was due to emigrate unexpectedly gave their ticket to another family member. In some cases, this was due to political reasons as in the case of Lily's Uncle Felix who emigrated from Newry, County Down to Philadelphia around 1920.

> The story goes that at that time it was the Black and Tans and all the problems and that kind of thing. And apparently, my daddy was going out to America and he had his fare … Felix was the youngest at the time … But anyway my daddy was going to go next, but he [Felix] was in trouble with the IRA or something, I'm not sure, but this is the story and my daddy give him his fare and then he went away out to Philadelphia, (interview, London, VMR–080).

Mark from Donegal reported the story of his father's older brothers who swapped places on the emigration boat at the last minute to join other siblings already in America:

> He had a brother who was about to emigrate and they had the fare for him and packed his bag and all the rest of it, and another brother went to see

him off at Cork – at Cobh. And eventually the man who was supposed to have gone came back home and had changed places with the younger fellow and the family were desperately upset about that. That this younger brother, who was very much the pet of the family had gone off to America and this older chap who was meant to have gone came back home. And he was always kind of – not exactly ostracised – but he was always kind of looked on as kind of the black sheep after that which was totally unfair. It was almost like a soldier who gets sort of cold feet and does a runner. He was meant to have gone, everything was prepared for his going, they'd adjusted themselves to that, and then the fact that he came back home and the lad who had gone to see him off had gone in his place. And he never came back again, the chap who went … The whole psychic then was sadness (interview, County Donegal, VMR–007).

Mark's narrative demonstrates the potential importance of the family effort in the migration process of an individual: to decide who emigrates; to raise the fare thus making communal sacrifices; to see the emigrant off; to receive the arriving immigrant in the destination; and to censure those who do not follow the approved family strategy.[8]

Siobhan, from Omagh, County Tyrone who now lives in Liverpool, told of her great-grandmother from County Limerick, who after giving birth to Siobhan's grandmother in 1899, left Ireland to join two sisters already living in America. She left her baby with her parents in Limerick. Siobhan explained:

I think the baby was to go out afterwards but she never did. And my grandmother had three aunts and an uncle who went to the States. Unfortunately, the uncle never made it, he actually went down on the Titanic … His wife survived and she was pregnant at the time (interview, Omagh, VMR–058).

Siobhan's great-grandmother came back to Ireland for one visit but as she had married in America and had a family out there, her first-born child – Siobhan's grandmother – remained behind in Ireland:

I think my great-grandmother obviously wasn't married when she had my grandmother which nobody ever knew in the family until my sister, after my grandmother had died, went and persuaded my mother to get her birth certificate. This was never talked about … Because the father was just written 'unknown'. But we think she was in service and were wondering … where did she get the money to go overseas? It would have been a lot of money. Although she did have two sisters there but she went on her own initially.

Siobhan speculated as to the reason her infant grandmother remained behind, but it is likely that going to America was the only possibility for her great-grandmother to have a normal life, to start over. The chances are that her new family in America knew nothing about the child back in Ireland. Certainly, there appears to have been no contact between Siobhan's grandmother in Ireland and the step-siblings in America. But Siobhan also surmised that there could be economic reasons which also factored into the events:

> I think often they sent money back for the children and maybe they [grandparents] didn't want to let go. Maybe they needed that money for the family. You know, a little bit from the States would have been a lot. We don't know that but possibly that was what happened to her. Maybe they got attached to the child and she [great-grandmother] had another family.

As Siobhan's story illustrates, disappearance, while regrettable on many levels, was a strategy some individuals, especially women, employed to escape the conservatism of Irish society. In most cases, it would appear they had little choice. Other interviewees reported similar strategies at play in their families. Jane from Belfast spoke at length about her beloved uncle who left Belfast for Zambia in the early 1960s and died there in the late 1980s. Although he remained in contact with the family, reflecting back Jane had come to believe that he was probably a homosexual and could not contemplate living his life in the conservative society of Northern Ireland (interview, Liverpool, VMR–050). William, from County Tyrone, talked about his aunt who married in Birmingham during the 1940s but when the marriage ended, she left for South Africa with a new partner to whom she was not married. The family never heard from her again after that (interview, Gortin, Co. Tyrone, VMR–008). Louise Ryan has referred to this strategy as 'managing emotions of shame' (2008: 306), citing the case of divorced women she interviewed who by not conforming to the social norms of Irish society did not meet family expectations. Thus, as her research and these narratives indicate, transnational family networks 'can serve as mechanisms of control or sanction' (2008: 306) and relationships can be highly conflictual rather than supportive and loving.

'It was all just land and trees': Narrating Settlement and Return

Another theme that emerged from the postmemory interview narratives relating to previous migrant generations was the extent and multidirectional type of movement in families. Far from the stereotypical notion of a single emigration event and then stasis upon arrival in the destination, interviewees recounted much more dynamic processes of multiple migrations: onward migrations; back and forth migrations; internal migrations (within Ireland); and return migrations often involving travel over great distances. These migrations frequently resulted in family members being born abroad and brought back to Ireland and the marrying-in of non-Irish spouses. Many families exhibited several types of migrations. Steve, for example, had two maternal uncles who migrated to Ontario in the 1960s. One of them stayed in Canada; the other returned to Northern Ireland with Canadian-born children after seven years. One of these children – Steve's cousin – subsequently went back to Ontario for six years but recently returned to Northern Ireland, although his line of work still requires him to spend several months each year in Canada (interview, Liverpool, VMR–053). Julia reported that her maternal grandmother from Fermanagh went to the United States in the early years of the twentieth century to train in nursing and then returned to work in Dublin while her paternal grandmother likewise went off to the United States as a teenager to be a companion to a young woman relation who was seriously ill. When the young woman died a few years later, Julia's paternal grandmother returned to Ireland (interview, Co. Fermanagh, VMR–031). Deirdre spoke of how her grandfather, like many Donegal men of his generation, took the 'Scotch boat' from Derry and worked in the Glasgow area while keeping the farm back home. Her father was consequently born in Scotland in the 1920s and brought back to Strabane where the family established but later on his brother – Deirdre's uncle – eventually went back to live permanently in Scotland (interview, Strabane, VMR–042). John from South Belfast reported how his father migrated to the United States in the 1920s and once established, John's mother went out to marry him. The family settled in Pittsburgh where John's father was employed in the steel industry and three of John's older siblings were born there, but the family returned to Belfast in the mid-1930s due to the Depression. John himself later migrated to the United States in 1968, moved on to Canada in the early 1970s and currently lives in Toronto (interview, Toronto, VMR–061). Similarly, Bill spoke of how his maternal grandparents and their family had emigrated from Belfast to Toronto in the 1920s and were joined by Bill's parents:

> They [parents] met through church and of course, they were married and came to Canada, I believe it was 1928. And of course, the grandparents had come before that – my mother's father and mother – and they lived and died in the Toronto area. My father of course took ill in 1930 and was advised to go home. When I look and study a little bit of history attached to that I think he was just purely homesick and he couldn't fight that. So consequently us three kids were born in Northern Ireland (interview, Toronto, VMR–059).

When Bill and his siblings emigrated from Belfast to Toronto during the 1950s, however, Bill's parents then re-emigrated to join them and this time they stayed in

Canada. Bill's mother formed an emigrant society in Toronto and his father was employed until retirement many years later by Eaton's Department Store, originally established by Timothy Eaton from Ballymena in 1869 and a well-known employer of Northern Irish immigrants. Paula reported how her parents emigrated from Belfast to Ontario during the early 1950s, where her father, a policeman in the Royal Ulster Constabulary (RUC), joined the Toronto Police Force. The adventure suited Paula's mother who had been forced to leave her civil service job because of the marriage bar but was able to seek employment in Canada.[9] After being abroad for a few years, several factors, such as the death her father's mother, the distance from her mother's family and her father's dissatisfaction with his police job, led the couple to return to Belfast. Paula recalled, however, that despite their return, her parents always viewed their emigration experience as empowering and this in turn influenced her own attitudes:

> One of the things that was very interesting about my mum and dad was that they also considered themselves to be quite modern and aware of the world because they'd spent these couple of years in Canada ... They were proud of those years of their life. Something would always come up in the conversation about well when of course we lived in Canada, x, y and z, so they very much kept that (interview, Liverpool, VMR–049).

Many of the migrants in previous generations emigrated from Ireland to rural areas abroad with the intention of farming. For those who went to regions, such as the Canadian west, they were often the first 'White' settlers on the land.[10] Edith originally from Lurgan, now living in the Toronto area, spoke of how her father and her mother's brother emigrated together from Northern Ireland to Manitoba during the 1920s where her mother's older sister was already established. They planned to set up in farming and when established to send for Edith's mother:

> So they went there and they got a bit of land. It was all just land and trees – there was nothing. So they cut themselves down these trees and all and they built a log cabin. And got it built – it took two years – my daddy was away for two years and then he got word to mommy the house was ready and come on out. There were no children by then, they had no children. So yes, come on out, the house is ready. But then [mommy's] mother said, 'No, you're not going. You're not going out of this house' (interview, Toronto, VMR–071).

So after two years of work clearing land and building a house, her father and her uncle left everything, sold up and came back to Northern Ireland.

Susannah from Belfast reported that her father's eldest brother, John, migrated to Canada around 1912, settling in rural Saskatchewan where he worked for the railway. Although her father and uncle wrote letters every Christmas, the last contact Susannah remembers is when her Uncle John's eldest son, Jim, visited the family during the Second World War:

> I can remember as a wee girl this big airman coming in to me – he was a very big man, in the Canadian Air Force – coming into the house and my father took him to see his Uncle Frank in Ballymena and so on. But he was killed on one of his first flights (interview, Kitchener, Ontario, VMR–066).

With the death of Susannah's Canadian cousin in the war, her grandfather's death in 1945 and her father's premature death a few years later, the two branches of her father's family lost contact. When her father's sister died in the mid-1980s, the family sent a letter to the last address they'd had in Saskatchewan and contact was re-established with her uncle's second son, Johnny, who invited Susannah to visit:

> Thinking on the plane on the way out, I don't know these people, but we just clicked right away. It was lovely. And their basement was nearly like a museum but he had a book of photographs from his father ... And also in this album there was I think it was a poem ... that my grandfather had written to his son when he was going to Canada. A lovely letter about going away – I think it was a poem about saying goodbye to his sister and all the rest. Yes, he had this in his album. Johnny kept it.

Harry reported the story of his aunt who married a Canadian soldier sent to recuperate in Belfast after having been gassed in the First World War. They left Ireland for Saskatchewan in 1919 where the demobilised soldier had received a land grant from the Canadian Government under the Soldier Settlement Scheme.[11] Harry marvelled at how his aunt, a middle-class city girl, adapted to life as a first White settler:

> They went out as fresh settlers. As they travelled up into where they'd been allotted, the ground been staked out for them. Building a house and living in tents ... They stayed there and they ranched. They had all kinds of tragedies like storms, like twisters which took their buildings away, and drought. Then they had a team of four horses to pull the ploughs. A horse disease came through, took the horses. You name it, they had it. They just about survived there (interview, Armagh, VMR–043).

Harry's aunt and uncle never had children so when his uncle died Harry went out to help his elderly aunt and brought her back to Northern Ireland. After three months, however, she decided to return to Saskatchewan where she died in 1987. Before her death, she contributed her story to an oral history project about first settlers in Saskatchewan:

Saskatchewan decided to do a book ... experiences of the settlers and of course, they came along to her with the tape recorder and spent several days ... Not only was she one of the oldest people left at the time they were doing this but she also had a big story to tell, like a very varied story.

'It was a culture shock': Narrating Generation and Immigration

In her investigation into Irish genealogy and diasporic identities entitled *Of Irish Descent*, Catherine Nash (2008) has noted that family stories of Irish emigrant origins may exclude the presence and significance of ancestors of other ethnicities. While this is undoubtedly true particularly in the diaspora, an important facet of the family migration stories in our studies was the revelation of the immigration and intermarriage of people of other ethnicities into Irish families. Not surprisingly, the British Empire and service in the imperial army played a significant role. Bríd from West Belfast spoke of how her great-grandfather had married a woman from Malta:

> My mother's father had been born in India. Her grandfather had originally come from County Carlow and had left home because there was a big family of them. He was only twelve or something and he left home and he walked to Dublin and he joined the British Army as a drummer boy and ended up in India. And then at one of the times when they were out, they sort of landed in Malta which was an old British port, and he met his wife there who was a woman called Philomena Greque that we believed was Maltese and he brought her back to Belfast. Know very little about this woman. Apparently she had very little English. My mother's father was called Michael, after her brother, but nobody knows who her brother was (interview, Belfast, VMR–019).

Bríd spoke of how members of her family had obtained the marriage certificate pertaining to this couple and that they planned to try to trace the Maltese branch of the family further. For her, however, the impact of the story was in the sense of loneliness and sadness that her great-grandmother never got back to Malta to see her family again and remained 'exiled' in a hostile climate:[12]

> I often think of her, what it must have been like for her because coming from a sunny place like that to Victorian Belfast ... Well even as a child I remember Belfast always being rainy and dirty and gray skies.

Clearly, the impact of this family story relates to Bríd's own migration narrative in which she detailed at length the loneliness, sense of exile and longing for home she felt during over twenty-years resident in Canada (Trew, 2005a). Patrick from Strabane, County Tyrone told the story of his parents who met in India. Patrick's father had joined the British Army Medical Corps and was on his way by ship to Burma when the Japanese invaded Burma. They were diverted to Bangalore, India where Patrick's father met his wife, a young woman from Goa of mixed Tamil and Portuguese descent:

> She was an Indian Catholic, her family was originally Goan from Goa. Because her name is Fernandez, her maiden name … Tamil was her native language but I mean I can't speak Tamil. She always spoke to us in English, in fact, she's got an Irish accent now (interview, Gortin, Co. Tyrone, VMR–020).

Patrick was born in Bangalore and the family returned to Strabane when he was about a year old. For his twenty-year-old mother, Ireland was a bit of an adjustment, particularly as the family was poor and first lived in a house with no central heating or running water:

> It was a culture shock to her, I think, because she came from a very, a fairly well off Indian family. Her father – my grandfather – worked for the British Indian, the East India Company; he was on the telephone, on communications. He was well off … She had two sisters and a brother she left. Her last sister's just died so she's the last of her family now.

But the multi-ethnic aspect of Patrick's family was not only due to having a Goan mother as became clear when he then related the story of his father's mother who was from Stranorlar in east Donegal where she and her siblings were raised in an orphanage. She left there as a teenager to work in Glasgow as a domestic shortly after the First World War.

> She got involved with a soldier there from the Canadian Army, got pregnant, had my father.
> JDT: So your father is half Canadian?
> Half Canadian, French–Canadian, that's why his name is Marcel … They never married and he eventually got posted back to Canada. But my granny – it must have been hard for her in them days having an illegitimate child in the 1920s.

His granny moved back to Donegal and eventually settled over the border in Strabane where she married the postman and had several more children. Although Patrick's father knew the name of his birth father he never traced him, but the French–Canadian legacy remains in the family.

I've got a brother called after my father, Marcel. And I've got a cousin – two cousins – called Marcel because he was their godfather.

Harry's grandfather from Wales was also in the British Army during the late nineteenth century and spent many years in Africa and India. It was only while he was on furlough in Liverpool, however, that he met his English wife and brought her back to India where several of their ten children were born. After retirement from the army the family moved briefly to Liverpool where Harry's grandfather owned two public houses which as Harry pointed out 'was a very wrong thing to do for an alcoholic'. After losing the businesses in the early years of the 1900s, Harry's grandfather took a job as manager of a chemical company on the Tolka River in Dublin where Harry's father was born and raised. As a British Protestant family in Dublin, several of Harry's uncles subsequently joined the British Army and went off to be killed in the First World War. His father also enlisted in 1918 but never saw active service abroad as the war ended, although his military service entitled him to privileges such as a civil service job in Dublin upon demobilisation. Harry explained:

> It was all British administered. It was the imperial civil service. They had a normal civil service and an imperial civil service. Now if there's one thing that an Irishman hates more than an ordinary Englishman, it's somebody from the imperial civil service because they administered the Empire. So he had got this privileged job in there and suddenly found that he was non persona grata south of the border when they started putting the border on (interview, Armagh, VMR–043).

As Harry pointed out his father lived through some very difficult times during the Irish war of independence and the years immediately following:

> So the imperial civil servants were given the option of joining the Irish civil service, the new one that was coming up – it hadn't been formed and they were forming one – or they were forming one in the North. With his background he knew he wouldn't live too long if he stayed down there so he went north and was a founding member of the civil service that you see today.

It is impossible to assess from the current vantage point whether Harry's father was in real danger or if the story simply fits in with a developed narrative of the forced expulsion of southern Protestants in the years following partition. Certainly, as noted in Chapter 2, statistical sources attest to significant numbers of Protestants who left the Irish Free State during the early 1920s; some to the North, some to Britain and others further afield. However, it is ironic that in Northern Ireland, Harry's family surname is usually associated with Catholics;

a perception which was later to cause Harry's generation considerable difficulty during the Troubles.

The majority of interviewees registered some form of immigration in their families in previous generations, most often involving a marriage whether the individual married abroad and brought the spouse back to Ireland, or married with the goal of migrating elsewhere as in the case of Harry's aunt who went to Saskatchewan. Most often the in-marrying spouse was of British Isles or European ancestry, but often enough ethnicities from the further reaches of the Empire were represented among the incomers.

Conclusion

These migration narratives of previous generations provide varied information about families, migration processes and societal constraints, and opportunities. Clearly, however, the stories also show that there are complex motivation factors and circumstances which are linked with national and global sociopolitical and economic forces in each generation and to which each migrant is subject. The narratives also demonstrate the extent and variety of multidirectional migrations and the long-term significance of immigration into Ireland and Ulster specifically. Perhaps most important, however, is the degree to which human agency, both individual and familial, is shown to operate within such national and global conditions.

While Louise Ryan (2008) and others have suggested that migrants tend to tell positive stories of their own migrations which depict them as active and empowered agents, this research would indicate that the stories or postmemories that the migrants themselves inherit from preceding migrant generations are often those of loss – a narrative inheritance of loss. But if so, what are the effects of these stories? What purpose do they serve? Perhaps, as Breda Gray has suggested, feelings of sadness about the absence of emigrants somehow keeps them alive and present and also 'functions as a form of acceptance of their absence'; consequently loss becomes a 'permissible emotion' – absolution – for those left behind who may have benefited from the emigration (2008: 943). As noted in Chapter 1, this would support the view that talking about negative events is particularly associated with well-being (McLean et al., 2007: 267; Pasupathi et al., 2009: 116–17). Analysis of emigrant letters reveals many of the same themes as these oral narratives of emigration and loss. Indeed, David Fitzpatrick (1994: 22–3) has rejected the claim that the bulk of emigrant correspondence testifies to the successes of emigration asserting that this cannot be substantiated. Rather, emigrant letters served several purposes, not least as missives of consolation, but their often guarded advice also functioned to regulate later migrations. Family postmemories of migration may serve similar purposes: although they are often narratives of loss, the stories frequently contain redemptive aspects which serve consolatory ends. Clearly, however, the narratives also function as cautionary tales. For in those tales that tell of 'failed' emigrations, of return, the events are often described as empowering and even fatalistic – certainly not disastrous – that the life recovered has then continued on at home.

Several of the interviewees, like Susannah and Roy earlier in this chapter, spoke of the importance of treasured 'migrant objects', such as diaries, photo albums, emigrant letters, or in my grandmother Roseena's case, a watch sent from America. Others like Paula spoke of practices enacted in her family that were not common in the Northern Ireland of the 1960s, such as the eating of 'Canadian' (sweet)corn on the cob and the persistent use of Canadian vocabulary. These objects or practices together with our narrative inheritance of migration ensure that whatever the decision to stay abroad or return, daily life in the here and now is always 'shot through' with other histories and places 'of residency' (Tolia-Kelly, 2006: 170).

Chapter 4

'Are you Catholic or Protestant?' Religion, Migration and Identity

Majorities and Minorities: 'Reality very often is not what you would wish it to be'

David was born in Belfast in 1940 to a father from County Cork and a mother from Dublin. His father, an elderly man when David was born, had in a previous marriage already reared a family; working in the insurance business for many years in Dublin, Liverpool and Twickenham, London before settling in Belfast during the 1930s. He was also a Baptist lay preacher, a Freemason and held strong Unionist beliefs. David's mother was raised in the Church of Ireland in which he himself was confirmed. In his childhood home, David remembered the photograph of King George VI on the living room wall, first in Belfast and later when they moved to Cork when he was in primary school. There the family lived in the city centre in the South Mall area; and David attended a Protestant school which catered largely for the sons of the Cork Protestant business community. Here he describes the people of their circle:

My father was a Freemason and what I didn't really grasp as a child was that as a Freemason we tended to know all the local businessmen. But as a child you accept all of that as being normal. It isn't abnormal. It was only afterwards I realised, why did we know these people? And I suspect it was because of my father's connections as a Freemason. I didn't see anything sinister in it then, nor, for that matter, now. It was just the people we mixed with ... I wouldn't want to bring class into it but I mean they were sort of respectable people, decent people ... You got to know the owner of the local bakery and the local printing works and so on and so forth. Because certainly in the forties and fifties it was a time when, shall we say, small businesses were more prominent than they are now. Big business hadn't arrived (interview, London, VMR–077).

As David adjusted to life in the South of Ireland, he was teased about his northern accent but he didn't recall this causing him any real difficulty. However, despite a secure upbringing David, an only child, was never completely anchored in Cork and always felt he belonged in the North. This, he maintains, was entirely personal, though possibly influenced by his parents Unionism, but he did not feel disadvantaged by being part of the Protestant minority in Cork, which he described as a privileged group:

> I suppose the Protestant minority was quite well off, relatively speaking. Not necessarily everybody but you were given courtesy by the authorities. People went out of their way to respect the churches and the religion, whoever they might be, the Garda Síochána or whatever. You were accorded certainly at least equality. They went to lengths to ensure that you got equality which meant that perhaps you got slightly better treatment.[1]

In a study of Protestants in West Cork (Butler and Ruane, 2009; Ruane and Butler, 2007), the issue of whether the Protestant community was a privileged or ill-treated minority was shown to be complex. While the authors concluded that Protestants were not exceptionally privileged in socio-economic terms, they, in accord with David's experience above, did not consider them as having been ill-treated, though they acknowledged incidents where discrimination was definitely at play. Crawford's study of southern Protestants (2010), on the other hand, has outlined many ways in which Protestants have been marginalised in the Republic of Ireland (ROI) while Baillie in her study of Presbyterians in Ireland has asserted that 'in the South Presbyterians have no difficulty with their loyalty to the Irish State and are proud of it' (2008: 217).

Due to a lengthy hospitalisation during adolescence, David never completed his schooling and at age seventeen, his father having died, he decided to return by himself to Belfast. It was the late 1950s and soon after his arrival David was dismayed to discover that Northern Ireland was a comparatively conservative society where Catholics were not treated as equals:

> I think where you start off you feel a need to return. But of course, you're returning to an image in your mind, not necessarily reality. When you get there you see the reality and the *reality very often is not what you would wish it to be* or expect it to be. I mean there were a number of things which I was uncomfortable with ... I'd sort of grown up in a society as part of a Protestant minority and I saw how we were treated as a Protestant minority ... And then of course returning to the North where the Catholic

minority were not treated in any way similar to the Protestant minority in the South. That is my experience.

David settled into digs in Belfast on the Donegall Road with a Protestant working-class family who treated him well and he began working as a clerk in an office in the city centre; a job that had been pre-arranged for him through family contacts. When the Stormont election of 1958 took place, David was surprised at some of the voting practices:[2]

> Somebody else who was sharing the same digs was the son of a magistrate and come polling day, he was very, very busy. He was the son of a pillar of the community. And on polling day he had four votes to cast which came as a bit of a novelty to me because he was registered at the university; he was registered at two sets of digs; and he was registered at home. So you know the little adage about the Unionist slogan, 'Vote early and vote often' [laughter]. I was exposed to that quite, quite soon. And they couldn't see anything wrong with it. I mean it was almost patriotic duty to go out and vote as many times as they could.[3]

David also noticed that as a Protestant he was expected to attend church regularly and to submit to the authority of the local minister. He felt that he had to be careful voicing opinions. Young Protestant men were also expected to join the Orange Order and to show deference towards the Royal Family. As he recalled:

> I was invited to join the Orange Order. I never said yes, I never said no, I just didn't do it. It had no attraction for me. And I got invited a second time to join the Orange Order and when I didn't take up the second offer, I felt that there was a little suspicion as to why I wouldn't. I mean I remember [in 1961] ... Mrs Queen, as I call her now, visited Belfast and I caused a certain amount of commotion. She was passing outside the place where I worked and everybody else was going over to wave and what have you and I couldn't be bothered to do it [laughs]. It was regarded as very odd behaviour, very odd behaviour indeed.

David was unable to settle in Belfast and after five years at 'home' he moved to London where he has since remained. Remembering his desire as a young man to return to Northern Ireland from Cork, David reflected:

> In many ways I just wanted to go home, in a matter of speaking. I didn't find it home. I found it a very claustrophobic society. You weren't encouraged to develop either personally or in any way. You were expected to conform ... And when it became apparent that you weren't really going to conform in that way, then you outgrew the North of Ireland quite, quite soon. There was no opportunity to develop in Belfast for me.

David's early move away from Northern Ireland, his parents' Unionism and perhaps his lack of identity with the southern Protestant community in Cork, led him to try to recover an Ulster identity. But he found he was between two worlds and did not fit there either. Now after a lifetime in England, David retains a strong interest in all things Irish and while he does not hold the pro-Union views of his parents, he identifies with the whole of the British Isles in a sort of dual British–Irish hybridity. Significantly, David's narrative highlights the majority/minority positions that Protestants and Catholics in Ireland may occupy simultaneously; an issue perhaps not well enough understood in the identity debate. But if as Kaufmann and Haklai (2008: 743) suggest, 'the world is in the midst of a long-term shift from dominant minority to dominant majority ethnicity', how will this play out in Ireland, the division of which was justified on the basis of consolidating a former dominant minority? What is the role of migration in this majority/minority paradigm, not only in terms of Northern Ireland's demographic balance, but also in the formation of northern Protestant and Catholic identities at home and abroad? These questions will be considered in this chapter along with a review of the statistics and assumptions that have been made about the emigration of northern Protestant and Catholic cohorts since partition. First, however, the chapter begins with consideration of majority and minority identities in Northern Ireland.

Majorities and Minorities in Northern Ireland

Amid a flurry of Loyalist protests in December 2012 over the decision by Belfast City Council to restrict the flying of the union flag at City Hall to designated days, release of the 2011 census results revealed that the proportion of Protestants in the Northern Ireland population had fallen below 50 per cent for the first time.[4] Although Protestants still form a small majority (48.4%), Catholics comprise a large and growing minority (45.1%) and are already a majority among children of school age.[5] Thus, the overturning of Protestant majority status appears inevitable in a relatively short time frame, rousing Protestant 'insecurity' and 'alienation'[6] while at the same time highlighting northern Catholic disaffection with the Irish state (Elliott, 2000, 2009; O Connor, 1993; O'Halloran, 1987; Phoenix, 1994). However, this majority/minority binary must also be considered historically in the context of all Ireland, where Protestants have always formed a minority (18% in 2011) while Catholics have comprised the large majority (73% in 2011).[7] Unionist anxieties about the eventual extinction of Protestants south of the border and fear of 'Rome rule' in the North have been fuelled by factors beyond simple demographics: the uncomfortable history of sectarian 'sorting out' during the 1920s; the dominance of the Catholic Church in independent Ireland and in particular the effect of the *Ne Temere* decree (1908), which most often influenced the decision for mixed marriage couples to raise their children as Catholics; and perceptions of anti-Protestant discrimination in the South fomented by northern politicians.[8] In whichever geographic context and position one chooses (e.g., majority/minority in all-Ireland, NI or the UK), neither Protestant nor Catholic groups are monoliths; indeed, in the case of northern Protestants, it is the diversity of identification and opinion – 'a majority of minorities' (Boal et al., 1991) – that has been characteristic of political reality in Northern Ireland.[9] Important recent research has examined national identity among northern Protestants in the context of denominational differences, especially with consideration of their impact on political policy-making (Ganiel, 2006; C. Mitchell, 2003, 2006; Mitchell and Tilley, 2004; Mitchell and Todd, 2007; Southern, 2005, 2007). Nevertheless, 'the fact that the overwhelming majority of Protestants support the Union regardless of theological disputes speaks to the importance of politics in the formation of Ulster Protestant identity' (Brewer, 2004: 266). Indeed surveys conducted since the Belfast/Good Friday Agreement (1998) support the view that the large majority of Protestants maintain a British national identity while a somewhat smaller majority of Catholics consider themselves to be Irish (see Figure 4.1).[10]

Taking pro-Union positions together (British, Northern Irish and Ulster) amounts to an over 89 per cent preference for Protestants for the three surveys listed in Figure 4.1, while Catholics selecting 'Irish' identity average 63 per cent, though the 2011 census shows a much lower percentage choosing Irish national identity overall. One must bear in mind, however, that unlike the most recent census much social survey research in Northern Ireland has permitted respondents to select only a single identity label from a fixed menu as per categories in Figure 4.1 and has not allowed for dual or hybrid identities, or for understanding the relationship between identity categories (Farrington and Walker, 2009: 137). Nor have the surveys enquired into the aspects of experience that might have influenced the choice. Among the respondents to these surveys, there were no doubt many differing interpretations of each of the categories; indeed the lack of accord in the UK on the meaning of 'Britishness' has become apparent in recent research as will be discussed a bit further on. It has also been suggested that interrogations into 'national' identity in Northern Ireland are misconceived because Ulster Protestants generally espouse a type of civic Unionism that 'has little to do with the idea of nation' (Aughey, 1989: 18).[11] However, in the European Values Study, when asked about the importance of identity, Protestants who chose 'British' and Catholics who chose 'Irish' had by far the highest, and approximately equal, adherence over those of either denominational group who opted for the other categories (Fahey et al., 2005: 64).[12] Since 1968, social surveys in Northern Ireland have shown a generally increasing preference for 'British' and 'Northern Irish' categories among Protestants and a decreasing inclination towards 'Ulster' and 'Irish' categories (Gallagher, 1995: 731).[13] Northern Ireland

Figure 4.1: National identity in Northern Ireland (%)

Surveys	British		Irish		Northern Irish		Ulster		British–Irish[1] (multiple response)		Other	
	Pr	RC	Pr	RC	Pr	RC	Pr	RC	Pr	RC	Pr	RC
European Values Study 1999–2000 (N=832)	75.8	8.0	3.0	63.6	8.8	14.3	5.1	1.8	6.5	11.6	0.9	0.8
Legacy of the Troubles Study 2004 (N=1556)	84.2	17.3	3.9	67.4	9.0	12.9	na	na	na	na	2.8	2.4
NILT 2010 (N=1205)	61	8	4	58	28	25	5	1	na	na	2	8
Census 2011 Nat ID[2]	39.9		25.3		20.9		na		8.9		5	

na = not applicable

[1] In the European Values Study the British–Irish category is reported as meaning 'sometimes British and sometimes Irish'. While it is possible to identify as Irish and be pro–union, the assumption here is that Irish identification cannot be taken automatically to be so; the same with British–Irish.

[2] There were several multiple identity options: British / Irish = 0.66%; British / Northern Irish = 6.17%; Irish / Northern Irish = 1.06%; British / Irish / Northern Irish = 1.02%. At time of writing (Dec. 2012), NISRA had not yet released cross–tabulations of 2011 census data (e.g. national identity by religious denomination). Another indicator of national identity can be ascertained via Table KS205NI: Passports held. Accordingly, those who held only a British passport (57.2%), Irish (18.9%), other (3%), while multiple passport holders comprised: British and Irish (1.67%), British and other (0.24%), and Irish and other (0.13%). 18.85 percent of the population did not hold a passport in 2011.

Life & Times (NILT) surveys of recent years, however, show a slight decline in 'British' identification among Protestants and a growing preference for the 'Northern Irish' label, which has also been increasing among northern Catholics, especially among the younger age group (eighteen to twenty-four).[14] The emerging preference for 'Northern Irish' identity is also evident in the recent 2011 census results, particularly if single and multiple responses are included together (British = 48%; Irish = 28%; and Northern Irish = 29%) and was strongest in Omagh (28%), Down and Strabane (each 27%).[15] These results would suggest that the 'turquoise tinge' of 'being Northern Irish' has become more neutral politically.[16] It may also be a sign that Northern Irish identity is perceived more and more as having value, perhaps as a badge of courage for having survived conflict or as bi-cultural apparatus that is useful for operating in the wider international context (see Gary's story in Chapter 5).

In the Irish context, several conceptual models have emerged from social identity theory (Tajfel, 1981) to cope with the complexity of identity positions: the 'double majority' (Cairns, 1982) or 'double minority' (Jackson, 1979) where Protestant and Catholic groups both exhibit characteristics of majority (positive self-image) or minority (insecure, threatened) behaviours; or even the 'triple minority' (Cassidy and Trew, 1998: 736) where northern Protestants exhibit minority characteristics in the multiple contexts of the island of Ireland and in Britain. Indeed, northern Catholics and southern Protestants have exhibited the features of majorities, each constructing a 'parallel universe' with their own institutions, newspapers, services, cultural events and even property transactions, but paradoxically both groups have also demonstrated the characteristics of minorities with long lists of real and imagined grievances (Elliott, 2009: 241). Consequently, the situation in Ireland provides a fine example of how 'a group constituted as a minority along one dimension of differentiation may be constructed as a majority along another' (Brah, 1996: 189).

While identities are formed in continuous interaction with environment, life history and social contact with others, change, especially of a sudden or violent nature (as with migration or conflict), provides the most significant challenge to identity. Stressful experiences can consolidate identities in majority and minority contexts because strong social identities (e.g., entrenched national identities) have been shown to be protective of individual identity and well-being, especially in times of change and even in the context of considerable political violence (Muldoon et al., 2009: 143). Thus, geographical contexts and societal conditions (especially involving conflict and violence) at particular moments in time all contribute to a group's sense of itself along a majority ↔ minority spectrum. Rather than two fixed positions, each group's position is flexible and reactive, and therefore prone to identity shifts (Bull, 2006; Hughes and Donnelly, 2003; Stevenson et al., 2007: 109; Todd, 2007; Todd et al., 2006).

The Demography of Northern Ireland Migration and Religion

Although the discourse surrounding migration has been muted in official circles in Northern Ireland (see discussion in Chapter 1), population movements have not entirely escaped the notice of sociologists and historians, and there have been several attempts to estimate the numbers of Protestants and Catholics that have left Northern Ireland since partition. Typically, emigration has been discussed in the context of other issues: economic instability, discrimination, sectarianism and the conflict as factors that have motivated departure; and for the period since the 1980s, as part of the discourse surrounding 'brain drain'; that is, the departure of young people, especially college-goers, to attend university in Britain. Accordingly, the discussion that follows is structured along these lines.

Religion, Migration and Conflict

Despite many assumptions made over the last half century concerning the emigration rates of Protestants and Catholics from Northern Ireland, in truth most migration data reveals little or nothing about the religious characteristics of migrants.[17] The census since 1861 (for Ireland and Northern Ireland) remains the most significant source on the religious composition of the resident population and, in more recent times, on the denomination of recently arrived immigrants.[18] However, there are two considerable problems inherent in using census data to determine the religion of emigrants in the calculation of net migration. The first is the issue of the reliability of the census counts concerning the size of the resident religious cohorts that form the basis of the net migration calculation due to significant rates of 'no religion' or 'religion not stated' in response to the religion question (1971= 9.4%; 1981= 21.5%; and 1991= 12.2%).[19] Consequently various strategies have been attempted with varying success to circumvent the non-response issue (e.g., inclusion from 2001 of a 'community background' or 'religion brought up in' question). The second problem in the use of census data to determine the religion of emigrants relates to the calculation of natural increase/decrease by religion as births and deaths are not registered by religious affiliation in Northern Ireland (Compton, 1991a: 159). Thus, fertility and mortality rates for each religious cohort over the inter-censal period must be estimated and it is precisely how these rates are arrived at that has come under considerable debate.[20] Nevertheless, this rather imprecise method is employed to calculate net emigration by religion, resulting in a variety of different estimates by several scholars over the period 1926–1981 which are presented in Figure 4.2 below. Barritt and Carter (1962: 107–108) accordingly stressed the approximate nature of their estimates, noting other factors that may affect the size of a religious cohort, in particular that there is no possibility of accounting for religious conversion.

They deduced that there had been a 9 per cent loss of Catholics and a 3 per cent loss of Protestants through emigration for the period 1937–1951 and for the following decade, 1951–1961, a 9 per cent loss of Catholics and a 4 per cent loss of Protestants. In total, the Catholic one-third of the population accounted for 55–58 per cent of total emigration from 1937 to 1961.

Figure 4.2: Some estimates of Northern Ireland net emigration by denomination

	1937–51 Barritt & Carter	1951–61 Barritt & Carter	1951–61 Compton (1976)	1961–71 Compton (1985)	1961–71 Compton (1989)	1971–81 Compton (1989)	1926–81 Rowthorn & Wayne (1988)
Total net emig.	67,000	92,000	92,000	69,000	61,000*	110,000*	441,000
Catholic	39,000	51,000	55,200	41,500	33,000	55,000	263,000
% Catholic	58%	55%	60%	60%	54%	50%	60%
Protestant	28,000	41,000	36,800	27,500	28,000	55,000	178,000
% Protestant	42%	45%	40%	40%	46%	50%	40%

* Compton's total net emigration estimates are actually lower than those of the Registrar General (1961–71= 69,222 and 1971–81 = 111,423).

From the estimates presented in Figure 4.2, we can assume that from the 1920s through to the 1970s the rate of Catholic emigration was likely over twice that for Protestants (based on the proportion of each cohort in the resident population).[21] Reasons for this include: discrimination in employment and housing against Catholics, and increasing Catholic disaffection; indeed the substantial emigration of Catholics may have been 'an overt policy goal of the Unionist administration' (McAuley, 1996: 58). The issue of discrimination against Catholics in Northern Ireland as a cause for unemployment and emigration, however, has been hotly contested over the years and most troubling has been the use of these inexact net migration estimates in the debate. This has occasioned some biting comment concerning 'the lengths to which some economists and sociologists will go to deny the obvious – the existence of direct and indirect discrimination – beggars belief' (McGarry and O'Leary, 1995: 485–6).[22] However, considering that unemployment has traditionally been an important cause of emigration, it is worth bearing in mind that even by 2001 unemployment rates for economically active males aged sixteen to seventy-four were still significantly higher for Catholics (11.2%) compared to the rates for other denominations: Presbyterian (5.6%); Church of Ireland (7.3%); Methodist (5.9%) or other/none (7.6%), with

Belfast and the Northwest the worst areas.[23]

A fascinating and hitherto neglected analysis of the relationship between emigration and sectarianism has been provided by Ronald Terchek (1984), based on survey data collected in 1968 by Richard Rose (1971).[24] Rose's survey included two questions concerning the desire of respondents to emigrate from Northern Ireland for which Terchek presented a detailed analysis of responses, profiled according to socio-economic characteristics, religion, education and value system of survey respondents to determine the type of respondent who would be more likely to emigrate in the context of prevailing sectarianism.[25] Terchek based his hypothesis on Hirschman's (1970) exit-voice polarity theory, that in the context of societal stress three options are available: to stay and protest for in-group interests (voice); to vote with the feet and leave (emigration, exit); or to stay and keep silent (accept the status quo).[26] Since younger people traditionally form the majority of protestors and emigrants in any society; the younger (rather than older) survey respondents in Terchek's analysis would be expected to favour both protest (voice) and emigration (exit) options. Among the intriguing results, however, were that young Protestants were almost equally divided between voice and exit options and that those who held the most traditional orthodox values were the most militant (i.e., likely to protest to maintain in-group Protestant interests = voice). Young Catholics, on the other hand, were much more likely to emigrate than to stay and protest but those who held traditional values were most likely to accept the status quo (i.e., neither emigrate nor protest). Among both Protestant and Catholic cohorts, those who were least committed to traditional values, displayed low levels of religiosity and possessed higher levels of education, were most likely to emigrate. In view of the significant emigration of the 1970s decade that subsequently took place following the collection of Rose's survey data, the implications of Terchek's analysis are striking: that the Protestants and Catholics most likely to emigrate tend to be also the most liberal of their cohort and with their departure they are not only 'taking with them orientations that could provide the basis for future accommodation', but their absence may well leave a more divided society behind (Terchek, 1984: 385). Thus, it would appear that emigration in the context of societal conflict is likely to delay conflict resolution by strengthening the old regime at home (Rose, 1971: 367), although the existence of expatriate or diasporic communities abroad may have an impact (positive or negative) on peace processes.[27]

Religion, Migration and 'Brain Drain'

Since the 1970s, emigration patterns have changed substantially with the proportion of Catholic emigration decreasing while Protestant emigration increased considerably, particularly among the young middle class.[28] This has been attributed to the migration of Northern Ireland college-goers to post-secondary institutions in Britain which grew to significant levels during the 1980s and 1990s (between 30 to 40 per cent), largely due to the lack of university places available within Northern Ireland for the fast-growing student population.[29] This, as mentioned previously, led to fears about a 'brain drain', given the general tendency for emigrants not to return, and especially that young middle-class Protestants represented about two-thirds of the departing cohort (Osborne, 2006; Schubotz, 2008).[30] Several studies conducted since the 1980s have examined student migration from a variety of perspectives, especially the likelihood of return (e.g., Cormack et al., 1997; Harmon and Walker, 2000; McGregor et al., 2002; Osborne, 2006; Osborne et al., 1987; Osborne et al. 2006, etc). Using data from several surveys representing cohorts that entered higher education in 1973, 1979, 1985 and 1991, Cormack et al. (1997), for example, confirmed that there was a general tendency among those who leave Northern Ireland not to return (see Figure 4.3).

Figure 4.3: Northern Ireland college-goers by destination 1979 and residence in 1991

	NI	*GB*	*ROI*	*Overseas*
Place of study 1979	64.7	30.6	4.7	–
Residence in 1991	56.9	35.6	2.9	4.6

Source data: Cormack et al. (1997, 82)

Examining 1991 college-goer cohort data on the basis of religion (see Figure 4.4) clearly shows the predominance of Protestants (43%) who chose to leave for study in Britain while the large majority of Catholics stayed in Northern Ireland for education. Only a tiny percentage overall chose universities in the ROI and Protestants were more likely attend the older British universities whereas the new

Figure 4.4: Northern Ireland college–goers by destination 1991 (% by row)

	QUB & UU	*GB*	*ROI*
Protestants*	55	43	1
Catholics	70	27	3
Other*	47	51	1

Source data: Cormack et al. (1997, 74) (*totals = 99)

universities (post-1991) tended to draw fairly equally from both Protestant and Catholic groups. The principal reasons cited by the cohort of 1991 respondents for their departure were the lack of available third-level places in Northern Ireland and the desire for adventure.

There are a number of factors that characterise students who are likely to leave to study in Britain ('leavers'). Based on a 1991 cohort of Northern Ireland college-goers surveyed in 1998, McGregor et al. (2002) found that leavers were more likely to have slightly higher A-level scores than those who stayed in Northern Ireland, be Protestant, have attended a grammar school, come from a professional-class background and after graduation were more likely to stay away and find employment often in the locality of their university where they earned on average a 13 per cent higher income level. They also found that those who returned to Northern Ireland after studying in Britain had performed generally less well in their degrees and experienced on average a 20 per cent drop in income upon return. Conversely, graduates of Northern Ireland institutions who left after their graduation for employment in Britain were also likely to have attended a grammar school and the Catholics in this group experienced the largest increase in income of 26 per cent (McGregor et al., 2002: 228).[31] Another study relating to a 1992 cohort showed that the probability of studying in Britain was higher for Protestants and women, but that Catholics and women were more likely to return to Northern Ireland and return tended to take place quite soon after graduation (Harmon and Walker, 2000). The data analysis also supported the notion that Protestants with higher A-level scores were more likely to leave for Britain and that the higher qualified tended to remain there. These trends may account for a larger proportion of Catholics than Protestants resident in Northern Ireland having third-level qualifications and that there has been a significant increase in the proportion of Catholics employed in the public sector (McQuaid and Hollywood, 2008: 75; Osborne, 2006: 337). Higher qualified Protestants from grammar school backgrounds ('determined leavers') were more likely to study in Britain while 'reluctant leavers' comprised those who lacked the grades to obtain places in Northern Ireland universities and were more likely to obtain places in post-1991 new British universities (Osborne, 2006: 337; Osborne et al., 2006: 2). Overall, student migration from Northern Ireland to Britain responded to relative unemployment rates and the availability of third-level places in higher education institutions (Harmon and Walker, 2000).

In more recent years the number of students leaving to study in Britain has dropped to near 30 per cent overall because of the increase in third-level places available within Northern Ireland (see Figure 4.5). Data analysis of graduate cohorts from 1998 to 2002 has confirmed the link between studying in Britain and staying there after graduation, however, there is in addition a tendency for graduates from Northern Ireland universities to go to Britain for employment, especially those with the highest level results (Hoare and Corver, 2010: 485–6). Recent data on Northern Ireland graduates of educational institutions in Britain showed: for the cohort in academic year 2010–2011, six months after their graduation, 56 per cent were employed in Britain while 38 per cent had returned to employment in Northern Ireland, 1 per cent were in the ROI and 4 per cent elsewhere; and for the cohort from the academic year 2006–2007, over three years after graduation, 45 per cent had returned to work in Northern Ireland.[32] Thus, Northern Ireland has long been and continues to be a significant loser of graduate employment to Britain. The propensity for Protestants to depart and Catholics to stay at home remains; the situation exacerbated by the lower level of Protestants in higher education generally (38%) and particularly low achievement among the Protestant working class (Purvis et al., 2011). However,

Figure 4.5: Northern Ireland school leavers who entered institutions of higher education in NI and GB by religion, 2005–2006 (School Leavers' Survey)

	2005	*%*	*2006*	*%*
Protestant school leavers				
In NI	2427	67.2%	2331	65.7%
GB	1187	32.8%	1217	34.3%
Total Protestant	3614	100.0%	3548	100.0%
% Protestant of Total		**38.5%**		**38.1%**
Catholic school leavers				
in NI	3986	79.7%	3852	77.0%
GB	1018	20.3%	1148	23.0%
Total RC	5004	100.0%	5000	100.0%
% Roman Catholic of Total		**53.3%**		**53.8%**
*Other school leavers**	776		754	
% Other of total		8.3%		8.1%
Overall total	9394		9302	

*Other includes Other Christian, Non–Christian, and No Religion

Source data: Department of Employment and Learning NI, Statistical Fact Sheets: Northern Ireland school leavers who entered institutions of higher education in Northern Ireland and Great Britain by religion 2006 (December 2008) and 2005 (March 2007) according to the School Leavers' Survey, at: www.delni.gov.uk/index/publications/r-and-s-stats/religion-higher-education-entrants-0506.htm (accessed: 26 Jan. 2013).

Figure 4.6: YLT (2008) 16-year-old respondents' intention to emigrate from Northern Ireland

YLT 2008 (N=941)	Total yes response %	% Protestant	% RC	% No religion
Will you leave NI	47	41	48	59
Leave for education	55	63	49	55
Leave for job prospects	37	35	37	38
Leave for better future	43	37	44	52
Leave because of The Troubles	3	5	1	5
Return to live in NI	51	50	57	37

when colleges of further education are included in the analysis, the situation is less stark with approximately 18 per cent of Protestants heading to Britain compared with 13 per cent of Catholics; and with Protestants averaging around 42 per cent of higher and further education and Catholics at around 50 per cent (averaged 2001–2007).[33] In October 2011, a motion was tabled in Stormont for a debate concerning the minority of Protestants attending universities in Northern Ireland, amounting approximately to only one-third of the 35,000 students.[34] Politicians Jim Allister of the Traditional Unionist Voice (TUV) and Gregory Campbell, Democratic Unionist Party (DUP), were both widely quoted in the media expressing concern that educational attainment was lower among working-class Protestants and that many university-bound Protestants chose to study in Britain.[35] By 2010–2011, 26% of third-level students (16,730) from Northern Ireland were enrolled at a university in Britain with a preference for Scotland (4,520) and the northwest of England (4,360), while 8,000 from outside attended Northern Ireland universities, approximately half of these from the ROI.[36] It remains to be seen how new fee structures recently introduced in the UK university sector will affect the outflow of Northern Ireland students to Britain over the longer term.

Attitudinal research, such as the annual *Northern Ireland Life and Times* (NILT) and *Young Life and Times* (YLT) Surveys, has also provided insight into the relationship between religious cohort and migration. In the YLT 2008 Survey (see Figure 4.6), for example, sixteen-year-olds were asked to consider whether they would leave Northern Ireland and for what reasons.[37] Education, especially for Protestants, was the major reason cited for emigration and both cohorts responded with a relatively positive attitude towards eventual return. It is apparent that for this post-Belfast/Good Friday Agreement generation, the conflict appears to have had little weight in their consideration.

In the NILT Survey 2010, when adult respondents were asked if they had ever lived outside of Northern Ireland for more than six months, 30 per cent answered in the affirmative. A breakdown of this 30 per cent can be found in Figure 4.7 below.[38]

Figure 4.7: NILT (2010) respondents who had lived outside of Northern Ireland for more than 6 months

NILT 2010 (*N=1205*)	*Total yes response %*	*% Protestant*	*% RC*	*% No religion*
Outside NI more than 6 months	30	23	33	39
Had lived in the Republic of Ireland (ROI)	14	6	23	*
Had lived outside the British Isles	41	39	42	*
Had lived in mainland UK	60	70	48	*

* Number is too small to permit calculation of percentage.

Over 38 per cent of those in the twenty-five to forty-four age group; 27 per cent of those aged forty-five to fifty-four; 22 per cent of the fifty-five to sixty-four; and 27 per cent of the sixty-five-plus groups had lived outside Northern Ireland, the figures demonstrate a preference for migration to Britain, especially for Protestants, but also for Catholics. The overall 'Yes' response to migration was weighted towards Catholics which would suggest a higher tendency for Catholics to return. It has been suggested (for the 1998 NILT Survey) that a higher proportion of those who claim 'no religion' tend to be Protestants (Brewer, 2004: 270) and if that is the case with the 2010 Survey, the Protestant emigration figure might well be higher. Brewer's supposition prompts several questions. Are Protestants more likely to drop their religious affiliation while abroad? If so, might this be an influence of the migration experience? Do Catholics do likewise? Or is it that those who are the least religious to begin with choose to depart as suggested by Terchek's analysis above?

Overall, the migration data from the surveys reviewed in this chapter generally demonstrates that those in both Protestant and Catholic cohorts who leave tend to be among the best educated, most liberal, and least committed to any particular version of ethno-national identity in Northern Ireland society. However, these surveys do not reveal why this is the case, nor anything about those who do not adhere to the general pattern. Thus, for the remainder of this chapter I embark on a discussion of interviewee narratives to examine more closely some of the particular factors that motivated emigration since the 1960s, including scrutiny of some general assumptions that have been made about the migration experiences of Irish Protestant and Catholic cohorts. For example, it has been assumed that Protestants have had an easier migration experience than Catholics; that Protestants have blended easily into host societies while Catholics formed ethnic enclaves and often faced discrimination abroad. The logical outcome of this assumption then is of voluntary identity loss for Protestants abroad and strengthened identity for Catholics. But what about the impact of background, class differences, reasons for departure, reception in the host society and meeting other Irish abroad from across religious, political and national divides? How have these experiences affected not only personal identity but attitudes towards larger political issues, such as Irish unity? The discussion which follows is therefore structured to shine some light on these questions.

'A big black cloud had lifted': Leaving the North

Pat, an only child, was raised in Bangor, North Down during the 1940s and 1950s. His father was a physician, but it was Pat's incarceration in the Purdysburn Fever Hospital as a ten-year-old for three months during the polio epidemic of 1951 that gave him the desire to become a doctor and he later attended medical school at Queen's University.[39] Although his family was middle class and his mother was English from County Durham, Pat felt that he had been indoctrinated in sectarian attitudes before he understood what they were. As he described:

> I grew up with a Presbyterian grandmother from Rasharkin [Co. Antrim] and you had to call it a pussy, not a cat, because cat was the first syllable of Catholic, she was that narrow. I had been taken by the hand to Orange parades on the Twelfth of July, I'd been taught to 'kick the pope', 'God bless King Billy' (interview, Holywood, Co. Down, VMR–087).

Nevertheless, living in a largely Protestant community, Pat was not all that aware of sectarianism and it was only when he got to medical school where the classes were integrated that he regularly interacted with Catholics. But even then, the cohorts were segregated for their hospital training: the Protestants assigned to the Royal Victoria and City hospitals; and the Catholics to the Mater. It was in September 1964 at the age of twenty-three when training in the casualty department of the Royal that Pat was first 'deeply affected' by real experience of violence that was 'utterly bloody mindless' as he assisted with treating injuries sustained by the protestors during the three days of the Divis Street riots.[40] However, it was economic opportunity not the conflict specifically, that was the principal motivating factor for his emigration to Canada. During the summer of 1969, Pat took the opportunity of going to fill a six-week locum contract at

Figure 4.8: Belfast International – Aldergrove Airport check-in, 1960s (National Museums Northern Ireland, Photograph Library, Yt5118)

a general practice in Alliston, Ontario, where he found that the conditions were good and the wages were much superior to what was then on offer in the UK. However, his first experience in Canada had a familiar 'parallel' dimension:

> It's good Ulster Protestant country. It's just up the road from Orangeville and the river that flows through Alliston is the Boyne River and halfway along the Boyne River is a farm called Ballymena Farm and if you go down Rural Route 11, the first place you come to is Cookstown (interview, Holywood, Co. Down, VMR–087).

Having been abroad for only six weeks, Pat was nonetheless struck by the increasingly difficult lifestyle and political instability when he returned to Northern Ireland and soon made arrangements to depart permanently for Canada with his wife and young son the following year, settling in Calgary, Alberta. Like Pat, Chris and his wife were both middle-class Protestants and doctors, though they had been raised in the Church of Ireland with fairly liberal values.

They left Belfast when they graduated from Queen's University medical school in 1972. While sympathetic to the civil rights movement, they had been too busy with their medical studies to get personally involved and did not really identify with the conflict. Chris recalled that it was the 'bombing every midnight and a lot of Troubles, a lot of violence that was influential in us deciding to go to England'. Prior to the civil rights movement, Chris had not been aware of sectarianism and fondly remembered a more peaceful time when for many years his mother had been the 'Protestant' GP in the working-class Catholic estate of Ballymurphy in West Belfast. During his secondary schooling at the Royal Belfast Academical Institution – known locally as Inst[41] – there had been only one 'conspicuous Catholic' – the son of one of the teachers – and one Jewish boy who 'were supposed to be a bit different but they weren't any different as it turned out … but for some reason they were labelled "a Catholic" and "he's a Jew"'. As emigrants, Chris and his wife were not unusual among the young medical fraternity as at their ten-year medical school reunion in 1982, for example, it was reported that 50 per cent of their fellow graduating class had left Northern Ireland. So many years later, Chris could easily remember how they felt at the time of their departure:

> When we did leave we did feel like there was *a big black cloud had lifted*. Yeah, we really did. It was really oppressive, the news, the TV, the physical things, the Troubles from 68 to 72 (interview, Ballynahinch, Co. Down, VMR–084).

Chris and his wife and Pat are examples of middle-class Protestant professionals from the greater Belfast area who left during the early 1970s. Growing up in Protestant communities, none of them had been particularly aware of sectarianism prior to the civil rights movement and they all felt somewhat removed from the conflict as if, to paraphrase another of the interviewees, 'it wasn't their battle' (VMR–034). By the same token, not wanting to deal with the political and economic instability of a conflict zone, it was relatively easy as professionals for them to leave and procure employment abroad.[42] For working-class individuals, however, leaving Northern Ireland was perhaps more of a risk, but there were also risks inherent in living in a conflict zone.

Laura, born in 1956, was from a working-class Presbyterian background in Lurgan, County Armagh, in an area which became known during the 1970s and 1980s as the 'murder triangle'.[43] Lurgan has been described as 'a bitter town … with an invisible dividing line through its centre'; Catholics tending to be located on the north side and Protestants on the south.[44] Laura, however, had memories of the pre-Troubles era in her community during the 1960s, noting that while there was only one Catholic family on her street, the neighbours got along well and the children played together. However, this was not to last. As sectarian tensions grew in Lurgan, people from outside their estate forced the Catholic family to leave and she remembered her parents and the neighbours being very unhappy but feeling powerless about the outcome.[45] The early years of the Troubles coincided with Laura beginning her secondary education at the state grammar school where she befriended the only Catholic girl attending in her year who subsequently introduced her to other Catholics. This was a key development in Laura's life and she credited her friend's courage and agency 'because she had crossed that boundary, it brought me, networked me, into a group which I wouldn't otherwise have known'. The friends socialised together, adopting Protestant or Catholic identities according to the pubs and clubs they frequented. By her late teens, Laura had already developed strong left-leaning attitudes and had become interested in feminism. She found the conservatism of Northern Ireland society too restrictive:

> I wanted to be somewhere that was more open to all sorts of different people and religions, and people from different places, and sexualities (interview, Liverpool, VMR–052).

But this was the 1970s and the escalation of sectarianism and violence made Laura even more anxious to get away. One night she was evacuated from a pub just in time before it blew up. She didn't see a future for herself in Northern Ireland:

> I just wanted to get away from it really and as quickly as possible. And it wasn't just because of the Troubles and all of that. It was partly probably because of similar reasons to the young people these days [who] want to leave. That narrow-minded sectarianism breeds a narrow-mindedness about most things in life.

When Laura turned eighteen in 1974 and came into a small inheritance, she decided to use the money to go abroad for a year as she had learned that you didn't need a lot of money to stay on a kibbutz in Israel where 'you could live and work in this setting that was reasonably safe'. Although from the present perspective Israel might seem an odd choice of destination for a young person with decidedly left-wing attitudes, it was quite different back then:[46]

> There were three levels of kibbutzim and I went to the most left-wing one which was largely agricultural. I remember having a one-way ticket and arriving in at 18 Leonardo da Vinci Street [Tel Aviv] – I remember the address – and they offered for me to go to the Golan Heights.[47] And I said, 'Look, I've just come from Northern Ireland, have you got somewhere any quieter?' So they sent me to the Negev desert. I got driving tractors and picking fruit and that kind of thing (interview, Liverpool, VMR–052).

Laura never returned to live permanently in Northern Ireland as after her sojourn in Israel, she decided to move to England. There wasn't much room for a Protestant who 'had left-wing sort of socialist sympathies. It almost didn't sit with your heritage.'

Like David at the beginning of this chapter, it was an early migration experience and the sectarianism in Northern Ireland that combined to affect Orla's identity in a formative way and ultimately to influence her eventual migration to England as a young woman. Originally from a working-class Catholic background, Orla who now lives in Liverpool, was born in Melbourne, Australia, in 1956, though she returned with her parents to Belfast when she was only four years old.[48] Among her earliest memories were their North Belfast neighbours cajoling her to talk so that they could hear her Australian accent. Thus, Orla was made aware of her difference early on but in the pre-Troubles era of her 1960s childhood, it made her feel special and may have led her to value difference in others. Of her two best friends during those years, one was Protestant, the other was Jewish and as Orla recalled, 'believe it or not, I was a Catholic and I went to Saturday Hebrew school with my friend Sharon and learned to speak some Hebrew and learned to write some Hebrew'. With the onset of the conflict, however, conservative tensions emerged and Orla felt the need to choose sides:

> I was quite proud to say I had been born in Melbourne, Australia, but I was very aware [of it] as I came into my teenage years and the Troubles began and a lot of stuff around identity kicked in for a lot of us as young people. What is this, the Troubles? What is happening? Who are we? Are we Irish? You know I had always felt very strongly Irish and so I dropped telling people the fact that I had been born in Melbourne, Australia because that felt as if it made me not Irish (interview, Liverpool, VMR–056).

Orla described her teenage years in North Belfast as living in a street that was 'under siege'. She recalled vividly soldiers bursting into their home late one night, seizing her father and tearing the house apart searching for guns, while she and her younger brother were held at gunpoint in the upstairs bedrooms. Her father was stunned at being a suspect as he had served in the British Army during the Second World War and Orla remembered 'the look on his face of absolute shock and disbelief as they took him out'. No guns ever materialised and her father was eventually released without charge, but there was never any apology to the family. Not long afterwards, a girl she knew from the neighbourhood was killed when the bomb she was planting at a shopping arcade exploded prematurely.[49] However, the most traumatic incident occurred one night in Belfast while walking back from the Queen's Film Theatre when Orla and her friend were caught up in a bomb explosion near Carlisle Circus:

They blew up the taxi place there as we were walking towards Carlisle Circus up towards the Antrim Road. And the whole thing blew up in front of us and it was like one of those slow, screen movies where you just see all this, bricks, mortar, building metal, coming at you from a distance away. In slow motion … I remember this sense of fear as it blew up and turning and running and running and running … There was great big metal things landing either side of us and I always thought, we just weren't meant to die that day. We weren't meant to die (interview, Liverpool, VMR–056).

Though Orla briefly held a job in the Northern Ireland civil service, she was the only Catholic in her section and felt excluded as her co-workers frequently discussed Protestant activities, such as parades. She was not sure 'whether it was something very definite about letting me know who they were and who I wasn't'. The violence and the sense of exclusion were factors which led Orla to leave Belfast and move to England permanently in 1982. 'I was scared and unsafe and knew I could die or anything could happen to me and I couldn't cope with it.'

Sectarianism, violence and exclusion were also factors that affected Paula, a Protestant raised in the Church of Ireland who was born in Belfast in the early 1960s, shortly after her parents had returned from a few years living in Canada. Her father, a former RUC police officer, opened a shop in a working-class neighbourhood on the 'peace line' in North Belfast; an area that became known as part of Belfast's 'murder triangle'. Paula's memories of her childhood and youth were of a family life that revolved around the Troubles. Because her father's shop was robbed and blown up several times 'by both sides', the family became partly dependent on the government compensation money as the shop was uninsurable. Thus, she described her family as lower middle class 'without any money' because they had the shop and a mortgage. Paula recalled that several people they knew, friends of her parents, were attacked and badly injured or killed during the 1970s; events she described as 'really awful, really unsettling, really, really terrible'. However, she also reported humorous events, recalling one incident in particular when gunmen robbed their shop and attempted to kidnap her father, in the end only succeeding in stealing their car. When the vehicle was recovered a while later, her mother went to collect it:

She [mother] goes up and says, 'Yes, yes, that's the car' and the army, they look underneath it and all the rest of it. But one of the things she said was that she was really aware that as she got into the car that the whole army patrol got down behind a wall just in case there was something in the car that they hadn't noticed. So she's in the car by herself turning the ignition and all the Brits are down behind the wall on their stomachs

107

[laughter]. So as I say, you couldn't make that up, could you? (interview, Liverpool, VMR–049).

Nevertheless, Paula recalled that during her teen years throughout the 1970s she had to 'live with an awful lot of fear and anxiety which really wasn't very good for me' and that 'we really did worry for our lives in lots of ways'. Because her family lived in an interface area and her father's shop served both sides of a mostly working-class population where there was a considerable degree of social deprivation, Paula became painfully aware of class issues and in particular found middle-class attitudes 'appalling'. At this time, she also got involved in cross-community youth work which allowed her access to Nationalist perspectives. Not feeling that she belonged to any religion or class group – 'there was something about my difference from people' – she described herself as 'too much of an observer to everybody' and that she 'didn't really fit'. But what 'tipped the balance' in terms of her decision to leave and stay away:

> was around being clearer then about my sexuality, about being gay …
> I was already in quite an uncomfortable position in terms of who I was
> and my politics but also the one thing that all of those groups have in
> common is that none of them much likes gay people (interview, Liverpool,
> VMR–049).

While the 1970s was a time for challenging social boundaries of all kinds in Britain and the United States, Paula's story is a reminder that once the conflict broke out in Northern Ireland, conservatism set in with a vengeance and there was little room for difference of any kind, including sexuality.[50] Class boundaries also remained firmly in place, as experienced by Gary, a practising Presbyterian from Sandy Row in Belfast, who now lives in Seattle, Washington. He described the Sandy Row of his childhood as a community where women like his mother worked, most of them nearby at Gallaher's Tobacco Factory, while the men were often unemployed, and he remembered a relatively happy childhood, despite the considerable poverty and social deprivation in the neighbourhood. Though from the present perspective it seems difficult to fathom, Gary insisted that two milestone events in his life occurred on the same day when he joined Short Brothers as an apprentice in 1974 at the age of sixteen – his first excursion into downtown Belfast and the first time he met a Catholic. Prior to that he had been relatively unaware of Catholics and of sectarianism, and during his pre-conflict primary school years had developed a positive view of what he now labels as 'Irish' culture. Gary recalled that even in Sandy Row during the 1960s, there was still some room for difference:

> I remember there was a teacher I had in primary school who was a crazy
> Orangeman. He was a big district master or something in that area. And
> he was very into the Irish culture and teaching culture to Protestant kids

which was something a wee bit forbidden, I think, at the time. But he would teach us all these old tales, Cuchulainn and all this kind of stuff, and stories about Queen Maeve and the Red Branch Knights. And I was always kind of fascinated by that. And he would play traditional music in the classroom when we were doing our work. And his reward system was, we all took on the name of a knight, you know, Ferdia or whoever it was. And you had to earn your sword and your shield and your garters, and as a reward you got on this Red Branch Knight sort of league, and if you got to the top, you got a prize (interview, Omagh, VMR–022).

Gary stayed at Shorts through most of the 1970s and 1980s but as a married man with a young family, he increasingly felt that he was living on a 'knife edge' because of the Troubles and consequently, the poor economy:

The fact that you were always under threat from your job and, it was clear to me, that Shorts was being subsidised just to keep men off the brew [social security] basically. But there was nobody going to put a new airplane contract in there, nobody was going to take that company over. The British Government was just handing us back and forth between departments and there was always lay-offs and threats of lay-offs. And the economic environment was being crippled, I think, by the Troubles really.[51]

Looking for opportunities he answered an advertisement in the newspaper and in 1987, moved his young family to the greater Los Angeles region to work for McDonnell Douglas.

The stories above reveal how segregation, sectarianism and the conflict affected the identities of individuals of different generations, class and denominational backgrounds, and motivated their emigration. Middle-class Protestants like Pat and Chris growing up in the 1950s and early 1960s were unaware of sectarianism and this was also the case for Gary from the very segregated working-class neighbourhood of Sandy Row. On the other hand, those from interface areas such as Laura in Lurgan, and Paula and Orla in North Belfast, all had significant experience of sectarian violence during their formative teenage years. Like David, at the beginning of the chapter, they all felt unable to fully develop or belong in Northern Ireland. For Paula, sexuality was the key issue, while Laura's left-leaning politics didn't appear to fit with her Protestant 'heritage' and she recalled how she felt prior to leaving, 'I'd wish I was a Catholic because at least it was a more acceptable face of Northern Ireland.' However, for Orla who was a Catholic, her birth abroad and the pressure to choose sides in the conflict resulted in her feeling that she wasn't authentically Irish and even years later living in England she remained reluctant to tell people that she had been born in Australia.

'Are you Catholic or Protestant?'
Religion and Identity Abroad

While daily life in Northern Ireland was a trial for many people, the move abroad didn't necessarily eliminate difficulties. For most the experience of migration was a journey of self-discovery during the course of which their views of Northern Ireland and their own identities were often challenged. The perception of them in the host society was a key factor in the development of their own identities. Migrants accordingly occupy 'diaspora space' (Brah, 1996: 201–10); places which have their own populations, histories and cultures, and which influence how they as immigrants are received and how in turn they perceive and interact with others. For the individuals who went to Britain, especially those who self-identified as British, they did not initially view their move as 'emigration' and thus did not expect to feel or be treated as foreign. Once arrived in England, doctors Chris and his wife felt that they were looked upon as 'refugees' by many of their medical colleagues and were annoyed at the predominantly negative portrayal of Northern Ireland, because they sorely missed the 'camaraderie, family and links' of home. Feeling like 'outsiders' in England and not content with wages and working conditions in the NHS, the couple took the opportunity in 1976 to go out as doctors on a six-month trial to New Zealand with their two young children and decided to stay.

For young middle-class Protestants like Susan, of a Presbyterian background, who arrived in London in 1976 to attend university, the general perception of her as Irish came as a shock:

> First time living there, total culture shock, total identity crisis. Oh yeah, because I mean you sort of thought, right, British, that'll be easy, London, you know, speak the same language, obviously I'm [from] the British part of Ireland. But you landed there and it was only then you realised you were Irish. That's the first time you are faced with that and then it becomes very clear that you're not English, you are Irish (interview, Belfast, VMR–034).

For many migrants like Susan, migration becomes, as Giddens would have it, a 'fateful moment' in the life cycle; one of the key defining periods or 'transition points which have major implications not just for the circumstances of an individual's future but for self-identity' (1991: 143); thus the natural impetus at these junctures for self-examination and adaptation, but also vulnerability to mental illness (Grinberg and Grinberg, 1989: 133).[52]

Julia, a nurse from Fermanagh of Church of Ireland denomination, who moved to Kent with her schoolteacher husband and two young children in 1975, assumed the move would be straightforward and was therefore greatly surprised to discover that they 'were considered to be foreigners'. This contrasted with the view from Northern Ireland of themselves as British. But as Julia pointed out, most people in England didn't go about proclaiming 'flag-waving Britishness' and those that did were considered to be extremely right wing:

> Growing up here we were considered to be British and it's very confusing. It's one of the reasons why I get so irritated with the people here [in Northern Ireland] who think they're British, you know, who feel so strongly that they're British. And it's not a kind of Britishness which people in England identify with or will have anything to do with … I mean the kind of people that identify with that kind of Britishness are probably very, very right wing. It's more a National Front type Britishness, I think (interview, Co. Fermanagh, VMR–031).

Julia's encounter in England with different interpretations of British identity has also been observed by informants in studies by Ní Laoire (2002), Mitchell (2003) and Harbinson (2010). This may well have to do with attitudes in England towards national identity; in particular the difficulty of disentangling English and British identities though interest in English identity has been increasing in recent years, likely influenced by devolution.[53] In their sample of English-born migrants living in Scotland, for example, Kiely et al. found that their respondents used both terms – English and British – but often in slightly different contexts, though overall they had a 'weak sense of being English' (2005: 156). Fenton's study of national identity among 1,100 mostly White English-born adults (age twenty to thirty-four) in Bristol found that 40 per cent of respondents were indifferent or even hostile to the labels 'English' or 'British', many identifying such expressions of nationality with right-wing groups. Only 15 per cent of respondents were enthusiastic about identity labels and another 45 per cent of respondents were neutral on the issue (Fenton, 2007: 329).[54] The Future of England Survey conducted in 2011, however, showed that attitudes have been changing and that there is a preference for English identity over British (40% versus 16%) across different regions of England and all social groups, with the exception of ethnic minorities who expressed a much greater preference for the British label (Wyn Jones et al., 2012: 3, 19).[55] This would indicate a perception that 'British' is a more inclusive identity than 'English'; however, 66 per cent of respondents claimed some level of British/English duality.

When Laura moved to England in 1975 after returning from her sojourn on the Israeli kibbutz, she was surprised and unprepared, like Susan and Julia above, to find that she was considered to be Irish. She blamed the state education system in Northern Ireland which had institutionalised her to be 'even more British than the British' by including very little Irish content in the curriculum (interview, Liverpool, VMR–052). Many of the interviewees, like Laura, who were perceived abroad as being Irish, reported feeling resentful and sometimes even a bit embarrassed to then discover that their own knowledge of Irish history and culture was sometimes inferior to that of the non-Irish people they encountered abroad. Some took measures to address this, like Stephen, a Presbyterian, who studied Irish history during the early 1990s while a postgraduate student in Canada. Responding to the regular queries about what it was like to live in Northern Ireland, Stephen became 'really fascinated with issues of ethnic identity and kept wanting to write term papers on ethnic identity' (interview, Belfast, VMR–015). Through his studies, Stephen (born 1966) came to realise that the withdrawal of Protestants from participation in Irish culture had been generational, that 'bits of common heritage have become seen as just Catholic heritage … they were part of my mother's upbringing but not part of my upbringing'. This shift towards an 'unshared' culture has been pinpointed to around the beginning of the civil rights movement in the mid-1960s (Vallely, 2008: 26–31). However, not all of the Protestant interviewees, especially more recent migrants, minded being labelled as Irish, like Steve from Carrickfergus of Church of Ireland background who moved to Liverpool in 1992 and now lives in nearby Widnes. Though he described his identity as 'Northern Irish British' he reported being frequently called by the nickname 'Irish' in his local community which he viewed positively. 'I like seeing myself as Steve from Ireland' (interview, Liverpool, VMR–053).

For Gary from Sandy Row who left his job at Shorts to work in the aircraft industry in the United States, he was liberated by the discovery that in America he wasn't branded as 'working class'; an identity which at home had limited his opportunities. The multinational aircraft companies he worked for in the United States operated on a meritocracy basis and provided him with ample prospects for advancement:[56]

> Nobody was hung up on structures or the formalities. Nobody cared about your background or your religion, or none of that, just 'Can you do what we need you to do?' 'Great, then do it' (interview, Omagh, VMR–022).

Though Gary perceived a bit of insincerity in the 'have a nice day' culture in the United States, he nonetheless felt that it made for an 'upbeat atmosphere' which empowered him.

> I kind of thrived in that, it made me optimistic, it made me want to do more things and see more things and attempt more things even within work that I hadn't done before. Take initiative. And I certainly realised that I didn't have to be told what to do all the time.

Fergal, a Catholic from Fermanagh who moved to Belgium in 1996, commented:

> It was almost like being free. It was fantastic! And because all the people

I was working with were from so many different places it didn't matter who you were or where you were from or what you did (interview, Omagh, VMR–033).

Although many interviewees reported that they preferred not to discuss the conflict or religion while abroad (this would usually be the case at home in Northern Ireland as well), they were often asked to explain the Troubles. Though he would not have openly discussed the conflict at home, in Belgium Fergal's discussions with non-Irish people allowed him the space to question and re-evaluate some of his old attitudes:

When people would ask me about, say, the Troubles, I was quite happy to talk to them about it and I would give them what I thought was a fairly balanced description of it whereas maybe in the past I wouldn't have.

Fergal contrasted this openness with the silence that closed in again when he returned to Northern Ireland in 2003:

Like at my own job now I have two colleagues who are Protestant and the two of them are gentlemen. But the Troubles or politics are never discussed. Never, never. And they have no idea on my views and I have no idea on their views (interview, Omagh, VMR–033).[57]

However, many interviewees felt defensive or even embarrassed while living abroad to have to explain a conflict they did not feel responsible for or have any real connection with:

I did not want to be quizzed about the bloody Troubles. You know the way you get that thing of, 'Why can't you people live together?' Like it's your fault. And I really didn't feel comfortable talking to English people about what was going on in Northern Ireland … And I didn't want to be associated with it. I didn't feel part of the conflict, I didn't feel responsible for it, I didn't want to have to answer for it (Susan, interview, Belfast, VMR–034).

Migration has often been assumed to be less problematic for Irish Protestants than for Catholics, in particular the notion that Protestants integrate invisibly into the host society, especially in the case of Britain, the Empire and historically in Colonial America.[58] Without exception, however, the Protestant interviewees in this study found that they were identified as Irish when abroad, even in Britain, and it was often the case that they were perceived quite negatively if their Protestant background was revealed:

I'd often find at parties, they'd say, 'Oh you're from Northern Ireland. *Are you Catholic or Protestant?*' Just like that, you know, they would ask.

And of course, I just generally didn't answer that one. It's not particularly relevant, is it. But if occasionally I did say, 'Well, as it happens, I come from a Protestant background,' you were immediately labelled as being a sort of – you know a bit like people just assumed White South Africans must all be racist – you were a nasty, evil oppressor (Julia, interview, Fermanagh, VMR–031).

The lack of apparent willingness in Britain to accept Northern Ireland Protestants as fellow citizens may lie in the historical legacy of Ulster's image of bigotry, intolerance and political extremism; features which contrast too starkly with the stereotypical characteristics of British identity: tolerance; humour; and compromise (Loughlin, 1995: 99–100). Richard, a young man in his mid-thirties from Cookstown, County Tyrone, who arrived in Toronto in 1998, was also often asked about his religion:

I often get asked if I'm Catholic or Protestant. I get asked that quite a bit. Not so much about the history of the Troubles, just are you Catholic or Protestant? And I'd be like, 'What's a nice Canadian like you asking such a question?' And then they would go, 'But I've no problem telling you what I am.' And I goes, 'Well I don't have a problem telling you or you knowing but why do you even ask in the first place? Would you go up to someone and say like, are you Hindu?' (interview, Toronto, VMR–072).

Richard mentioned that media attention in Canada over the protests against Orange marchers at Drumcree, County Armagh in the late 1990s and early 2000s had given a very negative impression of Irish Protestants and that he had been called upon several times to explain the marches.[59] In his explanations, he would often draw a comparison with English–French relations in Canada:

You do get the comments about the British treating the Irish badly and I would agree ... Northern Ireland under self rule was not exactly equal opportunities and I know that, I recognise that, I'm not defending it, I disagree with it. But of course you get people asking about religion and they do make that association, 'you hate the Irish', and that's not the case. If I hated them that much I'd be back there fighting them (interview, Toronto, VMR–072).

Deirdre, from Strabane, County Tyrone, of a Catholic background, left Ireland in the mid-1970s, after considerable involvement in the civil rights movement in Belfast. Locating first to London and later to Manchester, Deirdre established a career in community development and was very active in feminist circles. Deirdre's contact with northern Protestants and negative attitudes towards them that she witnessed in England, even in the greater Irish community, caused her to rethink her own politics. It dismayed her that few could understand that a Northern Irish Catholic might also claim British identity:

I had some friends who were [northern] Protestants. They were all people who were willing to be involved in women's issues and so on, in spite of what I found to be extreme discrimination against them, more so than against me ... Fascists! They were called fascists. On the left they were called fascists. And there was no understanding at all of them from ... British-identified English people, if you like. They didn't want to accept these people as British really. That's what I felt. They didn't want to accept me as British either particularly because I would say I was British–Irish or Irish–British which is the sort of thing I think it's safe enough to say in 2005. It wasn't safe enough to say then. Once or twice people asked me to come and present a paper on it in women's circles – feminist circles – and when I did I remember being described [introduced] as a Protestant ... because basically people couldn't cope with the complexity (interview, Strabane, VMR–042).

For other migrants, like Rosemary who grew up in the West Belfast neighbourhood of Ballymurphy during the 1970s and 1980s, the challenge to their identities took form in religious practice abroad and when this occurred it was usually quite unexpected. As a Catholic, Rosemary had always attended mass at home remarking, 'you never really thought about it growing up'. When she left Belfast in the early 1990s to attend university in London, however, like many students her weekly mass attendance dropped off, largely due to the demands of Saturday night socialising, though she explained, 'I always told my mum I still went ... because she'd be devastated if I didn't.' Rosemary stayed in London after she graduated and married a man of Scottish Catholic background. However, it was only when she had twins that Rosemary began to attend church with her children because she wanted them to have a Catholic upbringing. She was also keen that her children attend a Catholic school, but she insisted it was not because Catholic schools tended to be better schools but because she wanted the children to have Catholic instruction. This caused some surprise among her English friends, most of whom were nominally Anglican and only attended church services occasionally for weddings, christenings and funerals:

Friends sort of say to us occasionally, 'Are you Catholic?' They're very surprised and I don't know why they're surprised, they just are (interview, London, VMR–081).

Given the lax attitude towards religion that she had observed among English Protestants, Rosemary was very surprised at the commitment that was expected of her when she began to attend a Catholic church in London. In Northern Ireland, apart from attending mass fairly often, any further commitment was reserved for the more devout:

> My school friend [from Belfast] who's over at the other side of London, I remember her saying, 'I tell you what, it's awful hard to be a Catholic in England.' And I know exactly what she means now because you really have to make the effort to be seen. You do sort of have to go to church every week and they expect to see you there and they expect to see you bringing your children and see you making an effort in the parish which you never had to do in Northern Ireland.

Rosemary's experience of having to prove herself worthy of admittance to the English Catholic community, what historian Sheridan Gilley has referred to as 'English Catholic indifference or hostility to Irish Catholics' (2009: 238), demonstrates the controlling and assimilating influence of the English Church over Irish Catholics in Britain (Hickman, 1995; see discussion in Chapter 5). Julia, a Protestant who returned to Fermanagh in 1999, after living in England for twenty-five years, had the reverse experience. In England she had regularly attended services and social events at her local parish Church of England where the attitudes were generally very liberal and even the attire was casual. She noted that 'very few people go to church in England, but it's all very friendly and informal'. Thus, when she returned to Northern Ireland and decided to attend the local Church of Ireland, she was shocked by the conservative, hierarchical approach:

> It's still terribly old-fashioned here. The clergyman isn't called by his or her – rarely her – first name and they're kind of on a pedestal up there. They're totally obsessed with money. They produce lists every year of how much money people have given to the church ... I sent one of these lists off to our vicar in England and he just couldn't believe it! They seem to be totally obsessed with money. That was very shocking. So I actually don't go to a particular church now anymore, I pick and mix a bit (interview, Co. Fermanagh, VMR–031).

All of the interviewees in this study felt they were perceived as Irish while abroad regardless of their own denomination or the country in which they were resident. For those who migrated to Britain, however, this was unexpected and in many cases, caused distress and confusion, especially for migrants who self-identified as British. Indeed, as indicated by Deirdre's narrative, the association of Ulster Protestants with negative Loyalist stereotypes – as 'fascists' – was widespread, especially in Britain where public opinion has since the 1970s supported the withdrawal of British troops from Northern Ireland (Gallagher, 1995: 722).[60] However, living in 'diaspora space' meant meeting other Irish people from across the religious, political or national divide and these encounters often proved even more challenging to identity, especially for northern Catholics. It is to these encounters that we now turn.

'They don't see Northerners as Irish': Encounters in 'Diaspora Space'

For many of the interviewees, their migration abroad provided the opportunity to meet, sometimes for the first time, and engage with migrants from across the religious or political divide of Northern Ireland or with others from the ROI. These encounters often took place through Irish emigrant networks which were easily accessible due to the significant migrations of Irish since the 1950s to Britain, Europe, North America and Australasia. Although the term 'Irish diaspora' is often employed to denote the multigenerational communities of the Irish abroad, few of the Northern Ireland interviewees were aware of the concept, probably because most of them had emigrated prior to the term coming into public discourse in Ireland during the early 1990s. The interviewees were, however, aware of the generational aspects of Irish culture abroad and for the most part were fairly dismissive and rarely chose to engage with what I call here, 'Irish diaspora culture', which involved primarily the foreign-born Irish of multigenerational descent. Displays of 'shamrockery' such as St Patrick's parades appeared to have little appeal for Northern Ireland migrants and only a couple of the Protestant interviewees had ever been involved in Orange Order activities abroad, although a few had been active as Freemasons. Many born in Northern Ireland, both Protestants and Catholics, chose not to become involved in Irish organisations and when they did, it was most often the pubs, clubs, churches and societies that catered to the Irish-born. Several migrants rejected these emigrant networks with reasons given having usually to do with them being perceived as Catholic, Southern Irish or working class. Northern Protestants expressed concerns that they would not be welcomed or could even be in danger in these places (Trew, 2007: 33) and that Irish community events might be 'held in the guise of raising money for arms' for the Republican cause (Liz from Toronto, interview, Belfast, VMR–057). However, at times what would have been 'unthinkable' in Northern Ireland was possible in 'diaspora space' as was the case of Ken, a Presbyterian from County Londonderry, who moved to Fort McMurray in northern Alberta in the late 1970s and found himself sharing accommodation with two committed Republicans from south Armagh:

> I shared a flat with two guys that were in the IRA here. I'm Protestant and they knew it. But I got on better with them than they got on with a lot of people of similar backgrounds to them. I could not understand that. I

got on really well with them. But that amazed me, that amazed me! And you know, you'd go drinking together and all that and I would be the only Protestant among twenty or thirty Catholic people, whatever, and a row would start and the odd time there'd be a fight, you know and it would be pretty rough, a pretty mad house, and nobody would touch me. And I said, 'Hey boys, what's the matter? Why don't you guys ever touch me or hit me?' 'We can't hit you, you're a Protestant!' [laughs] (interview, Omagh, VMR–012).

Freddie, a Presbyterian from Ballymoney, County Antrim, lived in Zambia during the early 1970s where he met many people from the ROI especially through involvement with rugby. He remembered, 'we actually played Gaelic in the first half and rugby in the second half to celebrate St. Patrick's Day'. The Irish Government appointed an honorary consul in Zambia and as Freddie was dating the consul's daughter Margaret, when the consul was unavailable for official functions, Freddie and Margaret would attend on his behalf. On a trip back to Ireland, Margaret had even travelled up to Ballymoney to obtain a proper dinner suit from tailor Bryce Currie in order that Freddie could be properly attired for these events.[61] 'So I was going to the Russian Embassy, the Chinese Embassy and all these embassies as third secretary to the Irish consul' (interview, Ballymoney, VMR–025). Stewart, a Presbyterian from Derry city, who lived in England and in France for extensive periods during the 1980s and 1990s, also commented that his social networks were 'rugby, rugby, rugby, rugby, it's nearly all been centred around rugby' and he noted that religion was not an issue among the first and second-generation Irish rugby fraternity (interview, Derry, VMR–035).

However, Irish networks abroad were not always easily accessible to northern Protestants. Ciarán, a Catholic from West Tyrone, who had worked in construction in London, then in New York and San Francisco before moving to Sydney, Australia in 1989 described how the Irish pub served as the information hub for Irish immigrants to find work and accommodation. Upon his arrival in Sydney, he had asked the taxi driver to take him to an Irish pub and once there, he put his bag behind the bar and began talking to people. He was immediately told of a girl, also from rural Tyrone, who had a recently vacated room available in her apartment nearby and he arranged to move in that same evening:

It didn't bother me that I didn't know one person in the country or have an address for one person. It didn't 'faze' me in the slightest … I knew instinctively that I was going to meet some Irish person or some group of people that would be looking for someone to help them share their costs … It's a transient thing with people always coming and going (interview, Omagh, VMR–024).

However, Ciarán had noticed that Irish Protestants were not as comfortable in the Irish spaces he took for granted. He remembered meeting two Protestants who came into the Irish pub in London that he had regularly frequented and 'like Laurel and Hardy' pretended to be Catholics in order to make contacts. He described their pantomime:

> They were talking about like St. Patrick's Day and some other sort of Irish-y things … And one of the guys had made a slip-up and he called the other guy by his name, which was like Clarence or Nigel or some quite Protestant name, and then quickly tried to cover it up. It was a comedy of errors.

This experience led Ciarán to empathise with the plight of Protestant emigrants for whom the spaces of the Irish community abroad were not necessarily so welcoming:

> This myth that goes about here that only Catholics emigrated and Protestants got everything and Catholics got nothing, you know it sort of falls on its face when people had to try and do that because of a perception they thought others had of them (interview, Omagh, VMR–024).

However, occasionally it was Irish Protestant networks abroad that were not accessible to Catholics.[62] Herb, of Methodist denomination from the Shankill Springfield area of West Belfast, has lived in Toronto since emigrating with his wife and young son in 1957. Shortly after his arrival, he joined the Toronto police force, first as a beat cop, later working his way up to detective. Now retired, he described how he meets for lunch once a month with a group of retired Toronto police officers, all of them northern Protestants:

> There's a group of us, about twenty retired, and we're all emigrants from Northern Ireland – a lot of them were in the RUC … who meet once a month … And my partner on the [Toronto] police was a Catholic from Bangor, the nicest guy you ever met. Because one of these guys [policemen] – his brother was killed by the IRA – they would not let him [my partner] come to lunch with us. They will not let a Catholic come to lunch with us … They've even been over here [in Canada] and they've had their eyes opened and I guess they're more international in their outlook and there's still that strain … 'Quick to anger, slow to forgive, and never forget.' And that's the way the Irish people are (interview, Toronto, VMR–071).

Not all migrants wished to participate in Irish networks. Some, like Gary from Sandy Row, did not want to become 'ghettoised' in the United States. Similarly, Chris and his wife in New Zealand were very keen to integrate and 'made a point about not joining' their local Irish society in Hamilton:

mainly because we wanted to be New Zealanders and not to be sort of Irish New Zealanders, but to be integrated as New Zealanders ... But we'd always go to Biddy Mulligan's Pub on St. Patrick's night and that's great but the other 364 days we wouldn't, we would just be Kiwis (interview, Ballynahinch, Co. Down, VMR–084).

Others, such as Una, a Catholic from south County Londonderry, made a point of not participating in Irish activities in England because she felt they attracted people who were heavy drinkers or who just wanted to make money and go back home to Ireland. The sense of being different from people from the ROI was very common among the northern Catholics in the study and is a theme which has been raised by others (O Connor, 1993). In Una's case, her physiotherapy patients frequently enquired as to where she was from, often mistaking her accent for Scottish, but:

when they knew I was from Ireland and they'd say, 'Oh I know someone from Ireland' but it would be from Cork, I'd think no, I'm not from there. It made me feel proud of being Northern Irish and I was never really ... That's maybe more a Protestant way of thinking, you know, that there's a divide whereas I never really felt there was a divide before I left but when I left I felt there was a divide for some reason (interview, Larne, Co. Antrim, VMR–036).

For many northern Catholics, there was a sense of not being authentically Irish as with Rosemary in London who mentioned that in comparison to Southerners, 'maybe I don't feel proper Irish because I'm from the North, maybe I don't feel like the real McCoy'. Orla from Belfast, however, was clearer about where to lay the blame for the lack of acceptance. 'I have met Southern people who don't see me as Irish because I'm from the North. *They don't see Northerners as Irish.*' Thus, Orla, who at the time of her interview was chair of Irish Community Care in her area, was conscious of the importance of promoting the organisation as non-denominational and non-political to be inclusive of all Irish, from the North and South, and including those born in England. This meant taking care of practical concerns, such as the organisation's use of symbols (flags, colours and emblems) and protocol (anthems and prayers at public events). Orla was also aware that she was herself an embodied symbol of the organisation:

I am probably the first Northern chair of Irish Community Care so wherever I go, it's my accent that's speaking, it's a Northerner's accent that's coming out ... I do have a sense now that I am carrying the organisation with a Northern voice (interview, Liverpool, VMR–056).

Thus, interactions among Northern and Southern Irish migrants in 'diaspora space' were often complex and frequently provoked a rethinking of political, religious and national boundaries. For Protestants, accessing traditional Irish networks was often more difficult but for those, like Ken in Alberta and Freddie in Zambia, who crossed boundaries, such experiences often triggered a sense of commonality or identity with other Irish people. On the other hand, the experience of interacting with Southerners was often problematic for northern Catholics who were dismayed by the lack of a common culture and whose identity as authentically Irish was sometimes challenged. As with Una, Orla and Rosemary, this often brought about recognition of a Northern Irish identity. As Rosemary described:

> For years I called myself Irish but I think I'd probably call myself definitely Northern Irish now. If somebody asked me what was my nationality I'd be Northern Irish. I mean I have a British passport and for legal things and that I put down British because it covers Northern Ireland and I am technically British. But I would see myself as Northern Irish, probably as British people from Scotland would see themselves as Scottish. The same way. Very definitely (interview, London, VMR–081).

'There's nothing wrong with being British and Irish': Migration and Identity

The multiple nature of identity, as exemplified by Rosemary's statement above, which is not necessarily conflictual but is dependent upon context, reminds me of my Uncle Joe who emigrated from Belfast to Montreal in the mid-1950s. When quizzed by Canadians about his religion or politics I remember his reply, 'We're all Irish over here.' Uncle Joe had attended the Shankill Road Mission prior to his emigration and though a devout evangelical Protestant, he didn't appear to suffer any conflict between his British nationality – he always remained a British citizen and travelled on a British passport – and his Irish identity. When asked where he was from he would proudly reply, Ireland, Northern Ireland or Belfast, depending on the person asking. There was no reduction of his 'Irishness' despite an active lifetime in Canada where he was eventually buried, though 'home' was always still Belfast. This brings up a key point about the migration experience that was raised time and again in the research interviews. The migrants were generally of the view that they had achieved personal growth as a result of their migration experience, which if anything added to their identities, but they did not feel it subtracted anything. Thus, many expressed annoyance, even exasperation, that family and friends in Northern Ireland made assumptions about their identity having inevitably become diluted or reduced in some way. Consequently, their identities were not only challenged by reception in the host country, as discussed earlier in this chapter, but very much also by how they were perceived back home. This was experienced most keenly by those who returned to live in Ireland and was usually attributed to a lack of understanding on the part of people who had never lived abroad (see detailed discussion of return migration in Chapter 7). However, even for migrants who visited Northern Ireland regularly, they noted how their 'foreign' ways were pointed out and often mocked for fun; whether it was a change in their accent, use of 'foreign' expressions or words, 'strange' mannerisms or even attitudes they held.

Like my Uncle Joe above, the migrants did not necessarily experience conflict about British or Irish identity although they often gained additional perspective on it. For those who remained abroad especially, national identity issues often receded in the political sense and several reported fatigue with the topic. For Orla from Belfast who moved to England in the early 1980s, it was when she learned about the Omagh bomb in August 1998 that the futility of Irish identity politics hit with full force. She had been on a camping holiday and didn't find out about the atrocity until the following day when she went into a local shop to get a Sunday newspaper. She remembers it as 'a defining moment' that in front of everyone in the shop, 'in public in England' that she 'burst into uncontrollable tears':

> And it was in that one moment in that garage somewhere outside Buxton, that everything about being Irish for me just came home on me unbearably. I realised on that day that I just carried this pain and carried this pain and that morning I could not carry any more pain about the death of my people. It was that simple. These were all my people. Everyone in Ireland is my people, whether they identify as Ulster Protestant, British, whatever, they're all my people, whatever they choose as their identity (interview, Liverpool, VMR–056).

Others were quite content to live in Britain and retain Republican aspirations. Siobhan from Omagh had spent many years as a nurse in several African countries, first as a young single woman and later with her English-born husband and children. Having eventually settled contentedly with her family in the greater Liverpool area, she nevertheless maintained strong Republican views. She particularly objected to the change in Articles 2 and 3 of the Irish Constitution in which the ROI removed its claim on the territory of Northern Ireland:

> I have never in my life said I was British and that's just a product of the way I was brought up … I hold an Irish passport. I refuse to have a British passport because mum was born in the South. I don't want one, I won't have one although I am living in Britain quite happily … I wasn't best pleased when they changed the [Irish] constitution but I agree they had to (interview, Omagh, VMR–058).[63]

Rosemary from Ballymurphy described how the negative portrayal in England of the Nationalist side of the conflict had affected her during the 1990s. 'When I came here, if anything it probably made me have more Nationalist feelings than I ever had when I lived in Northern Ireland and lived in the Nationalist community.' However, since then with the effects of the peace process and devolution, she felt very positive about the future of Northern Ireland within a broad European context and was no longer committed to Irish unity:

> A united Ireland is a nice idea but I don't think it's a burning issue in my life and I don't think really it will be a burning issue for lots of people ... I could see a time when it will happen, not soon, maybe in my lifetime. Maybe. But not any time soon (interview, London, VMR–081).

Fergal from Fermanagh was not so optimistic about the future of Northern Ireland and he believed that the generation of his younger sister, ten years his junior, was much more militant about human rights and would never again accept second-class status for Catholics. Having been a strong supporter of a united Ireland scenario prior to his emigration in 1996, Fergal had since changed his mind, noting, 'I found that the longer I was in Belgium, the less bitter I was and the more understanding I was.' He spoke of how the need to 'persuade Protestants' would take at least another generation:

> It [united Ireland] used to be a very strong aspiration but I'm not so sure now. I suppose yes is the answer but sometimes I think it would be just better if they would just form a separate country and that would solve a lot of the problems, you know, just break away from the UK and break away from the Republic and just have a separate country here [in Northern Ireland] (interview, Omagh, VMR–033).

For Catholics like Denis from Andersonstown, Belfast, who lived in England and Scotland for twenty years before returning to Northern Ireland in 1999, 'being outside of the country' had occasioned a re-evaluation of his old attitudes with the realisation that 'if you stay where you are, you may not be aware of how much you are conditioned ... you may not be challenged.' In particular, Denis had re-assessed British–Irish relations:

> I think people should realise that you can be Irish and proud of being Irish without being anti-British. I have benefitted from British rule in Ireland and there's been disadvantages from British rule in Ireland. It's not clear cut, it's not black and white (interview, Belfast, VMR–038).

Most Protestants in the study seemed to feel that a united Ireland was inevitable in the longer term and many of them like Chris in New Zealand thought this could be quite a positive step and provide a more stable sense of belonging in Ireland:

> It's quite possible that it would be a united Ireland and I think that perfectly logical. And I think it would be a wonderful amalgamation really myself. My impression of the English in four years [of living in England], was that they didn't really see Ireland or Northern Ireland as part [of the UK]. It's the United Kingdom of Great Britain and Northern Ireland … I don't think they felt that Northern Ireland was part of it (interview, Ballynahinch, Co. Down, VMR–084).

As Chris pointed out, even the nomenclature sets Northern Ireland apart from the United Kingdom, and the British Government's acknowledgement of Northern Ireland's right to self-determination would also indicate that it is not integral to the 'British' nation (Gallagher, 1995: 722).[64] Paula from North Belfast believed that in another fifty years 'there's no longer going to be a Protestant majority anyway in the *six counties* … there's going to be no Unionist veto … hopefully that will be a good thing'. She assumed that inevitably this would lead to the border being removed but was not perturbed because, 'nowadays I definitely see it more as a whole island and I don't really see kind of the *six counties* so much really as I used to' (interview, Liverpool, VMR–049). Likewise, Laura from Lurgan, said that she visualised home as 'probably more Northern Ireland but sort of seeing that as part of a bigger island' and mentioned her view had changed substantially from the 'internal image … drummed into you as a child' when 'we were always told that it was Ulster, that it was Northern Ireland as if it existed aside from the South' (interview, Liverpool, VMR–052). Others such as Andrew, a medical consultant in Liverpool from an upper-class Belfast family, envisioned the future in a wider British Isles context. Claiming to have no politics or religion himself, Andrew self-described as 'Northern Irish' or as 'an Ulsterman' but qualified that also with 'I do consider myself part of Ireland, but I also consider myself part of the UK', acknowledging that 'the British Isles has always actually been a collective of people who cooperate and work together'. His encounters with people from Northern Ireland involved in business and medicine around Europe and in North America led him to believe that the Northern Irish had something particular to offer the world:

> We should be massively proud of ourselves and our heritage. And the truth is it's because we have both Catholic and Protestant traditions that we do have that massive drive and ability to see and to think way outside the box (interview, Liverpool, VMR–051).

Although Gary from Sandy Row and his wife and children were very settled in the United States and have a good circle of American friends of a variety of ethnic backgrounds, he still maintained a strong identity with Northern Ireland and was considering the possibility of eventually retiring 'back home'. While he admitted to sometimes being homesick, 'the only guy with my accent' and missed the humour and the 'kindness' of people in Northern Ireland, he was wary about returning to a conservative sectarian society that would force him to choose sides once again. Gary suggested the potential for a dual or hybrid British–Irish identity that need not be conflictual:[65]

> I've noticed that since I've been away, I've become more Irish in my outlook, I think, in terms of being proud of being Irish and seeing a lot of worth in that and seeing a lot of value in being Irish, as opposed to just being a British person, you know what I mean, or a Protestant or something like that, something narrow … And I think that my notion would be that *there's nothing wrong with being British and Irish* … And that same way you can be Irish and that's it. That's fair enough too (interview, Omagh, VMR–022).

Perhaps most poignant was the conclusion of Paula from North Belfast who expressed her difficulty with identity acknowledging that she was perhaps now more Liverpudlian than anything else and very grateful to the city she had found so welcoming. She related her feelings about identity with a sense of profound regret:

> One of the things that I haven't found so easy about my experience of having lived and grown up in Ireland is that at the end of all of that, I didn't really feel as if I had a nationality (interview, Liverpool, VMR–049).

However, for Protestants who had returned to live in Northern Ireland, especially those with liberal views, the identity issue was perhaps even more complex and is a reminder that the role for Protestants in Ireland remains ambiguous and unsettled:

> Because of the way this country was divided and the education system was divided, you were brought up institutionally to be British, to be Protestant. You didn't really, when you learned the history, you didn't want to be part of an Ascendancy or part of this thing that was keeping Catholics down. So what were you going to be in this country? So where was going to be the place for Protestants in this country? And it's still not clear, actually, where that place is (Susan, interview, Belfast, VMR-034).

Conclusion

This chapter has provided discussions concerning the impact of migration on the religious and national identities of Protestants and Catholics from Northern Ireland in multiple destination contexts over the last forty years. Though many left Northern Ireland because of sectarianism and violence, it is important to recognise that they did not necessarily suffer any loss of identity. Most of the migrants retained considerable loyalty to Northern Ireland and were often resentful of its unrelentingly negative portrayal in the media of other countries. Many spoke of how they, like Chris and his wife in New Zealand, missed the humour and 'the camaraderie' and several, like Paula, remembered humorous incidents that occurred in the midst of the violence. This paradox of Northern Ireland has been encapsulated in the words of well-known BBC journalist, Kate Adie who described it as, 'the only place I know where someone once told me a joke in the middle of a riot'.[66]

The migrants' narratives confirm 'the different repertoires of being Protestant' (Todd et al., 2009: 96), rejecting any notion of a fixed Unionist or Protestant identity, for in reality identity is fluid and in constant negotiation with others and therefore challenges any notion of fixedness. However, it is certainly the case that the conservative image of Unionism, which one interviewee described as 'xenophobic and drum-bashing' (VMR–015), has in the past been a contributing factor that has driven many young liberal Protestants to seek a life abroad. Although migration is generally assumed to broaden perspectives, in the case of many Protestants, as with David at the beginning of this chapter, they departed because the conservative nature of the society in Northern Ireland left no 'place' for their existing liberal views to develop further. Thus, perhaps the most significant effects of emigration from Northern Ireland have been: 1) the reduction of the Protestant majority which has consequently exacerbated Protestant 'insecurity'; and 2) that the over-representation of the young, liberal and higher educated Protestants and Catholics in the outflow who would be more likely to support change at home, has been a contributory factor to the slow pace and protracted progress of the peace process over the same period, thus confirming the hypotheses of Rose (1971) and Terchek (1984). However, individual lives rarely conform to grand theories or master narratives (Lyotard, 1989), thus, contrary to Rose and Terchek's hypotheses, several interviewees, like Gary and Stephen in this chapter, maintained their strong religious faith together with a liberal political outlook.

The position of northern Catholic migrants, as evidenced from this study, cannot be uniformly portrayed as either Nationalist or Republican, as necessarily supportive of a united Ireland scenario or as belonging intrinsically to the nation that is the ROI. Northern Catholics abroad were often dismayed to discover a lack of commonality – to sense a divide – with the rest of Ireland, while conversely Protestants often reclaimed aspects of their Irish identity while abroad. For Catholics and Protestants alike, reception in the host society, encounters with non-Irish, with Northern Irish from across the religious divide and with other Irish from the ROI occasioned much rethinking of the definitions of British, Irish and Northern Irish. As Northern Ireland migrants abroad confronted the daily reality of their dual British–Irish identities in the perceptions of others, they occupied 'majority and minority positions simultaneously' (Brah, 1996: 189). However, although it cannot be assumed that the migrant's 'diasporic positionality' will automatically 'assure a vantage point of privileged insight' (Brah, 1996: 9) as the case of the Herb's lunching Protestant policemen in Toronto attests, nevertheless, for most of the migrants in the study the experience of migration caused them to re-evaluate their politics and often resulted in significant shifts in their conceptions of self, other and home.

The next two chapters examine how Northern Ireland migrants have fared in the principal host societies; Britain and Canada, the latter generally assumed to have provided a more positive reception for Irish immigrants.

Chapter 5

'Doubly invisible': Being Northern Irish in Britain

'Northern Ireland's my soul': Home and Identity in Britain

February 2010. I receive a lovely card from Aimie, an elderly informant from Belfast who has lived in England since 1946. She writes, 'I am losing my sight. No more lovely books and poetry … I will never be able to go home again but have happy memories … these memories help to sustain us at sad times.' My own vision blurs with tears for Aimie is a woman who loves literature, poetry especially, and reading has been the only way over the past few years that she has been able to 'travel' home. Her words bring me back to our interview a few years previously at her apartment in Colchester, Essex, in London's commuter belt. Of all the people I interviewed, Aimie touched my heart most deeply. It is hard to explain the emotions in me that our encounter provoked but it was not because Aimie had had a sad life. On the contrary, she was quite content to be in England, living with her husband Arthur, near her children and grandchildren. She described her life as very average, the greatest sadness coming at the loss of an adult son six years earlier. So why when I boarded the train back to London after our interview was I hopelessly unable to stop the flow of tears?

Aimie had seen my advertisement for study participants in the *Irish Post*, a newspaper for the Irish community in Britain and asked her husband, Arthur, to contact me via email. As arranged, Arthur met me off the London train and we walked around the corner to their apartment building in Colchester. There I encountered Aimie who was not very mobile as she had contracted a serious infection after a routine procedure in hospital and had been under treatment for several months. Despite this setback, Aimie was full of life and cheer, and greeted me with a big hug as if we'd known each other for years. This set the tone for our visit and throughout the interview we talked and laughed easily together. She had also taken the trouble to write much of her story down, including important details of her family history and she gave me a copy to take away with me.

Aimie was born in the 1920s and grew up on Annadale Street off the lower Antrim Road in North Belfast. Because her father, a merchant seaman, was frequently away, she and her brother were raised primarily by their mother, a worker at the Milewater Mill in the docks area. Aimie acquired a good secondary education from Dominican College, where she held a scholarship and, in addition, she also earned a certificate in bookkeeping from the Irish Institute of Commerce. Nevertheless, as a Catholic, Aimie had difficulty finding employment in Belfast in the early 1940s:

> The usual thing when you went for a job in Belfast, 'What school did you go to?' So you didn't get the job. It wasn't said in so many words, 'You're a Catholic,' but you knew what it was ... You took no notice. You took it for granted that you didn't get it (interview, Colchester, Essex, VMR–078).

Eventually in desperation, her mother brought Aimie to see John Gordon, then Minister of Labour in Stormont, for whom she herself had worked during the First World War.[1] Gordon gave Aimie a letter to take to the employment office but nothing ever came of it and following the German bombing of Belfast in the spring of 1941, Aimie decided to join the army. Soon after her enlistment, she and her mother chanced to meet Minister Gordon on the street and he greeted them:

> [Mother] just looked at him and she took me by the scruff of the neck – I was in uniform too – and she said, 'They didn't ask her her religion when she joined the army!'

As a member of the Royal Army Ordnance Corps, Aimie was stationed at the Kinnegar Depot, Holywood Barracks on the shore of Belfast Lough. There she met her husband Arthur, who had been raised in an orphanage in London and was a Protestant. Describing the armed forces as an organisation where sectarian attitudes were not tolerated, Aimie said there had been no barrier to their marriage which was officiated by an army chaplain in November 1943. Pregnant by the time she was demobilised in 1945, she continued to live in Belfast with her mother as her husband Arthur had been stationed in Singapore. A year later, Aimie left Belfast with her baby son to join Arthur in Dagenham upon his discharge from the army and she remembered this period of her life as quite difficult. 'I can't explain Dagenham to anybody. It was grey, cheerless, cold ... I just felt I'd entered a grey world ... I still don't like it ... It gives me the horrors.' Financially things were very tough and there was rationing; all of this compounded by the famously cold winter of 1946–1947. However, with her sister-in-law providing childcare, Aimie soon found work packing Turkish cigarettes at the Godfrey Phillips Tobacco Factory on Commercial Street in east London. After a few years she landed what she described as her 'favourite job', inspecting newly printed bank notes at the Bank of England printing works on

Old Street. Later, when her children were in primary school she worked as a dinner lady and subsequently, when she was again ready to take on full-time work she was employed in a children's home run by the Hackney Borough Council. Aimie thoroughly enjoyed her working life and when I asked if she had ever experienced anti-Irishness in England, she could only remember one incident:

> I got on the bus once and in those days when you came to Colchester, it was 25p from the town [London] to here. And I had 25p in my hand, I put it on the [ledge] and I said 25p. And he done the ticket, the conductor, and he said, 'You haven't given me enough money.' I said, '25p.' He said, 'You asked for 35p.' I said, 'No, I'm sorry I asked for 25. Why would I ask for 35p when I've put 25 on the [ledge] for you?' So he said, 'Oh, bloody accents.' And that was the only time I came up against anything. But being me I said, 'There was nothing wrong with my accent when I joined the army.'

At the time of Lord Mountbatten's murder in 1979, Aimie had worried that there might be a backlash against Irish people in England, but nothing happened. In her experience, discrimination was something she had encountered regularly in her youth in Belfast, but not in England. Nevertheless, of all the interviewees, Aimie expressed perhaps the strongest attachment to Northern Ireland and her identity with it was undiminished despite the many years away. She described how she maintained her contact with home; in particular how much she loved reading the *Irish News* sent by her brother every week and poetry collections of Northern Irish poets which her husband ordered for her off the Internet.[2] Because of her difficulties with mobility, reading had become Aimie's principal vehicle for travelling home. Towards the end of our interview, I asked Aimie to self-describe in identity terms and she responded without hesitation with words that both surprised and moved me:

> *Northern Ireland's my soul.* I have to be honest, it is my soul. I never had many connections with the South [of Ireland] in that respect, I've got to be honest, except through meeting people or whatever. The North is me, it's my Ireland.

Aimie's story provides an example of how the actual life experience of migrants is multifaceted and often fails to conform to the common tropes of emigration as exile, discrimination and loss of identity among the Irish in Britain. Moreover, it also raises questions about issues of belonging and citizenship as they pertain specifically to migrants from Northern Ireland resident in Britain, whether Catholic or Protestant. For despite her husband, children and grandchildren all describing themselves as English, Aimie appeared to have suffered no loss of identity and was very proud about being 'Northern Irish'. Since her arrival in

England, Aimie had never lived in an Irish neighbourhood and she had socialised primarily with English people and non-Irish immigrants. Once her children were enrolled in the local Catholic school and she began working part-time there, Aimie's social world centred on the local Catholic community, where she attended a church comprised mostly of non-Irish members. She was acquainted with a few Southern Irish Catholics but she felt no special bond with them and had only once encountered anti-Irish racism directly though she was obviously conscious of the threat of it at times when tensions were heightened. Happily content in England, she was nonetheless aware at this point in her life of being physically unable to return to Northern Ireland. Though expressing fondness for the whole of Ireland, Aimie's identity was firmly anchored in Northern Ireland which she described as 'home' and she remained very connected with its culture and pleased by recent political developments, especially 'that at last hopefully Catholics will have their say in Stormont'.

Migrants from Northern Ireland living in Britain, like Aimie, occupy a space somewhere between the British and the Irish, as they share political union with one group and geographical union with the other. They are curiously positioned on an interstitial axis from which they can choose multiple alignments. However, in spite of a substantial body of research on identity issues within Northern Ireland, the rich potential of examining how Northern Ireland migrants experience identity on British terrain has been almost entirely overlooked and even more curious is that they have received so little attention in literature on the Irish in Britain. This chapter is intended to help fill this gap by exploring the very particular experiences of migrants from Northern Ireland in Britain and in so doing, serve to illuminate the wider Irish experience as a whole. First of all to provide context, data on Irish and Northern Irish migration to Britain is presented in the next section followed by a review of the principal theoretical constructs that have framed recent discourse on the Irish in Britain. Stories of Northern Ireland migrants follow, representing different generations, backgrounds and diverse experiences in Britain which may challenge some common misconceptions.

The Irish in Britain: Demography and Visibility

Until 2011, the Irish-born (thirty-two counties) comprised the largest born-abroad group in Britain since at least 1841 when country of birth information was first gathered in the census, at which time they comprised 1.8 per cent of the population of England and Wales, and 4.8 per cent in Scotland (see Figure 5.1) (Jackson, 1963: 7). By 1861, the Irish-born population in Britain had almost doubled comprising approximately 4 per cent of the total population; a peak not surpassed in actual numbers until 1961; though halved in proportional terms (2%). After partition, Britain became the principal destination for all migrants from Ireland,

Protestants and Catholics, North and South; the Irish-born population peaking in 1971 and gradually declining thereafter such that by 2001, it comprised 1.32 per cent of the population in Britain (57,103,927). Those born in Northern Ireland (hereafter NI-born) consistently maintained a significant and, in recent decades, increasing proportion of the Irish-born group, comprising by 2001 over one-third of the Irish cohort in Britain and over 60 per cent in Scotland.[3] In the most recent decade to 2011, the Irish-born population in England and Wales declined by over 10 per cent (to 622,345 or 1.1% of total population) with immigration from outside Britain and Ireland, particularly from the Indian subcontinent (to almost 1.4 million or 2.5%) and the new EU accession countries (to 1.1 million or 2%) accounting for the much of the population increase in England and Wales (71%), and in the UK generally.[4]

Figure 5.1: The Irish-born resident in Britain, 1841–2011

| Year Census | England and Wales | | | Scotland | | | Britain | |
	Irish-born	NI-born	% NI-born	Irish-born	NI-born	% NI-born	Total Irish-born	% NI-born
1841	289404	na	na	126321	na	na	415725	na
1851	519959	na	na	207367	na	na	727326	na
1861	601634	na	na	204083	na	na	805717	na
1871	566540	na	na	207770	na	na	774310	na
1881	562374	na	na	218745	na	na	781119	na
1891	458815	na	na	194807	na	na	635122	na
1901	426565	na	na	205064	na	na	631629	na
1911	375325	na	na	174715	na	na	550040	na
1921	364747	na	na	70623	88397	55.6	523767	na
1931	311033	70056	18.4	56391	67905	54.6	505385	27.3
1951	492056	134965	21.5	45653	43354	48.7	716028	24.9
1961	667088	187549	21.9	41904	37308	47.1	933849	24.1
1971	675870	215805	24.2	33365	32790	49.6	957830	26
1981	579807	209042	26.5	27044	33927	55.6	849820	28.6
1991	569750	218521	27.7	22800	26393	53.7	837464	29.2
2001	473027	222975	32	21809	33528	60.6	751339	34.1
2011	407357	214988	34.5	na	na	na	na	na

Source: Birthplaces of the people (tables): Census of Great Britain (includes Scotland), 1841–51, Census of England and Wales, 1861–2011, Census of Scotland, 1861–2001. 'Irish-born' includes all 32 counties before partition and 26 counties afterwards.

In 2001, over 90 per cent of NI-born residents in Britain were living in urban areas, with approximately 84 per cent in England; 3 per cent in Wales; and 13 per cent in Scotland. The main concentrations of the NI-born in England were in London and the southeast which accounted for over 29 per cent (75,119); the Midlands at 15 per cent (38,306); and the northwest at 13.6 per cent (34,879), of which some 38 per cent (13,283) were resident in Manchester alone.[5] In Scotland, the NI-born population was more evenly spread around the country, however, with notable concentrations in Edinburgh (5,607) and Glasgow (4,496). While Britain is the preferred destination for Northern Ireland migrants, it is particularly so for Protestants who have formed the majority of student migrants since the 1980s.[6] As noted in Chapter 4, due to the tendency to stay after graduation, it is likely that Protestants now comprise around half of the NI-born cohort overall, especially in areas in which the demand for professional labour is high, such as London and Merseyside (where the NI-born comprised 20% and 51% of Irish-born respectively in 2011).[7]

These figures, however, do not represent the total numbers of Irish or Northern Irish in Britain, as in addition to the figures for first-generation migrants above, one must take account of the larger numbers of second and subsequent generations whose place of origin is Ireland or Northern Ireland. This, however, is necessarily an approximate calculation due to the lack of quantifiable data about ethnic groups in Britain.[8] Because lower than expected responses in the census of England and Wales on ethnicity (2001 and 2011) and national identity (2011) amounted to lesser totals than for all Irish-born, these census categories revealed little about the size of the Irish multigenerational population. For example in 2011, only 150,722 acknowledged some form of Northern Irish identity and 388,083 claimed a category of Irish identity, while 409,065 held an Irish passport.[9] Consequently, we must content ourselves with estimates based on earlier data sets from 1971 to 1991 which put the second-generation Irish group in Britain at approximately 1.7 million and third generation at 3.3 million; a total of approximately 6 million (11% of total British population) overall for generations one to three (Hickman et al., 2001: 13).[10] Taking the average of NI-born in Britain over the period (1931–1991) as 26 per cent of total Irish-born and applying that to the figures above for Irish second and third generations, one arrives at a figure of approximately 1.55 million for the first three generations of the Northern Ireland group in Britain (i.e., NI-born in 1991 = 245,000; plus generation two = 442,000; and plus generation three = 858,000). Thus, the estimate of the Northern Ireland multigenerational group in Britain is close to the total population of the province in 1991 (1,607,300).[11]

The experience of the Irish in Britain is distinctive in the Irish diaspora for three important reasons: 1) the proximity of the two islands; 2) the historically asymmetrical power relationship between them; and 3) that Irish settlement in Britain dates to an earlier period than in other jurisdictions and is thus of much longer standing. Indeed, the populations of Ireland and Britain have for hundreds, if not thousands, of years been interconnected by migration back and forth. Though we know more about the Irish in Britain in the period after 1800, examination of court and parish records of the later sixteenth and early seventeenth centuries reveals that significant numbers of migrants from Ireland were even then in employment in labouring occupations in Britain and in the case of females, as domestic servants, while those without work often ended up as vagrants (Fitzgerald, 1992).[12] From the mid-eighteenth century, expanding opportunities of Empire through service in the British Military became an increasingly popular option for young Irish males as restrictions were eased concerning the recruitment of Catholics.[13] By 1830, the Irish comprised over 42 per cent of the British Military and were most numerous among the infantry, though their proportion declined steadily to approximately 13 per cent by the end of the century (Spiers, 1996: 337). Even as late as the 1970s, however, the Irish-born comprised in the order of 6 per cent of British Military personnel (O'Connor, 1972: 160). Regular emigration of ordinary citizens from Ireland to Britain also increased rapidly from the late eighteenth century and with the Act of Union in 1801 the Irish were formally incorporated into British nationality, though their loyalty was often under question. The onset of regular steamship travel from 1818 facilitated movement between the two islands (Jackson, 1963: 7), and the rapidly developing industrial economy and transportation infrastructure in Britain coupled with poor agricultural conditions and famine in Ireland drove the movement of people to epic proportions by mid-century.[14] In the era of mass migration, Britain became the principal recipient of Irish seasonal migrants and its port cities (especially Liverpool), the first stage of the emigration journey for Irish emigrants onward bound for destinations around the world. Following partition in 1921, citizens of the new Irish Free State maintained freedom of travel and work in Britain, though certain travel restrictions and the requirement for employment permits applied temporarily during the Second World War (Connolly, 2000; Delaney, 2000: Chapter 3). Despite changes brought about by new citizenship and immigration legislation in the post-war period, the Irish retained their 'special status' in Britain and continued to be exempted from immigration monitoring (Daly, 2001; Delaney, 2000, 2007; Drudy, 1986; Heuston, 1950; Megaw, 1949).[15] Thus, the Irish have for centuries occupied 'a curious middle place' (O'Connor, 1917: 32) in Britain, not quite aliens, not quite nationals.

Research on the Irish in Britain has consequently been framed in the context of segregation/integration/assimilation – these constructs often measured along a spectrum of perceived Irish visibility ↔ invisibility.[16] Simply put, studies of the Irish in nineteenth-century Britain have been largely concerned with their 'visibility' (i.e., racialisation and segregation) while in the twentieth it is their 'invisibility' (e.g., as in discourses of 'race' and 'whiteness') that has dominated thinking on the Irish. Certainly, the explicit and 'visibly' racialised portrayals in the printed media, stand as evidence of the alien status of the Irish in nineteenth-century Britain (Curtis, 1984b; Curtis, 1968; de Nie, 2004); this 'racial hibernophobia' later resurfacing during the interwar years (Douglas, 2002: 40). However, early studies of Irish settlement in nineteenth-century Britain, largely based on indices of residential segregation and institutional affiliation, have in recent years been complemented by a considerable body of literature examining Irish migrants over several generations in a variety of towns and cities demonstrating the participation of the Irish at all levels of society, and not only as the poor outcasts of Victorian cities (Swift, 2009).[17] The picture of the Irish that emerges depicts the variety and complexity of social relationships and identities, and begins to uncover the norms and values that constitute the fabric of community and belonging – 'the imagined community of the nation' (Hickman, 1996b, 7; following Anderson, 1991).

That Irish people might be lax in their religious practices or not spatially segregated from the general population, as in Aimie's case described at the beginning of this chapter, does not necessarily result in the lack of a distinct Irish identity or what Mary Hickman has called the 'myth of assimilation' (Hickman, 1995, 1996b). On the contrary, 'strategies of incorporation and denationalization' – educational, cultural and social – operated through the Catholic Church to expressly create a *veneer* of homogeneity, of a non-threatening Irish Catholic population indistinguishable from the host population (Hickman, 1995: 242; 1996a; 1999). This was achieved by multiple means. For example, the mostly state-funded Catholic schools offered an essentially 'Ireland-free' curriculum that was conspicuously silent on the Irish conflict, therefore transmission of Irish history, politics and culture was relegated to the home and community.[18] Irish Catholic children were segregated from the majority Protestant British population in separate schools, social life especially for women often revolved around church or Irish cultural activities (music, dancing, etc.), and working-class Irish men disappeared after work into the clubs and pubs frequented for the most part by their compatriots. Irish Catholics were essentially rendered 'invisible' and Irish women, often married to English men, became 'doubly invisible' (Walter, 1988: 7).

The increasing 'invisibility' of the Irish in post-war Britain was also due to emerging concerns about more 'visible' immigrants arriving in large numbers from the Indian subcontinent and the Caribbean. Ideological discourses of multiculturalism in Britain from the 1960s conflated race and ethnicity into a fixation with skin colour – a black/white binary – 'disconnected from questions of nation, nationalism and migration' (Mac an Ghaill, 2000: 140), thus race relations legislation failed initially to address issues of anti-Irish discrimination

(Hickman, 1998).[19] The Irish in Britain were 'cultural outsiders and racial insiders' (Gray, 2002c: 262; 2004, 136). In this new colour paradigm, White ethnic groups, with the Irish by far the largest, lost their distinctive ethnic differences in a discourse of 'whiteness' that emphasised civilising traits understood as being 'English' or 'British' (Hickman et al., 2005; Walter, 1998, 2004), especially a strong work ethic, tolerance, respectability and reasonableness.[20] The degree to how these 'whitely scripts' (Gray, 2002c: 257; 2004: 131) were enacted in daily life became especially critical in view of the introduction, shortly after the Birmingham bombings, of the Prevention of Terrorism Act in 1974.[21] With the new anti-terrorism legislation, the Irish were 'outed' as a 'suspect community' (Hillyard, 1993) and the pressure for their invisibility increased exponentially. Facing the hegemonic 'white' silence and the fallout from the new anti-terrorism legislation, several Irish community groups began to voice concerns over discrimination and anti-Irish racism and lobbied government agencies for studies and redress (Curtis, 1984a; Hickman, 1998). Largely as a result, a major study on anti-Irish discrimination (Hickman and Walter, 1997) was sponsored by the Commission for Racial Equality[22] (henceforth the CRE Report) and the perceived need for social data on the Irish community motivated their inclusion on the list of available responses to the ethnicity question in the census of 2001. However, the prevailing discourse of whiteness, concern about anti-Irish racism, and no option of choosing a hybridised British–Irish identity that might more effectively represent competing feelings of national belonging, may explain why 92 per cent of the second-generation Irish population chose not to self-identify as Irish ethnicity in the 2001 census (Hickman, 2011: 94; Walter, 2011: 1305), with little change apparent in 2011.

Academic sociological and historical discourses have also contributed to the invisibility of the Irish in Britain as, in addition to the colour paradigm, Britain's uncomfortable colonial history also factored into debates on difference. Conveniently, the 'forgetting of empire' (Mac an Ghaill, 2001: 181) in the particular case of Ireland fed into the discourse of whiteness and its 'myth of homogeneity' (Hickman, 1998: 299) where the oft-cited 'shared history and culture of the British Isles' forced inclusion of the Irish on cultural as well as racial terms. However, substantial differences in how that 'shared' history has been experienced and remembered have long plagued the relationship between Britain and Ireland (Jackson, 1963) and even more highly charged has been how the Irish living on British soil have continued to remember and commemorate that history. The positioning of the Irish as 'intimate betrayer within the historical memory of British–Irish relations' (Hickman et al., 2005: 179) has been especially problematic. In their interviews with Irish women in Britain, for example, Lennon et al. reported the frequent observation that British people did not appear to have a strong awareness of their own history, therefore the Irish 'obsession' with history was something that 'people in Britain often find mystifying' (1988: 12).[23] More recent concerns in Britain with immigration have overshadowed examination of its own history of emigration, Empire and the existence of its diaspora.[24] Therefore what:

> tends to be absent from the British popular imagination is that much of Britain's history has taken place 'outside Britain'. There is a sense in which 'post-colonial others' know more about the indigenous British than the latter know about themselves (Mac an Ghaill, 2001: 182).

Acknowledging this 'massive discrepancy', historian David Cannadine has contrasted the view of Empire from Britain, where 'ignorance of empire, rather than knowledge of it, emerges as its most marked feature', along with 'more malevolent' depictions by post-colonial writers who have 'experience of empire on the periphery' (2001: 197). Thus divergent collective memories of the supposedly 'same' history collide in a context where the former colonial power is the dominant group.

Structural reasons also contribute to the invisibility of the Irish in Britain and this is particularly true of the NI-born group and their descendants. In official UK Government sources, data on those born in independent Ireland (hereafter ROI) is usually listed among foreign-born populations while data pertaining to the NI-born is often subsumed under the UK category (annual population surveys, UK pensions data, etc.).[25] As a result there is a lack of general awareness of the full extent and complexity of the Irish-born population in Britain as references to the Irish often erroneously refer only to those from the twenty-six counties.[26] Thus for the Northern Ireland group, structural assimilation has rendered them doubly invisible in Britain, despite their significant proportion of the total Irish-born group. Though several recent academic studies on the Irish in Britain have included some statistical and interview data relating to NI-born individuals, the focus has nonetheless been on those originating from the ROI, mostly Catholics (e.g., Greenslade et al., 1991; Hickman and Walter, 1997; Kells, 1995; Sorohan, 2012; Walter, 2001, etc.).[27] Consequently, we know little concerning the NI-born and their attitudes regarding migration and settlement in Britain, especially the impact of their formative experiences of governance, education, identity, conflict and sectarian geography in Northern Ireland. How, for example, do northern Catholics or Protestants in Britain 'imagine the community of the nation'? Similarly, do migrants from the three other Ulster counties in the ROI – arguably another 'curious middle place' – experience migration to Britain any differently from their southern or northern cohorts? How may all these differently remembered histories and boundaries among the Irish in Britain contribute to their 'willingness to assimilate'? (Hickman, 1995: 253). In view of these questions, stories of migrants from Ulster are presented in several contexts in the remainder of this chapter in the hope of illuminating some neglected aspects of Irish life in Britain.

'No different than the nineteenth century': Being a Presbyterian Navvy

Ken, of Presbyterian background, was born in Derry in 1950 and grew up on a farm straddling the boundary of Counties Tyrone and Londonderry. His father was not himself from a farming background but had made money labouring in England as a young man and returned to purchase the farm in 1939. As the second of three sons, Ken was not expected to inherit the farm and was sent to grammar school in Coleraine where he boarded during the week. When his eldest brother unexpectedly went off to join the merchant navy, however, Ken was pulled from school where he had been preparing his A-levels and sent to Greenmount Agricultural College. He was not very keen on the course and resented the expectation that he spend all his spare time working at home on the farm which was still intended for the eventual return of his elder brother. In 1968, Ken took the boat to Liverpool and made his way to Manchester where he first found employment as a labourer laying gas pipes in a construction crew that was at least 'two-thirds Irish'; the men using assumed names working for cash wages:

> There was an awful lot of Irish people, an amazing amount, and actually quite a large proportion were farmers' sons because at that time there was no money to be made on a farm. Well, not much money. The 70s changed that a bit you know when Ireland joined the EC [European Community], income improved. But in the 60s, especially when there was three or four sons on a farm, the tradition was that the eldest son would get the farm but if the second son or the third son left school and there wasn't any work, he was working on the farm too ... The work at home was pretty rough, pretty hard ... You worked from seven in the morning until maybe eight, nine at night. You were expected to work practically for free as all farmers' kids at that time were. You didn't have a car, you didn't have anything (interview, Omagh, VMR–012).

Without any money, transport or spare time, Ken found it difficult to develop a social life at home. However, having left the pastoral idyll of a farm, he found life in Manchester a 'culture shock' living in a 'doss house' that slept thirty-six men, six to a room. Ken described his living conditions as 'no different than the nineteenth century' and remembered being almost constantly hungry; the owner of the 'doss house' complaining about Ken's 'huge appetite' and that 'it took the money he made from the other 35 to keep me'.

The construction crews were picked up by lorries near All Saint's Cathedral in Manchester by seven o'clock each morning and taken many miles away to their worksite. At fifteen pounds per week, Ken described the work as relentlessly breaking cobblestones all day until 'the pick was sticking to your hands'. The construction bosses were mostly Irish and the 'gangers' who supervised the work crews were 'brutal' and unsympathetic to the workers having themselves 'spent maybe twenty years on the end of a pick'. They often took a cut of the wages causing serious rows among the men. Ken's fellow workers came from all over Ireland and he was surprised that several were middle class including a young man from Blackrock College who had come to England because there wasn't such good money to be made in Ireland. After three months on the job, Ken found easier but lower paying factory work in Manchester and nicer digs with an Irish family from Westmeath who treated him well, but he eventually moved south to work on the building of the M4 motorway near Reading. Ken found that the working conditions in the south of England were much better than in the north and he described how the crew system in Manchester led many workers to become alcoholics:

> If it was a wet day, instead of going home, you went to the bar ... and there were maybe 12 in a crew ... You were expected to go up to buy 12 pints for your buddies. Well then, you just sat around till they all bought you a drink by which time you were totally plastered so you became an alcoholic yourself whether you wanted to or not. And if you didn't have the money you couldn't say 'Oh well I haven't got any money' because the gang man would give [lend] you a fiver. So in Manchester it rained three days out of five so when you got to the Friday, you had no money coming or just enough to pay your digs. You were trapped. You might have been 30 miles from home. You couldn't say you were going home because you had no way of getting home because the only way home was the lorry ... And a lot of those guys just disappeared up north because they didn't want their folks at home to know that they'd become an alcoholic.

In his history of the Irish navvy in Britain, Ultan Cowley has described nineteenth-century conditions when the navvy employment system encouraged drinking to the extent that navvies were commonly 'paid in beer' (2001: 52). Ken's story shows that working and living conditions for Irish navvies had changed very little by the late 1960s. Likewise, Ken's departure from Northern Ireland was motivated by primogeniture; the traditional system of land inheritance that had encouraged the departure of second and subsequent farmers' sons, Protestant and Catholic alike, for generations.[28] After eighteen months of hard labour Ken left England, lured by his father's promise that he would inherit half the farm, however, when his brother returned a few years later, the situation reverted and

Ken departed abruptly without telling his family, this time hoping for better working conditions in Canada. The tradition of temporary migration to Britain for the purposes of making money to bring or send back home, as with Ken and his father before him, was not unusual for Ulster families in the twentieth century, and indeed was made possible by the proximity of the two islands. When such migrations were extended to include spouses and children, however, there were unforeseen consequences and impacts.

'Pagan England': Family Migration to and from Britain

At the time of her interview, Kathleen had just turned forty and was pregnant with her third child. She, her American husband and two children were living in southwest Donegal near the town of Ballyshannon, the same area her parents came from and where she had partly grown up. Kathleen, the eldest of four children, had been born and spent most of her early childhood in England. The family had later returned to Donegal where Kathleen completed secondary education and eventually went on to university in Dublin. During the late 1980s, she took a job in Canada as a speech therapist because she was not able to find steady work in the ROI and after a few years, she moved on to the northeastern United States where she met her American husband. They returned to Donegal in the late 1990s to start a family.

Despite several years abroad in North America, however, it was Kathleen's experience as a child migrant in England and the legacy of multigenerational migration back and forth in her family which permeated her narrative and impinged on her identity. Her father came from a large family where his own father had worked away for long periods labouring in England while supporting the family on their small farm in Donegal. Many of her father's older siblings had also emigrated; several to England and one sister each to Australia and New Zealand. Kathleen's father had himself left home as a teenager and gone to England where he found work in the construction industry:

> He left school when he was fourteen or fifteen. He had older sisters who were out there in England and he went to them and he started off just working. He told me it was like on building estates and he used to go around and do the snag list. They would check things like the plaster and then he started off doing that and then he did his six or seven year apprenticeship to become the insulation man with asbestos and so forth (interview, Manorhamilton, Co. Leitrim, VMR–023).[29]

Having married in Donegal in the early 1960s, Kathleen's father brought his wife over to join him in London, where Kathleen and her sister were subsequently born. After a few years there, however, mother and children returned to Donegal while the father remained in England for work. Thus the generational pattern of back and forth migration between Donegal and England continued into Kathleen's generation and also the long periods of paternal absenteeism. In 1970, when Kathleen was about to turn five years old, her parents decided to move the family back to England, this time to Liverpool; a plan which caused some concern in the local Ballyshannon religious community surrounding the issue of Kathleen's first communion:

> *I remember* the nuns wanted me to make my first communion and I made it when I was really young. Oh God, I was just turned five. And the reason being that we were going back to as they called it, *'pagan England'* ... The nuns begged mum and dad, they said, 'Please let her make her first communion here.' And they set it out and they thought I was intelligent enough to do it. They tested me and I could answer all the questions. But there's a picture of me and all my teeth are, like, missing because you know I was only [five] ... I made it in the nuns' chapel and the only people there were me, my younger sister, mum and dad and my uncle Jackie who was home from Scotland from Aberdeen ... And *I just remember* that day because you know I had the dress and the veil and everything but it was Christmas day ... But that's funny that I should *remember* that now. But it was a really special kind of a thing because I didn't make my first communion then with any of my peers.[30]

Kathleen's story is thus a reminder that Irish attitudes concerning emigration 'from sinless Ireland to sinful England' (Ryan, 1990: 67) prevailed into the 1970s. Concern about Irish female immigrants in England since at least the 1920s and probably earlier, had 'reflected fears about sexuality, assimilation, and the abandonment of religious practice' (Daly, 2006: 285); indeed, England became a refuge for single pregnant Irish women (Garrett, 2000; and Redmond, 2008). In the post-war era, unease over the moral vulnerability of female immigrants in England prompted Catholic organisations, such as the Legion of Mary (established 1921), to regularly send chaperones to greet young Irish women arriving at English ports and railway stations (Daly, 2006; Earner-Byrne, 2003; Ferriter, 2009).[31] After Kathleen's family returned to England in 1970, the Northern Ireland conflict escalated and one of Kathleen's most vivid early memories was her first awareness of the Troubles. Kathleen's use of the words *I remember*, repeated here like a mantra, reveals the significance of the memory:[32]

> *I remember – I remember* the stairs in the house and everything. *I remember* being told to leave the room because there was a news thing [report on television] of something that had happened ... But *I remember* peeping through the keyhole because I knew I wasn't supposed to look. But

basically, it was pictures of people picking up body parts where *there'd been a bomb at home* and my parents told me to leave the room because they had said, you know, before the news item that this was going to have just graphic kind of – [images]. And *I remember* looking through the keyhole at that age and seeing it and knowing that that was *where we used to live* … That was what *I remember* and I don't have many early memories of many things, but *I do remember* that (interview, Manorhamilton, Co. Leitrim, VMR–023).

This account is a reminder of the impact of the Northern Ireland conflict on people living in border counties of the ROI, most especially Donegal which is almost entirely cut off from the rest of the ROI geographically. Thus, Kathleen even as a young child had experience of negotiating the border and identified the Northern Ireland conflict with home. While the conflict had a strong impact on Irish people living in Britain regardless of county of origin, it was no doubt worse for those with ties to Northern Ireland who bore distinguishing northern traits such as accent. For example, while Kathleen's mother had prior to the conflict 'loved living in England', she increasingly found the atmosphere intolerable:

I can still *remember* the house with all the 70s print curtains and everything … And then we lived in London and mum said she couldn't take it there anymore. And both my sister and I had very English accents and she didn't really worry so much about us at school and being teased about being Irish, but she just couldn't hack it anymore.

Bronwen Walter has noted how 'audibility is subordinated to visibility in discourses of racialisation' (2008b: 175) and that Irish women in Britain were most at risk of negative reaction to their accents as they tended to interact more with the host society in shops, at schools and in the community generally. In the case of Kathleen's mother, her Donegal Ulster accent did not escape notice; this doubtless exacerbated due to the volume of media broadcasting in Britain of events in Northern Ireland which after October 1968 increased 'beyond measure' (Butler, 1995: 61). Ulster accents became more recognisable and negatively associated with the conflict which meant that Northern Ireland migrants and those from border areas in the ROI could be easily identified and targeted. Indeed, a colleague from County Tyrone who lived in London during the early 1960s remembered how his accent was often mistaken at that time for a Scottish or even a Welsh accent, but when after a couple of intervening years at home he returned to work in London in 1970, his accent was immediately recognised and definitely not welcomed.[33] Not willing to 'hack it anymore' Kathleen's mother decided to take her two children back to Donegal for good, but this time Kathleen's father stayed to work in England for many, many years. Thus, the absence of her father had a strong impact on Kathleen who has only sporadic memories of him during her childhood and youth. The return migration also had an effect on the structure of Kathleen's family, resulting in what Kathleen described as a second family within her family:

> My parents had myself and my other sister in England and then it was like they had a whole second family when they came here [Donegal] because there's ... nine years difference between me and the next sister ... There's like 12 years difference between me and my younger brother. So it's almost like they had started a new family (interview, Manorhamilton, Co. Leitrim, VMR–023).

Kathleen's story demonstrates many different types of migration events that were not uncommon for Irish families in the later twentieth century and it also illustrates the motivating factors behind the migrations, which were both political and economic. Her memories of an unsettled childhood and the consequent ambivalence about her British–Irish identities, led Kathleen to consciously break the cycle of multiple migrations that she had embarked upon in early adulthood. She prevailed upon her American husband to return with her to Donegal to start their family even though his career prospects in Ireland were not promising and he subsequently experienced considerable difficulty finding steady employment. Consequently, Kathleen became the principal breadwinner in her family while her husband undertook the primary care of their children.

For Kathleen's working-class family in the 1970s, England provided a lifestyle where independence and freedom were tempered by anti-Irish racism. However, with substantial migration from Ireland to Britain throughout the 1980s and 1990s, especially of university students and young professionals – the so-called 'brain drain' – older Irish attitudes about 'Pagan England' gradually began to dissipate. For these young professional migrants, Britain had become a land of opportunity.

'Flying the flag': Doing Business in Britain

Gary, a very successful businessman in his early forties who lives in London, does not fit the traditional image of the Irish emigrant. For despite the downturn in economic fortunes, Gary's property development business has weathered the recession well and in addition, he is a successful author, public speaker and has been a popular presenter of property programmes on British television (BBC, Sky, Discovery, Five). The eldest of seven children, Gary was raised on a 'Nationalist' council estate in Dungannon, County Tyrone during the 1970s. He remembered a happy childhood with little money where the Troubles provided an exciting backdrop: a shoot-out between the IRA and British soldiers once took place behind his house and the homes on their estate were searched by army patrols on several occasions. With limited opportunities at home, Gary, like so many young Irish university graduates of the late 1980s and early 1990s, sought employment in Britain. He specialised in international property development working for several multinational companies based in Glasgow, London and New York, negotiating property deals all over the world. This provided him with the rare opportunity of executive-level involvement in business in several countries and eventually led him to start his own business in 2002.

As an 'Irishman' working in Britain, Gary claimed to have experienced little discrimination, though he mentioned a few occasions when he was shocked by anti-Irish or anti-Catholic attitudes in the workplace:

> It happened actually more in Glasgow than it did in London … In Northern Ireland they're quite conservative about asking if you're Protestant or Catholic or saying anything whereas in Glasgow because of the way the football works in the culture, they would sort of say something to you if they didn't like what you did … And I found in Glasgow a few things were said to me and in London a couple of things but not enough to hold me back (interview, London, VMR–082).

Gary's experience of sectarianism in Glasgow mirrors that of several respondents in a study of workplace sectarianism in that city where Catholics (mostly of Irish descent) reported obstacles to promotion especially in 'middle-class work' (Walls and Williams, 2003: 654). Gary noticed, however, that being Irish was a distinct advantage in America. He expressed the opinion that Americans were 'brilliant' at business and claimed to have learned his 'real hardcore business skills' from the Americans:

> I don't know what it is with the Irish and the Americans but we have an incredibly strong bond. I mean I've been in so many meetings where I'm so on the same page as the Americans, whereas the other guys from England and Europe aren't.

In Britain, however, Gary stressed that he had been fortunate to avail of many opportunities and he talked about the 'new' entrepreneurial Irish in cities, such as London, who were very different from Irish emigrants of previous generations. Even in the construction industry, a traditional employment niche for Irish immigrants, the situation had changed noticeably:

> Very rarely do you get Irish labourers now. You do get Irish tradesmen who are very skilled. You're more likely to get the Irish guys as the foremen, the owners and the property developers, and it's the Polish and Latvians and all these people who are doing the basic trades now and the labouring.

Nevertheless, when first working as a television presenter, Gary mentioned that the production company had wanted him to alter his Northern Irish accent and while he acknowledged that it was essential to speak in a clear manner that could be widely understood, he commented:

> I'm very proud of my accent. You know they did try to BBC me a little bit on doing the voice-overs. But I said no. I said this is the way I speak and if you guys don't like it, go find another presenter (interview, London, VMR–082).

In spite of Gary's assertion that he was 'flying the flag' with his Northern Irish accent on British television programmes that have been shown in several countries around the world, he admitted that the only hate mail he had received had actually come from Northern Ireland:

> I was disappointed to get these things and they really hurt me. I'm not sure if I can explain it. I don't mean to come across as cocky and that but at the end of the day, if you're on TV you're talking to millions of people, you've got to be assertive, confident.

Gary mentioned that especially since the Belfast/Good Friday Agreement he had noticed growing confidence in the ROI and in Northern Ireland as well as among Irish people living in Britain, though he also remarked that Irish people, himself included, had to work very hard on their confidence.[34] Noting that there were subtle differences between the Northern and Southern Irish, Gary expressed the notion that being from Northern Ireland was a definite advantage for doing business in Britain:

> I always find there's a little slight conflict between the Southern Irish and the Northern Irish. Not major, but I think it's almost a cultural thing. I think the Northern Ireland culture, whether you're Catholic or Protestant, is definitely more towards the British culture in everything, in all the ways we think and the way we do things. Because that makes sense. We're brought up in the British school system, the British laws, British money, all these things that you wouldn't actually think about but we're definitely towards that kind of culture.

Gary compared his experience of living in Britain with what he had observed as a lack of welcome towards immigrants in Ireland, especially in Dublin. He felt that the British were more open to outsiders and that British society had benefited greatly as a result. On the whole, Gary was very grateful for the opportunities he had availed of in Britain:

> I mean you have to hand it to the British people. They've opened up their

system for all of us to come in and do really well out of and because they've done that, it's created an atmosphere and opportunities for Irish to really thrive in (interview, London, VMR–082).

Gary represents the recent young generation of Irish business people and entrepreneurs who arrived in Britain since the late 1980s, though unlike many of them who have hit hard times in the recent economic recession, he has managed to turn this to his advantage, for example, by changing the focus of his television programmes from property development to house renovation in the credit crunch. For Irish migrants of previous generations, however, 'the atmosphere and opportunities for Irish to thrive in' as described by Gary were perhaps rarer and more difficult to access. Statistical data has shown that whether economic boom or bust, there has always been and continues to be a continuous flow to Britain of working-class migrants from Northern Ireland, many of whom live in poorer areas (Forsythe and Borooah, 1992). These migrants are particularly vulnerable to poor health, poverty, social exclusion and discrimination. Even in the first decade of the twenty-first century, there was evidence that anti-Irish racism 'hadn't gone away, you know'.

'The people with hair left': Social Exclusion in Northern Ireland and Britain

At the time of his interview, Terry was living with his wife and two children in a relatively deprived council estate off the Old Kent Road in southeast London. Born in Greenock, Scotland in the early 1950s, Terry had moved to the Dunmurry neighbourhood of Belfast with his NI-born parents and younger brother when he was only six, though even as an adult he still retained a memory of the large Irish community in the west of Scotland and the 'sense of being Irish even though you were born in Scotland'. Compared with his adult life spent mostly in London he felt that 'the experience [in Scotland] was very different from an Irish community in England'. He also contrasted his early childhood in Scotland with his youth and Catholic schooling in Northern Ireland where 'there was no reference to Irishness at all' and where fear and the threat of violence held sway even over his cohort of 'no softies' from working-class Catholic areas: the Falls; Andersonstown; the Markets; and the Short Strand. As a result, Terry recalled that his generation came of age in 'an explosion of rebelliousness' and many of them were attracted to the counterculture that thrived in Belfast during the mid-1960s; a movement, he stressed, that had nothing to do with local politics or sectarianism but was linked to the international youth culture prevalent in London and America where 'sex, drugs and rock and roll was basically it'. Terry's own involvement in the counterculture grew to some extent out of the particular lack of opportunity for young Catholics in Northern Ireland since he had much free time due to the lack of employment. However, it was only with hindsight that he came to understand the reasons for this:

> Like all my friends who were Protestant, they all had jobs and had the gear, do you know what I mean, in terms of dressing. Now I was never made to feel any different or anything but I look back on it now and realise I didn't get a job. And although they left school at the same age as me with the same qualifications if you like, i.e. virtually none, they all got good jobs in engineering, skilled apprenticeships and stuff. I didn't recognise that at the time and I don't think they did either. In fact I'm sure they didn't. But looking back on it, I can see why that was. This was the structural reality of the Northern Irish state (interview, London, VMR–076).[35]

Despite the lack of employment opportunity when he left school, it was the outbreak of the Troubles that caused Terry and many of his friends to leave Belfast for London in 1970. He described how violence destroyed the countercultural movement as pubs and clubs were bombed and the security forces clamped down on the population, especially young men:

> It was quite obvious to me for about a year Belfast was humming. There was a lot going on in Belfast, it was a very good place to be. And then really from August 1969 it just vanished over night and it became a very, very hairy place to be, if you had hair. There'd be one or two pubs, clubs in Belfast where people like that would meet from all different areas and from all different sorts of outlooks but basically their goal was to have fun and there was never any mention of all that [political] stuff and people got along very well. But in the end, even they were destroyed by bombs and what have you, like everywhere else was bombed. So I would say perhaps two generations, perhaps three, just vanished and went to England and wherever … The best way to express it really, the people with hair left.

Thus, as suggested by the studies of Rose (1971) and Terchek (1984), presented in the previous chapter, Terry along with other liberal-minded young people of his generation might have been most motivated to demand change had they stayed in Northern Ireland. Emigration in the context of late 1960s civil rights functioned as a 'safety-valve' impeding societal change; the greatest impact of the emigrants was felt in their absence. Belfast's loss however, may have been Britain's gain as Terry and his cohort became part of countercultural movements in British cities like London. Terry recalled how he and his mates squatted in several houses in the London neighbourhoods of Ealing, Perivale, Shepherd's Bush, Powis Square and the Portobello Road, and that they earned money by doing odd jobs, primarily house painting. They enjoyed the cultural scene and felt quite at home:

> Places like that now would be referred to as countercultural history, as it were. Yeah, people from Belfast predominantly everywhere. I'd see people from school and stuff with their hair down to their waist. All sorts of people. The whole of Belfast, that whole generation moved to Portobello Road, Notting Hill Gate, all around there. Huge. It was home from home.

During this period Terry didn't recall experiencing much in the way of anti-Irishness and remarked that in retrospect he and his friends 'were innocent and naïve at that time about being Irish'. One incident in particular, however, woke them up to the increasingly hostile attitudes towards Irish people in Britain; subsequently positioned as a 'suspect community' (Hillyard, 1993) due to the escalating Northern Ireland conflict:

> We had a house in Perivale and this police car pulled up at the garden and two guys in suits got out. We thought it was the drug squad. And you never seen an untidy room, living room, cleared up so quickly. All the drug paraphernalia was cleared away before the guy got to the door. They knocked on the door and I still remember the guy ... We were all sitting there apprehensive and he says, I swear, *'Detective Inspector Murphy of the Bomb Squad'* [imitating Dublin accent] ... Apparently there had been a bomb in the Post Office Tower and where were we that particular day? Well, we were so out of it that we didn't know there had been a bomb at the Post Office Tower. And he automatically, like he believed us. He apologised and he said, 'Somebody said there was a bunch of guys living here from Belfast and we had a phone call and we're obliged to check it out.'[36]

Convinced that he and his friends were not arrested that day because the police detective happened to be Irish, Terry was much more conscious from then on, not only of being Irish, but of being from Belfast. Indeed, this incident foreshadowed the wrongful arrests and imprisonment a few years later in 1974 of others who were targeted not only for 'being Irish' but most likely because of their specific association with Northern Ireland: the Guildford Four; the Maguire Seven; and the Birmingham Six.[37] Shortly after the close call with the police, Terry decided to return to Belfast where he worked for several years in maintenance at a local hospital and became active in his trade union.

Arriving back in London in 1980, Terry noticed that hostility towards Irish people had considerably worsened. He pointed to the 1981 Hunger Strikes as a defining moment when the Irish community in Britain, London especially, cohered in a way it had not done previously. Terry felt that the Irish community, including the second-generation cohort, was very politicised and he admired the work they did on the ground to document incidents of discrimination and anti-Irish racism within institutions and government agencies, including the NHS. He praised Ken Livingstone, the Greater London Council (GLC) and other borough councils which had supported the Irish community, and lauded the work of the Irish in Britain Representation Group in particular; noting that many who had worked hard for the betterment of the community had received very little public recognition. Terry was critical of the Dublin Government which in his view, only funded Irish agencies that remained out of the political arena and encouraged people to keep their heads down. However, among Irish groups funded in Britain, especially those that serve the middle-class Irish constituency, there has been 'reluctance to blame it all on the British' (Malone, 2001: 203) perhaps motivated by the need to remain neutral in political terms or by the desire to assimilate invisibly into the 'White' British mainstream.[38]

When asked whether he had experienced other incidents of anti-Irish discrimination, Terry was able to recount several in detail and a couple of these were relatively recent. A neighbour's complaint about a racial abuse incident from another neighbour had erroneously been laid at Terry's door by the local housing authority who didn't even offer an apology when their error was discovered.[39] Another example of negative Irish stereotyping concerned the health service. At the time of his interview Terry was in recovery from a rare medical condition and he recounted how he had initially been diagnosed with a drink problem even though he had insisted on repeated occasions that he didn't touch alcohol. Terry worried that people in Ireland were unaware that anti-Irish racism continued to exist in Britain and he expressed this repeatedly during his interview:

> I think the racism is so embedded here and I don't think Irish people in Ireland are aware of just how embedded it is. I don't think they're aware of how they're perceived here. People go on about Bono and people like that, and oh, you know, there's a new vision of Irishness. I think you can forget all that stuff here ... There's all this euphoria over the Good Friday Agreement and all but it affects people here because they're trying to pretend that all of this [racism] stuff has gone away overnight (interview, London, VMR–076).

Concerns about anti-Irish attitudes in the health service in Britain as raised by Terry, have been the subject of study since at least the 1970s (Greenslade et al., 1991), especially that such attitudes on the part of practitioners might encourage reticence among Irish individuals to seek medical advice or through lack of empathy, even result in serious misdiagnosis. Studies examining the health differential of the Irish population in Britain can be broadly grouped into three categories: 1) 'genetic-based' demographic studies which have identified but are unable to determine biological causes of poor health in the migrant population, for example, to substantiate the premise that less healthy individuals may have tended to migrate to the closest destination available (i.e., Britain); 2) behavioural approaches that consider culture and lifestyle factors which link health with 'problem behaviours', and; 3) identity-based approaches which attribute poor health 'to difficulties in developing and sustaining a positive Irish identity in England' (Walsh and McGrath, 2000: 471).

Demographic health research has shown fairly consistently over the last several decades, for example, that the Irish-born in England and Wales have poorer levels of physical and mental health with mortality rates that may exceed other residents by 20 to 30 per cent and are also higher than the non-emigrating Irish in Ireland (Adelstein et al., 1986; Balarajan, 1995; Bracken and O'Sullivan, 2001; Greenslade, 1994; Harding and Maxwell, 1997; Kelleher and Hillier, 1996; Marmot et al., 1984; Wild and McKeigue, 1997; Williams, 1992; Williams and Ecob, 1999). Perhaps most interesting is that the high-mortality rates have also been found to extend to the second and third-generation Irish in England and Wales, and there has been higher than average morbidity among Catholics of Irish descent in Scotland (Abbotts et al., 1997, 1999a, 1999b, 2001; Harding and Balarajan, 1996, 2001; Haskey, 1996; Raftery et al., 1990). This goes against the general assumption that immigrant groups tend to take on morbidity and mortality patterns of the host population over time (Walsh and McGrath, 2000: 469). Behavioural approaches have focused particular attention on mental health morbidity among Irish immigrants in Britain (Bracken et al., 1998; Cochrane, 1977; Cochrane and Bal, 1989; Cochrane and Stopes-Roe, 1979; Greenslade, 1991; Leavey, 2001; Leavey et al., 2007; Ryan et al., 2006; Walls, 1996) with some literature focusing on specific 'problem' behaviours such as smoking, alcohol consumption and suicide (Abbotts et al., 2001; Aspinall, 2002; Burke, 1976; Greenslade et al., 1995; Harrison and Carr-Hill, 1992; Leavey, 1999; Mullen et al., 1996).

Attitudinal or identity-based research has examined in-group attitudes (by ethnicity, religion, age, occupation, social class) that may have an impact on physical and mental health. For example, a survey comparing attitudes towards cancer among White British and first, second and third-generation Irish in Britain, found that the Irish group regardless of generation, tended to identify trauma or stress as a causal factor, including 'a sense of isolation – of "not belonging" or "not being wanted" in Britain' (Scanlon et al., 2006: 335).[40] The link between health and identity issues is also supported by evidence from the CRE Report which found that the Irish people in Britain who were surveyed believed that Irish people were much more positively perceived in Australia, Europe and especially the United States, than they were in Britain (Hickman and Walter, 1997: 221).[41] Identity-based health research has also been taken up by sociologists studying social mobility, poverty and exclusion among the Irish in Britain (Greenslade, 1997; Greenslade et al., 1991, 1997; Hornsby-Smith, 1987; Hornsby-Smith and Dale, 1988; Leavey et al., 1997, 2004; Leonard, 2005; Malone, 2001; Malone and Dooley, 2006; O'Sullivan and Murray, 2001; Pemberton and Mason, 2007; Tilki, 1994; Tilki et al., 2009, 2010); the problematic assumption underlying some of this work is that assimilation is viewed as the 'inevitable trajectory' for the multigenerational Irish population (Hickman, 2011: 81).

Curiously, the NI-born and their children remain for the most part 'doubly invisible' as only a few studies within the sociological and health literature on the Irish have specifically examined their position, even though a major cause of the negative image of the Irish in Britain since the 1960s has been attributed to the Northern Ireland conflict (Dooley, 2004; Hickman and Walter, 1997; Hillyard, 1993, etc.). However, one study based on 1970s data and therefore considering migrants from the 1920s through the 1960s, found that NI-born males had lower levels of social mobility than men born in independent Ireland, and that this was even more pronounced in the second generation. Thus, second-generation, working-class males of Northern Ireland background tended to remain in the working class. Women migrants from Northern Ireland fared substantially better becoming upwardly mobile possibly due to marriage with English men (Hornsby-Smith, 1987: 123–4; Hornsby-Smith and Dale, 1988: 536–7).[42] In a more recent study employing anonymised data from the 2001 census, the Irish population in England was disaggregated into ROI, NI and British-born Irish groups, and significantly the NI-born were further differentiated by self-identification as British or Irish; the results demonstrating an 'ethnic identity effect' on health (Clucas, 2009: 570).[43] First, the NI-born demonstrated a substantially increased risk of self-reported poor health and limiting long-term illness over and above the ROI-born and the host 'White' British population. Second, the NI-born who self-identified as 'Irish' were substantially more likely to claim poor health than those who identified as 'British', even after controlling for demographic and socio-economic factors (Clucas, 2009: 566). Similarly, the British-born Irish also showed increased risk of poor health compared to the ROI-born; thus, for the British-born Irish and the NI-born who self-identified as Irish, the study came to the intriguing conclusion that 'there is something more about being Irish which makes them more likely to report a poorer general health' (Clucas, 2009: 570). Another recent study by Tilki et al. (2009) as part of the 'Forgotten Irish' campaign targeted health and social concerns of the 1950s and 1960s emigrants in Britain. They noted the increasingly aging population among the Irish-born, that they are more likely to be single, live alone, be homeless or in poor housing, have long-term health problems or disabilities and have suffered from institutional abuse or domestic violence (2009: 1–3). They also reported that the NI-born had a higher rate of economic inactivity in the pre-retirement age group (over fifty) and that the conflict had had a significant impact on their mental health (2009: 21, 34).[44]

'Traumatised by being an Irish person in England': Suffering, Silence and Victimhood

Such was the case of Teresa, a Catholic, who grew up in North Belfast during the 1950s and 1960s. From a working-class background, she had been the first in her family to receive third-level education and witnessed the civil rights marches in the late 1960s that galvanised many students at Queen's University. She moved to London in 1973, shortly after her graduation, due in large part to the civil unrest and the consequent lack of available employment opportunities. Teresa first made contact with me by telephone in early April 2005, in response to a flyer about our return migration project that she had seen posted in her local community centre in south County Down. She had moved back to Northern Ireland only six months previously accompanied by her second husband who was English of Irish descent, though her adult children remained in England. As a recent returnee, she was still seeking employment. It was evident right from our first contact that Teresa was extremely shy and very nervous – not at all talkative – and during our initial telephone conversation, I tried to put her at ease. Teresa wasn't at all sure she wanted to participate in the project and indeed I was surprised when I rang her a week later that she had decided to go ahead with the interview. I sensed a profound uneasiness within her, an innate reticence to speak, and yet there was something she apparently needed to say. This became clearer when I arrived at her home in South Down on a beautiful sunny April morning and she greeted me nervously. Keen to settle the mood, I accepted a cup of tea and we began our conversation without the recorder running. Teresa explained that over the past couple of years she had begun to write short stories and had joined a local writers' group upon her return to Northern Ireland, but had been experiencing writer's block. Doing the interview with me was evidently a strategy to get the flow going and after we finished, Teresa described the process as having helped her 'to articulate a few things that have been rattling around in my head'.

During the first part of the interview we talked about Teresa's childhood in the Cavehill Road neighbourhood of Belfast, which she described as 'predominantly non-Catholic ... so most of our friends were Protestants' and where they played cricket and rounders in the street. She painted a colourful picture of sunny summers with 'complete freedom' where 'there wasn't the same fear ... that kind of a cloud', nothing that 'really darkened your whole kind of experience of being a child'. Teresa appeared quite relaxed as we discussed her childhood and youth leading up to her studies at Queen's, however, ninety minutes into the interview, when I asked what she had done after university, her manner, posture and voice all abruptly changed. Looking intently at the floor and speaking almost in a whisper, she began to describe the most devastating event of her life which had occurred shortly after graduation when she had just gone over to London to look for work:

> In 1973 my father was *murdered* in Belfast. And you know that was devastating. It was a sectarian *murder*. My dad was *murdered* [several seconds of silence].

JDT: And how old would he have been at that time?

> My dad would have been just 50. I came home for the funeral and it was just when I'd got back [to London] that I was offered my first teaching job. But I suppose I was so *traumatised* by it – *traumatised* by what had happened and *traumatised* by the whole Irish thing and *traumatised* by being an Irish person in England – that I tried just to be as quiet as possible about the whole thing. And it wasn't until years and years and years later that I could even say to people that actually, you know, my father was *murdered*. He was one of those – I'm one of the casualties really and he is one of the casualties and our family was. And the trouble was that you never had anyone to, kind of, talk to about it (interview, Co. Down, VMR–037).

Teresa's sudden change of posture and voice, and the reiteration of key words – '*murdered*' and '*traumatised*' – in her narrative are classic indications of significant trauma (BenEzer, 2002: 154–8). She spoke very quietly and almost apologetically about the murder; the classic victim suffering in silence, but as an immigrant in England during the period of the Troubles, this was compounded by feeling that she had to keep her head down. Throughout the 1970s and 1980s in England, Teresa had lived in dread of violent incidents perpetrated by Irish Republicans, sensing that others might blame her:

> I had no conversation with anyone else at that time so I had to keep my thoughts to myself … just being quiet and saying very little and just hoping that nothing else happened.

Indeed Teresa cited several occasions when she had suffered verbal abuse following terrorist incidents, such as the time of the Canary Wharf bombing in 1996, when she was dismayed to receive abuse from an elderly patient she had been caring for.[45] As she articulated, 'to *someone like me* that was really devastating' and 'the incidents stay in my mind'. Teresa felt that people from Northern Ireland living in England were doubly vulnerable, seen almost as perpetrators rather than the victims they really were, while on the other hand, there was little if any recognition of the British Government's role or responsibility in the conflict:[46]

> People don't stop and think, well hey, maybe she has suffered as well. There are people in Northern Ireland going through hell really and why are we putting them through hell again?

In their study of victims of the Northern Ireland conflict, Cairns and Mallett (2003: 20–21) found that those, like Teresa, who self-identified as victims, scored significantly lower in terms of psychological well-being, but their sample was comprised of residents of Northern Ireland who presumably might at least garner some general sympathy and support from the community. For victims in England, there was little chance of that. During the interview, Teresa made frequent references to the overwhelming fear and anxiety which had permeated her adult life; reporting that during the many years in England she had never spoken openly about her father's murder. Thus she had occupied a silent space of victimhood where her feelings of powerlessness were enhanced. Having recently returned to Northern Ireland, however, she found that the silence remained firmly in place. Unhappy with the slow pace of political change, she felt that she didn't have the right to criticise:

> Who am I to say to people who have been through the mill for the past thirty years, you know, 'It isn't good enough?' I can't say that because I haven't been here … I'd be very careful because I think I'm a coward. I think I'm an anxious person.

Like Teresa, most of the interviewees from Northern Ireland, Catholics and Protestants alike, reported having experienced some form of anti-Irishness while living in Britain, usually in the form of verbal abuse and often jokes relating to stereotypes, hinting at the threat of conflict. Indeed in Britain during the 1970s, 'books of Irish jokes achieved astonishing sales' (Curtis, 1984a: 227). The CRE Study reported that 80 per cent of the Irish migrants interviewed had been subject to verbal abuse which escalated following Republican attacks in Britain (Hickman and Walter, 1997: 191; Walter, 2001: 166–9) and there was a higher tendency for migrants from Northern Ireland to report racial harassment (Hickman and Walter, 1997: 188). Even middle-class migrants did not escape and many reported being refused service in shops and pubs because of their accent. Robert, a Protestant from Kilkeel who attended university in Birmingham during the late 1980s and early 1990s, remarked:

> I viewed in my imagination I'd be British, I'm one of them. You get there, you open your mouth and of course, you're really Irish and you'd get all the Paddy jokes, and you know, how thick you are … It was incredibly

strong and it really shocked me. These were the educated people in England. These were the top ten percent! (interview, Kilkeel, Co. Down, VMR–045).

Stephen, a Protestant from Belfast, who from the mid-to-late-1990s was employed as a lecturer at a well-known university in the north of England, was shocked at the level of anti-Irish racism in his workplace:

Being called Paddy by your colleagues I think is objectionable … And you know, jokes about, 'Don't annoy him, he'll plant a bomb on you' or something like that, those sorts of things which in an academic setting you certainly don't expect (interview, Belfast, VMR–015).

However, in addition to racial harassment, those from Northern Ireland also bore the added burden of worry about family and friends at home in the conflict and as Julia, a Protestant from Fermanagh who lived for over twenty years in Devon explained:

My aunt was actually killed in the Enniskillen bomb … and I'd known a girl in school that had been shot because she was in the UDR [Ulster Defence Regiment] and boys I'd been at primary school with had been shot … So we all knew someone. And it just used to strike me as extraordinary that the English had so little imagination that they didn't realise that it wasn't appropriate to make silly jokes about bombs and people being shot and so on, that it was actually quite personal (interview, Co. Fermanagh, VMR–031).[47]

As recently as 2007, however, Eileen, a Catholic from West Belfast who described her life in England as 'I love being here, I love London', nevertheless, reported that there were still 'plenty of people … who tell Irish jokes and think it's perfectly okay to do it … people that I know quite well would still think it's acceptable' (interview, London, VMR–079). Remarking that 'as the time's gone on, I try to say less about what's happening at home', Eileen was also disturbed by the view in England of Northern Ireland and its people:

It makes me feel bad that people think that people from home are small-minded and violent. Some of the best people I know grew up in Ballymurphy or Belfast and they're intelligent and they're eloquent and they're well read and they think about things and are very enlightened. Whereas people have this view of them as just being terrorists or violent.

In a detailed study of media coverage of Northern Ireland during the conflict, David Miller demonstrated that the 'key memories' that people in Britain had of the Northern Ireland conflict were experienced primarily through the media, that the tabloid press 'more often resorted to the language of irrationality and violence', and that television portrayed Northern Ireland as 'mostly violent' (1994: 177, 239). Facing this barrage of damning media portrayals of their homeland, their compatriots and their accents, many migrants from Northern Ireland, especially victims like Teresa, chose what seemed the only possible strategy: silence.

Conclusion

As the major destination for Irish migrants, North and South, during the twentieth century and into the twenty-first, Britain continues to play an important and fascinating part in the history of Irish migration and the development of the Irish diaspora. Clearly, the progress of British–Irish relations will be key to the future of trade, politics and peace on these islands and the visit of Queen Elizabeth II to the ROI in May 2011 signified the maturing of this relationship. It is also clear, that the Irish in Britain will continue to have a voice in British and Irish affairs, and that part of this voice belongs to migrants from Northern Ireland. Their inclusion is especially critical as Northern Ireland society heads further down the road towards reconciliation and perhaps even to the consideration of alternative constitutional frameworks. As a group that has been for the most part ignored in the history of Irish migration, Northern Ireland migrants remain largely 'invisible' in literature on the Irish in Britain, despite their significant proportion of the Irish-born group. While to some extent Northern Ireland migrants in Britain share common concerns (especially about the conflict), the 'curious middle' space they occupy between the Irish and the British, both in Ireland and in Britain is worthy of much further investigation in order to come to a fuller understanding of Irish experience in Britain.

The stories of Ulster migrants presented in this chapter illustrate the complexity of their experience in Britain over several generations since the Second World War. The cases here, however, represent only a small proportion of the research gathered for this book that in turn, represents only a minuscule part of the entire experience of Northern Ireland migrants in Britain. Nevertheless, from the evidence presented it is clear that Northern Ireland migrants are not easily categorised. Of the migrants interviewed, for example, Aimie, a Catholic, had lived in Britain the longest, had married an Englishman, had never lived in an Irish neighbourhood or been involved in Irish organisations, yet her 'Northern Irish' identity remained undiminished. The story of Kathleen, a returned child migrant to Donegal, born and having spent her early childhood in the 'Pagan England' of the 1960s and early 1970s, demonstrated several patterns and attitudes that have linked families in Ulster and Britain for generations. Similarly, Ken's story showed that even by the later twentieth century, migration from rural farming Ulster to urban labouring Britain was still common for Protestants and Catholics alike. Gary, a member of the younger generation of university educated entrepreneurs, consciously set himself apart from the traditional image of the Irish immigrant. He believed that his background and education in Northern Ireland were a kind of bi-cultural currency that equipped him well for operating successfully in business in the multiple contexts of Britain, the United States and Ireland. In contrast, Terry provided us with a reality check demonstrating that anti-Irish sentiment in Britain has not simply 'gone away you know' as a result of the Belfast/Good Friday Agreement and the peace process. Likewise, Teresa's experience is a sober reminder of the many victims that may still be living in anxiety and silence in Britain and in Northern Ireland.

Chapter 6

'A very tolerant country': Immigration to Canada

Brave New World

June 2007. I am in a taxi hurtling through the streets of Toronto en route to Pearson International Airport to catch a flight to London. My driver, an Iranian immigrant who has lived in Toronto since 1988 appears delighted to discover that I am genuinely interested in his country when I mention having recently read two books about Iran.[1] We stop at a red light and from under the journey log sheet on his clipboard he pulls out a folded Iranian newspaper, holds it over the steering wheel and begins reading aloud, translating from Farsi, moving his finger under the text from right to left to help keep his place while he resumes driving. The newspaper article speaks about the importance of Persian civilisation to the development of the ancient and modern worlds. I nod repeatedly in agreement to each significant point, making frequent eye contact with my driver through the rear-view mirror. We have several near misses with other vehicles but my driver remains unperturbed, reading, translating. Looking up from his newspaper, he abruptly interrupts his reading to tell me that his brother and his best friend were both killed in the Iran–Iraq War in 1986. That's why he 'got out' shortly after and cannot return unless there is a change to a more moderate regime. By the way, he asks, did I know that there is a Bobby Sands Street in Tehran?[2] I nod again at the mirror. He encourages me to visit Iran, says I could pass for an Iranian woman. Wouldn't my freckled face give me away, I ask? No matter, he insists.

July 2008. I am again in a taxi, this time driving sedately through the streets of Toronto en route to the airport to catch a flight to London. My driver, an immigrant from Pakistan, tells me he has a master's degree in mathematics and once held a prominent position in the Pakistan finance ministry. Eight years ago, he brought his family to Toronto where, he says, he can make much more money driving a taxi than he can at home in a good government job. He tells me he had hoped to get a job in Canada suiting his qualifications, but has been unsuccessful and has now more or less given up. Every month he sends money 'home' to his mother in Lahore.

January 2009. Once again in a taxi driving through the snow-slushy streets of Toronto on the way to the airport, my driver Mahmoud is a young British Asian from London who came to Canada three years ago. When he hears I am bound for his native city, he talks excitedly about London and how much he misses the UK – the football especially. He is considering return, though his family is now spread out around Britain, Canada and Pakistan. Initially Mahmoud thought he would have greater opportunity in Canada but he is now of the opinion that he would have done better had he remained in Britain. Not yet married, he knows he must soon make his decision to stay in Canada or return 'home' to the UK.

These brief insights into immigrant lives in Canada reveal universal themes which would not be unfamiliar among immigrants from Northern Ireland. The first narrative is one of political exile and speaks of the impossibility of return; the second is about economic opportunity and envisions eventual return; while the third narrative depicts the paradox of the second-generation migrant who having left his family's adopted homeland – his own birthplace – considers where is home. It is also clear that the migration experience for my three taxi drivers – all post-1986 'visible minority' immigrants to Canada – is constructed with the ideology of return.[3]

Over the twentieth century, Canada was the most popular overseas destination for migrants from Northern Ireland, however, the Canadian interviews in the VMR collection comprise part of a surprisingly small but growing body of narrative research on the life experiences of Canadian immigrants. Indeed much of the literature on Canadian immigration has tended to focus on policy implementation and the critique of multiculturalism initiatives.[4] Numerous studies concerning the adaptation of immigrants in Canada have tended to evaluate the economic upward mobility of ethnic groups or the lack thereof as the principal measure of successful integration of immigrants to mainstream Canadian life based on: analyses of geographical residence and mobility (Bernard, 2008; Newbold, 2001); educational attainment of offspring (Boyd; 2002; Corak, 2011; Ma, 2002; Picot and Hou, 2011); comparisons of income generation of immigrants and the Canadian-born (Frenette and Morissette, 2005; Li, 2000; Ornstein, 2006; Ostrovsky, 2008). Findings have shown the increasing phenomenon of 'new poverty' among recent immigrants, particularly among 'visible minorities', and somewhat unexpectedly that poverty rates may be even higher among some second-generation groups (Kazemipur and Halli, 2001).[5] Such findings fly in the face of standard assimilationist theory in which the longer the stay in the host country, the greater the expectation that immigrants will reduce cultural and linguistic barriers, increase their skills and begin the journey of upward mobility. Greater attention must therefore be paid to examining the social capital of migrants as revealed by their life experience in order to develop a fuller understanding of immigration processes that may contribute to inequality and social exclusion over the longer term.

In addition, while recent studies of immigrants in Canada have understandably tended to focus on visible minority groups and their experiences of discrimination and racism, this racialised discourse may actually mask the subtler aspects and problems of adapting to Canadian life shared by migrant groups regardless of ethnic background. Examining the migrant experience of groups assumed to face few barriers in Canadian society – those ostensibly absorbed into the White, English-speaking mainstream upon their arrival – may shed important light on settlement, integration and acculturation processes that otherwise might be overlooked, explained or even dismissed on the basis of racial factors.

Thus, this chapter presents a sample of experiences of immigrants from Northern Ireland, all of them White, English speaking and in religious terms, from broadly Christian backgrounds, Protestant and Catholic. In addition, the discussion considers their experiences in the context of different generations – individuals whose migrations to Canada occurred from the 1920s to the 1990s – with particular reference to new selective immigration and multiculturalism policies (1967–1972), in addition to deteriorating economic conditions in Canada after 1970 when the ease of entry for British and European migrants was greatly reduced. The consideration of different immigrant generations over time demonstrates how changing economic and political contexts both in the sending and host countries affected the motivations and attitudes of migrants towards emigration and their subsequent experiences of reception. From their own experiences of political unrest and violence in Northern Ireland, the interviewees also at times contested Canada's prevailing self-image as a land of peace and tolerance, which one individual characterised as 'the secret of Canada'. A brief review of British and Irish migration to Canada is first provided to set the scene.

Canada, British and Irish migration

Canada, as the senior dominion of the British Empire, received the largest number of British Empire migrants overall (over 4.75 million, from 1853 to 2000).[6] Although from earliest colonisation the French were the major European power controlling much of the territory that eventually became Canada, records show that the Irish were present in small numbers in the colony of New France (1534–1763), often as soldiers, merchants or servants. British immigration to Canadian territory began in earnest following the conquest in 1710 of Acadia (subsequently renamed Nova Scotia) and shortly after the cession to Britain of the French territories of Newfoundland and Hudson's Bay, dictated in the Treaty of Utrecht (1713).[7] Throughout the eighteenth century, British colonisation (including Irish settlers) grew steadily, but the large influx came after the Napoleonic Wars of 1812–1815 with the opening of lands in Upper Canada (Ontario). Indeed, official British-assisted emigration policy first occurred when the War Office organised military settlements in the Canadas after the end of hostilities (Snow, 1931: 243).[8] One of these, the Richmond Military Settlement of 1818 established along the Rideau River near what is now Ottawa, assigned land to Irish officers and soldiers of the 99th Regiment, including a significant number from Ulster (Elliott, 1988: 122).[9]

Immigration figures are patchy for the pre-confederation period (before 1867) in the Canadas, as reliable and comprehensive sources are scarce and it is not possible to distinguish passenger traffic from permanent settlers. One source puts British passenger traffic to British North America from 1815 to 1852 at 1,036,714 (Willcox, 1929: 627–8).[10] Another estimate puts the number of immigrants arriving in Upper and Lower Canada from 1827 to 1861 at 680,000, largely from the British Isles (Coats, 1931: 124).[11] Official estimates number outgoing Irish emigrants from Irish and British ports bound for British North America at over 416,000 from 30 June 1841 to December 1855, with some 97,000 arriving in 1847 alone.[12] Population growth in the Canadas between 1841 and 1861 was in the order of 1.5 million including natural increase, however, the overseas immigration figures are too low to account for it and there must have been in addition immigration overland from the United States for which there are few records for the pre-confederation period.[13]

With the confederation of Canada in 1867, followed shortly after by the addition of the provinces of Manitoba (1870) and British Columbia (1871), the need to attract settlers to the Canadian west became a priority.[14] However, a short-lived boom in immigration in the early 1870s was slowed by a worldwide depression that caused a continual decline in prices until 1896 (Coats, 1931: 126). To stimulate immigration, the Canadian Government in 1874 began selling land to private companies (the Hudson's Bay Company, railway companies, etc.) at reduced rates in order for them to encourage settlement, but until the cross-Canada railway was completed in 1886, immigration to western regions remained sluggish.[15] While about 1.5 million immigrants primarily from Britain and Europe arrived in Canada over an almost thirty-year period from 1867 to 1895, a great influx of over 2.9 million occurred in the years from the turn of the century until the First World War with more than 400,000 arriving in 1913 alone (Boyd and Vickers, 2000: 3; Li, 2003: 21). The marked increase in immigration was due to several factors. Scientific progress in agriculture from the 1880s, specifically the development of several new hardy varieties of wheat, was fundamental to the expansion of farming, accelerating the need for immigrants in the Canadian west (Hancock, 1942: 159–65; Porritt, 1913).[16] An economic boom from the turn of the century, owing primarily to western expansion, rapidly increasing industrialisation and urbanisation enabled by new transportation networks (Coats, 1931: 127), influenced an apparent redirection away from the United States of the majority of British emigrants bound for North America (Wells, 1981). As imperial ideology reached its apex at the turn of the twentieth century, the Laurier Liberal Government (1896–1911) contributed over four million dollars for programmes and propaganda to attract 'preferred' immigrants especially from Britain but also from Europe (Harper, 2008: 165).[17] The senior dominion saw itself at the centre of the Empire, merging imperialism with nascent Canadian nationalism (Jeffery, 2006: 52).[18] 'Imperialism was the road to the future' (Buckner, 2008: 73) and the Canadian advertising materials for the British market stressed the civilising and modernising advances underway in this part of greater Britain.

One advertisement which appeared in several local newspapers in Britain and Ulster in 1904 featured the heading, 'Prosperity awaits every willing worker in Canada' and it announced 'Free farms of 160 acres', 'good crops', 'healthy climate', 'light taxes' and 'free schools' with instructions to apply to the offices of the Commissioner of Emigration in London or Belfast. Below the advertisement's heading, an illustration of a (never) setting Empire sun on a large maple leaf was surrounded by five small line drawings of prosperous looking farms and 'modern' farm machinery.[19] Colourful immigration posters were also produced by Canadian railway and steamship companies for the British market with slogans such as 'Own your own home in Canada' and 'Ready-made farms in Western Canada' with 'virgin soil near the railway'; including such imagery as a woman with babe in arms or happy children surrounded by wheat sheaves, with pristine 'modern' house and farm buildings in the background.[20] At the same time in Britain, the *Daily Mail,* the newspaper with the largest circulation, openly encouraged emigration to Canada and coverage of the senior dominion in the paper exceeded that of all the other dominions combined (Wells, 1981: 246).[21] However, by the 1920s, concern about the type of immigrant required for the hardships of Canadian life was apparent in the slogan, 'The right land for the right man' that appeared on several immigration posters of the Canadian National Railway (see Figure 6.1).

That Canada was in such constant need of agricultural and domestic workers was due in part to the continual loss of significant numbers of immigrants and native-born Canadians over the border to the United States, where the draw to a faster industrialising economy provided more opportunities for higher wages and urban living.[22] An estimated 118,000 migrants entered the USA over the Canadian border in the decade from 1880 to 1890 and in the following decade the figure had risen to approximately 625,000 (Kuznets and Rubin, 1954: 74). From 1911 to 1921, 820,469 immigrants entered the USA from Canada (Stevenson, 1923: 352) and following the Johnson-Reed Immigration Act of 1924,

Figure 6.1: Canadian railway immigration poster, c. 1924, indicating the Belfast office (courtesy of the Canadian National Railway Company)

the 'leakage' of Canadian youth over the American border increased with the new barriers imposed on overseas immigration into the USA (Spender, 1925: 409).[23]

Canadian immigration data for the 1920s recorded the arrival of 67,951 Irish-born (North and South) and it is likely that at least two-thirds were from Northern Ireland (see Figure 6.2).[24] By 1931, the number of British-born in Canada had reached its peak for the twentieth century at 978,114, not including the Irish-born which added another 107,544, bringing the British Isles total to over one million or about 10 per cent of the total Canadian population of over 10.3 million.[25] Those claiming British ancestry comprised 51.9 per cent of the Canadian population (including Irish 11.9%; Scottish 13%; and English 24.4%). Analysis of the multigenerational Irish ethnic group in Canada in 1931 reveals that only 8.2 per cent were born in Ireland (first generation); 85.6 per cent were born in Canada; 3.8 per cent in the United States; and 1.1 per cent in England. Further analysis of the marriage patterns of males in the Irish ethnic group in this period demonstrates their overwhelming tendency to choose spouses within the British ethnicities: 43.3 per cent of spouses were Irish; 23.8 per cent English; 16.7 per cent Scottish; and 8.4 per cent French–Canadian (*Canada Year Book*, 1939: 160). While overseas immigration was greatly reduced in the 1930s due to the Great Depression, nevertheless, 9,152 immigrants from Northern Ireland (68% of the total Irish immigrant cohort) arrived in Canada during the decade.

Immediately following the Second World War, British immigration to Canada again surged. Of the approximately 168,000 British who landed in Canada during the 1940s, 87 per cent of the arrivals occurred in the immediate post-war years 1946–1949 and included approximately 42,000 British war brides and young children of Canadian servicemen.[26] In these years, those born in the six-county area (hereafter NI-born) amounted to 5,402 of the British contingent and in addition, there were 5,340 immigrants from independent Ireland. British

Figure 6.2: Family migration on ESA assisted passage was significant such as the Protestant Monteith family from Castlederg, Co. Tyrone on board the tender leaving Derry in April 1929, bound for Halifax, Nova Scotia (Bigger McDonald Collection, POR 14-09-2003/6/14, courtesy of Libraries NI).

immigration to Canada would have likely been even higher had it not been for British Government restrictions in the immediate post-war years on the amount of money that emigrants could remove from the country, followed by the devaluation of sterling in 1949 (Richmond, 1967: 9). Preferential immigration policies based on national origin were once again codified in the Canadian Immigration Act (1952) and British immigration to Canada continued to increase with 380,984 arriving during the 1950s, over 102,000 of these in the peak year of 1957 alone. The total number of NI-born arriving in Canada in this decade amounted to 24,830 with almost as many again (24,087) from independent Ireland, however, it is difficult to reconcile these immigration figures with the comparatively small population increase for the Irish-born in Canada. For example, the 1951 Canadian census recorded 56,685 NI-born residents in Canada and 24,110 Irish-born from the twenty-six-county area; by 1961, these numbers had only increased to 61,588 and 30,889 respectively, representing only 28 per cent of the 1950s inflow.[27]

British emigration to Canada continued strongly during the 1960s with approximately 333,000 arriving, almost 128,000 of them in the two-year period 1966–1967.[28] For the six years from 1960 to 1965 for which country of birth immigration data is available, Canada recorded the arrival of 8,967 NI-born and 5,990 Southern Ireland-born.[29] A noticeable difference in the two Irish cohorts is that approximately 30 per cent of Southern Irish immigrants in the post-war years came to Canada via another country, most likely via Britain or the United States while comparable figures for the NI-born are only about 7–8 per cent. The tendency towards direct migration to Canada from Northern Ireland reflects the migration history and continuing family ties between Ulster and Canada, the marketing campaign of the Canadian Government in the UK including eligibility for assisted passage and the availability in Belfast of Canadian immigration services.[30]

In summary, over the period 1930–1965, the NI-born made up 57.3% of the total Irish cohort that went to Canada. Projecting backwards on this basis to include the Irish cohort of the 1920s (not differentiated in the data between Northerners and Southerners), one arrives at the conservative estimate that over 87,000 NI-born came to Canada between 1920 and 1965 and 65,000–68,000 from independent Ireland.[31] Thus, the NI-born comprised just over 7 per cent of the UK immigrant cohort and 2.1 per cent of total immigration to Canada. In comparison, UK immigration to Canada over the same period comprised over 30 per cent of total Canadian immigration (English = 20%; Scottish = 8.25%; and Welsh = 0.9%). Despite the significant British and Irish immigration into Canada, however, growth in their numbers was slow due to their continuing emigration out of Canada. For example, in the decade from 1941 to 1951, almost 78,000 British and Irish-born left Canada, accounting for 20.5 per cent of all emigrants

(Canada Year Book, 1957–1958: 163)[32] and in the decade 1956–1965, a return rate of 19 per cent was estimated in a study of British migrants returning from Canada (Richmond, 1968: 264).

From 1962, the Canadian Government instituted new selection regulations which matched the skills and qualifications of applicants with employment need in Canada. This new policy was formalised into the 'point system' in 1967 and at that stage, the Immigration Appeal Board was created. Quebec took over the selection of its own immigrants the following year, employing the point system but with French-language competence emphasised.[33] The result of the new point selection system was a sharp decline in British and European immigration.[34] Nevertheless, out of the top ten countries of birth of foreign-born immigrants to Canada, the UK was still in first place in 1981 with 18,915 immigrants. By 1991, it had dropped to tenth position (6,451 immigrants), was absent from the top ten countries in 2001 and by 2009 was in fifth place (8,069 immigrants) with over three-quarters admitted under the economic category as skilled immigrants (Milan, 2011: 5–6).[35] The Canadian census of 2001 reported 614,610 UK-born residents of Canada and 26,210 from the ROI with approximately two-thirds of these immigrants having arrived prior to 1980. Data on the NI-born is not available in the Canadian census after 1961, but may be around 20,000 currently given recent youth emigration trends.[36] By the 2006 census, the multigenerational Irish were recorded as the fourth largest ethnic group (4,354,153) in Canada after the English, French and Scottish, with the 88.7 per cent of them claiming multiple heritage (i.e., of one or more additional ethnicities), while it is estimated that approximately 2.5 million Canadians are of 'Ulster heritage'.[37] Although figures in the 2006 census for Canada showed a reduction in both UK and Irish-born groups (592,355 and 22,825 respectively), this is likely to change due to the recent inflow to Canada of young Irish workers fleeing poor economic conditions at home.[38] Indeed, Irish community organisations in Canada, such as the St Patrick's Society in Montreal, have mobilised to assist incoming Irish people through the Irish Immigrant Integration Initiative, a joint project with the Emigrant Support Programme of the Irish Government.[39]

We turn now to examine the experiences of four generations of Northern Ireland immigrants to Canada, coinciding with major changes in Canadian immigration policy.

'Is this what I came to Canada for?' Interwar Immigration

Leo, a Catholic from Castlederg, County Tyrone, like many of the British and Irish emigrants bound for Canada in the 1920s, availed of an assisted passage scheme but in addition, had the support of family members already resident in Canada. With unemployment levels by 1925 at well over 20 per cent and few opportunities for young people in the rural areas of Northern Ireland, the plan arranged between Leo's mother and his aunt and uncle in Montreal was that once finished school, Leo be 'shipped off to Canada for so-called three years to make my fortune and go home again'.[40] He knew very little about the country. 'All I'd ever learned about Canada, I guess, in school was that the St Lawrence River was frozen six months of the year' (interview, Ottawa).[41] Thus barely eighteen, Leo left home for Belfast where he boarded the steamship *Letitia* of the Anchor-Donaldson Line, departing on 29 October 1926.[42] He arrived at the Port of Quebec on the 7 November and made his way by train to Montreal, noting that the weather was the coldest he had ever experienced in his life.[43] Though listed as a 'farmer' on the passenger manifest, no doubt in order to qualify for the assisted passage scheme, Leo evidently had no intention of working in agriculture.[44] His uncle had arranged a job for him in the shipping room of the Henry Morgan and Sons department store (later the Hudson's Bay Company) on Saint Catherine Street which as Leo described 'in those days it was *the* shop in Montreal' and he was well pleased to have such a clean indoor job.[45] His pleasure was short-lived, however, when a fierce blizzard blew in with the snow falling thicker and faster than Leo had ever thought possible:

> The arcade was out in front there of Eaton's and Morgan's [department stores]. The snow built up so high there that they called for recruits to go out and shovel it. This after I was on the job for about two weeks! I wasn't afraid of a shovel. I knew what a shovel was at home, certainly. But I stood up there and I thought, *Is this what I came to Canada for?* (interview, Ottawa)

Leo was only one of thousands of young people who left Northern Ireland during the 1920s on assisted passage schemes due to the poor economy and high unemployment at home, the luckier ones among them heading to join family members like Leo's aunt; herself part of the substantial emigrant outflow to Canada in the decade before the First World War. Most of these young people were intended as domestic, agricultural or other types of labourers and those that could usually tried to move into other forms of employment in retail or business as soon as possible. Leo was an accomplished fiddle player and managed to supplement his income by playing for dances in clubs in Montreal throughout the late 1920s and 1930s. He married into a French–Canadian family and eventually through a contact managed to obtain a clerical job in the Bank of Montreal where he worked for the remainder of his career, ultimately attaining the position of branch manager.

In the post-war years, due to changes in the Northern Ireland education system, migrants were better prepared for emigration and Canada was well placed with its growing industry to receive them. Providing they had good health and no criminal record, immigrants from the United Kingdom, Ireland and the 'White' Commonwealth could enter Canada without difficulty and assisted emigration schemes were again put in place to help them (Richmond, 1967: 10).

'The horizons go on forever': Post-war Immigration

By the end of the Second World War, the economic situation had changed dramatically and employment was much more easily available at home in Northern Ireland or nearby in Britain. Rapidly urbanising Commonwealth countries, such as Canada and Australia, were also in need of skilled immigrants and they actively sought them in the UK and Europe (Constantine, 2003). The revival of the 'ten-pound passage' assisted emigration scheme to Canada in February 1951 further facilitated travel for 'suitable immigrants ... employed in certain industries, including agriculture ... and most other trades and occupations' and instructions were given to apply to the Canadian Immigration Office on Chichester Street in Belfast.[46] Many among the young post-war generation in Northern Ireland who benefited from increasing opportunities for education and training – especially Protestants – were consequently well prepared to try their luck abroad.[47] So although emigration had been an inevitable outcome for many of the interwar generation like Leo above, the situation had changed markedly for the post-war cohort. Those that left for Canada during the 1950s and 1960s, for the most part, willingly chose to go, with reasons for their departure often cited as wanting to 'see the world' or 'have an adventure'.

Such was the case of Harry, whose aunt's story as a pioneer in northern Saskatchewan was presented in Chapter 3. Having joined the Air Ministry in London at the age of eighteen in 1947 where he was trained in meteorology, Harry had hoped to be stationed abroad and was very disappointed to be returned to Northern Ireland and stationed instead at RAF Aldergrove in County Antrim. Desiring adventure, Harry eventually left the service and began looking for opportunities abroad. Tempted by recruitment for the Palestine or Rhodesian police service that was on offer to those with military service, Harry changed his mind when he learned that 'the mortality rate was about 60 per cent ... you went in and you didn't last very long, it was far, far higher than ordinary army mortality rates during the war' (interview, Armagh, VMR–043). He opted instead to go to Canada, which he perceived of as 'somewhere where there's plenty of opportunity' to see if he could get training in aeronautical engineering. Thus Harry left Belfast accompanied by two friends, all of them availing of the Canadian ten-pound passage scheme, and boarded the steamship *Arosa Kulm* on 17 November 1952 when the ship called into Plymouth on its way from Bremerhaven to Quebec.

Like Leo a generation earlier, Harry arrived at Quebec in November, on the last ship to venture down the icy St Lawrence River that season before it froze over completely. He headed to Toronto where he searched for work at the employment exchange but found that his timing was poor as the place was filled with queuing outdoor seasonal workers – loggers and fishermen – who had come into the city to look for winter work. Indeed, winter unemployment in Canada was so severe that from the 1950s, government policy specifically aimed to discourage the arrival of immigrants during the winter months and by the 1960s efforts were made to attract immigrants for occupations not subject to 'seasonal slackening' (Canada Year Book, 1957–1958: 173). Harry soon found a job with an American aircraft company, based in the Toronto area that made jet engine parts which were supplied to the American air force, then actively involved in the Korean War. When the war ended soon after, so did the work and Harry was laid off with only four-hours-notice. Having previously trained in meteorology, Harry found work with the Canadian Meteorology Service and was sent to man an isolated weather station in the Arctic.

Like Harry, skilled female emigrants from Northern Ireland who benefited from the increasing availability of further education for women in the 1950s, were also well prepared to expand their horizons in Canada. Heather from the greater Belfast area had just graduated in 1958 as a physiotherapist and found employment locally, though she had a strong desire to see another part of the world before she 'settled down'. She noticed the regular advertisements for overseas posts in the monthly journal of the *Chartered Society of Physiotherapists* and since 'the only respectable way a young woman in Belfast could leave her father's roof was either to get married or to emigrate', she decided to apply for a two-year contract abroad. Though she definitely 'wanted to stay in the Commonwealth – that was a factor', she felt that Australia and New Zealand were too far away; that New Zealand in particular would just be 'going from one little island to another little island' (interview, Ottawa, VMR–074). Thus, she chose Canada and although there were several good immediate opportunities available in Vancouver, she had heard that the climate there was similar to Ireland and waited until she saw a post advertised for Alberta, where two great-aunts she had never met had gone out on homesteading schemes before the First World War. She procured a post in Edmonton with the Workmen's Compensation Board based on her references alone – no interview was required – and then underwent a medical examination at Canada House in Belfast which included a chest X-ray to scan for tuberculosis.

Having qualified for the Canadian assisted passage scheme, Heather, travelling alone, sailed on the *Empress of Britain* from Liverpool to Montreal arriving in June 1959. Heather's extraordinarily detailed account of the journey by ship and then overland by train testify to the momentous importance of this life-defining experience. As she described, 'the moment I set foot in Canada – the moment I set foot on the ship even – I found myself; I was suddenly my own person' (interview, Ottawa, VMR–074). She vividly remembered the stormy journey aboard ship and was thrilled to see icebergs as they approached Canada. Her overland rail journey across the country to Edmonton via Calgary through 'forests, forests, forests' was punctuated only by moose on the tracks, though once they got to the southern prairies where 'the horizons go on forever', she was amazed at the severity of the thunderstorms. Gadi BenEzer has suggested that migration journeys are in themselves vital aspects of the migration experience and he poses the question as to why they have received so little attention in migration literature. He suggests, as is evident in Heather's migration experience, that the journey itself becomes 'a unique part of their life story and sense of self' (2002: 8) and that its impact can be such as to influence their subsequent adaptation and integration in the new country. For Heather, the emigration journey was a precursor to an adventurous lifestyle.

After several months stationed in the Canadian Arctic, Harry travelled down to Toronto, married the German nurse he had met on board ship en route to Canada and brought her up to the Arctic where they remained for the next seven years, 1955–1962, first at Arctic Bay and later in Coppermines, Northwest Territories:

> Our first station together was Arctic Bay and we stayed there two years and that was the most isolated station in the whole of the Arctic and that included the other side, the Russian side. In the second year, we had three men and Renee [wife]. And there was a Hudson's Bay Company trader and there was no one else. South of us – about four hundred miles south – was a missionary, the Reverend Dalby and wife. But that station, the Eskimos didn't go north of that, they lived south of that (interview, Armagh, VMR–043).

At that time, Harry estimated there were probably only about one hundred 'White' people living across the Canadian Arctic. Significantly, the Inuit were then still living according to their traditional way of life, hunting and fishing, building ice houses in winter, travelling by dogsled and wearing outdoor clothing made entirely from animal skins. The 1950s–1960s was a period of enormous change for Inuit society and Harry believed that the influence of the Canadian Government specifically and of White people generally was very detrimental to the aboriginal way of life.[48] In a strange parallel with Northern Ireland, for example, Harry remarked that due to the influence of Presbyterian missionaries, the Inuit in the Coppermines region did not hunt on Sundays. He felt very privileged to have lived among the Inuit at this time, describing them as, 'the best people in the world'.

Soon after settling in Edmonton, Heather married and her adventurous life continued as the couple decided to head up north to the mining region near Yellowknife on Great Slave Lake in the Northwest Territories. She described in detail their hair-raising drive in May 1961 up the Mackenzie Highway – a rough dirt road at that time – crossing the thawing ice of the Mackenzie River near Fort Providence where their vehicle finally broke down.[49] Living in Yellowknife at 62 degrees latitude meant a short eight-week summer and then darkness and freezing temperatures for much of the year while living in a caravan as no other housing was available. There weren't many opportunities for physiotherapists in the north at that time and living in a frontier society meant poor educational standards for children, a high suicide rate and getting used to a certain degree of violence. Heather described an incident reminiscent of the poems of Robert Service when at eight-months pregnant she had to take cover on her hands and knees behind the bar at the Yellowknife Hotel because a fierce fight broke out between prospectors and miners over an insult to an aboriginal woman.[50]

Like many emigrants of the 1950s, Harry and Heather chose freely to go to Canada for opportunity and adventure, and both lived rather adventurous lives in Northern Canada. However, having children led both Harry and Heather to eventually leave Northern Canada because of the lack of adequate educational facilities. Harry and his family returned to Belfast where adventures of a different kind awaited them (see their story in Chapter 7), while Heather and her family relocated south to Edmonton. However, adventures were also to be had in Canadian cities like Toronto, especially for young naïve immigrants like Craig, from North Belfast.

From a working-class background, Craig had acquired few qualifications prior to his emigration, working at a variety of jobs in greater Belfast. Arriving in 1966 to be best man at his brother Fergus' wedding in Toronto, Craig decided to stay on and applied for Canadian immigration status. He was immediately given a temporary work permit while his file was under consideration.[51] Work in Canada was easy to find at that time, particularly if you were from a British Protestant background:

> In those days, the TTC – the [Toronto] Transit Commission – the insurance companies, the city of Toronto, all of those things were sort of run – coming near the end – but run by the Orangemen and a great Orange society here in Toronto which I didn't know until I came. So you just put your name in and you're on the right side of the fence and shuttled through (interview, Toronto, VMR–064).

The day after receiving his work permit, Craig had already lined up two job interviews. On his way from one interview to the other, however, he walked into the office of a credit company and asked about a job. The company manager, also of Ulster Presbyterian stock, hired Craig on the spot. Craig's job as a collection agent was to track down people who had defaulted on payments – this exposed him to a seedier side of life that he had no prior experience of:

And I'm telling you, for a guy who was a Presbyterian, who had gone to church three times through the week, didn't swear, didn't drink, it was like taking a cake and just cutting it down a slice. The things that I was exposed to in my life I just never knew existed.

He recalled being let into the apartment of a nice-looking young woman to enquire about her account payments. She said she was out of work, but when Craig got back to the office, he was informed that she was a 'hooker'. He had no idea what a hooker was and was shocked to learn that he had been in the apartment of a prostitute. Too naïve to realise fully the dangerous nature of the job, it wasn't until the day that someone pulled a shotgun on him that reality began to dawn. Nevertheless, for four years, Craig 'chased' members of Hells Angels biker gangs, muscle men that worked for mafia figures and even a famous murderer out on bail, known by the nickname Johnny Sombrero.

Craig next found an office job in a finance company where he was posted to a branch in the Italian quarter of Toronto. His contact with an Italian family there who more or less 'adopted' him was an important milestone in his life in developing an understanding of the sectarian conflict back home:

I became their adopted son and I was an Irish Italian Protestant and they were Catholic. That was my sort of eye-opener to people who didn't give a toss about what your religion was. Just good Christian people. They were just open, they fed me like their own son. I lived with them, I had a key to the house, a room – my own room – in their house, and they just accepted me as one of them. And like I said to you, Sundays, I would still go to church – I walked to the Presbyterian church, they'd go to the Catholic church, we'd come home and we'd have an Italian lunch. Everybody was talking ... everybody shouted at everybody else and the food was fantastic!

Following on from the finance company job, Craig heard that the major Canadian banks were recruiting employees from Britain; a source of young, educated English speakers who would fit in culturally. Craig once again used his British background to advantage, presented himself at a bank and suggested that as a Brit already in Canada they should hire him since they would not have to pay his way over. When asked for his qualifications, he said that he'd have to send away to Belfast for them and was hired conditionally. Craig explained how the Human Resources department would make contact every so often looking for his certificates, so eventually he used the Troubles as an excuse for not being able to obtain his documents:

'It's been blown up, like it's been destroyed over there. The place is in turmoil, I just can't get it.' But by that time, you're in the job for a year and you're doing the job ... And I wasn't the only guy that did that.

But if you were able to do the job – and I think that's what I found in Canada – that it wasn't like what school you went to, what your name was automatically said what side of the fence you were from, right, and then who do you know, like who sent you here. You didn't have to have those sort of things. If you could get in the door and show what you could do with the job, you could get ahead.

John like Craig left Belfast in 1966. Unlike Craig, however, John was from a middle-class background and left to undertake doctoral studies in psychology in the United States. Upon completion, he obtained a lecturing post at the University of Toronto and relocated there in 1972. He has since become a leading scholar in the field of cognition. Despite his middle-class background and considerable education John did not feel that as a Northern Irish person, he would have had the opportunities in Britain that were available to him in North America:

> I certainly grew up feeling I will not be given a fair shake in the rest of the United Kingdom … I felt I will get a much better shake and I will be much less conscious of myself as being from a particular place in North America. I'll be an invisible man here whereas I'll be a marked person in Britain … And I suspected that I would run into a lot of these glass ceilings (interview, Toronto, VMR–061).

The post-war period was a 'golden age' for British and Irish migration to Canada as at no other time was the process of immigration more favourable. Young skilled immigrants seeking opportunity and adventure benefited from preferential selection policies, availed of assisted passages and easily found employment. According to a contemporary immigration pamphlet, if immigrants were prepared to 'work more steadily with fewer tea and coffee breaks' and refrain from saying, 'we do it this way in Britain', then 'the rapid rise of competent and hard working men and women is the rule rather than the exception' (Beak, 1958: 20–21). Nevertheless, the return rates of British migrants in this period were consistently high enough to cause concern and stimulate investigation into the phenomenon (Richmond, 1966, 1967, 1968).[52] Family factors, such as the care of elderly parents in Britain or their children's education as in Harry's case, were found to be significant among the causes of return, rather than dissatisfaction with Canada. Those that chose to stay in Canada, like Heather, Craig and John, tended to do well in their careers, particularly working-class migrants like Craig many of whom became upwardly mobile in Canada.

For migrants who left Northern Ireland for Canada during the 1970s, the situation had changed markedly both at home and in Canada. The conflict (and the poor economy that resulted) became the principal reason for emigration. In Canada, the preferential selection of immigrants based on national origin had been abandoned in favour of a new points system (formalised in 1967) which selected immigrants on the basis of the specific requirements of the Canadian labour market. As the Canadian economy deteriorated after 1970, immigration targets were greatly reduced and more stringent regulations introduced that resulted in a more complex and prolonged application process.[53] The era of easy immigration for Commonwealth immigrants was over. Where one-third of immigrants to Canada in 1966 were from the UK, by 1971, it was only one in seven, with a substantial increase coming from Asia in particular (Pendakur and Mata, 1999: 6). Select British and Irish immigrants now had to pay their own way to Canada, only to find themselves in an increasingly multicultural environment and a tighter job market, as we shall see from the migrant narratives that follow.

'Second-class Canadian': 1970s Immigration

Cas and Colette are a couple from Lurgan, County Armagh who left Northern Ireland in 1974 directly due to the conflict after they had been caught up in several dangerous incidents in the early 1970s. On one occasion (24 November 1971), a bomb had been planted a few doors down from their house in William Street and Cas, a schoolteacher, remembered arriving in panic at the barricaded street, noting that the police had evacuated their Protestant neighbours, 'but they had not told Colette that it was there and they had not told the doctor who was Catholic that it was there for some reason'.[54] Moments later, the suction from the explosion sucked Colette down a staircase from the second floor of their house and the doctor's wife next door was sucked out of the bathtub. Nevertheless, it was only when Colette's successful hairdressing business was badly damaged by a bomb in June 1973 that the couple applied for Canadian immigration. They were admitted to Canada on the basis of the points given to Colette as a hairdresser, as Cas explained:

> When we went to the [Canadian] embassy, they said, 'We don't need teachers in Ontario, but we need hairdressers', which Colette was. When we did the interview, she got ten points and I got one point (interview, Windsor, ON, VMR–068).[55]

However when they arrived in Ontario, Colette was surprised to discover that her hairdressing qualifications were not accepted and she was forced to do the training courses all over again in order to work at her profession. Like other immigrants of the period who reported similar experiences, Colette could not understand how the country could admit her on the basis of her qualifications which were then not recognised for employment purposes:

I got the points for both of us ... But when I got here, they didn't recognise that. I could not get a job as a hairdresser. No way! ... I couldn't open my own business. I couldn't do nothing. I had to start from the word go. Right back to zero. And it was so hard because we came here with so little money and we wanted to buy a house because we didn't want to rent ... We had nothing. I had to go back to school.

Cas' qualifications as a teacher were not recognised in Canada, and as he described it, there was 'that sort of insinuation that you were always *a second-class Canadian*'. Reflecting back, he thought it might have been very difficult to find employment had it not been that Colette's cousin from Armagh was a vice president at the Hiram Walker plant in Windsor and arranged an interview for him.[56]

Bríd, from the Falls Road area of West Belfast had been active in the civil rights movement before she left Belfast at the end of 1974 with her husband and infant daughter. She had a degree from the Art College in Belfast and had been employed as an art teacher in a secondary school in the city. When she arrived in Toronto, she tried to apply for teacher's college, but they wouldn't accept her undergraduate degree:

When I went to apply for emigration, it was on a point system so I got a certain number of points: I was young, I got points for my education, I got points for higher education, all of that. When I got there [it was]: 'never heard of it', 'you'll have to go through university again' so it was to keep the universities open, to keep teachers employed. You got jobs at the bottom of the heap ... It's the best educated service industry in the world. I mean I had a degree and I aspired to waitress (interview, Belfast, VMR–019).

Liz left Northern Ireland with her English husband and two young children in February 1975, just a few months after Bríd. They had a very good lifestyle in Northern Ireland – Liz' husband was a company director in a large construction firm in Belfast and she ran a playgroup and was involved in many volunteer and social activities in the Lisburn area. Having lived through the terrible early years of the Troubles when Liz had been very conscious of the potential danger to her English husband, it was only after their daughter was threatened on her way home from school during the Ulster Workers' Council Strike of 1974 that they actively set about looking for emigration opportunities.[57] Liz' husband found a job in Toronto. Even though Liz nurtured the belief that the family would return after a few years once things in Northern Ireland had settled down, she was very upset about leaving:

I felt terrible. I thought I was leaving everything really. I didn't want to leave. I was an only child so I felt a bit guilty about leaving my mother and father. They [the children] were their only grandchildren … So I cried all the time before I left for silly things like I had planted hundreds of crocuses around the trees in the garden in the fall and never saw them come up to bloom because we left in February of that year. I cried about leaving the children in the playgroup, I cried about leaving my friends. Every time I turned around there was something to cry about (interview, Holywood, Co. Down, VMR–057).

With her husband in a pre-arranged job and friends from Belfast already established in Toronto, they soon settled in well. Though she had cried sorely at leaving Northern Ireland:

as soon as I got to Canada, I never shed a tear. All my homesickness was done before I ever left. I just thought I'd landed in Mickey Mouse land when I landed in Toronto. I couldn't believe how easy everything was.

It was also through the move and their 'easy' new lifestyle in Toronto that Liz and her husband came to realise the full impact that the Northern Ireland conflict had had on their lives:

Without realising we hadn't seen a movie for five years living here [in Northern Ireland] and at some subconscious level, we had just stopped going out without realising that we had stopped going out. The Troubles had infiltrated our lives to the point where you didn't go to restaurants for meals, you went to each other's homes for dinner parties … Our world had grown smaller here without us actually making conscious decisions that we were withdrawing from doing certain things. It only became apparent after we left that we had been unable to do a lot of things that we had taken for granted before the Troubles started.

Liz began clerical work in a real estate firm in Toronto and soon availed of the opportunity to study and obtain her license as a property agent. She eventually formed her own real estate company when her family relocated to Sudbury, Ontario where her husband took a job for Inco mines. But things did not always go smoothly. When Inco began lay-offs in Sudbury in the severe economic recession of the early 1980s, not only did Liz' husband lose his job, but the out-migration from Sudbury caused by the lay-offs resulted in her booming property business going bust.[58] Liz' experience is also a reminder that the opportunities of married women immigrants are often constrained by their husband's employment, even though they may strike out on their own as was the case of Sheila that follows.

Sheila had spent her early years in an orphanage in Omagh, County Tyrone and was eventually fostered by a family near Strabane. As a young adult she began nursing training in Omagh but transferred to the City Hospital in Belfast in 1971, just as the Troubles were greatly escalating. She was unprepared for the level of violence in the city and in her memory, 'the move from Omagh to Belfast was just horrific'. The period which began with the onset of internment in August and continued throughout the autumn of 1971 and into 1972 was one of the most violent in Northern Ireland history, with civilians, police and military personnel being killed on an almost daily basis in shootings or bomb explosions.[59] After the explosion at McGurk's bar in Belfast (4 December 1971), Sheila told the hospital matron that she couldn't 'cope with these daily explosions' and 'this level of turmoil because it was everywhere, we could never get away from it'.[60] Though she applied to go to Canada as a nurse, she duly received a reply from the Canadian authorities that Canada was not then in need of nurses and her application was rejected. Nevertheless, determined to leave Belfast she took a job as a nanny that she had seen advertised in the newspaper with a Jewish family in New York. This first real exposure to a different culture, religion and way of life was very influential. When she returned to Belfast after a year, she took up a job in a Barnardos children's home, but again found the level of violence horrifying. On the morning of her wedding day in May 1976, she was on her way to the hairdresser when she passed by the carnage of the Club Bar near Queen's University where a bomb had exploded the previous evening. Later at her wedding reception she found out that a friend had been killed in the explosion. She and her husband decided to leave Belfast shortly after, first for Cork where they stayed a few years, but in 1979 they moved on to Hamilton, Ontario, where Sheila's husband had accepted a postdoctoral position at McMaster University.

They arrived in Hamilton in December. Possessing only nylon motorbike gear, not proper winter clothes, the impact of the memory was still palpable as Sheila articulated the alienation she felt in the present tense, 'we're frozen and we're lonely and we're tired and we're cold'. While in Cork she had been surprised to encounter negative attitudes concerning the employment of married women and was unable to obtain steady employment, in the end only working 'informally' providing childcare for which she was paid on a cash basis. Thus when she arrived in Canada, Sheila was dismayed to discover that as the wife of a postdoctoral fellow, she did not have the right to work legally because she and her husband were not considered permanent immigrants. They also discovered that to become permanent immigrants they had to apply from outside the country. Unable to afford return to Ireland, Sheila was advised that they could apply from the United States so they drove over the border to Buffalo, New York and submitted their application for immigration from there. Thus during her first year in Canada, the only work Sheila could get was cleaning the houses of her husband's university colleagues for cash payment. Because of these experiences working in the informal economy in Ireland and in Canada, Sheila became 'consumed with my right to work' and was sensitised to the societal infrastructures that made women vulnerable to become economically dependent on men. Once her immigration had been approved, she left the marriage and got a job running a women's drop-in centre in Hamilton. As with Heather's story earlier, Sheila described the realisation that she could be her own person:

> I don't have to be a mother, I don't have to be a daughter, I don't have to be a wife, I can be a woman. It was so enlightening and sparkling and incredible and powerful (interview, Denman Island, B.C., VMR–085).

Sheila remembered this period of her life as a turning point when she became active in feminist, environmental and peace issues. In the mid-1980s, she moved to Vancouver and took a job with the Service, Office and Retail Workers' Union of Canada (SORWUC) which fought hard to improve pay and working conditions for women.[61]

Like many emigrants from Northern Ireland during the 1970s, regardless of religious affiliation, for Bríd, Colette and Cas as Catholics, and Liz and Sheila as Protestants, the conflict was an important factor in their decision to depart and all of them had close personal, or even life-threatening, experience of it. Though they were from working-class families, all but Liz had obtained either a degree or professional qualification before departure. Nevertheless, each of them experienced barriers to working at their chosen profession in Canada, thus their situations were considerably more challenging than those of earlier post-war British and Irish immigrants. Bríd and Cas were no longer able to work as teachers, Sheila was refused entry to Canada as a nurse and Colette had to retrain in hairstyling. Even Liz, who completed her education in Canada, then faced bankruptcy in the early 1980s when the economy began a downward trend with high inflation and unemployment. This was to herald even more difficult times for new immigrants as following a brief recovery, Canada's economy declined after 1986 and entered recession again in 1990. The timing of Martin's emigration from Belfast to Canada in 1987 was, as we shall see, even less favourable compared to those who had arrived in the decade prior to 1980.

'Amazing credentials and they don't get work': Immigration Since the 1980s

Despite being university educated with a degree in economics and having work experience as a manager in a manufacturing plant, Martin, nevertheless, had to wait eighteen months from the time he submitted his application before he received a phone call from the Canadian Embassy in London informing him that he had been accepted for immigration. Although he had planned to go to Toronto, Martin was told that he had been accepted by the Quebec Skilled

Worker Programme and therefore despite lacking French he would have to go to Montreal and apply for his Canadian social insurance number from there.[62] Fortunately, Martin had an aunt living in the Montreal area and he stayed with her when he arrived and began looking for work. He remembered his first full day in Canada:

> I just remember waking up the next morning freezing cold in my aunt's house in Montreal thinking, this is it, like I've got 700 bucks, what am I going to do? It's November (interview, Windsor, ON, VMR–068).

Finding employment proved elusive and Martin was soon very low on funds and had to contact his father to wire him more money. Once his Canadian documents were in order, Martin set out on the train to Toronto as he had been unable to find suitable work in Montreal, partly due to his lack of French. He subsequently obtained a clerical job in Toronto with an insurance company where he was treated poorly, but after a succession of 'hard knocks', he managed to get a job in the banking industry which enabled him to progress. At the time of his interview, Martin was working in the international investment banking sector for one of the country's largest banks where, like Gary the entrepreneur in the previous chapter, he found that his Irish–British identity was an asset in business:

> In my job I landed a great account last week. I know I landed it because when I went in there, the first thing the guy said to me was, 'Oh typical banker, he's British and he's a banker'. Because they've this image … I'm not [British] in my mind. I'm a mixture of Irish, I'm Northern Irish (interview, Windsor, ON, VMR–068).

However, immigrants were not always prepared for the 'hard knocks' of getting a career restarted in Canada. Eve, from Enniskillen, County Fermanagh was a successful filmmaker in Belfast, a partner in her own production company, when she emigrated from there to Toronto in 1994 to join her Canadian boyfriend, who she subsequently married. Of all the interviewees represented here, Eve's experience was perhaps the most difficult. Having previously served on an exchange programme working for three months in the Toronto film industry, Eve was unprepared for the reality of having to start her career over when she arrived in Toronto subsequently as a permanent immigrant. Like Colette and Bríd twenty years previously, Eve observed that although she had been given entry points for immigration based on her education and work experience, when she got to Canada, it was only 'Canadian experience' that counted:

> For a 26-year-old in Northern Ireland, I had a good c.v. and I had good tape [film portfolio]. You see when I came here? I may as well have put it in that bin (interview, Toronto, VMR–069).

Eve reported that despite having a portfolio of documentary films produced for the major television networks in the UK, she felt that no one was interested because the films had not been made in Canada. Due to her own difficulties, Eve became very aware of the position of well-qualified immigrants to Canada, especially those from visible minorities like my Toronto taxi driver from Pakistan, who could not find suitable jobs:

> But this is something about Canada, isn't it, and something about emigration. Like look at all those people that come here that are doctors that end up driving taxis. Like if you don't have Canadian experience you may as well not have it [qualifications]. Like I wanted to do a documentary about immigrants that come to the city with amazing credentials, and they don't get work because they don't have the Canadian experience. It's unbelievable!

This is what is referred to in the literature as a 'mismatch of skills', estimated to cost the Canadian economy around two billion dollars annually (CCSD, 2007: 25). Eve's impressions are backed up by several studies of recent immigrants to Canada who, like the Northern Ireland migrants in this study, had difficulty in getting their qualifications recognised. Examination of a sample of immigrants who arrived in Canada in 2000–2001 (LSIC data), for example, found that by the end of four years of residence, only just over 25 per cent had obtained recognition of educational credentials and 40 per cent had received recognition for prior work experience – the likelihood in both instances was higher for males, non-visible ethnicities (i.e., White) and those whose credentials or work experience had been obtained in English-speaking countries, such as the USA, the UK, Australia or New Zealand (Houle and Yssaad, 2010: 31).[63] These figures are especially surprising in view of the rising level of educational qualifications among immigrants generally. However, due to the increasing competition internationally for skilled immigrants, the Canadian immigration department has recently established a new programme to speed up the recognition of foreign credentials for targeted occupations and to facilitate access to permanent residency for temporary skilled workers and foreign postgraduate students already in Canada.[64] The immigrants surveyed in the LSIC Study cited that the main barriers to employment were: not enough Canadian experience (49.8%); lack of acceptance of foreign experience (36.6%) and foreign credentials (35.4%); lack of employment opportunities (32.4%); not enough Canadian job references (32.1%); and not able to find a job in their field (29.8%) (Schellenberg and Maheux, 2007: 8). Other studies have noted that racism, especially for visible minorities, remains a significant barrier and that the lack of 'Canadian experience' may actually be used as a screen by employers to racially discriminate (Hathiyani, 2007: 130).[65] These barriers have no doubt contributed to the increasing income gap evident between recent immigrants and the Canadian-born population.

Indeed, poverty rates for immigrants in Canada show that by 1991 those who arrived during the 1960s exhibited the least poverty (11%), for the 1970s arrivals it was slightly higher (15%) and for those arriving during the 1980s, reflecting the economic downturn, it had jumped substantially to 31 per cent (Kazemipur and Halli, 2001: 1144). Since then poverty rates for immigrants to Canada arriving since 1991 have continued to rise (Fang and Heywood, 2010; Frenette et al., 2008; Ostrovsky, 2008; Pendakur and Pendakur, 2004; Picot and Hou, 2003; Picot et al., 2007), however, a recent analysis has shown that there is as yet little evidence of residential ghettoisation (Hiebert et al., 2007).[66] Between 1980 and 2000, for example, the earnings gap between immigrant men and the Canadian-born more than doubled from 17 to 40 per cent and similarly, for immigrant women the gap increased from 23 to 44 per cent (Frenette and Morissette, 2005: 240). While British and Irish immigrants have fared, on the whole, considerably better than 'visible minority' groups (McGree and Esses, 1990; Rothon et al., 2009), they too have been subject to the same economic ups and downs, difficulty maintaining employment, falling wages and increasing skills atrophy as with Eve's experience detailed above.

Perhaps even more alarming according to the LSIC data, was that new immigrants showed a rapid health decline in the first two years in Canada and by four years the number who reported fair or poor health had almost trebled.[67] However, positive perception of the settlement experience correlated strongly with good health, underlining the link between good mental health and good physical health (Newbold, 2009: 330–31). A qualitative study of underemployed recent immigrants admitted to Canada under the Skilled Worker Programme found that the loss of income, the loss of skills (de-skilling) and the loss of status and identity associated with underemployment has lasting mental health effects on immigrants and their family members in addition to physical health issues related to stress and strenuous working conditions at 'survival jobs' (Dean and Wilson, 2009: 193–4).[68] Thus, it is perhaps not surprising that new immigrants admitted as highly skilled workers and especially those who have a university degree are much more likely to report dissatisfaction with life in Canada (Houle and Schellenberg, 2010: 25–6) and may account in part for the significant circulatory migration – 'brain circulation' – in and out of Canada of the highly skilled (DeVoretz, 2006: 18; King and Newbold, 2008).[69] Since the immigration experience for highly skilled immigrants to Canada evidently presents many challenges, it begs the question of how other categories of migrants fare, as for example, temporary workers or those attempting entry without skilled qualifications?

The experience of Richard illustrates the case. He first went over to Toronto in 1998 on a cross-community Wider Horizons (WH) Programme for young adults funded by the International Fund for Ireland. Due to the perception that the programme was funded by 'green money' there had been difficulty filling the quota of young working-class Protestants and this proved to Richard's advantage. Because of his love of outdoor pursuits, the organisation arranged an internship for him at a canoeing and sailing school on Lake Ontario. This proved to be such a positive experience that even though Richard spent much of the following year 'backpacking' in Australia, he hankered to go back to Canada and managed to obtain a temporary work visa for the sailing school the following summer. Having decided that he wanted to stay in Canada, Richard approached the coordinator of the WH Programme in Toronto – an Irishman from Cork – who after considerable negotiation with the immigration department arranged for Richard's employment as a 'foreign' worker to supervise the Irish interns coming over on the programme.[70] For Richard, this meant travelling to Ireland three or four times per year to meet with the WH interns before they embarked for Canada and then looking after them during their two-month residencies in Toronto.

At the time of his interview, Richard had applied for permanent immigration but was having considerable difficulty because his lack of formal qualifications meant that he had not attained the required minimum number of points in the Canadian immigration selection system. Richard's difficulty in gaining immigrant status is somewhat paradoxical in view of the fact that his grandmother was Canadian-born from Barrie, Ontario, and had emigrated from Canada to Northern Ireland in the 1920s with her new husband, Richard's Ulster-born grandfather, a returning emigrant. Through three generations the Canadian and Northern Irish sides of the family had stayed in contact and Richard's mother had herself worked in Toronto for a couple of years in the 1960s, living with her mother's sister. However, unlike Britain, the Canadian Government does not extend citizenship to the third generation (grandchildren) of the Canadian-born, so although Richard's mother was entitled to Canadian citizenship, this had no bearing on his own eligibility, in spite of having always felt a sense of belonging to Canada.

Though maintaining regular connections with Ireland in his work for the WH Programme, it is perhaps surprising that an athletic sociable young man like Richard chose not to participate in wider Irish community events or networks in Toronto. For despite Toronto's historical links with Ulster and its former reputation as an Orange city – indeed early in the twentieth century it was known as the 'Belfast of Canada' – Richard felt that Irish community organisations were not inclusive of British–Irish identities:

> Like a lot of the associations, it would be Gaelic this, or hurling, or there's a radio show that this guy Eamonn Loghlin does every Saturday morning but it's all Ireland Ireland, not your British aspect of Northern Ireland.

Now I have no problem with that, it's just that I don't identify with it. It's not as if I would find it intimidating, it's just I don't care about Gaelic, not because it's Irish, it's just it's a sport that I've never followed (interview, Toronto, VMR–072).

In response to a question about whether he had ever been involved with the Irish Canadian Rugby Club in Toronto which has both men's and women's teams, Richard's answer was a reminder that sport in Northern Ireland is not only a matter of denomination but of class and that rugby on both sides of the Irish border tends to be a middle-class pursuit:[71]

I didn't play rugby. It would be seen as a grammar school [sport] – like more of a Protestant sport, of course. The school I went to played field hockey, it wasn't a rugby school. Because in Northern Ireland your school either played hockey or they played rugby. I don't even know the rules of rugby.

Richard, nevertheless, maintained that he felt relatively free in Canada from the class 'conditioning' that had limited his choices and opportunities in Northern Ireland as a person from a working-class housing estate. He believed that at home he would never have had the opportunity to take up sailing, a pursuit of the middle and upper classes, and he worried that if he returned to Northern Ireland he might fall back into the old 'conditioning'. Ironically, although native-born Canadians, even those of British and Irish descent, would tend not to perceive class differences among Irish and British immigrants, within the first-generation immigrant group, as with Richard, old class 'conditioning' is immediately apparent through markers like accent and sports activities and can act as a barrier to participation in and cohesion of immigrant organisations abroad. Thus, Richard opted for integration into Canadian society rather than participating in Irish social networks; in a sense claiming his Canadian heritage by becoming a 'Canadian outdoorsman'.[72]

Two significant and related themes about Canada – peace and tolerance – which are an important part of Canadians' self-image were brought up in the interview narratives over and over again, either as a point of contestation or approval. The chapter thus concludes with consideration of some interviewee encounters in the 'peaceable kingdom'.

'A very tolerant country': Life in the 'peaceable kingdom'[73]

The depiction and critique of Canada as a peaceful utopia, first satirised by humorist and economist Stephen Leacock in the 1930s, now has a large literature.[74] Bríd, who had been active in the civil rights movement in Belfast before her emigration to Canada in 1974, disagreed with the peace-keeping image and believed Canadians on the whole to be rather passive politically:

> I just felt that most people avoided things, even the very government ... they always looked at what the Yanks were doing first. Any major thing that happened in the world, the Prime Minister never made a statement till the [US] President had made it or the Prime Minister in England. They never came out and said, 'We as Canadians'. There's no stance. I just see it very much as fence-sitting. I do believe that Canadians believe that they are the great peace-makers of the world and I often had people say that to me. But they're not great peace-makers, they just don't commit. But they actually believe that and the government sells them that bill of goods (interview, Belfast, VMR–019).

The image of Canadians and their country as tolerant and peace-loving dates back over fifty years to the 1956 Suez crisis when Lester B. Pearson, as Canadian Minister of External Affairs, proposed the development of a United Nations peacekeeping force for which he was awarded the Nobel Peace Prize in 1957.[75] Since then, the involvement of notable Canadians in mediation roles of peace processes around the world, recently including Northern Ireland, has continued to contribute to the peacekeeping self-image especially in English Canada and it remains a fundamental and unifying aspect of Canadian national identity.[76] However, most of the Canada-bound interviewees in this study felt that Canadians were neither interested nor informed about the Northern Ireland conflict. As Bríd described:

> I think they liked their causes far offshore ... It was all right to sing lots of songs about South America, you know Bruce Cockburn can sing *If I had a rocket launcher* ... but it was way down there ... Because you see the whole thing in Northern Ireland touched on their culture and they didn't want to know about it (interview, Belfast, VMR–019).[77]

When the causes were closer to home, according to Sheila who had arrived in Canada in 1979, peace-keeping soon went out the window. Sheila had relocated to Tofino, a village on the west coast of Vancouver Island, when she met her second husband in 1991 and they ran a bed and breakfast business there for several years. Being surrounded by such beautiful wilderness and living in close proximity with First Nations people, Sheila developed a keen interest in aboriginal spirituality and environmentalism. Her environmental 'awakening' coincided with the Clayoquot land use decision of the British Columbia Government, which in 1993 opted to allow clear-cut logging in two-thirds of the area of the old growth forest of Clayoquot Sound.[78] The decision sparked enormous opposition from First Nations people, local landowners and environmentalists the world over, including the Greenpeace organisation and the Sierra Club. To prevent logging access, thousands of protesters in the summer of 1994 participated in a blockade of roads into the Clayoquot area that lasted for four months and drew international media attention as over 800 people were arrested and 620 convicted of contempt. The Clayoquot protest – known as 'the war in the woods' – was the largest act of civil disobedience in Canadian history. As a key participant of the protest group, Sheila was arrested several times and eventually imprisoned for several months – the injunction to stop the protesters was named for her.[79] Sheila found the months in prison very hard and when she was released she was very ill for three months afterwards. Accessing her traumatic memories of that time was described in her narrative as a journey:

> Now I can remember, I mean I'm just going back there – it's a difficult time to go back to because being imprisoned was horrible. I mean it was terrible and I don't think I processed it fully, what that was ... Solitary confinement. I wouldn't wear a prison uniform. I said I'm not a criminal. Put me in a hole. It was an incredible experience. But Claire Culhane, Irish Jewish woman famous in Canada ... came to visit me. And Claire sent me a letter ... and I can remember that note just inspiring me. To get a note like that from someone like her was like, okay, she's right. And so I went through it (interview, Denman Island, B.C., VMR–085).[80]

In bringing the attention of the world to the potential destruction of Clayoquot Sound, the pressure to find a compromise was eventually successful and in 2000, Clayoquot Sound was declared a UNESCO Biosphere Reserve.[81] Following her release from prison, Sheila and her husband purchased a small farm on Denman Island, off the east coast of Vancouver Island, where they currently reside. Sheila explained that her interest and commitment to social justice and human rights was greatly influenced by her experience of the conflict in Northern Ireland and throughout her years in Canada, she has maintained a keen interest in the peace process. At a peace conference in Toronto in 1980, for example, Sheila asked Canadian Prime Minister, Joe Clark, to make a request to Margaret Thatcher to stop the British Army's use of plastic bullets in Northern Ireland and in 1990, she went on a peace walk across Northern Ireland.

The notion of tolerance also touches upon the discourses of immigration and multiculturalism. While Canada was the first country to develop an official multiculturalism policy (1971) and is as yet the only country which has enshrined it in its constitution (Kymlicka, 2010b: 261), critics have argued that the policy has been tokenistic in providing funding for the cultural expression of ethnic groups without incorporating multiculturalism into the country's key institutions and programmes (Bibby, 1990; Bissoondath, 1994; Li, 2003: 134, etc.).[82] Yet as Will Kymlicka and others have noted, the political participation rates of ethnic minorities in Canada are among the highest in the world (2010b: 261) though he acknowledges the many studies (cited earlier in this chapter) that have shown that immigrants since the 1980s have not done as well economically as those of previous generations (Kymlicka, 2010a: 21).[83] Running her own clothing shop in Toronto, Bríd noticed a change in attitude during the 1990s towards the new immigrants who were increasingly 'visible' and poor. She was also disturbed to realise that she was no longer perceived to be 'ethnic' because she was White and English speaking:[84]

> Because all of a sudden the ethnic minorities are all now visible … And all the Whites are moving … The first ethnic face in the area, they're gone. 'But we're *a very tolerant country* and we're not like the Americans, you know. They're really violent'. You see I think that Canada is violent in a quiet way. I feel it wastes people's lives and I think that's a violence (interview, Belfast, VMR–019).

Thus the image of tolerance somewhat masks the racialised discourse of diversity and multiculturalism in Canada, 'the notion of the model, law-abiding, respectable, multiculturalism-loving and peaceful Canadian citizen' (Austin, 2010: 21). Omitted from this narrative are the histories of colonialism, slavery and genocide in British and French Canada, especially in regard to aboriginals, the longstanding historical presence of Black communities and the shameful discrimination against Asians (Chinese, Japanese and 'Hindu') codified in Canadian immigration law that was repealed only in 1947! The 'problem of diversity', for which the blame usually falls on immigrants (especially non-Whites), is explored on an ongoing basis through government sponsored surveys and academic studies, employing methodology,

> systematically encouraging the articulation of 'racial' differences by conditioning respondents to choose preferences based on 'race', 'origin' or 'skin colour' … the legitimacy of asking such questions is engraved in the minds of people in their frequent recurrence in survey questionnaires (Li, 2003: 175).

Diversity thus presented is a 'problem' to be feared for the 'fragmentation' or dilution of Canadian identity and 'traditional' values it supposedly engenders, and 'integrative' multiculturalism is viewed as the means of resolving it. However, evidence has shown that immigrants have little resistance to conforming to Canadian institutions and ways of life (Li, 2003: 131; Walters, 2009). Indeed, recent surveys have demonstrated increasing public support for multiculturalism (e.g., Berry, 2006: 728; Wilkes and Corrigall-Brown, 2011), though some scholars have noted that there is little research on how Canadians and new immigrants actually understand the concept (Fries and Gingrich, 2010).[85] However, to achieve 'deep diversity' as advocated by Charles Taylor (1996), which recognises the multiple ways that individuals and groups may belong to Canada, necessitates a 'politics of equal recognition' (1992: 36) that counters the homogenising tendency of multiculturalism and promotes intercultural dialogue. The alternative model of interculturalism establishes negotiation as fundamental with the emphasis on the process of exchange (Bouchard and Taylor, 2008).

Like Sheila above, who was inspired by conflict in Northern Ireland to become an activist, Craig noted that Irish–Canadian business people have been active in promoting peace in Ireland through business development, raising funds for cross-community and cross-border programmes, such as the Wider Horizons initiative, that bring Irish youth out to Canada and in helping recent Irish immigrants to get established in Canada. During the worst years of the Troubles, this often meant providing a helping hand to those fleeing the conflict. As well as the Ireland–Canada Chamber of Commerce which promotes business and trade between Canada and Ireland, North and South, there is a less formal association of Irish-born businessmen formed around twenty years ago, whose goal has primarily been to aid peace and mutual understanding in Ireland. The principal remit of the association has been essentially educational; to provide a forum in the Irish–Canadian business community for the airing and discussion of Irish issues, usually at dinner events featuring guest speakers. These have included the likes of Gerry Adams, former Taiseaoch Bertie Ahern, former Tanaiste and Minister of Health, Mary Harney, several British cabinet ministers, leading academics and Canadians, such as General John de Chastelain and Judge Peter Cory, who have held important mediation roles in the peace process. Though membership is by invitation only, spouses and partners are also welcome to attend the dinner events which usually attract an audience of around seventy to a hundred people. A few years ago, the organisation sent a delegation to Ireland on a trade mission. Several members of the group are also active in the Ireland–Canada Chamber of Commerce, the Ireland Fund of Canada and were involved in the development of Ireland Park in Toronto, opened in 2007 by Irish President, Mary McAleese, which commemorates Irish immigration to Toronto during the famine of the 1840s.[86]

Craig felt that his attendance at group events had altered his previously held staunchly Unionist views. He was very hopeful about the peace process in Northern Ireland and was personally committed to doing his part, fully realising that social deprivation in his old neighbourhood was part of the problem and that business development that would create more employment had to be part of the solution:

I certainly have tried to promote business back and forth to the North ...
[I'm] direct at saying, 'Yeah, the war is over, it's open for business.' I have

a certain influence in my circle and I try to direct business to Belfast. I could have taken it to Dublin, I could have taken it to New Brunswick, I tried to direct it to Belfast. And would I be doing that if I was a Canadian who had forgotten about Ireland, cutting off the Irish ties? No, I wouldn't have done that.

'The secret of Canada': Conclusion

For interwar immigrants to Canada like Leo, helpful contacts, hard work and marrying into a Canadian family were all factors that enabled upward mobility. For post-war immigrants of the 1950s and 1960s, such as Harry, Heather, Craig and John, from different class backgrounds, Canada generally proved to be a land of opportunity, adventure and available employment. Immigrants who arrived during the 1970s, such as Cas and Colette, Bríd, Liz and Sheila were subject to increasingly restrictive immigration and employment policies, including the point system of immigrant selection. Thus their situation was considerably more challenging and all of them underwent changes of career in order to remain employed. For Martin and Eve, highly educated people who emigrated in the late 1980s and early 1990s respectively, finding steady employment was much more difficult. In his interview, Martin described many hard knocks and periods working in lousy jobs before eventually managing to get into investment banking, which despite its status is high pressure, strictly performance-dependent and therefore inherently precarious. Yet Martin was very positive about Canada and one has the sense that this was in part driven by his experience of having overcome tough obstacles. Over the twelve years in Canada, Eve had had difficulty finding steady employment in the film industry and was often out of work for lengthy periods. Unlike most of the others Eve had the impression, like my taxi driver Mahmoud at the beginning of this chapter, that she would have done better in the UK than in Canada. She also missed the support of her family especially since the birth of her son in 2002. Likewise, Cas and Colette in Windsor Ontario, whose only child, an adult son, lives in England, expressed the anxiety of growing old away from family:

> I had a wonderful life over there [in Northern Ireland], I really had. And like had we stayed over there, financially we would have been much better off. We did it [emigrated] because we felt emotionally and politically and culturally things weren't working out in terms of the social dimensions of that time. But as you get older you don't have family. Like I've lost all the experience of nephews and nieces and brothers and sisters and so on and so forth – they all live their own lives. And as we get older, at the end of the day I'm here and I've no family. We've no family (Cas, interview, Windsor, ON, VMR–068).

Nevertheless, Cas felt that despite their initial difficulties, their overall experience in Canada had been positive. While he and Colette had both established careers in Ontario, in social terms they had also been instrumental in their community, as founding members of their local Irish society, as founder organisers of an annual Irish cultural festival and many charitable events. In this way, Cas looked at migration as a two-way street; that as immigrants with a good Northern Ireland education, they were well-equipped to avail of Canada's opportunities but in turn have themselves as immigrants made a significant contribution to Canadian society:

> I think we have done ourselves proud in many ways. And you know it's been a real pleasure – not a pleasure – but a privilege to have been a member of Canadian society coming from Northern Ireland because I think that basis, that foundation, that that society has given us has been a wonderful sort of platform for us to do what we can do (interview, Windsor, ON, VMR–068).

A year after his interview for this study, Richard from Cookstown informed me with apparent relief that he had at last been granted permanent resident status which gave him the right to work in Canada and to apply for Canadian citizenship after three years. Ironically, of all the migrants in our study that went to Canada, it was Richard, with direct Canadian ancestry (his grandmother) who experienced the most difficulty in gaining entry to Canada because his lack of formal qualifications didn't rank him highly enough in the point system of immigrant selection. Without the help of his Irish contacts who provided him with 'Canadian work experience' and assisted him through the application process, it is unlikely that Richard would have been granted permanent residency.

In spite of his good fortune in Canada, Craig remained emotionally ambivalent about his identification with it. As he pointed out, his family was spread out all over Canada. His two children live in Saskatchewan and his parents, who moved to Canada from Belfast when they retired, are buried in British Columbia, where Craig's sister lives. In his words, they might as well be buried 'on the moon'. He asked the poignant question, 'Where is home anymore?' (interview, Toronto, VMR–064). Notwithstanding John's position as a prominent academic, his relationship to Canada was also rather ambivalent: he firmly rejected the description of himself as 'Irish–Canadian' and admitted that he took out Canadian citizenship recently 'purely for convenience'. However, John believed that Canada's tolerant politics – 'the dulling of politics to uncreative mediocrity' (Torrance, 1986: 103) – might provide a good model for conflicted societies like Northern Ireland:[87]

> Because I think anytime there was a crisis, this place would set up a committee and it would turn into something incredibly boring. That's *the*

189

secret of Canada [laughter]. Everybody has to be respectful and talk about it and try to find a solution and they would end up with a compromise ... In Northern Ireland people tried to be dominant over the other and certain people like me felt, well, a plague on both your houses. I don't like the Montagues and I don't like the Capulets.[88] Why don't the Montagues and the Capulets respect each other and get on and have boring committee meetings? ... A little less excitement, please, yeah, less fury (interview, Toronto, VMR–061).

Although from the late 1960s, Northern Ireland immigrants to Canada lost their official status as 'preferred' category immigrants and many encountered difficulties related to employment and career progression, the experiences of our interviewees has demonstrated that they, nevertheless, retained informal privileges in comparison to visible minority immigrants in that they did not face discrimination based on race, religion, class or language. Accordingly, their situation differed considerably from that of their compatriots who migrated to Britain. Comparatively, those bound for Canada discovered that 'the secret of Canada' was 'a very tolerant country' indeed. Conversely, the next chapter treats the experiences of migrants who returned home to a not so 'tolerant country' – Northern Ireland.

Chapter 7

'I'm back where I belong': Return Migration

Returning Home: 'I'm back where I belong'

Marie, a woman in her late sixties, grew up in the prosperous south Dublin suburb of Blackrock. Her mother, Catherine, born into a Fermanagh farming family that worshiped in a Plymouth Brethren congregation, had decided at the age of eighteen after a life-threatening experience to convert to Catholicism. As a result, Catherine was expelled from the family home in Fermanagh forbidden ever to return, so she travelled to Dublin where she made her conversion official and subsequently married a man from a middle-class Catholic family. Marie was born the following year but when only two years old, her mother Catherine died suddenly of a congenital heart condition and Marie's father, unable to cope with a young child, left her with a local shopkeeper in Blackrock who raised her. Her father's family wanted little to do with her because they considered her a 'Protestant', her mother's Fermanagh family likewise because to them she was a 'Catholic'. The confusion surrounding Marie's identity persisted throughout her childhood and while attending a convent boarding school, she felt the nuns attributed her every failing and misdemeanour to her 'Protestant' background. Marie, nevertheless, apparently put all this behind her when she left school: she lived through a troubled first marriage, raised eight children and in the mid-1980s emigrated from Dublin with her second husband first to Spain, then to England and back again to Spain where they ran several successful businesses. In 2003, Marie and her husband returned to Ireland because she felt a strong pull to be at home. Although they returned to Dublin, Marie felt unsettled and delayed purchasing a house. One day she persuaded her husband to get into the car and drive to Enniskillen. She described her feelings on arriving in Fermanagh for the very first time. 'I had this feeling now that I'm here, I'd come back. Now *I'm back where I belong.*'

They made an immediate decision to relocate to Fermanagh and only a few days after moving into their house outside Enniskillen, Marie answered a knock at her front door to a man who introduced himself with, 'Hello, I believe I'm your cousin David.' Since then Marie has become acquainted with her Fermanagh family and is thus known locally by association as a Protestant, although she does not hide the fact that she remains 'officially' a Catholic. For her, however, the specifics of denomination are unimportant; what is vital is that she understands how her ties to this Fermanagh place, to her people and their Protestant identity, have had such a huge impact on her own identity and lifelong feelings of alienation and migrancy:

> When you do all the travelling we've done, you don't belong anywhere. You really don't belong anywhere. I find out where the library is and where I get my groceries and I'm in. That's it. That's all it means to me normally, but this is different. This has taken over from Dublin and Blackrock and Killiney and all the places I used to love. This is my place here and this is where I am going to stay. Now I've got to the point, I have a grave in Dublin and I think I'm going to be buried in Enniskillen. How about that for commitment! ... I'm not leaving it ... The pull is here, the pull is here. I don't know what it is but there. And I can't deny it. I don't want to deny it. And I get all weepy about it and I think if I had to leave it I'd die. I'd shrivel up and die (interview, Omagh, VMR–030).

Of all the stories told to me during the research process, Marie's story epitomises most the paradox of Irish identity, illustrating the complexities of belonging to a country, to people, to family and of how each of us may be connected to places over generations. Such emotional geographies (Anderson and Smith, 2001; Pile, 2010) – which in Marie's case included postmemories of County Fermanagh, a place she had never even visited – are bound up with family history and identity as the places described in stories, their place names repeated, are passed down the generations. The emotional connection to place so characteristic of 'diaspora memory' (Chamberlain, 2009) is thus depicted in family narratives of leaving and returning over generations, often imbued with power that is beyond explanation or expression. In some instances, it may even impel individuals to action which may appear to others as ill-conceived, as with Marie's apparently sudden decision to relocate to Fermanagh.

The issue of return is complex, multi-layered and usually remains ever present for the emigrant through the lifespan and often for their descendants as well. It not only raises questions about where one should live and where to raise children and grandchildren, but perhaps even more poignantly, about where one should die and be buried. Indeed, such practical concerns about life and death were raised time and again during the research process with migrants who had returned to Ireland and most particularly, with those who had not. Through their stories, it has been possible to examine return from a variety of perspectives and experiences. In the case of the returnees, they spoke of their decision to return, their arrival back home and the reception they received from family and friends; the process of integration which included searching for employment and the settling of spouses and children, many of whom were not Irish-born. While the focus of the research was on people of working age, some interviewees had returned for retirement or early semi-retirement and had left children and grandchildren abroad. All of the returnees related their impressions and opinions about change in Ireland, North and South, which included their views about economic development and modernisation and most specifically about the Peace Process in the North. Emigrants or non-returnees still living outside Ireland were also consulted about whether they would consider returning to live in Ireland and their reflections gave especially valuable insights into the decision-making process surrounding return. Before turning to their stories, however, a brief summary of the typologies of return is presented.

Return migration: definitions

Return migration has long been a significant aspect of European migration. While the reverse flow of emigrants from the 'new world' to the 'old' since the earliest days of exploration and settlement has been noted, study of this phenomenon has received less attention from scholars than the topic of emigration for several reasons. The lack of reliable quantifiable data on return flows coupled with the unwelcome critique of the destination 'settlement societies' that return might suggest have made study of return a difficult task.[1] Nevertheless, increasing intra-European migration since the Second World War in which the return of migrant workers was a significant component began to generate interest in the topic as far back as the 1960s, resulting in the organisation of an international OECD seminar and publication of a major report (Reverdy, 1967).[2] Since then, several surveys of the literature and methods employed to investigate return migration have been undertaken, particularly relating to Europe.[3] In addition, there is a growing literature relating to the emigration and return of specific European national, ethnic and class groups, and some scholars have attempted to define typologies of return migration within the overall perspective of multi-directional migration processes.[4] Most recently, the concept of 'return mobilities' encompasses the many forms of return located theoretically within mobilities, transnational and diaspora approaches (King and Christou, 2011).

Return migration is usually defined as a person's return to place of origin or 'homeland' after a period resident elsewhere. Re-emigration then occurs when the returnee emigrates away from the home country once again to reside back in the host country. From the host country's perspective this phenomenon, increasingly common in settler societies like Canada, has been called return immigration

(King and Newbold, 2008). When the movement between the home and host country becomes more frequent it is often called circular migration or seasonal migration when it occurs on a regularised basis. 'Transilient migration' (King, 1986: 4–5; Morawska, 1991: 277) or 'transient migration' (Dustmann and Weiss, 2007: 238) refer to the process where the migrant rather than returning to the place of origin moves on to yet a third or fourth country, and so on. Return migration may also take place within national boundaries (e.g., from northern to southern Italy) and thus be a form of internal migration. Another important type of return migration takes a multi-generational form when children or descendants of original emigrants return to the ancestral place of origin. Hence, this has sometimes been called 'ancestral return' (King, 1986: 6; Nash, 2008) or 'diasporic return' (Tsuda, 2009: 1); the concept here brings to mind organised political returns that are often as a result of conflict, the redrawing of national boundaries and/or the creation or recreation of nation states (e.g., repatriation of Jews to Israel). These incidences of return may be forced rather than voluntary as was the case of the exchange of people of Greek origin from Asia Minor, now Turkey, and those of Turk origin from Greece in 1923 – the displacement of some two million individuals.

Another way of framing return migration is based on the economic balance between home and host societies. The most common scenario is the return of migrant workers employed in developed countries back to less industrialised home countries, thus movement from first world back to third world. A second type, colonial or multinational return, represents a relationship where elites return from former colonies or resource rich countries under development by multinational corporations (for oil, minerals, etc.), thus from third world back to first world. British and American citizens working for extended periods abroad in the employ of multinational oil companies, in places like West Africa or Indonesia, are an example of this form of migration. Third, an emigration and return flow that takes place between relatively equal first-world countries (e.g., the United Kingdom and the United States) represents the scenario that is the focus of this chapter.

The investigation of migrant intentionality in which migration is viewed from the perspective of length of stay abroad, or stage in the life cycle of the migrant, represents another way of framing the study of emigration and return. Thus, temporary migrants are defined as those who had always intended to return. Their duration of stay may be short or long periods; however, sometimes the return gets postponed until retirement (Malcolm, 1996). There are also migrants who always intended to return and thus maintain an 'ideology of return' (Brettell, 1979), that is, a dream or 'myth of return' (Anwar, 1979) but who in the end for a variety of reasons never return to live in the home place. Then there are the migrants who intended to remain abroad but who decide to return sometimes due to family circumstances (death), improving circumstances in the home economy or failure to adapt to the host society, what Cerase (1974: 249) in his study of returning Italians called the 'return of failure'. Seldom discussed are the migrants who intended to remain abroad permanently and did not consider returning. Individuals who fit this category of migrant are included in the present study. Of course it is important to point out that many migrants (probably even the majority) emigrate on a trial basis without concrete future plans. It is also important to consider the reasons for the return, in terms of push and pull factors in the home and host societies, which can be influenced by economic conditions, social circumstances especially concerning family, personal attitudes to nationality and culture, and environmental factors such as landscape and climate.

Another framework employed in return migration studies has been to examine the impact of the returned migrant on the home society. This includes consideration of the remittances sent prior to return; money and capital brought back and spent or invested upon return; impact of returnee skills and attitudes as potential modernising influences on the economy or social and political development of the home society; and the influence of the returnees on further emigration from their home communities.

Finally, the points above prompt the question of whether return is even possible, inasmuch as the returnee is greatly changed by experience from their former self at the time of departure and the place to which they return is not the same place they left.[5] This is suggested by some of the experiences detailed in this chapter which demonstrate a need to transcend simplistic models of return in order to account for circulatory, multi-directional and multigenerational processes of mobility (King and Christou, 2011: 460). Mindful of the role of memory in this process, the discussion now turns to an exploration of the return mobilities of migrants from Northern Ireland. Like looking through a prism, consideration of return afforded migrants the examination and interrogation of home and host societies from many angles and heightened their awareness of identity issues, societal change and conflict.

Dream of Return: 'Nobody knows me there'

Discussion of return among populations of expatriates has often been framed by constructs such as the 'myth of return' (Anwar, 1979; Ganga, 2006; etc.), the myth of no return (Burrell, 2006; Sarna, 1981) or the vision or dream of return:

> I think everybody who leaves Ireland - maybe it's the same with every emigrant – has a yearning or maybe a desire, dream of some kind of going back at some point (Kevin, Toronto, VMR–063).

In the particular case of migrants who depart the homeland due to political or sectarian strife, some can have no dream of return; for others return may only be envisioned in terms of future conflict resolution. What became clear among our informants was that even for those who could not or would not contemplate return, the decision in no way lessened their sense of Irish or Northern Irish identity. In the study of non-returnees, a pre-interview questionnaire sent out to all participants prior to interview included the question, 'Would you consider returning to live in Northern Ireland?' Of the forty-eight non-returnees, nineteen ticked 'no', seven selected 'yes', three chose 'only for retirement' and thirteen ticked 'maybe' in the response boxes provided. Six individuals did not respond to the question, possibly an oversight. The issue of return was then discussed during the interviews. As the participants weighed the pros and cons of return, concerns were raised about the impact on children and other family members, finding employment, retirement, climate and environment, political accommodation and the Peace Process. Significantly, issues surrounding death and burial were often raised spontaneously by participants. For many emigrants like Ciaran, who spent the 1980s working in the construction industry in England, the United States and even for a brief period in Australia, it was the example of older emigrants from the previous generation that motivated his decision to return home:

> One of the reasons I could never stay away was because I met old emigrants who lived in England in the pubs and they were so sad and they would say, 'I can't go back home, all my family's dead. They wouldn't know me if I went back.' Or in America, I used to meet old Irish people and they would say the same, or they would say, 'Sure look, my kids are all American now, my grandkids are American. I'm not American although I've lived here sixty-five years ... I'm Irish, but I can't live in Ireland because *nobody knows me there*'. And I found that so sad that I remember saying consciously to myself, 'I'm never going to be like that person there. I'm never going to wind up in that situation if I can manage it' (interview, Omagh, VMR–024).

Many of the interviewees, like Ciaran, felt that there was a time limit to being abroad after which point – 'now or never'– a definite decision about return had to be made. While the desire for adventure and employment prospects often featured largely in decisions to emigrate, it was primarily family issues that fuelled the question of whether or not to return. Several of the non-returnees, for example, who thought they had made permanent decisions earlier in their lives to remain abroad, found that the issue of return came up later due to a change in personal or family circumstances, especially involving divorce, remarriage, the birth of children or illness and death.

Failed Return: 'Take your political views and shut up'

Many of the non-returned group also revealed experience of what has often been called 'failed return'; in other words they had actually returned to Northern Ireland at an earlier period in their lives but later re-emigrated. In most of these cases, the conflict was the principal factor motivating the individuals who chose to re-emigrate.

Larry from East Belfast set out with a friend on the steamship *H.M.T. Asturias* of the Orient Line departing from Southampton bound for Australia on 28 November 1951 when he was nineteen years old. He travelled around Australia and worked at a variety of jobs which included being a bus conductor in Melbourne; a sorter in a candy factory; labouring at a potato research station in Victoria; picking fruit in Queensland; and being a boundary rider on horseback at a sheep station in New South Wales. Larry loved Australia, especially working in the outdoors, but after two years he made good on his promise to his mother to return home to Belfast for a visit where he stayed for several months working at a local grocery shop, nurturing the firm intention of returning to Australia. While at home and upon a chance meeting, he decided to accompany a friend who was going to Canada and from there intended to make his way back to Australia. His mother was not pleased that he was leaving again:

> I had to tell her I'm taking off again but I'm going to Canada. And I can remember her remark was, 'Oh well that's not so far.' Yeah, but I'm thinking of going on back to Australia again. She didn't like that. That was too far away. But anyways, that was that and was my intention (interview, Guelph, ON, VMR–067).

Larry recalled that shortly after he arrived in Toronto in November 1954, he arranged his onward passage to Australia which involved going to San Francisco by train and then getting a ship from there.[6] As luck would have it, after a few months in Canada, Larry met his future wife – a Canadian – and shortly after he cashed in his ticket to Australia.

Several years later while employed in Toronto for an international business headquartered in Birmingham, the firm requested that Larry come to England for a year. Not wanting to be separated from his wife and children, he rented out their house in Toronto and moved the family to Bangor, near Belfast, where his parents and brother lived. Larry commuted from Belfast to Birmingham for several months and was at home in Bangor every weekend but this was 1972, the Troubles were in full fury and adjustment to the tense situation was difficult for his Canadian family who had no experience of such conflict. Though Bangor was less affected by the Troubles, there were over the years several serious incidents, including two bomb explosions in the main street in March 1972, the time

197

Figure 7.1: Passengers boarding airplane, Aldergrove Airport, County Antrim, c. 1970 (National Museums Northern Ireland, Photograph Library, Yt5141)

Larry's family was in residence.[7] When his wife became seriously ill and was hospitalised due to what Larry described as a 'nervous breakdown', he arranged to move the family quickly back to Toronto.

Brian also returned to Northern Ireland in 1972. He was only in his early twenties and had spent a couple of years in Liverpool when his brother became seriously ill with kidney failure. Brian returned to help his widowed mother manage the situation which involved transporting his sick brother to and from the City Hospital for dialysis several times per week. His brother would be dropped at the hospital in the afternoon and would not be ready for pick-up until one in the morning. Brian recalled, 'I can remember sitting in the car park there listening to the gunfire coming across.' Brian stayed in Belfast for a couple of years and witnessed the terrible violence of the time. He remembered being deeply affected by the bombing of the Abercorn Restaurant in March 1972[8] and some months later the terror of the day known as Bloody Friday when bombs went off all over Belfast:[9]

> The bombs were going off all around you so it was pandemonium. The difficulty describing that is that because of my politics I was one

of these people who would have been sympathetic to the objectives of the Republicans at that time but not committed towards – I always have been a pacifist. I would have said the way they're doing it is wrong but their objectives and the sort of things which are driving all this are understandable, unemployment in particular. I always thought unemployment was the engine of the Troubles (interview, Liverpool, VMR–054).

After two years at home, Brian gave up his job in Belfast and returned to Liverpool. Despite the terrible violence he had witnessed during his stay, he recalled that probably due to his youthful age at the time it was not the physical threat that worried him. Rather, it was ideological difference and the sense that he would be silenced that impelled him to leave:

> You would have had to *take your political views* and put them in your back pocket *and shut up* about them probably. I don't mean Nationalist views, I mean wider political views where you're saying where there's injustice it should be put right.

Brian has since built a career in the social care field and has particular experience working with adolescent males who have 'social' problems. While he has been quite active in his community on social justice and environmental issues, Brian does not believe that he would have been free to be an activist had he stayed in Northern Ireland. Despite his middle-class background – his father was a doctor (GP) – and having an uncommon surname that was more likely to be perceived as Protestant, he nevertheless felt that even as a (non-practising) Catholic, his life choices would be limited:

> So I do feel now that that sectarian situation – the way Northern Ireland society was set up – has really impacted a lot on my life chances and so on, certainly in the first half of my life … That first half of my life was very reactive to the fact that there was a label put on me about where I was from and what I was by other people. And that was also, all of that social pressure was dictating things to do with what I could believe in, where I could socialise, what career I could have, and all those things. And I just felt I've got to get out of this and go to someplace where all that doesn't exist and where I can be free to develop the way I want to.

Brian and his wife, who is of Irish descent, have toyed with the notion of return, but not to Northern Ireland. In the mid-1990s, they bought a house in County Galway with the idea that they might return permanently and find jobs there. So far they have only used the house for holidays and rented it out when they were away. Thus, Brian's dream of return is entangled with the myth of the rural west of Ireland; the wellspring of real Irishness where the Irish abroad over generations have come to recharge their cultural batteries.[10] However, having grown children in Liverpool has been a deterrent to returning to Ireland, but also, the significant friendships that Brian has built up over the years there. This is particularly important for him since he remembers a childhood when as the only Catholic family in their neighbourhood, he and his brothers had few friends.

Although Brian had not considered permanent return to Northern Ireland because of his experience of the conflict earlier in his life, for those like Larry who had initially left Northern Ireland in the 1950s, the Troubles did not appear to feature in their decision to return but was very much a factor in their decision not to stay. Such was the case of Heather whose story of emigration to Canada in 1959 appeared in Chapter 6. Heather currently lives in Ottawa, Ontario and worked as a physiotherapist for most of her adult life until she took early retirement several years ago. Having originally emigrated in 1959 from Belfast to Edmonton, Alberta, she lived an adventurous life in western Canada including several years working in a largely aboriginal community in the Northwest Territories. When her mother died in 1987, Heather, herself a widow, had envisaged the possibility of returning to Northern Ireland permanently upon retirement to be close to her brother. In preparation for this possible move, she used her inheritance to purchase a house in the Castlereagh area of South Belfast and began to spend summers there. She remembered that by the mid-1990s the conflict appeared to be settling down and 'there was a positive outlook and things were definitely looking better'. Thus, she was very disappointed when political activities took a turn for the worse and disturbances began in her neighbourhood. The marching season in the summer of 1996 was particularly bad. She was shocked when the corner shop was burned down and young rioters ran up and down the streets throwing missiles. Heather couldn't bear to sit in her front room looking out at the mayhem:

> I remember just closing the door and going into the back room, turning the wireless on, and being cosy and thinking, I'm just going to shut that world out. And then I thought to myself, if I'm going to shut that world out I might as well give up this house. And I did, I sold it. I wasn't willing to go back over there and face that. *I didn't grow up with that …* And I wouldn't go back and volunteer to face that kind of friction again (interview, Ottawa, VMR–074).

Having grown up in the 1940s and 1950s – the post-war years often remembered as relatively free of sectarian violence – Heather distanced herself from what she believed was a conflict concocted by others after she left Northern Ireland and for which she bore no responsibility. Despite the rather negative experience of return, however, Heather continues to visit her brother and friends in Northern Ireland on a regular basis. She has closed the door, however, on the possibility of permanent return despite having few family ties in Canada:

> I doubt now that I would ever return permanently. I don't think I would. But I'm sure I will keep up very regular visits and contacts because I love my brother, I love my friends ... I still like going over. Could I reintegrate? I probably could reintegrate if I were going but I think I would choose not to bother.

Heather's decision against returning to Northern Ireland was also connected with her feelings about cultural identity. Having been involved with an Irish drama group in Ottawa which stages one or two productions every year, she was unsure whether she would have the same freedom to choose her cultural activities in Belfast because of the politics:

> To be able to do these things without any political agenda is wonderful. To feel that you belong to the whole of Ireland. And I don't think I'd ever not feel that I belonged to the whole of Ireland even though my background is Scots-Irish ... You know when people ask me where I come from I say Ireland. I definitely say I come from Ireland.

Several interviewees mentioned that experience gained abroad was not beneficial to finding employment in Northern Ireland. While most felt that they had gained from their experience, many also felt that it actually counted against them upon return. Susan left Belfast in 1976 to pursue university education in London. From there she went on to Brussels and Paris and then back to London where she worked as a French teacher in what was known as a 'tough' comprehensive school in the Shepherd's Bush district where the student body was largely comprised of ethnic minorities and new immigrants. She also took some time off to travel extensively in India and Nepal. In 1984, with the intention of returning home permanently, Susan began applying for teaching jobs in the Belfast area:

> I thought on paper I'd brilliant experience, having travelled to India and Nepal after I'd done my teacher training ... and then taught in London. I thought that was fantastic experience (interview, Belfast, VMR–034).

However, this was the mid-1980s and times were tough so in addition to filling out application forms, Susan headed to Belfast and began visiting schools in the hope of getting an interview. She found that the school officials were not at all interested in her experience outside Northern Ireland and she was dismayed by the 'strong Christian evangelical element' in the state school sector.

'What were you doing in India? Were you visiting mission stations?' one principal asked me … And then [me] saying, 'Well no, but I did visit a school in Nepal' but they didn't want to talk about that.

From a middle-class Protestant background, Susan had been raised with liberal values and was interested in the different religions and cultures she had encountered in her London school and on her travels. Unable even to obtain a formal interview for a teaching job in Northern Ireland, Susan, nevertheless, nurtured a strong desire to return home. She decided to stay in England a while longer and train in the IT field, thinking to make herself more employable in Northern Ireland. Though she eventually returned to Belfast some years later, overall she felt that in Northern Ireland work experience abroad 'doesn't actually get you economic success, it doesn't get you a lot of recognition' though she acknowledged that, 'it makes you the person you are':

> But if people get left behind and stay here, and a lot of people do, they're a bit jealous and a bit threatened by people who've been away and come back with these big ideas and funny accents.[11]

These examples of 'failed' or 'attempted' return illustrate some of the real difficulties faced by Northern Ireland returnees. The atmosphere of conflict in 1972 was too difficult for Larry's Canadian family members to adjust to and he regretted ever having brought them to Northern Ireland. The desire to return home was paramount for Susan and though the conflict did not factor in her decision-making, the lack of employment opportunities in Northern Ireland kept her in England. For Brian and Heather, while issues of physical threat were apparent, it was primarily the continuing sectarianism and the lack of political, cultural and social freedom that made return to Northern Ireland too restrictive. Belonging to Ireland 'as a whole' was easier from abroad.

No Return: 'Not in my name'

Mary, aged in her late fifties, from a small village in south Armagh, moved to the Greater London area in 1971 to take up a teaching post where she married a northern Protestant whom she had met while a student at Queen's University in Belfast. For Mary, there could be no dream of return. Because of her mixed marriage and unfavourable conditions at home, she felt strongly that they could not raise Catholic children with a Protestant surname in Northern Ireland and she didn't ever plan to return to live there.[12] She felt fortunate not to have experienced direct hostility in England as a result of the IRA bombing campaigns, probably due to her professional position as a teacher, but she recalled feeling a sense of shame and responsibility, and empathised with the current situation of Muslims in Britain:

We just felt very embarrassed about being from Northern Ireland ... And while all those bombings were going on in England, the Guildford bomb and all the rest of it, I was working in Surrey at that time and nobody ostracized me in my work or anything. But you felt so bad ... Like those slogans on the anti-war march '*not in my name*' you felt that people were almost bound to be associating you with that ... We can identify with how Muslim people feel because we know what that felt like in a much less difficult way (interview, West Sussex, VMR–083).

Margaret, the youngest of four children, grew up on a farm in southwest Tyrone, which her father, himself a returned emigrant, had purchased in 1932 after many years in the dry goods business in Scotland and New York. Growing up with their father's stories of his travels, Margaret described that she and her siblings were 'raised with a spirit of adventure' and how from an early age she had nurtured the desire to emigrate. Thus, shortly after her marriage in 1968, even though they were both employed, Margaret persuaded her husband to emigrate with her from Northern Ireland to Toronto. They had just purchased but not yet moved into their first house there in 1973 when Margaret's husband was suddenly killed in an accident at work. With three children under five and only a small amount of insurance money from the accident, Margaret was encouraged to move the family back to Northern Ireland. From her former boss in Tyrone she received the offer of her old job and Margaret's mother found out that benefits for widows were far superior in Northern Ireland to what was then on offer in Canada. Still, Margaret was uneasy about the move, not, she insisted, because of the onset of the Troubles, but rather due to the conservative nature of the society. Though at first she felt inclined to leave Canada, she decided not to rush into the decision:

I knew that if I went back with three children as a 30-year-old widow that I was going to be monitored and watched very carefully. And I didn't want that. I had great freedom here. This is a very free society to live in, in Canada, and I didn't want to be part of that again. I had grown away from that and didn't want to go back to it (interview, Toronto, VMR–070).

By the end of the year, Margaret had decided to stay in Toronto and put all the compensation money into paying for the house. A few years later, she remarried and went on to have three more children. Over the years, Margaret has been very active in the Irish community in Toronto, as a founding member of the Tyrone Association and an active member of the Action Grosse Ile committee which lobbied to have the immigration station designated as the Irish National Memorial Historic Site.[13] She has remained in close contact with her sister in Tyrone and visits Northern Ireland every few years.

After over forty years in Canada, Herb and Edith visited Northern Ireland for the first time since they'd left West Belfast in 1957. The trip was a gift from their four sons who 'wanted to send us home'. Despite the huge amount of change in Northern Ireland in the intervening years, Herb and Edith were both struck by the beauty of the country and the smaller scale of the geography than they remembered. While they enjoyed the trip enormously, neither had any desire to return permanently, though for Edith it awakened strong feelings. 'You were home or something. It was just a feeling of home. Oh, I loved it.' Herb spoke about the impracticality of returning home which also had a lot to do with the reasons he left in the first place:

> I never was into this sort of sectarian thing. And like I never voted
> Unionist ... When I started to vote the Labour Party was trying to make
> a bit of an inroad and I could never understand people being manipulated
> on their religious grounds and like voting in blocks ... I didn't get into
> that scene, you know, as far as the Protestant Catholic thing. So that was
> another reason I was glad to leave Northern Ireland and another reason
> why over the years I would never consider going back to Northern Ireland
> because it got worse after I left. I was walking up the Springfield Road one
> night and they threw a hand grenade at a policeman outside Springfield
> Road Barracks. We were just down the street from it. Almost killed the
> guy ... I thought what is this all about? Such a beautiful country! And
> they managed to get everybody turned against each other (interview,
> Toronto, VMR–071).

Richard, in his mid-thirties from Cookstown living in Toronto since the early 2000s, was concerned that he would not have the same opportunity in Northern Ireland as he would in Canada because of what he called the class 'conditioning'. Despite the fact that at the time of his interview he was experiencing difficulties with the immigration process in Canada due to his lack of formal qualifications, it was in Northern Ireland that he felt this would be more harshly judged and in addition, that his Canadian work experience would not impress. He also mentioned that since most of his cohort of friends now lived in England it would be difficult for him to integrate socially if he returned. However, the sectarian attitudes he remembered, which he admitted to once harbouring himself, were of most concern. For despite the political and social changes there in recent years which he acknowledged, Richard also felt that those same old attitudes remained underneath and the past still retained considerable power:

> I know Northern Ireland has changed in terms of the day to day tension
> with the politics, however, you still have the psyche of three or four
> hundred years that may never go away. But so long as we're not killing

each other, great ... Like will I go back to a more narrow viewpoint or entrenched way compared to the way I operate out here? I don't know. I would like to think that I wouldn't. But when you go back into your formative years' environment, who knows? That could trigger everything back the way it had been (interview, Toronto, VMR–072).

While reasons for not returning to Northern Ireland varied considerably among the emigrants, the political situation and the conservative nature of the society were the two principal reasons militating against return. Just as most of the emigrants had not left for purely economic reasons, financial concerns were not the primary factor in their decisions to stay abroad. This is particularly evident in the case of Margaret, the young widow who would have had much more financial and family support in Northern Ireland than in Canada. Similarly, Herb had been employed in a good post office job when he and Edith left Northern Ireland with their young son, but for over forty years they had never experienced any desire to return, preferring to bring other family members over to live with them in Toronto. Mary felt that the difficulties of coping with a 'mixed' marriage in Northern Ireland were insurmountable thus return was simply not an option. However, it is disquieting that for a young migrant of the post-conflict era like Richard, it is fear that the past might still be strong enough to pull him back to sectarian ways of thinking that keeps him away.

After Return: 'We found we were in trouble with both sides'

For many people return to Northern Ireland, and most especially to the Belfast area, meant returning to a place of conflict; those who returned did so primarily for family reasons and in spite of the ongoing sectarianism. After seven years of living in the Canadian Arctic, Harry, however, returned to Belfast in the mid-1960s with his German-born wife and two children, prior to the outbreak of full conflict. They returned somewhat reluctantly for their children's education and immediately missed the outdoor lifestyle, close community and the Inuit people they had come to admire. In comparison, life in Northern Ireland at first appeared rather tame, but this was not to last as the civil rights movement got underway and sectarian unrest began to surface. Around this time, Harry and his brothers bought a haulage firm and a little while later purchased the Great Northern Mineral Company which had large premises on the Shankill Road in West Belfast. They moved the haulage business to their Shankill Road location and immediately began to experience difficulties because most of their drivers were Catholics. Not wanting to lay off their employees they decided to sell the haulage part of the business, employees, contracts and all. Because their family name was perceived as a Catholic name in Northern Ireland, Harry and his brothers also put out the word in the local community that they were actually a Protestant family in the hope that this would reduce sectarian tensions. The strategy did not work, however, as the general belief that their company was owned by Catholics persisted. The irony was that the family name came with Harry's grandfather from Wales to Dublin, that Harry's uncles served and died in the British Army during the First World War and that Harry's father, a Dublin Protestant whose story was presented in Chapter 3, had come north as a political exile at the time of partition to help establish the first Northern Ireland civil service. But as Harry described, the conflict was bad for business and *'we found we were in trouble with both sides'*:

> Because it [mineral bottling company] was where it was [Shankill], most of those drivers were Protestant. And some of them were way out Protestant. We had a case where the police rung us up and told us, 'Get the hell out quickly and rescue one of your vans which is besieged in the Falls Road flying two Union Jacks.' For a starter how much more stuff were we going to sell on the Falls Road with that? … People had turned against us down in Belfast and they actually burned us out in the end. Our lorries were taken out into the barricades (interview, Armagh, VMR–043).

Harry's family eventually managed to sell the Shankill Road premises and transferred their mineral bottling business to the town of Armagh, from where for many years they had a monopoly supplying bottled drinks along the border from Newry to Rosslea.

Return in the context of conflict was a difficult adjustment for those, like Harry, who had left during more peaceful times or for others who had left areas relatively untouched by unrest only to come back to neighbourhoods where disturbances were quite frequent. In some cases, people had simply forgotten or become unused to sectarian ways of thinking and behaving. One interviewee likened his feelings upon return to 'putting on an old suit of clothes which did not fit right anymore and wasn't comfortable' (VMR–033). Although return migration always requires a period of adjustment, in a situation of ethnic conflict, issues are more complex and the consequences may be very serious.

Christine reported that her first real encounter with the conflict was as an adult, after she returned to Belfast from Reading with her English husband in the autumn of 1999, both of them to take up professional jobs. Born in the early 1970s and having grown up in Bangor in North Down, Christine was too young to remember the bomb incidents that had terrified Larry's family. She was adamant that the Troubles did not factor significantly in her memories of her youth even though she had attended secondary school at Methodist College in South Belfast and the train on which she had commuted to and from Bangor was regularly disrupted by bomb scares. For despite its proximity to Belfast, North Down as a stronghold of middle-class pro-Union politics was one of the areas in Northern Ireland seemingly least affected by the conflict.[14] Indeed, in her book *Northern Protestants*, Susan McKay (2005) has presented a damning portrayal of North Down as a bastion of middle-class Protestant complacency and political irresponsibility.[15] In the spring of 2000, a few months following their return, Christine and her husband purchased a house 'that looked absolutely beautiful, 1930s setting' in Greenisland on the north shore of Belfast Lough near Carrickfergus, and they moved in shortly after. But as Christine remarked:

> We only went to look at it in April and if we'd gone back, maybe, in June or July, we probably would have got a better sense of what the area was like because it was incredibly Loyalist – you know, painted kerbstones, flags, the lot! (interview, Belfast, VMR–016).

Based on conflict-free memories of growing up in middle-class Bangor, Christine was unprepared for the atmosphere of her new middle-class neighbourhood in Greenisland:

> Where we'd lived – Bangor – rarely has much trouble and certainly at the stage when I'd lived there when I was younger, didn't. So [Greenisland] was really almost kind of my first sort of close at hand experience of it.

That summer of 2000 the Twelfth celebrations were particularly fraught, the protests were on again at Drumcree and tensions were generally high. Christine's Greenisland neighbourhood was sealed off on several occasions and one day she came home to find her street barricaded. She and her husband moved to her parents house in Bangor for a few weeks until the 'celebrations' were over. One particular incident that summer was especially alarming and intolerable:

> There was a house across the road from us that was rented and a family moved into that and within, like, about a week or so, there was suddenly a crowd of people outside throwing stones through the windows. I don't know whether they'd been relocated from somewhere else or what but they weren't wanted, whoever they were, in the area.

After just six months they put their beautiful house back on the market and rented a house in Helen's Bay on the North Down side of Belfast Lough while they considered moving back to England. Living in a less overtly sectarian area gradually gave them the confidence to stay and they eventually purchased another house, this time in Bangor.

Like Christine, Stephen had also grown up in North Down, in Holywood between Belfast and Bangor, where despite having traumatic childhood memories about Bloody Friday in Belfast (July 1972), he had had little direct experience of the conflict in his own neighbourhood. After several years of living in Canada and then in England, Stephen returned to Belfast in July 2000 with his American wife. He was very annoyed at having had to pay an 'exorbitant' price for a house in a street without 'sectarian display'. However, the flags soon began to encroach:

> I remember in the first year, flags went up in our street that year and I was really incensed about that and they were on public lamp posts and I thought my taxes are partly contributing, an infinitesimal amount, but it's contributing to that public lamp post. So I tried to find out who to contact ... So eventually I found the right department and my letter gets forwarded and then I get a standard response ... 'We think it's going to cause more problems if we remove it than if we leave it there.' And there was a number count at the bottom of the letter and I think this must have been the ten thousandth letter or something like that that they'd sent out (interview, Belfast, VMR–015).

When she separated from her American husband in 1996, Elizabeth returned to the Belfast area following eight years in California. She bought a house in Carrickfergus, a bit further east along the shore from Greenisland. Though she had been back in Northern Ireland for nine years at the time of her interview, Elizabeth was still quite ambivalent about her return, saying, 'I can't say I'm glad, no' but also 'I can't say I hate it here.' She loved the easy familiarity of being understood in her own accent, but was dismayed that after so many years of the peace process, sectarianism was still rife. Her description of 'sectarian display' as a foreboding presence is palpable in her narrative:

> You're driving along somewhere and that does something to you, the flags and kerbstones. It makes you feel uncomfortable, it makes you feel you could get beat up here. There's *that territorial thing that is trying to mark its territory* ... Because the opposite side of that is you're driving along in this lovely countryside, thinking oh isn't that beautiful and free. You feel a freeness. When *that thing's there* then it's the opposite, you don't feel free, you feel you're being told something. You can't even *get away from it* (interview, Carrickfergus, VMR–040).

Christine, Stephen and Elizabeth are typical of the generation of middle-class Protestants born since the 1960s who object to ethno-religious labelling and sectarian display, and want a more secular and multicultural society. The display of flags and painted kerbstones, often described as 'lowering the tone' of a neighbourhood, is also a concern because it affects the price and marketability of property and may discourage business. Though associated with lower and working-class neighbourhoods, such displays are occasionally found in middle-class areas, usually Protestant, though it would be difficult to find anyone in these areas responsible for doing the painting. Indeed the *Northern Ireland Life and Times* survey (NILT) in 2008 found that 84 per cent of those surveyed objected to flags on lampposts and approximately 68 per cent believed that they were put there by members of paramilitary organisations. Approximately 40 per cent of respondents said they were less likely to shop in an area that featured such displays.[16]

For Nick in his early fifties, a former missionary priest who had grown up near the border in Clones, County Monaghan and spent over thirty years abroad in South America, sectarianism had not been an important issue since his return in 2004 to Northern Ireland with his Ecuadoran wife and three children. Having left Ecuador because of the very volatile economy, Nick as an older father with young children believed that the UK social welfare system was superior to that of the Republic of Ireland (ROI) and would better ensure his family's future well-being in the event of his own illness or death. Though his own father had been born in Rosslea, County Fermanagh, Nick admitted that as a young man, he had not been supportive of British governance in Northern Ireland and had never considered living there, thus he was surprised to be so readily accepted by the government social services staff who went 'absolutely out of their way' to help him and his family obtain initial welfare benefits to assist their settlement:

> We were basically on everything we needed within a month. Quite solid already. In fairness it is one of the great things about Her Majesty's Government ... I'm very appreciative of the UK Government and how they've dealt with my family while we've been here. Absolutely terrific (interview, Omagh, VMR–028).

At the time of his interview, Nick was employed to work with ethnic communities in County Tyrone and was familiar with the challenges of integration from several perspectives: that of the immigrants he worked with; his own experience helping to integrate his foreign-born spouse and children; and of having himself been an immigrant in a foreign-language environment in South America. Noting that attitudes in Ireland, North and South, had become much more open to outsiders since he emigrated in the 1970s, he was, nevertheless, amazed at the welcoming attitude of the teachers in the integrated school system towards his Spanish-speaking children. However, he believed that the major barrier to integration facing adult immigrants was language and that more language classes were needed especially for them:

> We have to start getting them into language skills. I think that's the biggest gift we can offer them at the moment. The jobs are there, okay, the services are there. There's very little discrimination which people might suspect, but actually there's very little of that as such. The problem is language.

Nick's views are supported by a recent study which noted that since the Belfast/Good Friday Agreement, the Northern Ireland Government's 'Racial Equality' (OFMDFM, 2005); 'Shared future' (OFMDFM, 2006); and 'Cohesion, Sharing and Integration' (OFMDFM, 2010) strategies have not given enough attention to 'the issue of language and language barriers as a cause of non-societal participation' (McDermott, 2011: 252).[17] Overall, however, Nick's experience in Northern Ireland was very positive and he believed that any lingering sectarianism would soon fade away.

For the returnees, return to Ireland was generally constructed as a definite move forward, not as a backward step, as each of them made important career and life changes once settled again in Northern Ireland. Most of the emigrants felt that they had gained substantially from their experiences abroad in terms of personal growth and the acquisition of new skills even when these did not transfer into employment opportunities at home. Many of the returnees experienced considerable difficulties during their resettlement period, most often with employment and housing, and sometimes on a social level as well. In a land where emigration has been the norm, return was not well understood by family, friends and neighbours, and many individuals were greeted with a less-than-positive reception, as in the case of Ciaran, a construction worker, who reported the reaction of the locals in his home village when he returned in the early 1990s:

> 'You must be crazy. How much you were earning? My God! And now you're back here on 30 pounds a week on the dole and the pay is crap here.' The construction industry was flat on its face here in the early 90s (interview, Omagh, VMR–024).

While repatriation could be interpreted as a validation of the home place, it was more often perceived by others as 'failed emigration' and sometimes viewed with suspicion that returnees might be reclaiming rights or property they would have been presumed to have given up when they emigrated. In many cases, emigration had provided a convenient solution to issues surrounding inheritance or the fierce competition for local jobs and many who stayed behind benefitted from the departure of others. However, considering that in 2011, approximately 6.6 per cent of those born in Northern Ireland, resident in the state, claimed to have lived elsewhere – almost half of whom had returned since 2001 – clearly, the positive reception and successful reintegration of returnees is economically and socially important to future prosperity.[18]

Deirdre from Strabane returned to Ireland in 2001 after twenty years in England. For a few years prior to her return, however, she had been involved in managing European Union community development projects in the northwest of Ireland and during that time had travelled to the region on a regular basis. Rather than return to Northern Ireland, Deirdre had built a house on land in

Donegal that had belonged to her grandfather. Despite her ancestral ties to the land, and having been raised only a few miles down the road in Strabane right on the border, she was surprised to find that the locals viewed her as a 'six-county Northerner':

> In spite of coming here [regularly], being based here and so on, I found that when I came back to live it had changed even more than I had realised from that contact. I think there's a lot of resentment and jealousy … I have found that there is. You know, I'm a Northerner. I still have a Northern accent. So I'm a Northerner who's been away and who travels (interview, Strabane, VMR–042).

Deirdre remarked, however, that the people who had encouraged her to come back were of the older generation and that acceptance was harder to achieve among her own age cohort:

> The peer group is tricky and I don't know about the younger generation yet. Having said that, I mean I've made friends and been accepted and it's changed in the four years I've been there obviously. I mean I'm well able to do what I have to do to be accepted, part of the community. But I find I've had to work at it.

The majority of the returnees expressed disappointment with the political situation in Northern Ireland upon their return and many experienced considerable difficulty as a direct result of the conflict. Having returned from the Arctic where their basic survival had depended on vital government supplies and the 'ingenuity' of the native people, Harry found it paradoxical to have come back to a land of plenty only to struggle for economic survival in the midst of ethnic conflict. For several others who returned either after the ceasefires (1994) or following the Belfast/Good Friday Agreement (1998), the peace process was a definite factor that had encouraged their return. Like Christine, Elizabeth and Stephen, however, many were surprised and disturbed by the embedded sectarianism still evident on the ground. All of the returnees, even Deirdre who returned to the ROI, found that their identities were challenged and their freedom somewhat curtailed. Having all resided in societies that were more multicultural and secular than Northern Ireland, they were frustrated to rediscover the conservatism and old attitudes they had left behind when they emigrated. For Nick and his Ecuadoran family, however, coming from a much poorer country, the social security system available in Northern Ireland, especially education and healthcare, far outweighed any concerns with residual sectarianism.

Transnational Returning: 'A dream that I would have'

While many emigrants feel at some level a sort of multiple belonging, most of them have had to privilege one location as place of residence for practical or emotional reasons. Subject to means and opportunity, however, for some migrants the ideal is to have a foot in two worlds, to enjoy the benefits of each location and to be able to maintain close and active social networks in each country. For these people, their 'dream of return' is the plan to have a base in each location and to divide their time accordingly. For some, this can be a way of 'trying out' a move home or acclimatising over time before making the decision of permanent return. Earlier in the twentieth century, however, a different form of transnationalism occurred as men who worked abroad in Britain left families to be raised in Ireland. Often as in the case of Kathleen's father presented in Chapter 5, the men made it home only once or twice per year, for a couple of weeks of summer holidays and if lucky, maybe a week at Christmas. In my own family, my grandmother Roseena's brother Joe, left Newry as a young man in the early 1920s to work in a factory in Birmingham. According to our family story, Joe made it back only one week per year, usually at Christmas and Roseena, with the help of her children, had the front room repapered each year to welcome her brother home. Joe even married a local girl who always remained behind in Newry and they adopted a daughter to keep her company. After forty-years away, Joe returned to Newry upon his retirement but sadly died within the year.

Michael from the market town of Ballynahinch, County Down, recounted a similar story of his grandfather who worked much of his adult life at Pilkington's glass works in St Helen's, Lancashire. He remembered how the house would be cleaned from top to bottom in time for his grandfather's annual two-week summer holiday at home and when the man himself arrived, these were 'weeks of merriment, lots of hard drink and enjoying himself'. But as happened with many other families, Michael's family eventually discovered a second family:

> We found out later in life that he had a son who was not known to us until the [19]60s who was brought up in England. And this son who died three years ago, to my mind's eye, was very similar in both his life, attitudes and lifestyle to my recollection of my granddad … you know, devil may care, and going off, quite adventurous (interview, Bangor, VMR–046).

Kevin, an internationally known classical musician from North Belfast based in Canada since 1994 regularly travels around the world performing with orchestras and opera companies. He has made over forty recordings for a well-known classical music label, including several that have won international awards. In recent times, his work has brought him regularly to Cork in the ROI for several months each year, but he has not worked much in Northern Ireland. When asked whether he would like to return to Ireland, Kevin articulated at one and the same time the desire and the impossibility of return:

> I would love to go back there and immerse in the culture that I never had a chance to. Like I never really learned Irish. I would love to be living there and being part of a community learning that, being really part of the writers and the music and everything. That's *a dream that I would have* (interview, Toronto, VMR–063).

However, an established career and the cost of living have favoured Canada thus far and Kevin commented that Northern Ireland, in particular, has not supported or promoted the arts adequately, citing as an example that there was no music conservatory of high standard in Belfast, nor were there many opportunities for performing artists in Northern Ireland. Despite his evident pleasure at working in the ROI and lack of opportunity in the North, Kevin in the event of potential permanent return, nonetheless, expressed a preference for Northern Ireland especially Belfast, not only because his family is there. He explained:

> I feel very much at home, more at home with Belfast sensibility than the Republic. I don't feel a foreigner down in the Republic, I can quite happily still feel I'm Irish. But I feel more of a Belfast man, you know, and I feel that when I'm in Belfast.

Despite his fondness for Cork and having cousins there, Kevin's identity was very much tied to the North and he expressed the view that northern Catholics were more 'Nationalist' than Southerners who took their identity for granted:

> I prefer the drivenness of the people in the North. They've had to fight for something, they've had to fight for their identity. There was never a moment of taking anything for granted. And I feel a little bit that that's moulded who I am and that's why I'll always be somebody from the North ... I don't care whether Ireland is a united Ireland. It's just a bit of land ... I would rather that we'd all compromise and lived in peace and got on. That's more important to me. But I would go back to the North.

Liz originally from East Belfast, always missed Northern Ireland since she, her English-born husband and two children had left Lisburn for Toronto in 1975 because of the Troubles. In semi-retirement, with their children grown, Liz and her husband decided that downsizing their home in Toronto would allow them the opportunity to travel and to set up a second base in the Belfast area. They sold their house and purchased an apartment in downtown Toronto, and then in 2003 purchased another in a large house that had been converted into flats overlooking Belfast Lough in North Down. Their intention was to spend half the year in each location, with plenty of opportunity to visit other family members in England and spend time with their daughter who lives in Barbados. While Liz loved being back in Northern Ireland, she noticed that there was much intolerance in the society, what she described as the 'not an inch' mentality towards new immigrants, racial minorities and gay people, that also applied to many aspects of daily life, even when driving the roads. She was disappointed that sectarianism was still so prevalent and in fact, in spite of the removal of most of the visible signs of conflict (barriers, barbed wire, army vehicles) didn't feel that things had changed much:

> From what I've seen going up and down past housing estates, I would say the level of intolerance is just as bad now as it was when we left in the 70s. I see no difference (interview, Belfast, VMR–057).

Liz realised that the realities of aging and illness will inevitably require her and her husband to eventually settle in one location. She is not yet ready, however, to make that decision and acknowledges that future circumstances, such as medical care and the location of their children, may dictate their ultimate choice. For now, she is happy to have the freedom to avail of the best of both worlds.

While back and forth migration and return is not a new phenomenon in Irish culture, air travel has in recent years made truly transnational lifestyles possible. In some cases, as with Kevin above, mobility is a requirement of the chosen career and is not unusual in the performing arts or in the increasingly globalised business world. It is striking, however, that in spite of Kevin's mobile lifestyle, which has recently included regular periods based in the ROI, his Irish identity is so firmly anchored in Northern Ireland. From his international perspective, however, he is not concerned about eventual political solutions in Ireland, though he continues to value and strongly identify with Irish culture. Liz's story is, however, a reminder that transnationalism is temporary and that the realities of life and death eventually lead to settling permanently abroad or to ultimate return.

Ultimate Return: 'I don't want to go home to live, I want to go home to die'

It is a sunny warm late Saturday afternoon in mid-September 2006 and I am on a commuter train travelling from downtown Toronto on my way to meet Craig, a banking consultant originally from the Oldpark neighbourhood of North Belfast, now living in a Toronto suburb. Craig had responded the previous June to an advertisement seeking interviewees for our migration project and made initial contact via email. Since then we had corresponded several times and spoken on the telephone twice. I was on my way to join Craig and his wife for dinner at their home after which we were to record an interview about Craig's migration experience and life in Canada. Upon arrival at the train station, Craig was there to meet me. A tall man who easily looked a decade younger than his sixty-odd years, Craig exhibited a friendly and relaxed manner; as we got into his car I already felt as if I had known him for some time. Chatting easily about the train trip and the beautiful weather, we drove slowly out of the station parking lot. At the intersection with the main road, Craig stopped the car, looked over at me and abruptly changing the subject, exclaimed, 'Well, it's great to live here, but now burial, that's another matter! I'm not too sure about burial.'

Many of the non-returnees brought up the subject of death and dying during their interviews in relation to whether they might eventually return to Ireland. Although the issue of the return of elderly emigrants has been recognised by the ROI which provides some funding to elderly returnees who qualify through the Safe-Home Programme, an organisation founded in 2001, there is no specific assistance given to emigrants in Northern Ireland relating to return.[19] The Aisling Return to Ireland Project, based in London, also helps isolated emigrants reconnect with Ireland by regularly sponsoring group visits and in some cases assisting in resettlement, however, it and other Irish emigrant organisations at home and abroad are for the most part geared towards return to the ROI and many are linked with the Catholic Church.[20] Thus, their assistance is not applicable to most Northerners, especially Protestants, who wish to return to Northern Ireland.

Craig in Toronto struggled with the idea of burial since his parents, who had retired to Canada to live near their emigrant children, had been buried in British Columbia where Craig's sister lives, while his teenage son had died of cancer a few years previously and was buried in Ontario (interview, Toronto, VMR–064). Several informants had experience of returning to Ireland for the death of a parent, sibling or close relation and this had often provoked thoughts about their own death, especially the desire to be buried in Ireland. Eilísh came home to Derry from New Jersey to look after her elderly uncle in his last year and made the decision to take early retirement and stay after he died (interview, Derry, VMR–005). Rose from rural County Tyrone told of how she had been sent by her family to New York to collect an uncle, diagnosed with a brain tumour, and bring him back home to die (interview, Gortin, Co. Tyrone, VMR–013). Chris, a doctor from Belfast, who lives in Hamilton, New Zealand was persuaded by family members in Ireland not to return for his father's funeral, suggesting he might be of more use to his mother if he came back at a later point. But this had unforeseen consequences on Chris and for the first time, made him keenly aware of the great distance:

215

I probably had a delayed grief reaction for about nine or twelve months where I wasn't really able to grieve properly. Because of the distance I wasn't able to support my mother except the phone calls and the letters and so it was quite a difficult time. But we went back at twelve months after his death and I think that was very helpful (interview, Ballynahinch, Co. Down, VMR–084).

Barry, who lives in Liverpool, began to think of death as he approached the age of fifty, despite the fact that his own parents were still alive and well. Though very youthful and athletic, Barry admitted that the process of aging was having an impact on his attitudes. It was a worry that if he died suddenly, his teenage children would not know what to do. He was just being practical, not morose, he insisted, and where to be buried was a 'huge dilemma' for him. He remembered as a child the feeling he had when they'd read the deaths out in church:

You'd hear in mass somebody reading out the death list and 'blah, blah, blah died in England' and that's such a removed, huge thing … It just seemed somebody who was lost, maybe. Lost. That's the word that came into my head just now. Somebody who was a bit lost (interview, Liverpool, VMR–047).

Nevertheless, Barry and his English-born children were well settled in Liverpool and he didn't think it realistic that the children would ever live in Ireland. He thought the only practical way to resolve the issue might be to be cremated:

Ireland is home … so I *imagine* part of me there. But I'd also want a bit here for my kids. So that's why I think if I ever dropped dead in the morning I'd want to be cremated, leave some of the ashes here, some of the ashes over there.

Still, it wasn't only the issue of burial that concerned him but also the issue of where to live out his last years and die. He couldn't imagine himself as an old man living in England, but he also realised that it would be too late to wait until he was in his seventies to relocate back to Ireland. Though not a practicising Catholic, Barry spoke in religious terms:

When I'm 70, 75, I want to be there then, you know, I want to go home to die or something. I can see that as a strong pull. *I don't want to go home to live, I want to go home to die* … It's my soul really. At the end of the day it's my soul.

Emigration later in life and family situation may have a bearing on the significance of burial location, as with Pamela who was in her forties when she emigrated, leaving two grown children in Northern Ireland. Pamela had left Belfast in 2002 to join her second husband, a Belfast-born banker who lived in the greater Toronto area. Although she had spent most of her adult life in Belfast, Pamela was four years later already calling Canada 'home'. Clearly, Pamela linked her concept of home with the establishment of her career and achievement of financial independence. Still, she was quite convinced that she wanted to be buried in Ireland:

> I think somewhere about six, nine months ago there was this transition where suddenly Canada's home ... When I first came to Canada, it was like I'm going to be here for two years and then we are going back to Ireland, right ... This was always temporary. Whereas as things have gone on, and now I can have my financial independence, I have a job. If [husband] wasn't on the scene, I can make it as a person, I'm not dependent. And that was the turning point. Now I'm not going back to Ireland yet. I might eventually and I certainly want to be buried there, but I'm not going back yet. This is home and there's too many places here I want to see, I want to experience (interview, Toronto, VMR–065).

When pressed a bit more about burial, however, Pamela made it clear that in fact even within Ireland, the only burial site that would be acceptable was her family's plot in her 'home' cemetery in the east Donegal village where she had grown up:

> I said I wanted to make it perfectly clear that if I die in Canada, I do not want to be buried in Canada. Though this is home, I want to be buried in St. Johnston, in the grave in St. Johnston, because that's where I'm from.

For many of the interviewees, concern about their final days and resting place became more of an issue with age and none had ever considered this particular consequence of emigration when they were first setting out. Significantly, in their discussion of death, funerals and burial, the interviewees' narratives were intensely visual with detailed imagery, and it was apparent that they each seemed to possess a mental vision or video clip of what they ideally anticipated. Thus, the importance of the specific burial location may be linked with ancient ideas of blood ties to the land, belonging to a very particular place or simply the availability of family members to visit the grave. This was central to Pamela's vision of ultimate return to east Donegal. For Barry, despite being very happily settled in Liverpool, the idea of being buried away from his home community where his family was known for generations was linked in his mind with being lost or displaced. In addition, the desire to spend his last years in Ireland had become part of his vision or dream, or perhaps ultimately his myth of return.

Epilogue: 'I can't see myself leaving and I can't see myself going back'

June 2009. I received an email with the shocking news that one of my interviewees was dead by suicide. Stunned and unable to believe it, I immediately rang my email contact who confirmed the horrible news. The interviewee had died in Northern Ireland a few weeks previously while on a visit to her family home.[21] The evening I spent in her house abroad remains vivid in my mind. She very hospitably made me dinner and while she cooked, I read a story to her child. Later we chatted easily over the meal, eventually beginning the formal interview. She referred over and over again during the interview to the importance of her family and how she missed them, worried that her child was being denied the experience of growing up with an extended family unit and a close community:

> If I had have known how hard it was, I probably would never have done
> it. Especially now with [child], particularly. That has been the hardest part
> of emigrating is having a child … Like the guilt I feel that [child] doesn't
> have family, doesn't have cousins, doesn't have friends. Even though I grew
> up in a town – we didn't have a garden or any of that sort of thing – there
> was community, there was friends, there was cousins (interview).

While she also spoke at length of the difficulties of emigration in her own life, it was most especially the struggle to belong that loomed large in her narrative. She recognised that Northern Ireland was changing and that she herself had changed and this saddened her. She expressed a strong sense of loss that she was no longer a part of life in Ireland and yet was still struggling to belong in her new home:

> Some days I wake up and I think where the hell am I? In many ways it's
> so alien. I don't know where that's going to lead to. I don't know if some
> day I'm going to go, screw this I'm away home. But I know now that it's
> changed so much at home, that it's not what it was when I was growing
> up, or it's not what it was like when I was in my twenties. I've changed,
> it's changed. Life's just different.

When I asked her whether she would likely return to Ireland, somewhat prophetically she could not envision the future. 'The future I don't know. *I can't see myself leaving and I can't see myself going back.*' Again, at the forefront of her experience was the sense that she was in limbo – 'this horrible feeling of not belonging anywhere':

> That feeling of belonging, you know, you grow up in Northern Ireland
> and where you belong you don't even think about it because it is what it

is and it is where you are. If I was still living in Northern Ireland ... if somebody had said to me, where do you feel like you belong? I'd go, 'Away and catch yourself on, where do you think I belong?' I never even asked those types of questions, I didn't know they existed. But I definitely knew they existed when I came here.

During the interview the subject of death came up several times. She spoke of the devastating effect of the sudden death of her father when she was only seven and later the similar sudden death of a friend who had mentored her and had been, she said, a surrogate father figure. She spoke of her anxiety as her own husband approached middle age, worried that he would die suddenly as well. While other interviewees were concerned about where they would be buried, she was more much more concerned about the funeral and again it is her need of community that comes through in her narrative:

Who's going to come to my funeral would be a big one for me. Like I don't really give a shit where I'm put. But who's going to come to my funeral? Like you know what funerals are like at home. They're bloody huge ... You can tell how liked a person was in Ireland by the size of their funeral.

On a fine spring day in her home town in Northern Ireland, a large gathering assembled to attend her funeral.

Postscript

Lost generations

October 2012. Just as I am making final revisions to this book, my uncle informs me that he has unexpectedly found a few things belonging to my grandmother Roseena (whose story opens Chapter 3). In a brown envelope along with a few letters and some photographs of my mother, my brothers and me taken in Canada the summer before Roseena's death, is her treasured watch, long assumed lost, a gift from her brother James sent from America. The fine inscription engraved on the back, 'From James to Roseena Aug 20th 27' provides another intriguing clue to her migration story. Though their plan to meet had been thwarted by the American authorities who repeatedly denied Roseena entry to the United States at several crossing points along the Canadian border, it would appear that the siblings had been touch over that period. The date on the watch, five months after Roseena's arrival in Canada and more than a year prior to her return to Northern Ireland, suggests that James sent the watch to her at a Canadian address. This is strangely comforting in view of the tragic outcome that they were never to see each other again. Ironic too, that just as I was laying this story to rest, it comes to life once more – this engraved timepiece like Barthes' *punctum* – a point of memory intersecting between past and present to 'puncture through layers of oblivion' (Hirsch, 2012: 61).[1]

In spite of the tragedy of her brother's disappearance, Roseena's migration story is one of courage, daring and self-actualisation; her Canadian adventure, a resource she drew on throughout her life that helped to sustain her. Exactly thirty years later in 1957, fortified by her mother Roseena's story, my mother too embarked on a new life in Canada with a spirit of optimism and adventure, undaunted at the prospect of living and working in a French-speaking city. I am conscious of how their stories – Roseena's as a returned migrant, my mother Margie's as an emigrant – resonate with my own, a Canadian-born immigrant (or ancestral returned migrant) to Ireland. Though I have a strong sense of the shared experience among three generations of migrant women in my maternal line, I am equally aware of the very different contexts in which our migrations occurred. For while Roseena freely chose an adventure in 1927 facilitated by an assisted Empire migration scheme for domestic workers, thirty years later my mother Margie had few options but to emigrate with her Protestant husband because of the insurmountable difficulties a mixed marriage in Northern Ireland then presented. An elopement to Scotland for the wedding, which was not celebrated by either of their families, was followed by an assisted passage as skilled migrants aboard the *Empress of France* of the Canadian Pacific Steamship Line from Liverpool bound for Montreal. Over another thirty years later in 1993, I left Canada as the country was beginning to emerge from recession. Already university educated, I had undoubtedly the best prospects of the three of us as I boarded the airplane. But it turned out that there were other unforeseen costs.

January 2009. Ottawa, Canada. It is a brilliantly sunny but bitterly cold day, so dangerously cold at minus 24° Celsius that we have asked only family members and close friends to venture outside. Walking the short distance from the chapel through the snowy cemetery I am being supported by a dear friend, himself the child of Polish immigrants. We arrive at an open grave and I am amazed that it is possible to dig in such hard icy ground. To the sound of prayers a few minutes later, my mother's coffin is lowered into the cold earth and I ask myself how can I leave her – she who hated the harsh Canadian winters – in this inhospitable frozen wasteland so far from the place she called 'home'. I want to cry out and stop it but remain silent, numb. For my mother, ever the practical organiser who managed our family's several migrations, pre-arranged this, her last one. Over the days and months that follow, my mind returns unbidden to this blinding, white, frozen scene that will continue to haunt me. With the end of my mother's life story the stark reality of migration becomes all too apparent; that in spite of its many benefits and opportunities there are also unbearable costs, some of which may endure over several generations.

October 2012. As I write, the media in Northern Ireland has been reporting on a 'new' phenomenon – the 'lost generation'.[2] For thousands of young people are again leaving due to high youth unemployment which passed the one million mark in the UK in November 2011, and now amounts to one in five young people in Northern Ireland, aged sixteen to twenty-four. Emigration is a viable option for many of the young unemployed, especially university graduates who leave to seek work in Britain, Canada and Australasia. But as the review of migration in Chapter 2 has shown, this state of affairs is hardly new or even surprising. That emigration is at last receiving media attention in Northern Ireland is likely down to the economic downturn which is now affecting the children of the middle class. If this is a 'lost generation', then by the same definition Northern Ireland has 'lost' several generations previously – at least three in its relatively short history, during the 1920s, the 1950s and the 1970s. As before, issues of economic sustainability, increasing inequality and ongoing sectarianism in Northern Ireland continue to have the greatest impact on young people. In addition, the lack of public discourse about migration has thus far resulted in little if any effort within Northern Ireland to avail of its opportunities – to harness the goodwill, expertise and linkages provided by our emigrants and immigrants that could be of enormous benefit. Therefore, as we once again contemplate the costs of another 'lost generation', it is perhaps time to learn from the stories of those who have been 'leaving the North' over many decades; not only to acknowledge their departure but in the hope that we might welcome the opportunities that migration and diaspora may present.

Notes and references

Notes to Introduction

1   The VMR oral archive is part of the online resource, *Documenting Ireland Online: Parliament, People and Migration* (DIPPAM), which also includes the Irish Emigration Database (IED) and the Enhanced British Parliamentary Papers on Ireland (EPPI). Dippam was funded by the Arts and Humanities Research Council (AHRC) and is available at: www.dippam.ac.uk

2   The concept of a 'usable past' or of 'using the past' as 'a reservoir of experience' is from the important book on public history by Rosenzweig and Thelen (1998: 37–8) and is also discussed in an essay by Bernard E. Jensen (2009).

3   Arthur's activities have been reported in a considerable number of books about politics at the turn of the twentieth century in Belfast. Most useful are Patrick Maume's article on Arthur Trew in the *Dictionary of Irish Biography* Vol. 9 (2009): 488–9; and J. W. Boyle, 'The Belfast Protestant Association and the Independent Orange Order, 1901–10', *Irish Historical Studies* 13 (1962–1963): 117–52.

4   Lily Trew Edens, interview by author, Shankill, Belfast, 25 August 2006, sound recording.

5   The riot took place on 9 June 1901 and is reported in the *Belfast News Letter* the following day 'Roman Catholic Procession: Disturbances in the city' (10 June 1901, p. 6). The trial took place on 23–24 July 1901 and is also reported in detail in the *News Letter*: 'Assize Intelligence. The Charge of Conspiracy' (24 July 1901 p. 10); and 'Assize Intelligence. The Alleged Conspiracy' (25 July 1901, pp. 5–6). Arthur's triumphant release from the jail a year later, 'Release of Mr. Arthur Trew. Popular Demonstrations', is reported in the *News Letter* (19 July 1902, p. 7).

6   The name of Richard Trew appears in the Kilnwick Percy Estate Papers, relating to land in Bielby, Yorkshire, 2 December 1556 (DDKP/5/1). The name is also found in Lancashire and Wales. The surname is very rare in Ireland and is only found in County Armagh in the eighteenth and nineteenth centuries. In Griffiths Valuation for Armagh (1864), there was only one Trew, first name of John (Arthur's father). Trew is sometimes spelled 'True' in the military records relating to the same individuals.

7   This was a substantial amount of land and they were most likely sub-letting parcels of it out to tenants as was the local practice.

8   I am unsure which Thomas this is as there were at least two: the brother of Andrew aged eighteen in1788 and another Thomas at Bhurtpoor who was aged eighteen in 1805. A freeholder either owned his land outright or held a lease for the duration of his life or the lives of those also listed on the lease. The Freeholders' Lists contain the names of people entitled to vote: from 1727 to 1793 this meant Protestants with freeholdings with the minimum value of forty shillings; after 1793 Catholics with the minimum freeholdings value were included. From 1829, however, the minimum amount was increased to ten pounds, thus many freeholders were made ineligible for the vote. Freeholders records may be searched online on the Public Record Office of Northern Ireland (PRONI) website at: www.proni.gov.uk/index/search_the_archives/freeholders_records.htm

9   Thomas Trew served from 1803 to 1805 (WO 121/78/1) and James Trew from 1807 to 1823 (WO 97/1120/148 and 149).

10 Arthur Trew is found in the Muster of the 101st Regiment of Foot dated October 1794–March 1795. This is believed to be the regiment raised in Ireland by Colonel William Fullarton (1754–1808) and stationed in Dublin and Cork. It appears that Arthur was promoted into Colonel John Ogle's regiment (128th Foot) on 6 March 1795 (*London Gazette*, 7–11 April 1795, No. 13768, 321) and on 2 February 1796 to the 1st Battalion of the 41st Foot (Commander in chief's memoranda, WO 31/143) and stationed at Cork from 1796 to 1799, at which point the regiment left for Canada.

11 Commander in chief's memoranda, Colonel Thomas Stirling to Adjutant General Harry Calvert, dated 8 October and approved 19 October 1804, WO 31/169. Captain Arthur is reported to have died in Canada on 8 March 1811. See Regimental muster rolls, WO 12/5404–5415. My thanks to Jonathan Collins for his assistance in researching this story.

12 Captain Arthur's command at Fort St Joseph is discussed briefly in Abbott et al. (2000: 75).

13 PRO, WO 97/4045/068. John Trew enlisted at Markethill in the 3rd Regiment of Foot in 1857. By the time of John Trew's retirement from the army in 1890, the Irish-born comprised approximately 14 per cent of British Military personnel recruited from all over Ireland (Jackson, 1963: 10) and, as in John's case, it was not unusual given the expansion of the British Empire during the nineteenth century for military personnel to be assigned to serve in the colonies for extended periods of their career. John Trew is listed as the leaseholder of a farm in the townland of Drumatee in Griffiths Valuation of Armagh in 1864. The farm can't have been very prosperous since John's occupation was listed as a weaver on his army enlistment papers and his father Samuel was employed as a gardener, probably on the nearby Gosford estate. At some point during his army career, John must have divested himself of the farm (or more likely the lease expired) since upon discharge from the army in 1890 he was registered as living in Belfast where he appears in the census of 1901 and 1911.

14 RUC reports on Arthur's public speeches were filed during 1923 and 1924,

demonstrating the concern by the fledging state authorities with Loyalist political activists.

15 The 'narrow ground' comes from the title of the well-known history of Ulster by A. T. Q. Stewart (1977: 12) which he in turn borrowed from the writings of Sir Walter Scott of his visit to Ireland in 1825. It has since been borrowed by many other writers and historians as an epithet for Ulster or Northern Ireland.

16 Academics bear some responsibility for this. For example, there has been a tendency to either organise conferences entirely devoted to Northern Ireland (especially the conflict) or to ghettoise Northern Ireland issues or interests into separate 'Northern' or 'Ulster' sessions at Irish studies conferences. The use of display maps at these events is especially noteworthy: often the six-county 'island' in the first instance or the map of an all-island Ireland with the six-county area as a blank space (usually white). In my experience, the use of these maps has always passed without comment.

17 This is also true of the changing boundaries of Ulster over time (see Elliott, 2000, especially Chapter 1).

18 The understanding is that 'Ireland' is the official name of the state, but the usage of the other terms is purely for clarity (especially relating to statistics or historical context) to differentiate the two jurisdictions on the island.

19 This follows directly from the work of my colleagues, Patrick Fitzgerald and Brian Lambkin, of putting migration back into Irish history (2008). Their work in turn follows from the larger project of putting migration into world history (Hoerder, 2002; Lucassen and Lucassen, 1999; Manning, 2004; Rodriguez and Grafton, 2007) into European history (Bade, 2003; Page Moch, 2003 [1992]) and into North American history (Rodriguez, 2004).

Notes to Chapter 1: History, Memory, Migration

1 Nafisi (2010: xx).

2 There is in addition to these sources a large and growing literature on diaspora, but see especially Brah (1996); Brubaker (2005); Clifford (1994); Gilroy (1993); Safran (1991); Sheffer (2003), Soysal (2000); Tötölyan (1996); and Vertovec (2009). Literature on the Irish diaspora has been surveyed by Akenson (1993); Bielenberg (2000); Delaney (2005, 2011); Delaney et al. (2006); Doyle (1989 and 1994); Fanning, (2000); Gray (2000, 2002b, 2004); Hickman (2002, 2005); Kenny (2003); Lee (2005); O'Sullivan (1992–1997); Walker (2007).

3 There is a large literature including: Blethen and Wood (1997); Griffin (2001); Hanna (1902); Hume (2011); Kennedy (2001); Leyburn (1962); Marshall (1944); Paisley (1976); Vann (2008); Webb (2004); Wilson and Spencer (2006); Woodburn (1914), etc.

4 For studies on the Orange Order, see Houston and Smyth (1980); MacRaild (2005a); Senior (1966, 1972); and Wilson (2007); and for emigrant letters, see Fitzpatrick (1994); McCarthy (2005, 2006); Miller et al. (2003); Parkhill (1997, 2005); and Wells (1991). In addition, recent work has examined Ulster emigrants

from multi-denominational perspectives in the nineteenth and twentieth centuries (e.g., Hume, 2005; Mageean, 1991; Patterson, 2007; Phillips, 2007).

5 Perhaps the first published use of diaspora in the Ulster context was 'Hopes of Ulster diaspora', the heading of the editorial page (*Belfast Telegraph*, 21 April 1998, p. 10), which featured letters from three Northern Ireland Protestants living abroad (two in England and one in Greece) who wrote in support of the Belfast Agreement. The editor evidently took his heading from a sentence in the letter of Dr David Green of Athens who wrote 'When the Agreement is ratified on May 22, I would ask that a large orange and green candle be lit in the foyer of Stormont Buildings to act as a beacon to those of us in [the] Ulster diaspora who would like to come home and help rebuild and develop our beloved province.'

6 As represented in Thomas Ryan's well-known painting, *The Departure of O'Neill Out of Ireland* (1958). The 'flight' from Rathmullan, Donegal of Hugh O'Neill; Earl of Tyrone; Rory O'Donnell; Earl of Tyrconnell; and the Maguires of Fermanagh with their families and followers, is also taken to signify the end of Gaelic order in Ireland.

7 Fitzgerald credits the important contribution of Lorraine Tennant's unpublished MPhil. thesis, Ulster Emigration, 1851–1914 (University of Ulster, 1988), for data and analysis of this period based upon the annual returns of the Registrar General for Ireland.

8 The first Northern Ireland Prime Minister, James Craig, made an unofficial holiday visit to Canada in 1926 which received much media attention (Fedorowich, 1999: 1174–5) and an official visit to Australia and New Zealand in 1929–1930 (Jeffery, 2008). Sir Basil Brooke, third Prime Minister of Northern Ireland undertook a well-publicised tour of North America in 1950. While there Brooke met with trade representatives and government officials and with Protestant Irish emigrant organisations in New York, Philadelphia and several more in Canada, notably Toronto. In the USA, Brooke had to tread carefully in view of Irish Nationalist sympathies thus the visit was mostly confined to trade meetings. Conversely in Canada, Brooke was greeted with great warmth by his former Unionist countrymen and women, and was able to voice his partitionist stance quite openly in public speeches (Smyth, 2007).

9 The later 1950s and early 1960s saw the establishment of organisations and institutions which reinforced an image of nation inclusive of the Northern Ireland 'diaspora' as evidenced by the provision of heritage and tourism organisations and institutions. For example, the Ulster Historical Foundation (originally the Ulster-Scots Historical Society) an organisation that encourages research into family history and transnational connections, was founded in 1956 at the behest of Sir Basil Brooke (Lord Brookeborough) (Ulster Historical Foundation, 2007). The Ulster Folk Museum was created by an Act of Parliament in 1958, while the Museum Act (NI) of 1961 formally renamed and recognised the Ulster Museum as the 'national museum' of Northern Ireland, effective 1962.

10 From analyses of Northern Ireland census data, most especially the census of 1961, it became apparent that since partition, Catholics had been emigrating at approximately

twice the rate of Protestants and concerns were raised in Stormont (see discussion of 1961 census report, Parliamentary Debates, Northern Ireland, 27 February 1962, Vol. 50, 1971–1994; and Barritt and Carter, 1962: 107–108). This in turn prompted investigations into the reasons for this trend which helped to highlight the Northern Ireland Government's discriminatory policies in employment, education and housing. The Report of the Cameron Commission (1969) was the first official government document that acknowledged and described the discrimination against Catholics in Northern Ireland (see CAIN Archive at: http://cain.ulst.ac.uk/hmso/ cameron.htm (accessed 20 October 2012)).

11 The Northern Ireland Parliament at Stormont was prorogued in March 1972 and direct rule for Northern Ireland was first legislated in the Northern Ireland (Temporary Provisions) Act 1972. Parliament was formally abolished by the Northern Ireland Constitution Act 1973.

12 New immigration since 2004 has also had an impact on the sectarian body count, especially the perception that the majority of recent immigrants have been Catholics (e.g., Poles, Lithuanians, Portuguese, Filipinos) that has contributed to anti-immigrant abuse in Loyalist areas, such as the Village neighbourhood in Belfast where cheaper housing has attracted newcomers. Recent attitudinal research has found that Protestants and Unionists have a higher tendency than other groups to hold prejudiced views towards immigrants (Pehrson et al., 2012) and that this may be amplified if the immigrants are known to be Catholics (van Rijswijk et al., 2009).

13 A truly intercultural approach requires negotiation between both host society and immigrants in seeking reasonable accommodation. However, although some sectors (libraries, churches, schools) in Northern Ireland have made considerable effort, the sense in official government policy is that the onus is placed on the immigrants who are expected to conform as soon as possible after arrival to Northern Ireland norms (see the recent critique by McDermott, 2011). Although attracting foreign direct investment has long been a strategy of the Northern Ireland Government (see Chapter 2), there is little information available about how Northern Ireland emigrants might be contributing to international commercial relations; rather the concern has been with 'brain drain' (see Chapter 4). For an impression of the type and range of Northern Ireland professionals working abroad, for example, the social media network (LinkedIn) has a discussion group, Northern Ireland/Irish Professional People Living in Exile (Nipple) with over 600 members signed up (January 2013).

14 Jarman has pointed out that while new immigrants were included in the *Racial Equality Strategy for Northern Ireland* (OFMDFM, 2005); they were not mentioned in the *Economic vision for Northern Ireland* (DETINI, 2005).

15 'Space-time' or 'time-space', as connoted here refers to the geographical concept for which there is a large literature (Hagerstrand, 1973; Harvey, 1990).

16 Diasporas may play positive or negative roles in relation to conflict. While they may influence peace processes, they may also raise funds for armed conflict and especially in the case of forced migration, they could reignite conflict with demands

to reclaim land. There are several examples of this in relation to conflicts in the Balkans and in central Africa, especially Rwanda and the Democratic Republic of the Congo. There is a growing literature which treats the contribution of the Irish abroad to the peace process: F. Cochrane (2007); Dempsey (1999); Dixon (2006); Guelke (1996); Hazleton (2000); MacGinty (1997); Ó Dochartaigh (2009); Ruane and Todd (1996); and Wilson (1995, 1997, 2000).

[17] The International Passenger Survey for Northern Ireland measures the flow at Belfast and Larne seaports and at three airports: Belfast City – George Best Airport; Belfast International – Aldergrove; and City of Derry Airport.

[18] In 2011, overseas travellers into Northern Ireland for the purpose of visiting friends and relatives (VFR) comprised 58 per cent, holiday travellers averaged around 20 per cent; while business travellers accounted for around 18 per cent; and those travelling for other reasons at 4 per cent of the sample (N = 973,000). Travellers from Britain, Canada and Australia/New Zealand were most prominent in the VFR category. DETINI, 'Results from the 2011 Northern Ireland Passenger Survey', 22 March 2012 at: www.detini.gov.uk/2011_annual_nips.pdf (accessed 6 January 2013).

[19] The exception was Richard Rose (1971); see discussion in Chapter 4. There is a vast literature concerning social identities (national, political and religious) in Northern Ireland and it is not possible to provide a comprehensive review of this material here as it has been done elsewhere (Coakley, 2007; Elliott, 2009; Loughlin, 1995; C. Mitchell, 2006; Muldoon et al., 2009; Stevenson et al., 2007; Trew, 2007). The literature generally falls into two principal approaches: psycho-sociological and historical, and it is relatively rare for scholars in one area to cite the literature of the other, as Peter Mandler (2006) has similarly noted about the literature on national identity in British historiography. The psycho-sociological approach focuses primarily on behavioural aspects of identity, including adherence to political parties, while the historical treats cultural narratives, collective memory and geographical/ spatial aspects. This second approach includes research in relation to Ulster migration and Ulster-Scots/Scots-Irish/Presbyterian/Protestant identities in the eighteenth and nineteenth centuries, notably by Kerby Miller (see especially his collection of essays, 2008; and Miller et al., 2003), as well as a large literature considering the impact of historical narratives (e.g., 1641, the Siege, the Somme) on Irish and Ulster identities into the present. In this book, I am informed by both historical and psycho-sociological approaches.

[20] I use the term Ulster-Scot(s) advisedly as it is nomenclature of the later nineteenth and twentieth centuries, not the eighteenth. An early example of the term's appearance in print was the newspaper column 'Ulster Scot's letters' penned by the Rev Henry Henderson (1820–1879) that appeared in the *Belfast Weekly News* during the 1870s. Thanks to Dr Frank Ferguson for alerting me to Henderson. James Greer's, *Three Wee Ulster Lassies* (1883), a rather remarkable attempt to explain Irish history to English schoolchildren, features a chapter entitled 'The Ulster-Scot.' By 1912, another writer who signed himself 'an Ulster Scot' in the *Irish Review* discussed the nomenclature relating to Ulster Protestants noting, '"Ulster Scot" now

appears to be the favourite term' ('The Denial of North-East Ulster', p. 228). James Woodburn's *The Ulster Scot* published in 1914 would bear this out.

21 For example, recent film documentaries on this theme aired on Northern Ireland television in March 2011, 'Are you related to an American president?' based on the book, *In Search of Buchanan* by Irene Martin (2011); and 'Born Fighting: How the Scots-Irish Shaped America' based on former American Senator James Webb's book of the same title (2004). Another version of the Ulster-Scots story was presented in the theatrical production *On Eagle's Wing*, dubbed Ulster's answer to Riverdance, which premiered in Belfast in 2004.

22 In his review of the survey research on ethnonational identity conducted in Northern Ireland from 1968 to 2005, John Coakley (2007: 584–5), noted studies that reported the potential shift in self-identification affected by travel abroad. In her study of northern Protestant identity, Mitchell included interviewees who happened to be returned migrants, concluding that migration 'can have implications for a British identification' (2003: 619). A study of national identity among English-born respondents living in Scotland (Kiely et al., 2005) noted the impact of migration on shifts in identity and feelings of belonging. In a wider international context, a recent survey of thirty-two countries found that individuals whose lives were connected 'transnationally' across borders in relation to work, family or friendship networks, were less committed to a national identity based on ethnic or ancestral heritage (Ford et al., 2011: 9).

23 The Northern Ireland Executive rejected involvement in The Gathering initiative of the ROI; a 'homecoming' tourism campaign targeted at the diaspora to encourage them to visit Ireland in 2013 with many special events organised around the country. Instead, Northern Ireland sponsored its 'Our place, our time' campaign in 2012 to coincide with anniversaries of the Titanic and the Ulster Covenant, hoping to increase overseas visitor numbers by 20 per cent. However, despite spending almost five million pounds, the first quarter of 2012 saw a drop in tourist numbers especially from Britain. See 'Short-sighted North fails to join in Irish diaspora tourism plan' and 'Meanwhile, despite multi-million-pound "our place, our time" promotion, number of overseas tourists drops by 13 percent', both stories in the *Irish News*, 17 July 2012, pp. 8–9. That Northern Ireland has thus far been largely absent from the discourse of the Irish diaspora is also due to the reluctance on the part of academics on both sides of the border to engage with the 'other' jurisdiction. The complexities and sensitivities surrounding the conflict in particular make it difficult for those located outside Northern Ireland – and most especially those located in the ROI – to contribute to the debate. Unfortunately, partition is not only a matter of geography in Ireland, but also of academic and intellectual discourse.

24 The Good Friday Agreement (10 April 1998), also known as the Belfast Agreement, was agreed by both British and Irish Governments and supported by majority votes in referenda held in Northern Ireland and the ROI. Key to the Agreement was the commitment to the self-determination of Northern Ireland by peaceful means and the establishment of a devolved Northern Ireland Assembly. Full text of the

Agreement is at: www.nio.gov.uk/the-agreement.

25 Most recently, the dispute over the installation of 'Welcome to Northern Ireland' signs at border crossing points was reported in the Nationalist *Irish News*, 7 August 2012, as, 'Welcome to Northern Ireland border road signs cause anger' and 'Border signs taken down within hours.' On the same day in the pro-union *Belfast News Letter* the story was reported as, 'Border signs welcome visitors.'

26 The Black Pig's Dyke is a series of ancient earthworks (ditches) running east from Bundoran, County Donegal and said to form the old boundary of Ulster. There are various versions of the legend relating to it; perhaps the most complete of these in *The Fate of the Children of Tuireann* (see Joyce, 2000 [1879]). For an overview of the legends surrounding the Black Pig, see Hull (1918); and Williams (1987). This old boundary is also the setting for the play *At the Black Pig's Dyke* by Vincent Woods (1998) first produced in 1992 by the Druid Lane Theatre in Galway.

27 On the roots of northern Catholic disaffection, see especially O Connor (1993); Elliott (2000, 2009); and O'Halloran (1987). Another key question is to what extent prior to and during the period of conflict surrounding partition did southern Protestants perceive of Ulster as the homeland/refuge for British Ireland? Early twentieth-century Loyalist/Unionist claims included the entire territory of Ireland, eventually withdrawing to the six counties of Northern Ireland (Fitzpatrick, 1998: 32–5).

28 Unlike many other European countries, Ireland does not permit Irish-born citizens resident abroad to vote in elections at home. It is in this sense that the Irish diaspora exists discursively. The de-territorialisation of the Irish diaspora was originally suggested by Irish President, Mary Robinson, in her 'Cherish the Diaspora' speech addressed to the Houses of the Oireachtas (Dáil and Seanad/Senate) in 1995. Breda Gray has suggested that this was intended to open up the discourse and destabilise 'the territorialized politics of nationalisms in Northern Ireland' (Gray, 2002b: 125). The argument put forth here, however, is that such discursive endeavours, while laudable, have thus far had little impact 'on the ground'.

29 NMR was a cross-border, all-Ireland Study (2004–2006) about return migration involving researchers at University College Cork (UCC); the University of Limerick, Queen's University Belfast (QUB); and the Mellon Centre for Migration Studies (MCMS). The NIEN Study (2006–2008) was funded by the AHRC and based at QUB and MCMS. The author conducted the Ulster interviews for NMR and all interviews for NIEN. Both studies drew on the example and experience of a previous Irish migration study (2000–2002), Breaking the Silence: Staying at Home in an Emigrant Society, based at UCC (see Gray, 2002a, 2007, 2009).

30 An approach also taken by psychologists Grinberg and Grinberg (1989) in their ground-breaking study based on the interviews they conducted with migrants in several jurisdictions.

31 However, note DeMartini's (1985) critique of Mannheim in which he argues that political activism may actually link generations.

32 Portes (2010: 1557) notes that in migration studies there is a tendency to take

either a short-term or very long-term migration time frame; the former providing rich detail of migration-in-process while the latter shows the 'durable effects' of migration. He suggests rather that a 'middle time frame encompassing two or three generations' is preferable.

33 In Morrison's view, 'rememory' has energy of its own – it does not go away – and is often strongly associated with places. It is comprised of traumatic memories that are debilitating as they transcend normal past and present temporal dimensions, repeatedly ambushing the individual at unexpected moments, demanding to be re-enacted in the psyche.

34 Raczymow's 'La Mémoire Trouée' has been translated into English and published in *Yale French Studies* Vol. 85 (1994): 98–105.

35 Theatre of Witness was founded and directed by Teya Sepinuck. The production and tour of 'We carried your secrets' was funded by the Holywell Trust and Donegal County Council. A film of the production (fifty-four minutes) directed by Declan Keeney and produced by John McIlduff was premiered in Derry on 12 May 2010. Website: www.theatreofwitness.org/ (accessed 12 May 2010). A second production featuring the stories of women entitled, *I Once Knew a Girl: Unheard Stories of Women*, toured in the autumn of 2010.

36 As the area of autobiographical memory in the field of psychology has an enormous literature associated with it, it is not possible here to reference the subject comprehensively. The works cited, however, include substantial reviews of relevant literature.

37 See also the other articles in this special issue of the journal *Memory* (Vol. 16, No.3, 2008) devoted to the relationship of individual and collective memory, especially the Introduction by Barnier and Sutton. In addition, see Wulf Kansteiner's (2002) useful review of collective memory studies.

38 Jansari and Parkin (1996) have suggested that the RB may be formed earlier (i.e., from six to fifteen years) however, McAdams (2001) places the reminiscence bump between the ages of fifteen to twenty-five years. Holmes and Conway (1999) have suggested that there may be two sub-RBs occurring during the ten to thirty-year-period which serve different functions: the first from ten to nineteen years, exhibiting more recall for public events and thus contributing to the formation of generational identity; and a second sub-RB from twenty to twenty-nine years that demonstrates more recall for private events, contributing to personal identity formation (e.g., formation of relationships, establishment of own home, career, etc.).

39 Several explanations have been posited for this phenomenon: 1) that cognitive capacities are at their optimum during these formative RB years thus allowing greater memory encoding; 2) that it is a time of identity formation when the adult identity emerges; and 3) cognitive mechanisms allow for increased encoding of first time and novel experiences, a large proportion of which occur during the RB years and consequently demonstrate a higher degree of memory retrieval.

Notes to Chapter 2: Northern Ireland: Migration History and Demography

[1] The Census Act (Ireland), 1920, provided that a census should be taken in Ireland on 24 April 1921, but it was postponed indefinitely because of 'disturbed conditions prevailing in the country at that that time' (Finance Minister H.M. Pollock, Parliamentary Debates, Northern Ireland, 19 April 1923, Vol. 3: 431).

[2] Letter reprinted in G.B. Kenna (1997 [1922]: 118), a pseudonym for Father John Hassan who witnessed the violence in Belfast and wrote this contemporary account (see also Parkinson, 2004). In total, seventy-four people were killed between July and December 1920 and from 1920 to 1922, there were in total 455 people killed and over 2,000 wounded (Kenna, 1997 [1922]: 101). My own family was to some extent victimised in this violence when on 26 August 1920, the riots spread to Ballymacarett in East Belfast and Catholic businesses on the Newtownards Road and Seaforde Street were attacked and looted. Stephen Conlin's illustration, 'The Troubles in Ballymacarett', clearly shows my grandfather's shop (B. Devlin) on Seaforde Street with an angry crowd gathered outside (Bardon and Conlin, 1985: 24–5).

[3] Because population counts were based on the most recent census data then available which dated back to 1911, the figures were greatly disputed in many communities. The recommendations of the Boundary Commission were never implemented and the report was shelved. See Terence Dooley (2000: 51–7); Michael Kennedy (2000: Chapter 1); Kieran Rankin (2001, 2007, 2008, 2009); and Paul Murray (2011) for discussion of these issues.

[4] In a bid to make the best migration estimates possible, it has been necessary to avail of several data sources including: the Northern Ireland census (1926–2011); the annual reports of the Registrar-General for Northern Ireland (since 1922); the *Ulster Year Book* (1922–1985) – all make use of Board of Trade data; population estimates from the Northern Ireland Statistics and Research Agency (NISRA); census and demographic data from the Central Statistics Office (CSO) in Dublin, the Office of National Statistics (ONS), General Register Office for Scotland, Statistics Canada, Australian Bureau of Statistics, Statistics New Zealand; and publications from government departments including the UK Department of Work and Pensions (DWP), the Home Office and several departments of the Northern Ireland Government.

[5] Vaughan and Fitzpatrick (1978: 3). A first unsuccessful census was attempted in 1813–1815 under the supervision of William Shaw Mason. For the censuses of 1821 and 1831, returns were filled out by enumerators and are considered to be less accurate than those from 1841 onwards when householders filled out the forms themselves (i.e., presumably those who were literate). See 'Census of Ireland (1821, 1831 and 1841 compared)', *Dublin University Magazine* Vol. 23, No. 137 (May 1844), at: www.libraryireland.com/articles/CensusIrelandDUM23-137/index.php (accessed 8 September 2012); and also Froggatt (1965); Ian White (2012).

6   The total population of Ireland in 1841 was 8,175,124 and by 1851 had declined to 6,552,385.

7   The corresponding all-Ulster population figures for these years are 1841: 2,386,373; 1851: 2,011,880; and 1891: 1,619,814 (Vaughan and Fitzpatrick, 1978: 16). Between 1841 and 1951, the six counties that became Northern Ireland experienced a 17 per cent decline of population while the twenty-six-county area lost almost 55 per cent of its population (Bradley, 1999: 43; and Mjøset, 1992: 222).

8   Calculated from figures provided by Vaughan and Fitzpatrick (1978) from the Board of Trade emigration returns and census data.

9   Figures from Kennedy (1994: 23, Table 21); Munck (1993: 85); Sexton (2003: 799); and author's calculations based on Northern Ireland census 1926–2011; NISRA, mid-year population estimates; Ireland, census 1926–2011; CSO, PEA01: Population estimates by age group, sex and year (1950–2012); and PEA09: Annual population change by year and component (1987–2012). Northern Ireland outflow rates for 1971–1981 and 1981–1991 may be slightly lower if, as is NISRA's recent practice, the revised 1981 and 1991 census figures are substituted with mid-year population estimates.

10 Registrar General Northern Ireland, *Annual Report for 2009* (2010: 8). Hereafter, RG Report 2009, etc.

11 NISRA, 'Report: A demographic portrait of Northern Ireland', *Population Trends* 135 (spring) 2009: 91–97; idem, 'Census 2011: population and household results for Northern Ireland' [press release], 16 July 2012 (Belfast: NISRA).

12 Annual net migration figures for this period are: 1998 (minus 1,800); 1999 (minus 4,800); 2000 (minus 2,200); 2001 (minus 1,100); 2002 (plus 1,000); 2003 (plus 200); and 2004 (plus 1,600). NISRA, 'Rebased population and migration estimates Northern Ireland (2001–11) – statistical report', 30 April 2013, Table 2.

13 In the year ending June 2007, net migration amounted to 10,900 while natural increase totalled 9,300 (source as in note 12).

14 Net migration figures for these years were: 2008 (7,700); 2009 (3,700); 2010 (1,200); and 2011 (minus 1,500) (source as in note 12). BBC Northern Ireland broadcast a television programme on the issue in their Spotlight series, entitled 'Lost generation', 31 January 2012, in which several young people were interviewed who had recently emigrated or were planning to emigrate. By late 2011, approximately one in five young people aged eighteen to twenty-four in Northern Ireland were unemployed. See 'Youth unemployment soars by 155%', BBC News Northern Ireland, 17 January 2012, at: www.bbc.co.uk/news/uk-northern-ireland-16587735 (accessed 1 February 2012). See also the front page story, 'Exodus of our middle-class: fears grow as hordes of talented young professionals quit Ulster to find work', *Belfast Telegraph*, 20 February 2012.

15 NISRA, 'Census 2011: population and household results for Northern Ireland' [press release], 16 July 2012.

16 The 2011 census estimates give the total UK population at 63,181,775 (NI = 1,810,863; England = 53,012,456; Scotland = 5,295,000; and Wales = 3,063,456). ONS, UK census 2011: www.ons.gov.uk/ons/guide-method/census/2011/uk-census/index.html (accessed 17 December 2012). Migration proportions based on figures for 2010, see ONS, *Migration Statistics Quarterly Report* (November 2011): 20.

17 NISRA, 'Census 2011: population and household results for Northern Ireland' [press release], 16 July 2012; 'Census 2011: population and household estimates for local government districts in Northern Ireland' [statistics bulletin], 19 September 2012.

18 Department of Enterprise, Trade and Investment (DETINI). *Monthly Labour Market Report, October 2011*. Belfast: DETINI: www.detini.gov.uk/ (accessed 5 November 2011).

19 DETINI, *Northern Ireland Labour Force Survey Quarterly Supplement: April–June 2011* (31 August 2011) p. 10: www.detini.gov.uk/ (accessed 5 November 2011).

20 Some estimates are higher, e.g., 22.6 million leaving the UK between 1815 and 1914 (Bridge and Fedorowich, 2003: 4).

21 These were the self-governing dominions: Canada; Newfoundland; Australia; New Zealand; and Union of South Africa (from 1910). While the Irish Free State acquired dominion status from 1922, it was never considered an 'overseas' dominion.

22 As the Board of Trade only distinguished permanent migrants from passengers in the annual migration figures beginning in 1913, care must be taken with migration estimates prior to that year (Plant, 1951: 174–5; Snow, 1931: 242).

23 Some estimates of British emigration are: 1880s = 1,640,000 (Constantine, 2003: 19); 1900–1909 = 1,670,198 (Bridge and Fedorowich, 2003: 4). For the 1920s = 1,816,618 (Constantine, 2003: 19); 1,811,553 (Plant, 1951: 174–5); or 1,742,000 (Mitchell, 2007: 138).

24 Ronald Hyam (2010: Chapter 1) has noted two distinct approaches to scholarship on the British Empire: economic determinism (as with Hancock's influential 'men, money and markets' model, 1942: Chapter 3) that has a focus on trade as the fundamental rationale underlying Empire; and geopolitical models with a focus on international relations and the elites involved in decision-making. I would venture that another more recent approach via literary accounts and personal narratives considers the lived experience of Empire and Commonwealth among ordinary people.

25 For an illuminating discussion of the development of British social reform in this period, see Offer (2006), especially Chapter 5 on the tensions between idealist and non-idealist thought.

26 It was later called the Oversea Settlement Board. The OSC was formed upon recommendation of the Dominions Royal Commission (1917) initially to contend with the settlement of soldiers demobilised following the First World War. Its final report was issued in May 1938.

27 Following Canada's development of nationality legislation in 1946, effective from 1947, the members of the Commonwealth agreed in 1948 to establish their own nationality legislation: United Kingdom (1948); Australia (1948); New Zealand (1948); South Africa (1949); and Newfoundland (joined Canada 1949) (Mansergh, 1968 [1958]: 382–7).

28 Under the provisions of the Aliens (Exemption) Order, 1935, the Irish Free State exempted the countries of the Commonwealth (UK, Canada, Newfoundland, Australia, New Zealand, South Africa and India) from alien status. See Hancock (1937: Chapters 3 and 6); and Mansergh (1968 [1958]: Chapter 6), for discussion of Irish constitutional and citizenship legislation in the period leading up to Ireland's secession from the Commonwealth.

29 Preferred selection of immigrants by ethnic or national group ceased in Canada in 1962, in Australia in 1973 and in New Zealand by 1974, though in South Africa it continued until 1994 (Constantine, 2003: 27). Conversely, the United Kingdom brought in the Commonwealth Immigrants Act (1962) and the Commonwealth Immigration Act (1968) to restrict immigration from Commonwealth countries, especially from the Caribbean and the Indian sub-continent.

30 Mitchell (1988: 84) provides total annual emigration figures by citizenship (1964–1980 = 3,091,500 UK citizens), however, the emigration figures relating to destination are by 'country of last residence' (including UK citizens and non-citizen residents).

31 A recent estimate puts the UK-born population of South Africa at 212,000 in 2006 (Sriskandarajah and Drew, 2006: 17). Comparative figures for Irish-born (e.g., twenty-six-county area) are Australia (50,259); New Zealand (6,885); and Canada (22,825) (Census for Australia 2006; Census for Canada 2006; and Census for New Zealand 2006). In 2001, over 70 per cent of the UK- and Irish-born residents of New Zealand had by that time lived there for over twenty years (Census for New Zealand 2001, People born overseas, Table 6: birthplace and sex by years since arrival in New Zealand, at: www.stats.govt.nz/Census/2001-census-data/2001-census-people-born-overseas.aspx) (accessed 28 December 2012). For characteristics of British emigrants, see ONS, 'Emigration – a short story' [article] (24 November 2011: 4–5). Note that France and Spain have been primarily destinations for retirees but the numbers have diminished significantly since the economic downturn in 2008. From 2006 to 2010, the top five destinations for non-British citizens leaving the UK have consistently been in order of preference: Poland, India, France, the United States and Australia.

32 Statistics calculated at: www.dwp.gov.uk/ (accessed 9 September 2012).

33 Thousands of British and Irish immigrants arrived in Canada each year via the land border with the United States. Thus in any given year Canadian figures for incoming British immigrants tend to be higher than UK figures for outgoing British emigrants to Canada as supplied by the Board of Trade. Canadian immigration data for the 1920s recorded migrants by country of birth, racial origin and nationality, however, Northern Ireland was not recognised as a distinct place of birth in the

data until 1930. The numbers of 'Irish-born' immigrants during the 1920s would indicate that all have been included under 'Ireland'. Census data of the principal receiving countries has not consistently included distinct categories for those born in independent Ireland and Northern Ireland and there is no way of knowing whether Northern Ireland respondents have chosen to self-designate on census question-naires as British or Irish. Prior to 1951, the Canadian census did not distinguish the resident population born in independent Ireland from the NI-born (Historical Statistics of Canada, Section A: Population and Migration, Table A297–326: Country of birth of other British-born and the foreign-born population, census dates, 1871 to 1971, at: www.statcan.gc.ca/pub/11-516-x/sectiona/4147436-eng.htm).

[34] However, a central aspiration of assisted migration was to stimulate the further chain migration of other family members, friends and neighbours who would for the most part be self or family financed. In this, the schemes were largely successful (Harper and Constantine, 2010; Johnston, 1972; and Moran, 2004).

[35] The scheme was extended to include ex-Royal Irish Constabulary officers, some 1,436 of whom emigrated overseas in the period 1919–1923 (Fedorowich, 1996: 105).

[36] Caution must be exercised on the subject of interwar unemployment rates in Britain as a substantial percentage of the population was not then eligible for national insurance. While the official rate of insured unemployed from 1921 to 1930 averaged approximately 12.5 per cent and only dipped below 10 per cent in 1927 (9.7%), C. H. Feinstein (1972) has provided widely recognised estimates on the rates for all unemployed (insured and non-insured) which are consistently lower, averaging to 8.6 per cent over the same years with a rate for 1927 of 6.8 per cent. Both sets of British unemployment rates are included in Mitchell (1988: 124).

[37] There was also concern to address the gender imbalance in Britain in the 1920s of over one million 'surplus' females due to the high rate of male casualties during the First World War (Noakes, 2012: 26).

[38] Organisations included: the Society for the Oversea Settlement of British Women; YWCA; Girls' Friendly Society; Canadian Council of Immigration of Women for Household Service; and the Salvation Army (Barber, 1991; Blakely, 1988; Gothard, 1990).

[39] Lettice Ilbert Fisher (1875–1956), a lecturer in economics and history, was the wife of H. A. L. Fisher, historian and President of the Board of Education (1916–1922) under Lloyd George.

[40] British Oversea Settlement Delegation to Canada (1924: 5). The report documents interesting cultural differences, for example, Canadian organisations requested long trousers for winter wear instead of short pants for boys (p. 7).

[41] Northern Ireland women desiring domestic training to go to Australia were sent to the Australian Government training centre in Market Harborough, Leicestershire (*Ulster Year Book*, 1929: 112).

[42] This letter was published in 1911. The *Imperial Colonist* was the serial publication

of the British Women's Settlement Association (formed in 1901 and a precursor to the Society for the Oversea Settlement of British Women, established 1919).

[43] Increasing concern over the falling birth rate in particular led to the appointment of the Royal Commission on Population (1944–1949) (see Redington and Clarke, 1951).

[44] The ESA was renamed the Commonwealth Settlement Act in 1957.

[45] The Canadian scheme required the emigrant to pay ten pounds up front towards the passage with the Canadian Government providing an interest-free loan for the rest (approximately fifty-five pounds) which had to eventually be repaid in full ('Assisted emigration to Canada: New scheme announced', *The Times*, 1 February 1951: 3).

[46] These immigrants were assisted with reception and finding employment but they were expected to pay their own way (Hill, 1948: 20). The cost of the flight was approximately sixty-seven pounds. The Ontario Government claimed that 'many hundreds of members of their families have followed by sea' and announced cancellation of the air immigration scheme on 25 March 1948. (Ontario, *Journals of the Legislative Assembly of the Province of Ontario, from the 3rd March to 16th April 1948: fourth session of the twenty-second legislature of Ontario*, Vol. 82 (3): 84. Toronto: Baptist Johnson, King's Printer).

[47] Imperial Economic Conference Ottawa, 1932: Notes on matters specially affecting Northern Ireland. 16 June 1932, PRONI, CAB 4/302/1, p. 13. (Memoranda prepared by Ministers of Agriculture and Commerce).

[48] Indeed, from partition until the renewal of conflict in the late 1960s, the British House of Commons only devoted a mere two hours per year on average to Northern Ireland affairs (Howe, 2000: 72).

[49] Imperial Economic Conference (1932: 13). During the autumn of 1921 as the Anglo–Irish Conference negotiations were underway, the British proposal to create an all-Ireland Parliament with Dominion status resulted in James Craig's counter-proposal in a letter to Lloyd George, dated 17 November, that if Northern Ireland were to be fiscally separated from Britain, would 'it not be better to grant to Ulster the status of a separate Dominion'? Lloyd George, however, was vehemently opposed to the creation of two Dominions in Ireland ('Correspondence between His Majesty's Government and the Prime Minister of Northern Ireland relating to the proposals for an Irish settlement', pp. i, 83 [Cmd 1561], H. C. 1921: 10). James Loughlin (1995: 149) has noted that the matter of potential Dominion status for Northern Ireland was raised again in 1948, demonstrating the desire of the Northern Ireland authorities for increased powers. The irony in all this, as James Mitchell (2006: 56) and others have noted, is that Ulster had been the strongest anti-home rule region of the UK. Mitchell has also pointed out that the finance structure for Northern Ireland as set out in the Government of Ireland Act, 1920, was really intended to provide a revenue-raising structure which would have allowed for more autonomy, however, the subsequent development of the welfare state made this unfeasible. Financial responsibilities were generally apportioned and negotiated between the British Treasury and the Ministry of Finance in Northern Ireland, with input from the Joint

Exchequer Board established under Section 32 of the Government of Ireland Act, 1920. W. D. Flackes (1983: 294–5) noted that some British ministers considered the Stormont system 'as nearer to Dominion status than simple devolution' because of the established convention that Westminster MPs were not to raise issues that were within the remit of a Stormont minister. See also M. W. Heslinga's discussion of Ulster as a 'separate nation' (1979: 55–66) and for the history of Dominion status, see McIntyre (1999).

[50] Loughlin (1995: 101) has argued, however, that as Ireland was after partition still within the Empire, Northern Ireland's external image was often 'culturally indistinguishable' from the rest of Ireland. Certainly, the documentation of Irish migrants in immigration and census data of countries outside the UK would indicate the slow pace of recognition of Northern and Southern Ireland as separate entities.

[51] Hancock (1942: 95) lists a series of pamphlets in support of the Empire. Intriguingly, one which bears the title: *A Self-Supporting Empire: With a Foreword by Sir Edward Carson* was published in 1918 and written by E. Saunders (possibly the Canadian agronomist Sir Charles E. Saunders, the inventor of Marquis wheat).

[52] They were William Massey (NZ) in 1923; J. G. Coates (NZ) and Walter Stanley Monroe (Newfoundland) in 1926; and R. B. Bennett (Canada), James H. Scullin (Australia) and George W. Forbes (NZ) in 1930. For descriptions of their visits to Northern Ireland, see Jeffery (2008).

[53] Imperial Economic Conference, 1932: 15–20. Tariffs were placed on many manufactured goods, including: oatmeal, maize products, woollen cloth, clothing, footwear, soap, candles, jam and baked goods.

[54] Imperial Economic Conference, 1932: 14.

[55] For 1922 and 1923, emigration statistics for Northern Ireland were collected at sea ports by the Royal Ulster Constabulary and provided to the Board of Trade. These did not include those who departed or arrived via ports in the Irish Free State nor was any information collected concerning immigrants (RG Report, 1922: 7). From 1924 until 1963, statistics concerning overseas 'British' migrants – those arriving from or departing Northern Ireland to 'countries outside Europe' – were collected by the Board of Trade and supplied to the Registrar General for Northern Ireland for its annual reports. Data on movement between Northern Ireland and Britain was not recorded for much of the 1920s, though an estimate for the years 1926–1937 for the flow with 'countries within Europe' was provided in the NI census 1937. Judging by the large numbers of NI-born recorded in the censuses for England, Wales and Scotland in 1931, 1951 and 1961, it is safe to assume that the large part of the European flow was actually with Britain. It is assumed here that those defined by the Board of Trade as 'British nationals' in their data for Northern Ireland were largely the NI-born and their families and therefore the inflow data of this group from overseas destinations in large part represents the return migration flow. Calculating emigration and return flows specifically relating to Northern Ireland migrants is problematic since they are counted as 'British' in the census data of most destination countries and not distinguished from other British nationals in much

UK demographic data. The ROI and New Zealand are exceptions to this.

56 Total based on estimates presented in Parliament for 1922–1923 = 16,000; Board of Trade overseas emigration data 1924–1926 reported in the 1926 census = 29,761 (NI census 1926, General Report: xxv); 1927–1937 overseas emigration data reported in the 1937 census and the *Ulster Year Book* = 48,557 (NI census 1937, Preliminary Report: 2); total = 94,318. Data on overseas destinations of emigrants is only available from 1925 to 1937. The Board of Trade estimated *net emigration* from Northern Ireland at 4,500 for 1922 and 9,000 for 1923. However, the Minister of Finance, Hugh Pollock presented estimates in the Northern Ireland Parliament on the numbers of overseas emigrants as: 1922 = 6,000; 1923 = 10,000; and 1924 = 8,000 (Parliamentary Debates, Northern Ireland, 5 May 1927, Vol. 8: 1179).

57 Source data for Figure 2.3 from the Board of Trade as reported in the *Ulster Year Book*. These outflow statistics are probably conservative as net migration figures for the 1926–1937 inter-censal period as reported in the 1937 census give the total net outflow of 57,643: to Britain/Europe = 34%; and overseas = 66% (NI census 1937, Preliminary Report: 2). Note that the Board of Trade data represents the actual flow of individual migrants while net migration figures are calculated on population growth as indicated in the census, taking account of natural increase/decrease. Net migration estimates therefore only represent how many people are missing from the expected population count or are surplus to it. The figure of 57,643 reported in the 1937 census was later revised slightly and appeared from the 1951 census forward as 57,651 (NI census 1951, General Report: xviii, Table 1).

58 For 1924–1926, overseas inflow represented only 16 per cent of the outflow (NI census 1926, General Report: xxv). From 1927 to 1929, overseas emigration averaged 11,606 per year, although by 1932 there were only 610 emigrants; the average for 1932–1936 being only 687 per annum. Overseas inflow into Northern Ireland averaged just under 1,700 per year from 1927 to 1929, jumping to over 2,600 per year from 1930 to 1933, with a peak of 3,219 in 1932.

59 Census for England and Wales, 1931 and 1951; Census for Scotland, 1931 and 1951 (Birthplace Tables). In 1931, there were 70,056 born in the six Northern Ireland counties resident in England and Wales plus 67,905 in Scotland, amounting to 27.3 per cent of the total Irish-born population resident in Britain. By 1951, there had been a substantial shift in the emigration of NI-born towards England and Wales (134,965) and away from Scotland (43,354); the total amounting to a quarter of the Irish-born population in Britain. Although employment data charting the movement of the UK labour force has been available since the 1940s, it has recorded only the movement of workers, not their accompanying non-employed spouses and children. It also remains difficult to accurately assess the undoubtedly significant numbers of NI-born who over the century returned from overseas destinations to mainland Britain, rather than Northern Ireland.

60 Letter of 24 May 1932 from the Office of the Registrar General and Statistician, Ministry of Finance, Government of Northern Ireland to C. H. Martin, GRO, London (file T.H.302), at: www.histpop.org (accessed 5 December 2012). Delaney

(2000: 88) cites a memorandum by demographer A. M. Carr-Saunders of October 1930 in which he claimed that migration from Northern Ireland to Britain had recently declined due to worsening economic conditions in Britain.

61 Lobo and Salvo (1998: 258) report that between 1932 and 1945 the average flow from independent Ireland into the United States was fewer than 400 per year.

62 Birthplace tables in the Northern Ireland census provide the principal source of information concerning immigrants, especially prior to 1971. The earlier censuses also included a category for those born at sea which is included here under foreign-born. In addition, there are usually a few thousand returns in every census for which no place of birth is stated, although the 1981 census reported an uncharacteristically high proportion (17,400 or 1.2%) (Compton, 1995: 19). Some early censuses include information about length of stay of immigrants (e.g., 1937, 1951 and 1961), but censuses since 1961 have included information about migrants who have relocated to or within Northern Ireland within the year prior to the census (address one year ago). In 2011, new questions relating to migration were introduced: lived outside Northern Ireland; last country lived in; date of most recent arrival in Northern Ireland; intention to stay in the UK; and passports held. See NISRA, 'Comparability of the census questionnaire in Northern Ireland between 2001 and 2011', December 2012.

63 NI census 1926, Preliminary Report: xxv. A fascinating private census of 2,117 incoming Protestants to County Fermanagh in the years 1920–1925 was compiled by solicitor James Cooper of Enniskillen and provided to the Boundary Commissioners in May 1925. The document, which was republished in the *Clogher Record* (Dooley, 1996), demonstrates that many southern Protestants went north and purchased farms and businesses with the intention of permanent settlement.

64 Ireland, Census 1936, Vol. 3: Religion and Birthplaces, p. 3; Table 1A. Note that Sexton and O'Leary (1996: 301) have calculated that as many as 90,000 Protestants left the Irish Free State between 1911 and 1926 but their estimate includes approximately 30,000 British Government and Armed Forces personnel stationed in Ireland. Terence Dooley (1996: 87) has suggested that approximately 25 per cent of the southern Protestants who left the twenty-six counties were affiliated to the British Army or the police (e.g., RIC). See also Kent Fedorowich (1996) on the disbandment and emigration of RIC personnel in the 1920s. Robert Kennedy (1973: 121) has suggested that the inter-censal outflow figures for Protestants which include the foreign-born (most from Britain) has somewhat masked the full extent of the decline of native Irish-born Protestants, especially notable between 1926 to 1961, though the 'long retreat' of Protestants in Ireland has a much lengthier historical trajectory (Kennedy et al., 1991). For Ulster as a whole, the non-Catholic (largely Protestant) proportion of the population in 1911 amounted to 56.3 per cent, forming majorities in Belfast Borough (75.9%) and in the counties of Antrim (79.5%), Armagh (54.7%), Down (68.4%), and Londonderry (58.5%); large minorities in Fermanagh (43.8%), Tyrone (44.6%), and Derry Borough (43.8%); and significant minorities in Cavan (19%), Donegal (21.1%), and Monaghan

(25.3%) (Ireland, Census 1911, General Report: xlvii–l and 211).

65 Lynch cites, 'Reports on Recruits leaving Northern Ireland to join Irish Free State Army' ('Secret Series' files, PRONI, HA32/l/168). Even in the present day, there are over 10,000 Northerners living in southern border counties who consider themselves to have been 'displaced' because of the conflict (Combat Poverty Agency, 2005: 5).

66 All rates based on insured unemployed. Sources: for Great Britain's rates (Mitchell, 1988: 125) and for Northern Ireland rates (*Ulster Year Book*, 1926–1947). Note that Mitchell provides unemployment rates for Northern Ireland that vary somewhat from those provided in the *Ulster Year Book*.

67 In 1927, Unionist MP John F. Gordon, then Secretary to the Minister of Labour, stated in the Northern Ireland Parliament that since May 1922, 28,102 men had been employed on 792 relief schemes at a total cost of £4,750,962. The average period of employment was only three months (Parliamentary Debates, Northern Ireland, 4 May 1927, Vol. 8: 1149).

68 Michael Roe (1995: 211) has suggested that Northern Ireland was not fully included in the ESA during the 1920s, however, assurance on the issue was sought in Parliament in a query by the Unionist MP for Antrim, Robert Crawford, addressed to the Minister of Labour, J. M. Andrews, who gave assurance that Northern Ireland was indeed party to the ESA, and although there had been some delay on the part of the Australian Government in accepting applications from Northern Ireland, he believed that recent negotiations with the Australian authorities would resolve the issue in short order (Parliamentary Debates, Northern Ireland, 9 April 1923, Vol. 3: 473).

69 While emigration data does not provide characteristics of emigrants on the basis of religious denomination, clues may be found in the census population counts. For example, in the inter-censal period, 1926–1937, there was a decline by 10.5 per cent (minus 2,443) of the resident population claiming Presbyterian denomination, notable in view of the percentage increase of the other principal denominations (RC – plus 33.9%; Anglican = plus 29.1%; and Methodist = plus 24 1%), though part of a general decline in Presbyterian numbers since at least 1841 that was reversed between 1937 and 1951, with an increase of 21.2 per cent (reported in the NI census 1951, General Report: xlii–xliii).

70 Parliamentary Debates, Northern Ireland, 13 March 1924, Vol. 4: 137. Although MPs in this period usually took care not to mention religion during parliamentary debates, the subject, occupation or local area under discussion, as in this instance, usually provided adequate indication. The farmers' sons in question would have been Protestants.

71 Nationalist MP Joseph Connellan noted that by 1929, people were referring to the training centre 'by the odious name of the Richhill Emigration College' (Parliamentary Debates, Northern Ireland, 10 June 1929, Vol. 11: 389–90).

72 The Australian Government was expected to pay or provide loans for the passage for their trainees (Parliamentary Debates, Northern Ireland, 4 May 1927, Vol. 8: 1154).

[73] Parliamentary Debates, Northern Ireland, 27 October 1926, Vol. 7: 1953.

[74] Canada was relatively late in bringing in its Unemployment Insurance Act of 1941 under which 42 per cent of workers were insured. Employers and employees each paid 40 per cent and the Federal Government 20 per cent of contributions. The system was revamped and greatly expanded under the Trudeau Liberal Government in 1971.

[75] Parliamentary Debates, Northern Ireland, 27 October 1926, Vol. 7: 1983.

[76] Parliamentary Debates, Northern Ireland, 4 May 1927, Vol. 8: 1167.

[77] Jack Beattie, Parliamentary Debates, Northern Ireland, 4 May 1927, Vol. 8: 1164.

[78] Parliamentary Debates, Northern Ireland, 5 May 1927, Vol. 8: 1185–6. Dehra Chichester (1882–1963), known after her second marriage in 1928 as Dehra Parker, had been born in India and named for her place of birth (Dehra Dun). She also spent part of her childhood and youth in the United States and Germany, and was Unionist MP for Londonderry from 1921 to 1929 and for South Londonderry from 1933 to 1960.

[79] J. M. Andrews, Minister of Labour, Parliamentary Debates, Northern Ireland, 25 November 1930, Vol. 12: 2402.

[80] Vaughan and Fitzpatrick (1978: 267) report Board of Trade data until 1938 and from 1947 onwards. However, data for 1946 is reported in the NI census 1951 and in the RG Reports, 1951–1963.

[81] Canadian immigration data is reported in the *Canada Year Book*.

[82] The total net outward movement from Northern Ireland recorded for the 1937–1951 period was 67,267 (59.7% male and 40.3% female); the large majority destined for Britain/Europe (minus 57,333) with only a small proportion heading overseas (minus 9,934 or 15%). The figure for Britain includes losses in the British Armed Forces and mercantile marine during the war years, however, Board of Trade data relating to the overseas movement was unavailable for the years 1939–1945 (NI census 1951, General Report: xviii–xix).

[83] The British Government required travel permits for Irish citizens from 1940 to 1946 and it actively recruited Irish labour from August 1941. See Delaney (2000: Chapter 3) for a detailed explanation of the permits and recruitment processes.

[84] These figures relate to the army, air force and women's auxiliaries. An additional 5,000 are estimated to have served in the British Navy.

[85] Calculated using the difference between the population estimates of December 1945 and 1951. However, the Board of Trade figures for 1946–1950 as reported in the 1951 census differ somewhat from the Isles and Cuthbert analysis, indicating that 14,748 individuals emigrated overseas while 4,380 British nationals returned from overseas and from this we might infer a return rate of approximately 30 per cent (NI census 1951, General Report: xviii–xix).

[86] The annual net movement overseas was 2,959 and to Britain/Europe of 6,226. Actual overseas movement monitored by the Board of Trade for the decade recorded 40,979 emigrants and 11,391 incoming, suggesting a return rate of around 28 per cent (NI census 1961, General Report: xxvi).

87 The large increase of Irish-born (+171,283) and NI-born (+46,538) resident in Britain is evident in the country of birth tables in the Census for England and Wales, 1961; and Census for Scotland, 1961.

88 The unemployment rate in Northern Ireland reached 10.3 per cent in 1952 and rose again to 9.3 per cent in 1958 (Mitchell, 1988: 126).

89 NI census 1961, General Report : xxvi.

90 Parliamentary Debates, Northern Ireland, 27 February 1962, Vol.50: 1989–1990. Captain Terence O'Neill (1914–1990) served as MP for Bann Side (1946–1970) and as Prime Minister of Northern Ireland (1963–1969).

91 Parliamentary Debates, Northern Ireland, 27 February 1962, Vol.50: 1992–1993. David Bleakley (born 1925) was Labour MP for Belfast – Victoria from 1958 to 1965.

92 The NI census recorded 1,086 from the Indian subcontinent (India, Pakistan and Ceylon) in 1951 and 1,316 by 1961 (NI census 1951, General Report: 21, Table 16: Birthplaces; and NI census 1961, General Report: 26, Table 15: Birthplaces). The first Chinese restaurant opened in Belfast in 1962 (Northern Ireland Museums Council, 2005: 18 and 20).

93 NI census 1951, General Report: xli, 22, Table 18: Persons born outside Northern Ireland by religion and duration of residence.

94 NI census 1961, General Report: L, Table XXII; and 28–9, Table 17: Persons born outside Northern Ireland by religion and place of birth. Sects included under 'other denominations' were: Jewish = 1,191; Hindu = 316; Sikh = 62; 'Mohammedan'/ Islam = 272; Mormon = 371; Greek Orthodox = 51; Bahai = 32; Spiritualist = 56; Buddhist = 50; Singh = 12; and 'Chinese religion' = 15. The larger Protestant denominations listed in this category include: Brethren = 16,847; Baptist = 13,765; Non-subscribing, Reformed and Free Presbyterian = 10,881; and Congregationalist = 9,838.

95 RG Report 1964: 41.

96 Because of the large population movements of the 1950s, limited censuses were conducted in England and Wales, Scotland and Ireland in April 1966 and in Northern Ireland on 9 October 1966. Within the UK, only Northern Ireland conducted a full population census, the others were on a 10 per cent sample basis, however, the NI census questions were limited in scope, omitting those on religion, place of birth and nationality while adding a few relating to movement within Northern Ireland, including the distance commuters travelled to work (NI census 1966, Preliminary Report: 3). In the five-year period 1961–1966, there was a net outward movement from Northern Ireland of 37,701 (54% male and 46% female) and another 31,521 from 1966 to 1971. Beginning with the 1971 census, the output format was streamlined and the reports included much less analysis than earlier large format census documents.

97 As the data is recorded by country of last residence (not of birth), these were not necessarily all NI-born migrants.

98 Data analysis in this section is based on Board of Trade data for the overseas flows

to and from Northern Ireland for 'British' migrants from 1925 to 1938 and 1954 to 1963 as reported in the RG Reports.

99 Irish migration has generally been considered as exceptional among European countries in having an almost equal proportion of emigrants by gender. For example, among European emigrants to the USA from 1870 to 1920, 60–70 per cent were male (Storhaug, 2003: 71). Analysis based on immigration and alien outflow data from the annual reports of the US Commissioner-General of Immigration, 1908–1923, however, showed that Irish females comprised approximately half the Irish emigrant flow but less than half the return flow (Gould, 1980: 60, Table 3). 'T Hart (1985: 226) found in her earlier sample of Irish return migration data, 1858–1867, that two-thirds of the returnees were male, but in the period 1895–1925, between 52.2 and 56.7 of the Irish returnees were female.

100 Occupation data on a sample of Northern Ireland immigrants to the USA in the period 1956–1966 shows similar patterns (Boyle, 1968: 422). Over 15 per cent were professional/managerial; 22 per cent skilled trades; 14.5 per cent clerical/sales; 5 per cent services; just over 4 per cent domestics; only 4.5 per cent labourers; and over 34 per cent reported no occupation, namely housewives and children.

101 In the overseas flow for the 1920s and 1930s, for example, children and youth under eighteen comprised 24 per cent of the emigrant flow and 22 per cent of the return group, with children under twelve the large majority of under eighteens in both flows (65% of emigrant youth and 86% of returnee youth). Similarly, during the 1950s and 1960s, 32 per cent of emigrants and 28.5 per cent of returnees were under twenty; with under fifteens comprising 81.5 per cent of emigrant youth and over 87 per cent of the returnees. The proportion of under fifteens is documented only for the years 1961–1963 but the over 80 per cent figures are probably a safe enough assumption for the period. 'T Hart found that families returning with only one child under five years of age comprised a significant proportion of the returnee cohort in the 1860s (1985: 227–8); and Fitzpatrick has noted the prevalence of family groups in nineteenth-century Ulster migration (1996: 616 and 651, Map 7).

102 The Northern Ireland Education Act of 1947 made secondary education compulsory until age fifteen (although not widely enforced until 1957) and grants were also introduced to make third-level education more widely available. More equitable funding for Catholic schools, however, did not come on stream until the Northern Ireland Education Act of 1968. In the South, free secondary education was only made available in 1969.

103 The EU8 (formerly A8) countries that joined the EU on 1 May 2004 are: Czech Republic, Estonia, Hungary, Latvia, Lithuania, Poland, Slovakia and Slovenia. Their citizens were required until May 2011 to register for work in the UK under the Worker Registration Scheme (WRS). Malta and Cyprus also joined the EU on 1 May 2004 but are considered separately from the EU8 as they were not subject to the WRS requirements ('Long-Term International Migration Estimates for Northern Ireland, 2005-2006', NISRA, 2007: 2).

104 NISRA, 'Population and migration estimates Northern Ireland (2012) – statistics

press notice, 26 June 2013. In the twelve months ending in March 2009, applications to the UK Worker Registration Scheme (WRS) from EU8 countries had greatly declined (141,000) from the same period ending in March 2008 (215,000) and March 2007 (239,000) (Home Office, *Accession Monitoring Report,* May 2004– March 2009: 1).

[105] Concerns were raised about the reliability of the data in the censuses of 1971–1991, principally under-enumeration and the rates of non-response on the religion question. Problems with the 1981 census count centred on the under-enumeration of the population as a whole (over 3%) and in addition, that a significant number of respondents (18.5 per cent of the returns) refused to identify religious denomination. The under-enumeration which was concentrated in particular areas was first estimated at 19,000 persons by the Registrar General, soon after revised to 74,000 by the Policy Planning and Research Unit. The most recently agreed 1981 census count was 1,532,600 (Registrar General Report 2000: 22), however, NISRA has chosen to substitute the 1981 mid-year population estimate of 1,543,000, which would imply a lesser though still significant outflow rate. Kennedy (1994: 23) estimated the net migration flow for the 1970s at minus 6.7 (per 1000), though Munck (1993: 85) arrived at minus 7.2, while Sexton (2003: 799) presumably using the revised 1981 census figure above arrived at an estimate of minus 7.3. These calculations indicate that the outflow was greater than initially reported. See also Chapter 4 and discussions of census issues by Anderson and Shuttleworth (1994, 1998); Compton (1985); Doherty and Poole (2002); Morris and Compton (1985); O'Grada and Walsh (1995); and Shuttleworth and Lloyd (2006).

[106] Delaney (2000: 70) and Fitzgerald and Lambkin (2008: 236) have made this point with regard to Irish migration history in general. Concern over the 'polarisation' of Northern Ireland communities on denominational grounds due to sectarianism and violence has generated several reports and studies over the years (Community Relations Commission, 1971; Hughes et al., 2007; Murtagh, 2002; Poole, 1999; Poole and Doherty, 1996; Shirlow and Murtagh, 2006; Shirlow et al., 2005; Shuttleworth and Lloyd, 2006, etc.). A recent large-scale study on the internal mobility of the Northern Ireland workforce (employing data gathered from 1996 to 2001) noted the continuing effect of sectarian boundaries on access to employment in spite of policies put in place to encourage spatial mobility, thus demonstrating the difficulty of separating economic factors from the history of sectarian conflict (Shuttleworth and Green, 2009). In a related vein, Denis O'Hearn has recently argued that despite the peace process, the dividend for the Northern Ireland economy so far has not achieved the anticipated prosperity. Sectarian boundaries continue to ensure the marginalisation of a significant sector of the community, income levels are still lower than the UK, and the promised increase in foreign direct investment from the United States has been slow even though it is a 'major basis of economic legitimacy for the devolved assembly' (O' Hearn, 2008: 113).

[107] See, for example, Compton (1992, 1995); and with Power (1991). An exception is Ronald Terchek's Study (1984) discussed in Chapter 4.

108 See Bew et al., (1997: Chapter 4) for a discussion of these positions.

109 O'Grada points out that 36,000 jobs were lost during the period 1973–1986 in foreign-owned enterprises established in Northern Ireland from 1945 to 1973 (O'Grada, 1997: 135).

110 Part of this outflow was redistributed to the suburbs (Lambkin et al., 2013).

111 In the years ending in April 1987 and 1988, for example, annual emigration from the ROI amounted to 27,000 and 32,000 respectively where it had averaged 14,400 from 1981 to 1986 (Corcoran, 1989: 29). See the edited volume by Mulholland and Keogh (1989) for statistics and analysis of this period in the ROI.

112 Between May and August 1981, ten Republican prisoners in the Maze Prison died on hunger strike. Throughout the spring and summer there was significant civil disturbance in the form of protest marches, rallies and rioting.

113 Data on emigration from the ROI in this period also shows a marked preference for Britain (Corcoran, 1989: 33). Average yearly inflow from the ROI to the United States from 1972 to 1995, for example, amounted to only 3,997 or a total of 96,933 over the period, with approximately 39 per cent locating to New York and New Jersey. However, looking at this data year by year shows that the inflow was actually very low until the late 1980s, with 1,496 per year from 1972 to 1977 (total of 9,348) and only 1,155 from 1978 to 1986 (total of 10,394). The marked increase to 8,577 per year from 1987 to 1995 (total of 77,191) was largely due to those entering the USA on the new visa schemes (e.g., Donnelly and Morrison visas) who accounted for 79 per cent of the total ROI immigrant flow (Lobo and Salvo, 1998: 275).

114 The Labour Force Survey (LFS) is conducted by the ONS for Great Britain and for Northern Ireland by NISRA on behalf of the Department of Enterprise, Trade and Investment (DETINI). Because of a sample size of approximately 2,700 addresses per year in Northern Ireland of which only a small sub-sample are migrants, NISRA advises that as a source for information about migrants, LFS estimates are prone to sampling errors. See: www.detini.gov.uk/deti-stats-index/stats-surveys.htm (accessed 20 January 2013).

115 A survey of 1,000 emigrants leaving Northern Ireland by air and sea at the end of the New Year holidays in early 1988, most of whom were resident in Britain, with professionals and Protestants over-represented in the sample.

116 Analysis of data on four cohorts of university graduates from 1998 to 2002.

117 Dr David Marshall, NISRA, personal communication, 10 August 2009. The IRA declared its ceasefire on 31 August 1994 and was followed by a UDA/UVF ceasefire on 13 October 1994.

118 CSO, 'Population and migration estimates, April 2012, Table 4: Estimated Migration classified by Sex and Country of Destination/Origin, 2006–2012' (15 September 2012), p.5.

119 RG Report 2011: 10; and NISRA, 'Rebased population and migration estimates Northern Ireland (2001–11) – statistical report', 30 April 2013, Table 2. Unless otherwise indicated, UK statistics for this section, including the quarterly reports

on migration, are taken from the ONS population statistics area on their website: (www.ons.gov.uk/) and statistics hub: (www.statistics.gov.uk/hub/index.html); for Northern Ireland, population statistics and reports, international migration statistics and mid-year population estimates are available on the NISRA website: (www.nisra. gov.uk/archive/demography/); as are the Northern Ireland census tables for 2001 and 2011: (www.nisra.gov.uk/Census/) and the RG Reports. However, caution must be advised for Northern Ireland mid-year population estimates for 2001–2011 which have been revised by NISRA in light of the significant discrepancy with the estimate for June 2011 of 1,806,900 that was over 4,000 fewer than the 2011 census total of 1,810,863 taken on March 27.

120 The Polish population of Northern Ireland was estimated at 15,000 in 2011. ONS, 'Polish people in the UK. Half a million Polish residents', *Migration Statistics Quarterly Report* (August 2011); and ONS, *Migration Statistics Quarterly Report* (August 2012), Tables: Population by country of birth and nationality report; Table 1.4: Estimated overseas-born population resident in the United Kingdom by country of birth, January 2011 to December 2011 (accessed 2 September 2012).

121 ONS, *Migration Statistics Quarterly Report* (August 2012). Note the definition of British nationals employed by the ONS: '"British nationals" are people who have British citizenship, either because they were born with it or have been granted it since. Nationality is not necessarily determined by country of birth. In the year to September 2008 a total of 40.9 per cent of UK residents not born in the UK had British nationality. And of those UK residents who didn't have British nationality, 5.3 per cent had been born in the UK' (ONS, *Migration Statistics Quarterly Report*, May 2009: 11).

122 ONS, 'News Release: Increased emigration of Central and Eastern Europeans' (20 May 2009); and ONS, *Migration Statistics Quarterly Report* (August 2012): 8–9.

123 ONS, *Migration Statistics Quarterly Report* (August 2012).

124 Figures are 255,000 (2008); 228,000 (2009); 203,000 (2010); and 201,000 (2011). ONS, 'Emigration – the short story', 24 November 2011; *Migration Statistics Quarterly Report* (August 2012): 6.

125 These sources include: census data for NI, the ROI, Scotland, England and Wales, and other countries; National Health Service (NHS) transfers, new registrations and de-registrations; employment data; the School Census; and the International Passenger Survey. It is important to bear in mind that much of this data will overlap.

126 NI census 1971, Migration Tables, Table 1A; NI census 1981; Migration Report, Table 1; NI census 1991; Migration Report, Table 1; and NI census 2001, Table EXT20040628A: Country of address one year ago by Country of Birth (All Migrants), supplied by NISRA upon request. The total inflow figure for 2001 is less 4 (total = 18,970) from the total inflow recorded in Tables S376, S388A and S388 (= 18,974). Migration data for 2011 had not been released before going to press.

127 NI census 2001: Migration Tables, S376: Sex and age by migration; S388A: Religion

247

by migration; and S388: Community background by migration. Outflow statistics from Northern Ireland to the UK differ only slightly from the inflow, with 17 per cent aged under sixteen and just over 2 per cent of pensionable age. Data on religion is not available for outflow statistics.

128 All data in the above paragraph is from the NI census of 2001, Table EXT20040628A. Immigrants born in other regions include Europe (5.5%); Asia (4.4%); North America (3.3%); Africa (2.1%); and Oceania (1.9%). Figures provided for ROI-born do not include the category Ireland (non-specified).

129 NISRA, Mid-year population estimates, June 2007, Table 2.10: Estimated net Great Britain and international migration (July 2000–June 2007); and Mid-year population estimates, June 2011, Table D: Resident population estimates mid-2011: Components of change (data under revision). These estimates are based on patients reregistering with NHS doctors in other parts of the United Kingdom. Flows are measured by the receiving country, thus the Central Health Index (CHI) for inflow to Northern Ireland, and outflow to GB is measured by the National Health Service Central Register (NHSCR) for England and Wales, and the Scottish National Health Service Central Register (SNHSCR). One issue with the NHS estimates is the underestimation of males eighteen to thirty-six due to their tendency to delay reregistration. Students may also fail to reregister away from their family home. For guidance on using NHS statistics, consult: 'Quality report/User guide: Northern Ireland population estimates', NISRA, Occasional Paper No. 32 (September 2011) (accessed 15 December 2012).

130 In the year to 2001, the census for Scotland reported that 2,602 migrants came in from Northern Ireland. See General Register Office for Scotland, 'Scotland's census 2001 statistics on migration', Occasional Paper No. 11 (2005): 28, Table 3A. See 'NHSCR inter-regional migration movements within the UK' [Tables from 2002 to 2010]: (www.statistics.gov.uk/hub/population/migration/migration-within-the-uk/index.html). For details of migration between Scotland and the rest of the UK, see 'In and Out Migration between Scotland and rest of UK, 1991 to most recent': www.gro-scotland.gov.uk/statistics/theme/migration/mig-stats/scotland-rest-of-uk.html (both sites accessed 1 September 2012).

131 CSO, Population usually resident and present in the State in each province and county classified by birthplace: Census 2011 (Table CD612); Census 2006: Vol. 4, Table 37); Census 2002: Vol. 4, Table 38); and Census 1996: Vol. 4, Table 31). These figures for the NI-born include Donegal residents born in the city of Derry, but usually or always resident in the ROI. From 1926, the census figures for those born in NI but living south of the border (1926 = 35,132) showed a very gradual decline until 1971 = 26,183, followed by a sharp increase notable in 1981 = 40,557 reflecting the North's high outmigration of the 1970s, then declining again by 1991 = 35,986. A steady increase evident in figures from 1996 to 2006 no doubt reflects the economic boom in the ROI; that the increase has continued to 2011 is surprising in view of the economic downturn.

132 CSO, Population aged one year and over usually resident in the state, whose usual

residence one year previously was outside the state, classified by former country of usual residence and distinguishing those born in Ireland (Republic): Census 2011 (Table CD603); Census 2006: Vol. 4, Table 11); Census 2002: Vol. 4, Table 11); and Census 1996: Vol. 4, Table 11).

133 NISRA, Mid-year population estimates, June 2010, Table D: Resident population estimates mid-2010: Components of change (accessed 24 February 2012). Caution: these figures will be revised in 2013.

134 NISRA, Resident population estimates mid-2000 to mid-2012: Components of change. These figures include migration with the ROI and rest of world.

135 New National Insurance Number Registrations (NINo) rose from 5,826 in 2004–2005 to 19,680 in 2006–2007 and over the period to 2011, almost 63 per cent were awarded to EU8 nationals, though a sharp decline was evident from the third quarter of 2008. Some 2,071 registrations were also issued to EU2 migrants (NISRA, International Migration Tables, Table 1.17: Non-UK Nationals Allocated National Insurance Numbers (NINo) by Nationality, April 2004–March 2011). Northern Ireland received approximately 4 per cent of EU8 workers under the UK Workers Registration Scheme (WRS) which operated from May 2004–April 2011, with the Dungannon, Craigavon, Armagh and Newry and Mourne regions receiving the largest numbers per capita (NISRA, International Migration Tables: WRS Table 1.2: Northern Ireland Worker Registration System (WRS) Registrations by Local Authority of Employment, May 2004–March 2011; and Table 1.3: Northern Ireland Worker Registration Scheme (WRS) Registrations by Nationality, May 2004–March 2011). The Work Permit Scheme (WP) allowed employers to specifically recruit and match over 12,000 individuals from outside the European Economic Area (EEA) to specific jobs in Northern Ireland. From November 2008, it was replaced by the Points Based System requiring employers to be licensed as sponsors and to obtain certificates of sponsorship rather than work permits for non-EU employees. From January 2008 until the end of June 2011, some 358 worker cards and 940 registration certificates were also issued in Northern Ireland to EU2 nationals (from A2 countries Bulgaria and Romania which joined the EU on 1 January 2007, for whom certain work restrictions apply). See ONS, *Migration Statistics Quarterly Report* (August 2012): 23; NISRA, International Migration Tables, Table 1.5: A2 Approved Applications for Accession Worker Cards by Nationality, UK and NI, 2007–2011; and Table 1.6: A2 Approved Applications for Registration Certificates by Nationality, UK and NI, 2007–2011 (all Tables accessed 1 September 2012).

136 ONS, *Migration Statistics Quarterly Report* (August 2012), Table 1.4: Estimated overseas-born population resident in the United Kingdom by country of birth, January 2011 to December 2011; NISRA, International Migration Tables, Table 1.36: NI Health Card Registrations from Non-UK Nationals by Country of Last Residence (January 2005–December 2011); Table 1.17: Non-UK Nationals Allocated National Insurance Numbers (NINo) by Nationality (April 2004–March 2011); Table 1.3: NI Worker Registration Scheme (WRS) Registrations by Nationality (May 2004–March 2011); Table 1.19: First Language of Children with

English as an Additional Language in Year 1–Year 7 at Schools in Northern Ireland, 2005–2011 School Census; Table 1.20: First Language of Children with English as an Additional Language in Post Primary Schools in Northern Ireland, 2005–2011 School Census; and NISRA, International Migration Tables: and WP Table 1.11: Number of Work Permits Issued by Nationality (April 2004–March 2009) (accessed 7 September 2012).

137 DENI, Number of Newcomer Pupils at Schools in Northern Ireland: www.deni. gov.uk/index/32-statisticsandresearch_pg/32-statistics_and_research_statistics_on_ education_pg.htm (accessed 15 December 2012); and RG Report 2011: 11.

138 Portugal, India, the Philippines and China dominated the immigration stream from 2001 to 2004 (Jarman, 2006: 48). NISRA, International Migration Tables: Table 3.2: Estimated Net International Migration, by Local Government District (July 2004–June 2010) (accessed 6 September 2012).

139 NISRA, International Migration Tables, Table 1.38: NI Health Card Registrations from Non-UK Nationals by Reason for Coming to the UK (2010 and 2011) (accessed 1 September 2012).

140 See also Kempny (2011) and Odhiambo and McDermott (2010) for narratives of new immigrants and the difficulties they face in Northern Ireland.

141 Chris Gilligan, 'Northern Ireland: the capital of "race hate"?', Spiked [website], 18 June 2009 at: www.spiked-online.com/index.php/site/article/7043/ (accessed 17 January 2012) for discussion of this event and note the association between Loyalism and racism directed at immigrants (Chapter 1, footnote 12).

142 'Give jobs to locals not immigrants: DUP MLA', *Belfast Telegraph*, 6 October 2009. After Finance Minister, Sammy Wilson, made the link between migrants and unemployment in a statement which was widely criticised, the director of the Northern Ireland Council for Ethnic Minorities, reported that graffiti appeared on the Donegall Road: 'British jobs for British people and Poles out!' (Patrick Yu, 'Opinion – accommodating diversity key to North's recovery', *Irish News*, 19 August 2009).

143 Ethnic minorities 'new victims in the Troubles-free Northern Ireland', *Belfast Telegraph*, 23 December 2009.

144 'Here comes the bill – PSNI "sorry" for mistaken wedding-day couple arrest', *Irish News*, 23 July 2011. PSNI = Police Service of Northern Ireland.

145 The Equality Commission in Northern Ireland (ECNI) has published several anti-racism strategies on education (2001); health and social care (2003); and the implementation of Section 75 of the Northern Ireland Act (2007). The Office of the First Minister and Deputy First Minister has published three strategies for improving community relations: *Racial equality strategy; Shared future;* and *Programme for cohesion, sharing and integration* (OFMDFM, 2005, 2006, 2010). See Peter Geoghegan's (2010) discussion and critique of anti-racist strategies at the local level in Northern Ireland.

146 Home Secretary, Theresa May, announced in Westminster on 26 March 2013 that the UKBA was being split up and immigration services re-organised (www.gov.

uk/ government/speeches/home-secretary-uk-border-agency-oral-statement).

147 Michael McHugh, 'New detention centre for immigrants opens', *Belfast Telegraph*, 6 July 2011. The UK Coalition Government promised in May 2010 to end the detention of refugee and asylum seeking children, however, it is not clear how this is being managed in Northern Ireland (IPPR, 2010). See Geraghty et al. (2010) for a discussion of the specific issues facing these children in Northern Ireland. Information on Larne House at: www.ukba.homeoffice.gov.uk/aboutus/ organisation/immigrationremovalcentres/larne-house (accessed 6 September 2012).

148 Ciaran Barnes, 'BNP takes hate message to Larne with fake picture', *Belfast Telegraph*, 5 October 2010.

149 Statistics concerning the number of detainees have never been consistent and the available figures were most likely an underestimation of the actual numbers. In Northern Ireland prisons between January 1999 to June 2000, for example, seventy asylum seekers (fifty-seven men and thirteen women) were detained for periods of anywhere between one and over ninety-one days, while in the period July 2001 to December 2002, there were similarly eighty-two detainees (seventy men and twelve women) (Threlfall, 2003: 10). The Northern Ireland Prison Service website lists weekly population reports and in 2009–2010, there were between one and six immigration detainees in Maghaberry and Hydebank Wood Prisons at any given time. Since 11 July 2011, immigration detainees have been held at the new detention centre in Larne. For the stories of those detained in Northern Ireland, see Wilson (2010). Prison population reports: www.dojni.gov.uk/index/ni-prison-service.htm (accessed 15 December 2010 and 6 September 2012).

150 Other relevant organisations include: The Northern Ireland Community of Refugees and Asylum Seekers (NICRAS); Embrace NI; The Northern Ireland Council of Ethnic Minorities (NICEM); The Refugee Council (UK); and the Information Centre about Asylum and Refugees (ICAR) at King's College, London.

151 Calculations based on census counts and annual population estimates for Ireland and Northern Ireland, though figures for 2011 are preliminary only. In Ireland, a somewhat limited census was also conducted at the five-year interval (from 1946, 1956, etc).

Notes to Chapter 3: Migration, Generation and Family History

1 John McParland is listed as a bread server in the census of Ireland for 1901 and 1911.

2 Also known as the Johnson-Reed Act (1924), it established the system of national origin quotas.

3 The following year the *Montrose II* did indeed hit an iceberg in heavy fog near Saint John, New Brunswick and two of the crew were killed and the ship damaged (www. theshipslist.com/ships/lines/cp.html). This was the second ship called Montrose, launched in 1922; the first Montrose, aboard which the famous murderer Dr

Crippen was captured in 1910, was wrecked in 1914. Listed as Rosena McParland on the Montrose passenger manifest (Board of Trade passenger lists available from: Findmypast.co.uk) and as Roseena McParland on the record of her entry into Canada which can be accessed on the database of Immigration Records 1925–1935 on the Library and Archives Canada website at: www.collectionscanada.gc.ca/databases/immigration-1925/ (both sites accessed 3 January 2013).

4   The parable of the prodigal son can be found in the New Testament book of Luke 15: 11–32.

5   John Grenham, 'Irish roots' [column], *Irish Times*, 21 March 2011.

6   As reported in the *New Zealand Herald*, 15 February 1865, under the headline 'Arrival of the Ganges from London and Cork', the ship carried 434 passengers and there were fifty-six deaths during the passage, fifty-four of them children most of whom succumbed to an outbreak of whooping cough.

7   Roy Hewitt most generously lent me Jennie's 1913 diary which was transcribed by her nephew Robert J. L. Finley of Pakuranga, New Zealand in 1999. Ruby, Jack and Jennie set sail from Wellington aboard the *Ionic* on 15 May 1913.

8   Loss may also motivate migration, especially traumatic loss of a mother in childhood, as in the case of Ellen (VMR–004) who left Donegal in 1966 aged barely sixteen, a few years after the tragic premature death of her mother from an asthma attack.

9   Although the marriage bar on women in permanent posts in the British civil service was lifted in 1946, it remained in place in the Northern Ireland civil service until the 1970s (Sales, 1997: 206, footnote 18).

10   For an overview of European settlement on the Canadian Prairies, see the collection by Cavanaugh and Mouat (1996).

11   The Soldier Settlement Act of 1917 (revised 1919) provided demobilised soldiers with free quarter-sections of land in Manitoba, Saskatchewan or Alberta plus entitled them to $2,500 in interest-free loans. While some 25,000 Canadian veterans applied (Fedorowich, 1999: 1151), approximately 4,000 of them took up residence in rural Saskatchewan. This had an adverse affect on the native people of the Prairies (Carter, 1999). See article, Solder Settlement Act, in *The Encyclopedia of Saskatchewan*, at: http://esask.uregina.ca/entry/soldier_settlement_act.html (accessed 4 January 2013).

12   Bríd's story resonates with the story of my Barbadian-born great-great-grandmother Elizabeth Newsam Trew, who accompanied by her Irish-born husband and three children, including my great-Grandfather Arthur, left sunny Barbados in the late 1870s for Ireland.

Notes to Chapter 4: Religion, Migration and Identity

1   For historical perspectives, see Bowen (1983) and McDowell's (1997) insightful discussion of 'ex-Unionists'.

2   This was the probably the election of 20 March 1958 when the Ulster Unionists under Basil Brooke, 1st Viscount Brookeborough, won thirty-seven of fifty-two seats.

3   Sidney Elliott (1999) presents a rather uncritical analysis of former electoral

procedures in Northern Ireland, but see Barritt and Carter (1962: 120–25); the Cameron Commission Report (1969: Chapter 12); and Farrell (1980: Chapter 4) for discussion of the impact of gerrymandering. While franchise in local government elections was restricted to owners, principal tenants and their spouses, it was restricted further by the Representation of the People Bill, NI (1946) by removing the vote from lodgers who were not ratepayers, which included adult children living in their parents' homes. Thus, due to the severe housing shortage during the 1950s, many young married couples who had little choice but to reside with their parents were deprived of the vote. By 1961, it was estimated that more than one-quarter of the electorate were deprived of the local government vote (Cain: Introduction to the Electoral System in Northern Ireland, at: cain. ulst.ac.uk/issues/politics/election/electoralsystem.htm). Stormont (from 1929) and Westminster elections were structured on the basis of universal suffrage in a first past the post system, with two exceptions. First, until the Electoral Act, 1968, limited companies were awarded up to six votes depending on valuation which were exercised at the discretion of company directors in local government and Stormont elections. Second, for Stormont and Westminster there was a Queen's University constituency; four seats for Stormont (abolished in 1969) and one seat for Westminster (abolished in 1948); these elected by proportional representation by Queen's graduates, although the Westminster seat was contested only once (in 1945) (Wallace, 1971, 28–30). Although David remembered the election he describes here as the Westminster election of 1959, it would have had to be a Stormont election (probably 1958) in order for his co-lodger to have been eligible for a university vote in this period. It was certainly possible, however, that David's friend, in addition to his university vote, may have had a vote on behalf of his father's business and been registered for votes at multiple residences (at his lodgings and his father's home) due to the imperfect system at the time of tracking addresses. Election policies in Northern Ireland for much of the Stormont era therefore favoured Unionists who were the majority of property and business owners, and were discriminatory against Catholics and young people. They were evidently set up to maintain the status quo and did not lend a propensity for change. David's view that Protestants didn't see anything amiss in this system is also supported by Anna Bryson's research into community relations in the mid-Ulster region. She noted that local Protestants thought of the post-war period as a 'golden era' of community relations, but that Catholics remembered how Protestants 'ruled the roost' and that relations were fine as long as Catholics 'didn't ever put a foot wrong' (Bryson, 2007: 51).

[4] The vote to restrict the flying of the union flag at Belfast City Hall to designated days was held on 3 December 2012 and sparked protests which continued over several months.

[5] NI census 2011, Table KS212NI: Religion or religion brought up in; Ireland census 2011, Table CD702: Population usually resident and present in the state classified by religion and nationality.

[6] This is evident in the titles of research publications, e.g., Dunn and Morgan (1994); Finlay (2001); Hayes and McAllister (2004); and Southern (2007).

[7] In 2011, the population recorded in Ireland, North and South, as having no religion, none stated or other religion (i.e., neither Catholic nor Protestant) amounted to almost 10 per cent. After 1991, the gradual decline of the Protestant population in the ROI was reversed and most denominations showed increases by 2002 and again in 2006 and 2011, due principally to immigration. Although the proportion of Protestants in the ROI population has risen to approximately 5 per cent, their actual numbers increased by over 24 per cent from 2002 to 2011. Similarly, while Catholic numbers have increased by 369,259 over the same period, their proportion of the population has decreased by almost 5 per cent (to 84%).

[8] For sectarian sorting out, see Dooley (2000: 42–50). *Ne Temere* was introduced under Pope Pius X on 10 August 1907 and took effect from 19 April 1908. It was supported in Irish law in a judgment in the case of Tilson versus Tilson (1952) and was most notoriously enforced in Fethard-on-Sea, County Wexford in 1957, the story of which is depicted in the film *A Love Divided* (Parallel Films, 1998). See Elliott (2009: 230–32) for a description of these cases. Awareness of *Ne Temere* among ordinary Protestants was a feature of the interviews and focus groups conducted by the Opsahl Commission in 1993 (Elliott, 2002: 172). An important study of the decline of the Protestant population in Longford and Westmeath has shown the complexity of factors that have contributed to what has been a gradual decline over a long period of time. The authors concluded that while political and sectarian troubles were significant, socio-economic factors were largely responsible for the decline (Kennedy et al., 1991: 56).

[9] One could add that in their minority context, each group would be a minority of minorities. There is a large literature on Loyalism and Unionism.

[10] European Values Study 1999–2000 as reported in Fahey et al. (2005: 60); *The Legacy of the Troubles* (Muldoon et al., 2005: 50); ARK, *Northern Ireland Life and Times Survey,* 2010 [computer file] at: www.ark.ac.uk/nilt/; NI census 2011, Table KS202NI: National identity, Classification 1; Table KS205NI: Passports held. The NILT 2010 Survey identity question (NINATID): 'Do you think of yourself as British/Irish/Ulster/Northern Irish?' Of the total respondents (N = 1205), 47.6 per cent were Protestants; 36.2 per cent Catholics; 13.1 per cent no religion; and 3.2 per cent 'Other religion'. In the Legacy of the Troubles Study, 57 per cent of respondents were Protestants; 43 per cent were Catholics, while in the European Values Study 434 were Protestants and 398 were Catholics. The category 'Northern Irish' was first included in survey research in 1986 (reported in Whyte, 1990: 69). Despite the prevalence of Ulster-Scots cultural activities in Northern Ireland and the public monies, North and South, spent on them (e.g., via the Ulster-Scots Agency), academic social survey research does not usually include Ulster-Scots as an identity category.

[11] Civic versus ethnic concepts of nation have also been recently explored in the British context by Heath and Tilley (2005) based on the British Social Attitudes

Survey 2003. They concluded that the younger generations are tending towards a civic identity.

12 Cassidy and Trew (1998), however, found that among their young adult respondents personal aspects of their identity based on relationships with family and friends were more important in their self-description than either religion or nationality.

13 Despite efforts south of the border to 'rehabilitate' the term 'Ulster', its historical and current prevalence in Unionist and Loyalist nomenclature, especially that of paramilitaries (Ulster Defence Association, Ulster Volunteer Force, Ulster Freedom Fighters), has made it repellent to northern Nationalists.

14 Loughlin (1995: 219) has commented that this may be due to the increasing numbers of middle-class Catholics whose economic security may be tied to the continuing link with Britain, thus they too espouse a sort of 'civic' Britishness.

15 Total of single and multiple responses will be greater than 100 per cent.

16 Alex Kane, 'Politicians risk North falling into the abyss', *Irish News*, 12 December 2012. In the *Young Life and Times* Survey 2007–2010, however, the results have been more polarised among the 16-year-old respondents with an average of 41 per cent of Protestants choosing 'Northern Irish' identity since 2007 but only 16 per cent on average of the Catholic cohort over the same period [www.ark.ac.uk/ylt/2010/Identity/NINATID.html]. For young Protestants, this is a marked increase from an average of 33 per cent in the years 2003–2006 and one might pose the question if this is an impact of devolution and having a working assembly. The Northern Irish label is probably interpreted differently among Protestants and Catholics; likely the expression of a pro-Union identity for the former, though this cannot be assumed for the latter.

17 The Board of Trade migration data (1922–1963), for example, reveals nothing about the denomination of migrants, nor do the mid-year population estimates (which include estimates of net migration per year).

18 The census for England and Wales did not collect data on religion until 2001 (except for the religion census of 1851 which recorded church attendance). Other countries vary in their approach. For example, Fitzpatrick (1996: 611) reported that the 1911 census in Australia recorded 29 per cent of the Irish-born population as non-Catholic, although not all of this was of Ulster origin. Similarly, he reported that the 1931 Canadian census recorded fewer than 25 per cent of the Irish-born and only one-third of Irish ethnicity as Catholic with the majority of Irish Protestants likely from Ulster.

19 The 1991 figure includes general under-enumeration (1.1%), responses that claimed 'no religion' (3.8%) and non-responders (7.3%); the 1981 figure includes non-responders (18.5%) and under-enumeration (3%); and 1971 comprises only non-responders (9.4%) (Doherty and Poole, 2002: 77). By reallocating total non-responses, McGarry and O'Leary (1995: 502–503) estimated the 1991 census population as 42.9 per cent Catholic and 56.9 per cent Protestant with 0.2 per cent non-Christian. Similarly, O'Grada and Walsh (1995: 264) estimated the 1991 Catholic population at 42 to 43 per cent, the highest since the famine. By a reallocation of non-responses in the 2001 census by the method of donor

imputation, the figures arrived at were: Protestants (53.1%); Catholics (43.8%); no religion (2.7%); and other religions (0.4%) (Geoghegan, 2010: 65). In the NI census 2011, just over 10 per cent claimed 'no religion' and 6.75 per cent did not respond to the question on religious denomination (KS211NI), however only 5.59 per cent claimed not to have been brought up in any religion (KS212NI). Until 1961, non-response rates on religion amounted to less than 2 per cent so these censuses are considered more reliable on the issue. See sources above and also Anderson and Shuttleworth (1994, 1998); Shuttleworth and Lloyd (2006) for discussion of using religion data in the census as a determinant of ethnicity.

[20] The calculation of fertility rates has been discussed at length by Paul Compton (1976, 1978, 1985, 1989, 1991a, 1995) who suggested matching baptismal records of the *Annuario Pontificio* with birth data from the Registrar General for calculating Catholic births (Compton, 1991a: 159) although there is no equivalent documentation for Protestants. Previously, Compton criticised the use of church membership records for estimating Catholic numbers (Compton, 1985: 203). O'Grada and Walsh (1995: 266) noted that Catholic fertility rates dropped substantially between 1971 and 1991 but remained, nevertheless, well ahead of the general Protestant rate.

[21] Rowthorn and Wayne (1988: 209) estimated that from 1926 to 1981 the emigration rates were 6.7 per 1000 for Catholics and 3.1 per 1000 for Protestants (based on 1981 census estimate of 1,535,000, having allocated the non-responses). Simpson (1983: 102) calculated emigration rates by denomination for 1961–1971 at 6.9 per 1000 for Catholics and 2.8 per 1000 for Protestants, but did not provide the figures upon which these rates were based. This is problematic as there was a non-response on religion in the 1971 census of over 135,000 (9.4%). Compton (1985: 207–8) reallocated the 135,000 non-responses in his estimates, however, O'Grada and Walsh (1995: 269–70) have argued that census-based estimates of the Catholic population in Northern Ireland from 1971 to 1991 must be considered approximate precisely because it is impossible to accurately determine the denomination of the non-responders. In the census of 1991, for example, although non-responders and those who claimed 'No religion' correlated strongly with living in Protestant areas, examination of fertility rates among this group and response on the Irish language question would indicate that many may have actually been Catholics.

[22] McGarry and O'Leary have reported on one such debate at a seminar in Belfast (1995: 485–6). Compton has argued, somewhat controversially, that the disadvantage experienced by Catholics in employment was due to 'the structure, attitudes and aptitudes of the Catholic population' and that it was 'neither caused nor is it the responsibility of the Protestant population' (Compton, 1991b: 75). Boyle (1977) however, found that the occupational disadvantage of Catholics was not due to an inferior education system but to social background and traditional infrastructural conditions such as the lack of Catholics in higher status industries, thus supporting earlier findings by Aunger (1975). These findings were then confirmed again in Moxon-Browne's survey of 1978 (published 1983; see also discussion in Moxon-Browne, 1991). In his survey of the literature on conflict in Northern Ireland, Whyte

(1990: 7) concluded that the Unionist authorities had consistently discriminated against Catholics. See also Elliott (2000: 383–94).

23 NI census 2001, Table: EXT20031707A: Unemployment rate by religion.

24 Rose employed survey questionnaires with a random sample of 757 Protestants and 534 Catholics from March to August 1968, therefore, just prior to what has been recognised as the outbreak of the Northern Ireland conflict. The civil rights movement, however, was well underway by then and there had been numerous incidents of protest and violence since at least the early 1960s.

25 There are two questions on Rose's extensive questionnaire that concern migration. Question 1g) Have you ever thought about emigrating? and; Question 1h) How would you feel if you had to leave Northern Ireland? To which 55 per cent of Protestants and 60 per cent of Catholics said they would be either very unhappy or somewhat unhappy (Rose, 1971: 475–6).

26 In the study definition, protestors may be seeking change to address inequalities and injustices or their protest may be of a 'repressive' nature in order to maintain the status quo.

27 Rose also suggests another possible interpretation: that those who leave are indifferent to conditions at home, while those who stay are emotionally committed to the society (Rose, 1971: 367).

28 Boal (2006: 83, footnote 19) has noted that the emigration flow must have been disproportionately Protestant in the period from 1971 to 1991 in order to produce the dramatic changes in the Protestant–Catholic population balance recorded in the 1991 census.

29 Analysis of data from the British Household Panel Survey 1991, revealed the significant presence of young NI-born in Britain who were generally much better educated than British-born or ROI-born residents (Halpin, 2000: 96–7).

30 Compton and Power in their 1988 survey of 1000 New Year travellers who had left NI found that 51.6% were Protestants and 39.6% were Catholics, the rest not having stated denomination. Only about a quarter of the students surveyed intended to return to Northern Ireland (1991: 6–7).

31 In 2008–2009, 42% of post-primary students in Northern Ireland were enrolled in grammar schools. This is an increase of 2% over ten years (DENI, School census, Table: Number of pupils attending educational establishments in Northern Ireland by school type, 2008–2009).

32 Department of Employment and Learning (DELNI), 'Destinations of leavers from UK higher education institutions: Northern Ireland analysis 2010/11'; and 'Destinations of leavers from higher education: longitudinal survey of 2006/07 qualifiers – Northern Ireland analysis', at: www.delni.gov.uk/es/index/statsandresearch/higher-education-stats/he_destination_of_leavers.htm (accessed 26 January 2013).

33 The 'other' category comprises approximately 8% per year.

34 Figures obtained for the 2010–2011 academic year as published in the *Irish Times* were that there were 20,995 (59.3%) Catholic students and 14,410 (40.7%) Protestant students enrolled at the two universities and two teacher-training colleges

in Northern Ireland. In addition, 57.6 per cent of the students in the primary and secondary schools were Catholics versus 42.4 per cent Protestants. Obviously, there will be serious implications for the future majority/minority balance in Northern Ireland in the not too distant future (Gerry Moriarty, 'Catholic majority in Northern Ireland to present dilemma for Britain and Republic', *Irish Times*, 4 January 2012).

35 Some of the media headlines were: 'Just one-third of Northern Ireland students are Protestant', BBC News, 17 October 2011; 'Jim Allister says NI universities must address Protestant imbalance', BBC News, 18 October 2011; 'Concern over fewer Protestant students', *Belfast Telegraph*, 19 October 2011; 'Alarm over student numbers', *Irish Echo*, 19 October 2011; 'University "fails" to enrol Protestants', *Irish Times*, 20 October 2011; '20% of Magee enrolments are Protestant', *Londonderry Sentinel*, 20 October 2011.

36 DELNI, 'Enrolments at UK Higher Education Institutions: Northern Ireland Analysis 2010/11' at: www.delni.gov.uk/index/publications/r-and-s-stats/higher-education-enrolments/he-enrolments-2010-11.htm (accessed 26 January 2013).

37 *Young Life and Times* survey at: www.ark.ac.uk/ylt/ (accessed 26 January 2013).

38 Totals of more than 100 per cent per category indicate residencies in multiple locations (e.g., an individual may have resided outside the British Isles and also in mainland Britain). Note that some of these numbers fluctuate quite widely from year to year, likely due to the small sample size. For example, in 2008, 58% of Catholics in the survey said that they had lived in mainland Britain as compared with 48% in 2010 (NILT, www.ark.ac.uk/nilt/ accessed 26 January 2013).

39 The Purdysburn Fever Hospital, not to be confused with the adjacent Purdysburn (mental) Hospital, opened in 1906 and was renamed the Belvoir Park Hospital in the 1960s when it became a centre for cancer care. It was closed in 2006.

40 This event is also known as the Tricolour Riots (see Boyd, 1969: Chapter 11). The RUC were ordered to remove an Irish tricolour flag flying from the headquarters of the Republican Party in Divis Street and three days of rioting ensued. Ian Paisley was among the loudest voices of those protesting against the flag and was blamed by some Unionists and Nationalists for fomenting violence.

41 The Royal Belfast Academical Institution, known locally 'Inst', is a boy's grammar school that officially opened in 1814. It caters primarily to the non-Catholic population. In its early years prior to the opening of Queen's University in 1849, the school also functioned as a university (www.rbai.org.uk/index.php).

42 Greta Jones (2012: 143) has pointed out that medical graduates from Queen's University, benefited from the easy recognition of their credentials as British-qualified doctors. Irish medical schools south of the border did not receive the same level of credential recognition abroad certainly in the post-war period even though their curricula met the requirements of the British General Medical Council and many of their external examiners were faculty of British medical schools. Thus, Jones makes a convincing argument for migration as a factor motivating change in Irish medical education.

43 There were at least two murder triangles in Northern Ireland, one in North Belfast

and the other in the area bordering southeast Tyrone and northwest Armagh. Even in more recent times, Lurgan has been the site of notorious sectarian murders: that of lawyer Rosemary Nelson in 1999 and *Sunday World* journalist Martin O'Hagan in 2001. For census purposes Lurgan has been combined with the neighbouring towns of Portadown and Craigavon to form a district, however, by calculating its electoral wards the population was estimated at 23,534 in 2001.

[44] Susan McKay, 'Faith, hate and murder', *The Guardian*, 17 November 2001.

[45] Popular memory of conflict in personal narratives often ascribes the blame for incidents of violence or sectarian hatred on outsiders, sometimes with perpetrators and victims colluding in the maintenance of a more bearable myth. For example, Susan, a Protestant from Belfast, described a local myth accepted in her own family surrounding the burning out of her family home in Donegal during the Irish War of Independence that had been blamed on marauders from County Monaghan. Further investigation into the story uncovered that the perpetrators were most likely locals, some of whom had been employees of the family (VMR–034).

[46] Laura's story is particularly interesting in view of the more recent association of Loyalism with the Israeli side of the Israeli–Palestinian conflict. It is not uncommon to see Israeli flags flying in Loyalist areas in Northern Ireland. See Guelke (2008); Hamber (2006); and Hill and White (2008) for discussion of this phenomenon.

[47] Much of the Golan Heights territory, also known as the Syrian Heights, was captured by Israel during the six-day war in 1967 and has been under Israeli occupation ever since. From 1944, it had been part of Syria which maintains its claim, though Jewish settlements in the Golan date from around the 1890s. The Golan has been the site of some of the worst violence of the Arab Israeli conflict, including battles during the Yom Kippur War in 1973. The Israeli -Syrian disengagement Agreement of 31 May 1974 ended skirmishes and Syrian shelling in the Golan and established a United Nations buffer zone. Hence for Laura, the Golan in 1974 would have been going 'from the frying pan into the fire'.

[48] Orla's parents had gone out on the 'ten pound' assisted passage scheme in the early 1950s but returned because Orla's mother in particular was very unhappy living in the temporary housing in what she called a 'migrant camp', which had the appearance of a concentration camp (described in Hammerton and Thomson, 2005: Chapter 5).

[49] This was Rosemary Bleakley, aged nineteen, who was killed planting the bomb on behalf of the IRA at a shopping arcade in North Street, Belfast on 13 January 1976.

[50] This can even be seen in the popular television programmes of the period, such as ITV's *Love Thy Neighbour* (1972–1976) and BBC's *Till Death Us Do Part* (1965–1975), and its American spin-off on CBS, *All in the Family* (1971–1979), which in turn had spin-offs in *Maude* (1972–1978) and *The Jeffersons* (1975–1985). These sitcoms all challenged ethnic, racial, religious, class, feminist and gender stereotyping and bigotry.

[51] Short Brothers PLC, known locally as Shorts, was established in London in 1908. It opened its Belfast location in 1936 on Queen's Island adjacent to the present

George Best Belfast City Airport and near the shipyards, and has been traditionally an important employer of Protestants. Shorts was sold by the British Government to the Bombardier Corporation of Quebec, Canada in 1989 and is still in the aerospace business. At the time of the sale, Bombardier was perceived as the saviour of the company and it promised to pursue an equitable hiring policy. Despite new equality legislation, however, as reported in early 2011, its workforce was still overwhelmingly Protestant (Paul Ainsworth, 'Bombardier is 83% Protestant', *Andersonstown News*, 27 January 2011).

52 There is a large body of literature that links migrants with a higher incidence of mental illness, some of which dates back to the nineteenth century (reviewed in Ødegaard's groundbreaking study of mental illness among Norwegian immigrants to the United States published in 1932). Morgan et al. (2010) recently reviewed literature linking migration, ethnicity and psychosis; much of it focuses on particular racialised ethnic groups. However, a recent study analysing historical data from 1902 to 1913 concerning British and European immigrants admitted to psychiatric institutions in British Columbia, has suggested that even a century ago, migrants were similarly vulnerable to the development of psychosis even when they were assimilating into a host society of similar ethnic origin to their own (Smith et al., 2006). Incidence of physical and mental illness associated with migration is discussed in Chapters 6 and 7.

53 For recent discussions of English and British national identity especially in the context of devolution, see Aughey (2007); Bechhofer and McCrone (2007, 2010); English (2011); Heath and Tilley (2005, 2007); Kumar (2006); Mandler (2006); and Wellings (2007).

54 Population of the survey area (Bristol) is 91 per cent White, with 87 per cent born in England.

55 The Future of England Survey was conducted from 27 July to 2 August 2011 with sample of 1,057 adults across England in addition to three booster samples: the north (750); the Midlands (756); and London (750).

56 Gary has worked for McDonnell Douglas, Boeing, Lockheed Martin and several other subsidiary aircraft design companies.

57 According to David Gardiner (2008: 2), the title of his report about Protestants in the Diocese of Clogher entitled, 'Whatever you say, say nothing' (taken from the poem by Seamus Heaney), is the phrase that best describes the behaviour of Protestants living in the Tyrone and Fermanagh border areas during the Troubles. But this lack of willingness to discuss politics in public is common throughout Northern Ireland.

58 Compton and Power (1991: 8), for example, mention 'the relatively greater ease with which Protestants merge into British society'.

59 During these years, several Canadian observers attended the protests at Drumcree and this drew the attention of the Canadian media. One notorious incident in July 2000 which got extensive coverage on Canadian television showed Canadian observers Svend Robinson, a well-known MP from British Columbia, and Warren

Allmand, former Liberal Cabinet Minister under Pierre Trudeau, with American politician and activist Tom Hayden, getting hit by RUC police batons along with the Garvaghy residents protest group on the Garvaghy Road (email communication from Svend Robinson, 16 September 2011).

60 Gallagher has also noted that it is quite rare for groups, as is the case of Ulster Protestants, to 'claim to belong to a larger nation whose own members do not see them as co-nationals' (Gallagher, 1995: 722).

61 Of the firm W. J. Currie, Draper and Boot Merchant listed in the 1952 street directory for Ballymoney.

62 Irish Protestant networks operated into the early twentieth century (Jenkins 2002–2003, 2003; MacRaild, 2002–2003, 2005a, 2005b). Membership of the Orange Order in Britain and Ontario is now predominantly comprised of the non-Irish born (Houston and Smyth, 2007; Kaufmann, 2007). Whereas, through to the early 1970s, Irish Protestants could fairly easily join the Toronto Police Force – a good number were former RUC officers – the more recent emphasis for police forces in Canada and Britain is on the recruitment of non-Whites. The closure of the Eaton's department store chain (1869–1999), founded in Toronto by Timothy Eaton of Ballymena, County Antrim, saw the end of another former Irish Protestant employment network.

63 Siobhan is referring to the change in Articles 2 and 3 of the Constitution of Ireland (Nineteenth Amendment, 1999), that followed from the Belfast/Good Friday Agreement (1998) and the North–South referendum, removing Ireland's automatic territorial claim on the six counties of Northern Ireland.

64 The British Government acknowledged the principal of self-determination for Northern Ireland in the context of potential Irish unity in the Sunningdale (1973); Anglo-Irish (1985); Downing Street (1993); and Belfast/Good Friday (1998) agreements.

65 A recent study of the place branding of Northern Ireland in the USA found that the Irish Tourist Board employed a dual identity strategy depending on whether they perceived the host environment as 'British-friendly' or 'Irish-friendly' (Gould and Skinner, 2007: 100).

66 Kate Adie, interviewed by Dave Fanning on the Ryan Tubridy programme, RTE Radio One, 5 July 2009. Adie's career as a journalist has been largely spent covering conflicts around the world, including Northern Ireland during some of the worst years of the Troubles.

Notes to Chapter 5: Being Northern Irish in Britain

1 John Fawcett Gordon (1879–1965) was an Ulster Unionist MP in the Northern Ireland Parliament for Antrim, 1921–1929; and Carrick, 1929–1943. He also served as Minister of Labour from August 1938 until May 1943.

2 The *Irish News* is a daily newspaper published in Belfast understood primarily to serve the Nationalist/Catholic community in Northern Ireland.

3 Country of birth tables: Census of England and Wales 2001 (Table UV08); Census of Scotland 2001 (Table S015).

4 2011 census figures available for England and Wales only (at time of going to press) show that the leading countries of birth abroad (outside Britain) were: India (694,000); Poland (579,000); Pakistan (482,000); ROI (407,357); Germany (274,000 – including children of British Armed Forces personnel previously stationed there); Northern Ireland (214,988); and Bangladesh (212,000) (Census of England and Wales 2011, Table KS204EW: Country of birth; ONS, 'International migrants in England and Wales', Figure 2: Top ten countries for non-UK born residents of England and Wales, 2001 and 2011, 11 December 2012). Recent data on UK births to ROI-born mothers reveals a gradual decline in numbers relative to other immigrant groups, with Ireland no longer among the top ten countries from 2007 (ONS, 'Parents country of birth', Table 2: Live births for the ten most common countries of birth of mother for non-UK born mothers, 2002–2011', August 2012, available at: www.ons.gov.uk/ons/publications/index.html accessed 31 August 2012).

5 In 2011, there were 206,735 NI-born residents in England and 8,253 residents in Wales. Although overall numbers were down, the proportions had increased in these areas: London and southeast (68,118 or 33%); the Midlands (34,806 or 17%); and the northwest (36,767 or 18%), of which some 37 per cent resided in greater Manchester and another 23 per cent in Merseyside (Census of England and Wales 2011, Table KS204EW).

6 R. D. Osborne, 'The North's brain drain', *Irish Times*, 6 February 2007.

7 Census of England and Wales 2011, Table KS204EW. In 2001, 40 per cent of the Irish-born in Merseyside were NI-born and yet they comprised only 16.5 per cent of those who claimed 'White Irish' ethnicity in the census (others were ROI-born = 61% and British-born = 22.5%); the implication being that a large number of the NI-born claimed 'White British' ethnicity and the majority of these were likely Protestants (Pemberton and Mason, 2007: 1444).

8 An ethnicity question was first introduced in the 1991 census for England and Wales but did not include 'Irish' as a response category, however, it was amended in the 2001 census questionnaire to include the Irish after much lobbying on the part of Irish organisations in Britain (Walter, 1998). Low response in 2001 on ethnicity (641,804) was attributed to confusion about the question (Hickman, 2011; Walter, 2011), however, response to the adjusted ethnicity question in 2011 was also low ('White Irish' at 531,087, plus 57,680 'Gypsy and Irish Traveller'; a detailed breakdown on white/mixed race categories not yet released) (Census of England and Wales 2011, Table KS201EW: Ethnic group). The census of 1971 included a question about parents' place of birth, thus providing valuable information on the extent of the second-generation Irish group and the degree of intermarriage with other ethnicities. The censuses of 1851–1961 included a question on nationality, which was dropped, but again added in 2011 as was a question about passports held. After the much disputed religion census of 1851, questions on religion were not included in the census for England and

Wales, and the census for Scotland until 2001 (Southworth, 2005).

9   Specific responses were: NI only = 113,577; NI + British = 18,205; NI + other = 16,500; Irish + NI = 1,355; Irish + NI + either British/English/Welsh/Scottish = 1,085; Irish only = 348,638; Irish + British = 11,313; Irish + either English/Welsh/Scottish = 25,692 (Census of England and Wales 2011, Table KS202EW: National identity; Table KS205EW: Passports held).

10 Datasets included were the General Household Survey; the Labour Force Survey 1983 (which included a question on parents' birthplace); the 1970 British Cohort Study; and the Office of National Statistics Longitudinal Study (which included data from the 1971, 1981 and 1991 censuses). Based on 1966 census statistics, Kevin O'Connor (1972: 173) estimated the Irish multigenerational group conservatively at four million, noting that at least half of the number was comprised of generations one to three.

11 Mid-year population estimate for 1991 (NISRA, 'Historic population trends 1841 to 2011 – Northern Ireland and Republic of Ireland' [Table]). The estimate for the multigenerational Northern Ireland group here is somewhat simplistic as it assumes a single fertility rate for the Irish group as a whole.

12 In sixteenth-century England, the growing number of beggars and vagrants, many of whom were Irish, motivated the Tudors to introduce a variety of 'beggar' and 'poor relief' legislation over the century with the eventual establishment of formal poor law in 1597 and 1601.

13 Spiers (1996: 337) reports that in 1868, 28.7 per cent of British Military personnel were Catholics, declining to 17.7 per cent by 1898.

14 See Ruth-Ann Harris (1990) for work on seasonal migration between Ireland and England before the famine and Anne O'Dowd (1991) for the classic work on seasonal labourers.

15 The British Nationality Acts of 1948 and 1981; the Commonwealth Immigrants Act 1962; the Commonwealth Immigration Act 1968; and the Immigration Act 1971, have all maintained the special status of the Irish in Britain, excluding them from immigration control. In the post-war period concern about immigration was largely focused on new Commonwealth countries though more recently it has shifted specifically to Asian and Middle Eastern immigration.

16 The terms 'assimilation' and 'integration' have slightly different meanings and uses in American and European discourse. See the Introduction by Schneider and Crul to the special issue on assimilation and integration theory, *Ethnic and Racial Studies*, Vol. 33, No. 7 (2010): 1143–8. Patrick Fitzgerald and Lambkin (2008: 62–8) have proposed another theoretical model to describe the experience of immigration: segregation/integration/modulation; the latter acknowledges that the process of belonging entails continual negotiation between home and host destinations with the potential for multiple homes and identities.

17 A summary of this large literature, much of which dates since the late 1990s, is beyond the scope of this chapter, but see Roger Swift's (2009) review; and note John Belchem's (2007) history of the Irish in Liverpool into the twentieth century which

provided helpful context for this study.

18 The second-generation Irish participants in the Irish2 Project reported that knowledge of Irish history passed down to them within the family was generally only of a fragmentary nature (Walter et al., 2002: 208).

19 The Race Relations Acts of 1965 and 1976 were conceived primarily to address discrimination against the Black population. A more comprehensive human rights approach in recent equality legislation (2010) addresses need based on race, ethnicity, religion, gender, sexuality, age, disability and social exclusion.

20 For historical critique of the discourse of 'whiteness' in relation to the Irish, see the special issue of the *Journal of British Studies*, Vol. 44, No. 1 (January 2005).

21 The Prevention of Terrorism Act was passed on 29 November 1974 after a series of bombings in England. Two pubs in Guildford were bombed on 5 October 1974 killing four soldiers and one civilian and injuring sixty-five others. The King's Arms Pub in Woolwich, London was bombed on 7 November killing one soldier and one civilian. Two pubs in Birmingham were bombed on 21 November, killing 21 people and injuring 182.

22 The Commission for Racial Equality (CRE) was established as a result of the Race Relations Act 1976 and though mandated to examine discrimination from many perspectives; its primary focus was on race. In 2007, the CRE was replaced by a new government body, the Equality and Human Rights Commission www.equalityhumanrights.com/ which has jurisdiction in England, Wales and Scotland. Northern Ireland has its own Human Rights Commission established in 1998, following from the Belfast/Good Friday Agreement (www.nihrc.org/).

23 Northern Ireland Protestant migrants often reported 'discovering' Irish history when they were abroad as they had learned mostly British history in the Northern Ireland state education system. Considerable resentment was expressed in the interviews on this topic and it is perhaps partly why many did not feel 'qualified' to claim Irish identity. It is also the case that many people from Northern Ireland have a negative view of history, blaming it for years of conflict (Bell et al., 2010).

24 There has been growing interest in the concept of diaspora in relation to the British and English. Richards (2004) and Bueltmann et al. (2012) provide historical context, and for recent analysis of the contemporary British diaspora, see reports by Sriskandarajah and Drew (2006); and Finch et al. (2010).

25 The same is also true for most other countries where data on the NI-born is usually subsumed under the UK category. New Zealand is an exception as it maintains a category for NI-born in its census.

26 For example, in Khalid Koser's useful introduction to the subject of international migration, he provides an estimate for 2003 of only 'about 375,000 Irish in the UK' (Koser, 2007a: 105); a figure that is about 120,000 lower than the number of ROI-born in Britain recorded in the 2001 census, thus evidently not inclusive of the NI-born. At an international migration conference in 2008, the representative of an important policy think-tank in London delivered a keynote presentation about immigration to Britain displaying figures only for the ROI-born, though

acknowledging the oversight afterwards when asked about the NI-born.

27 Exceptions to this are studies of Northern Ireland migrants in Britain by Compton (1992); Forsythe and Borooah (1992); Morgan and Walter (2008); Ní Laoire (2002); and most recently, an unpublished M.Sc. dissertation graciously made available to me by the author (Harbinson, 2010).

28 Primogeniture was the feudal system of property inheritance among the nobility of Western Europe including Britain, in which land and any associated titles were inherited by the eldest male heir (usually a son). A system of partible inheritance known as 'gavelkind' in which land holdings and property were divided equally among male heirs also existed in many areas. In Ireland, the Gavelkind Act (2 Anne, c. 6, 1704, repealed 1778) required Catholics to divide land among their male heirs while Protestants adhered to the tradition of primogeniture which gradually became the norm and was an important mechanism leading to the land consolidation that was greatly accelerated at the time of the famine in the 1840s (Byrne, 2004: 132; but see also Dowling, 1999; Elliott, 2000: 35–45; and Stout, 1996).

29 Kathleen's work was spread over a wide region so we arranged her interview in Manorhamilton, a mutually convenient location.

30 Irish Catholic children are usually aged seven years old by the time they take their first holy communion. They are prepared for it with their class at school, the ceremony most often held in May or June.

31 John Charles McQuaid (1895–1973), Catholic Archbishop of Dublin, was throughout his long career very influential in providing assistance to Irish Catholic emigrants in Britain. To this end, he established the Catholic Social Welfare Bureau in 1942 which catered especially for the moral and spiritual welfare of female emigrants. In the mid-1950s, he appointed two social workers to investigate the situation of the Irish in Britain and set up a series of missions formally instituted in 1957 as the Irish Emigrant Chaplaincy Scheme. McQuaid's initiatives contrast sharply with the Irish Government's non-intervention during the period (Daly, 2006; Delaney, 1998; and Ferriter, 2009).

32 In their study of victimhood and the Northern Ireland conflict conducted in 2001, Cairns and Mallett (2003: 22–4) asked respondents to recall two events in Northern Ireland over the last fifty years. For 91 per cent, the memories had to do with the conflict and for over 50 per cent, specific violence.

33 John Bradley, personal communication, 4 April 2011. Ulster accents could also come in handy. A cousin of mine remembered that as a young man living in London in the 1980s, he had on occasion identified himself as being from Belfast, making his accent more pronounced than usual, to ward off would-be aggressors and thus escape being dragged into pub brawls. It is interesting that in the literature on the Irish abroad, there appears to be for the most part an unquestioned assumption that people in host countries are incapable of differentiating Irish accents. However, Ulster dialects (including syntax, modality and pronunciation) are more often confused with Scottish dialects and are distinctive from those in the southern half of Ireland. This is not only due to the Scottish and English plantations in Ulster

but also the influence of Ulster Irish (see Braidwood, 1964; Corrigan, 1999; Gregg, 1985; Kallen, 1999; McCafferty, 2003).

34 In a recent study of economically inactive Irish people in Merseyside, their reported lack of confidence was attributed to factors such as discrimination, 'difficult social environments' and 'cultural shock from arriving in the UK' (Pemberton and Mason, 2007: 1455).

35 See discussion of structural discrimination in Chapter 4.

36 The Post Office Tower bomb exploded in the men's toilets in the Top of the Tower Restaurant on 31 October 1971 and is generally attributed to the IRA.

37 The Birmingham Six were taken into police custody on 21 and 22 November, immediately following the bombing. The Guildford Four, the first people to be arrested under the provisions of the Prevention of Terrorism Act in late November, were followed shortly by the Maguire Seven on 3 December. Three of the Guildford Four (Gerry Conlon, Paul Hill and Paddy Armstrong) were from Belfast, the fourth, Englishwoman Carole Richardson, was Armstrong's girlfriend at the time of the arrest. Of the Maguire Seven, Annie and Patrick Maguire, Annie's brother Sean Smyth and brother-in-law Giuseppe Conlon, were all from Belfast and were arrested with the two Maguire sons, both underage and Patrick O'Neill, a family friend. Of the Birmingham Six, five were from Belfast (Patrick Hill, Gerry Hunter, Billy Power, Hugh Callaghan and Richard McIlkenny) and one was from Derry (John Walker). See Moran (2010: Chapter 7) for a description of the Birmingham bombings and analysis of their impact on the Irish community.

38 In a recent small-scale study about the Irish in London, it has been suggested that the 'widespread backlash theory' has been 'overplayed' (Sorohan, 2012: 94), despite the rather large body of evidence to the contrary. This conclusion appears especially premature in view of the lack of prior research on the experience of Northern Ireland migrants in Britain who were most vulnerable to such a backlash, which sometimes came from their Southern Irish compatriots.

39 When Terry and I took a break during the interview and went out down the road to get some biscuits in the local shop, we chanced to meet a representative of the housing authority who had evidently come by to speak to Terry about the incident in question.

40 The Irish group also reported a higher measure of distrust of the medical system and held traditional beliefs and attitudes about the disease; all factors which would tend to have a negative impact on health-seeking behaviours. The researchers did not differentiate between Southern Irish or Northern Irish but acknowledged the possibility of the existence of important differences in their attitudes towards cancer.

41 The AESOP Study (Aetiology and Ethnicity in Schizophrenia and other Psychoses) among the Black and minority ethnic population in Britain (i.e., non-White groups) found that perceived disadvantage was an important factor in the higher incidence of psychosis in this population (Reininghaus et al., 2010: 47–8).

42 Hornsby-Smith (1987: 124) noted the propensity for Irish Catholic women to marry outside the Irish ethnic group; a significant proportion also marrying non-Catholics

(one-third in the first generation and two-thirds in the second). Based on analysis of data from the British Household Panel Survey, 1991, Halpin (2000: 97) concluded that the NI-born (especially males) were happier about the state of their health than the ROI-born, however, the NI-born sample was very small and skewed in favour of a younger age cohort.

[43] SARS (individual licensed samples of anonymised records) extracted from the 2001 census for England and Wales represents approximately 3 per cent of individual records pertaining to 1.84 million people.

[44] Most recently, Maynard et al. (2012) in their study of suicide rates among eight ethnic groups resident in England and Wales over the period 1979–2003, found that males born in the ROI and Northern Ireland had significantly higher rates of suicide than those born in England and Wales, India, Pakistan and East Africa. Note that the resident population of Northern Ireland has a much higher level of mental ill health morbidity than populations of the ROI or the other UK jurisdictions. For example, in 2006 the number of people claiming Disability Living Allowance in Northern Ireland due to mental ill health (2.9%) was three times the number in Britain (Gray and Horgan, 2009: 27) and there is a growing body of research which suggests that this may be the outcome of over thirty years of conflict (Fay et al., 2001; O'Reilly and Stevenson, 2003).

[45] The London Docklands bombing also known as the Canary Wharf or South Quay bombing occurred in the early evening of 9 February 1996 and signalled the end of a seventeen-month IRA ceasefire. Two people were killed and thirty-nine injured, the damage was estimated at eighty-five million pounds.

[46] Patricia Walls (2005: 12–13) has documented that even after the Belfast/Good Friday Agreement, a substantial number of Northern Ireland migrants to Britain claimed to have left because of violence or threats of violence from paramilitary organisations.

[47] Also known as the 'Poppy Day Massacre', a bomb planted by the IRA exploded near the Cenotaph in Enniskillen, County Fermanagh, during the Remembrance Day service on 8 November 1987. Eleven people were killed and sixty-three injured. No one has yet been found guilty for the bombing. In their study of the relationship of the memory of the Enniskillen bomb to mental health, Cairns and Lewis (1999) found that Protestants were more likely to mention the bomb as a key event in their lives and for those that did, they scored higher on the General Health Questionnaire (indicating poorer mental health). This would be compounded for those like Julia who were closely related to victims of the incident.

Notes to Chapter 6: Immigration to Canada

[1] The two books I had read about Iran were: Nafisi (2004); and Molavi (2002).

[2] Bobby Sands (1954–1981) was a member of the Provisional Irish Republican Army and leader of the 1981 hunger strike in the Maze Prison organised as a protest against the removal of Special Category status. He was elected Member of the Westminster

Parliament for Fermanagh/South Tyrone in April 1981 but died on hunger strike shortly after.

3 Statistics Canada currently employs the definition of 'visible minorities' in the Canadian census and other government documents as it appears in the Employment Equity Act (1986): persons (apart from aboriginals) who are neither Caucasian in race or White in colour (www.statcan.gc.ca/concepts/definitions/minority01-minorite01a-eng.htm). However, the United Nations Office of the High Commissioner for Human Rights (OHCHR) criticised Canada's use of the term as discriminatory (OHCHR, 'Committee on Elimination of Racial Discrimination considers report of Canada' [press release], 21 February 2007, at (www.unhchr.ch/huricane/huricane.nsf/); 'Term "visible minorities" may be discriminatory, UN body warns Canada', CBC news, 8 March 2007, at: www.cbc.ca/news/canada/story/2007/03/08/canada-minorities.html (sites accessed 24 January 2013).

4 There is an enormous literature on multiculturalism, much of it specifically within the Canadian context. During the 1990s, after over twenty years of immigration and multiculturalism policies which saw Canada's population becoming increasingly multi-ethnic, most particularly in regards to 'visible minorities', the debate on multiculturalism raged following the release of the Spicer Commission Report in 1991 (Spicer, 1991). Writer Neil Bissoondath's critique (1994) from a visible minority perspective was answered by several advocates of multiculturalism, notably Will Kymlicka (1995). Since then, the Canadian Government, primarily through its department of Immigration and Citizenship and Statistics Canada, has sponsored many studies of immigrants and their integration into Canadian society. The Quebec Government likewise has also sponsored several studies and an important commission in 2007–2008, *Consultation Commission on Accommodation Practices Related to Cultural Differences,* co-chaired by Gerard Bouchard and Charles Taylor, and known as the Bouchard–Taylor Commission (full report at: *http://web.archive.org/web/20110826201006/http://www.accommodements.qc.ca/documentation/rapports/rapport-final-integral-en.pdf* (accessed 24 January 2013).

5 Recent research has shown that second-generation offspring of non-visible minorities are likely to have earnings on a par with the offspring of Canadian-born parents, however, this is not the case for visible minority offspring who fare markedly worse (Palameta, 2007: 14). Studies of social cohesion factors have shown that some second-generation visible minorities score even lower than the first generation despite improved economic prospects, suggesting that even if economic factors improve, higher levels of social inclusion do not necessarily follow (Reitz and Banerjee, 2007).

6 Estimated from Board of Trade statistics reported by Mitchell (1988: 84); Plant (1951: 177); Willcox (1929: 636–7); and Canadian immigration data reported in the *Canada Year Book* and in Li (2003: 32). This estimate has compensated for the somewhat inflated figures for the period until 1853 to April 1912; that is, before passengers were distinguished from migrants in the Board of Trade returns. After the Second World War, the focus of the Empire emigrant flow switched to Australasia.

7 Literature on the settlement of Newfoundland is summarised in Trew (2005b).

8 Fedorowich (1995: 6) reports that prior to the Napoleonic wars there was less formalised British soldier settlement in Halifax in 1749 and also the settlement of United Empire Loyalists (Americans), including those who had fought for the British, in New Brunswick and along the St Lawrence following the American Revolutionary War.

9 Elliott reports that of the 125 Irish-born in the 99th Regiment who became settlers in Richmond, seventy-five were from Ulster, most originating in the western counties of Londonderry, Tyrone, Cavan and Fermanagh.

10 Errington (2008: 141; based on figures by Carrier and Jeffery, 1953: 96) comes up with a similar figure estimating the number departing British and Irish ports from 1815 to 1854 bound for British North America at 1,136,087. Most of the passenger traffic in this period is assumed to be permanent settlers.

11 Based on the foreign-born registered in the census of Upper and Lower Canada, 1851–1852 and 1861.

12 Census of Ireland, 1851, Part VI: General Report, Appendix, cii–ciii, Tables XVIII and XIX (published 1856). See also discussion in Harkness (1931: 265).

13 Robert H. Coats (1874–1960), Canada's first Dominion Statistician, suggested that the immigration figures for the pre-Confederation period were too low to account for the population increase recorded in the census of Upper and Lower Canada, 1861 (Coats, 1931: 125).

14 The new Canadian Federal Government, which had taken control of immigration policy from the provinces, followed the American example of the US Homesteader Act (1862) and enacted the Dominion Lands Act in 1872 to provide 160 acres of land to adult males in return for a registration fee of ten dollars and minor residency requirements. From 1874 to 1896, an average of some 3,000 homesteaders per year availed of the scheme, including some British and European settlers, however, the majority were established Canadians from central and eastern Canada who moved west.

15 Manitoba was first joined by rail to eastern Canada in 1883 and the first transcontinental railway in Canada was completed in 1886.

16 Settlement of the Canadian west was largely promoted by Clifford Sifton, Minister of the Interior in Laurier's Government. In 1901, the combined territories of the province of Manitoba and of what became the provinces of Alberta and Saskatchewan (from 1905) had a population of 114,000; by 1911 this had grown to 326,000 (Coats, 1931: 127).

17 'Oriental' immigration, which denoted immigrants from China, Japan and India, was severely restricted by legislation, and such exclusionary practices were to characterise Canadian immigration policy until the 1960s. The Chinese Immigration Act (1885, repealed 1947); the Immigration Act (1906); and the Immigration Act (1910) which came out of the Royal Commission on Oriental immigration and labour report authored by W.L. Mackenzie King (1908) and submitted by him as his doctoral dissertation to Harvard University in 1909, all codified these exclusionary policies. King (1874–1950) served as Canadian Minister of Labour (1909–1911)

in the Laurier Liberal Government and later as Prime Minister (1921–1930 and 1935–1948).

18 Jeffery notes that the design of the Canadian stamp issued upon the inauguration of the imperial penny post in 1898 featured a map of the Empire with Canada placed at the centre and above the map, the words, 'We hold a vaster Empire than has been' from *A Song of Empire* written by Welsh poet, Sir Lewis Morris, for Queen Victoria's Diamond Jubilee in 1897. The point has been made by Mark McGowan (1999) that Irish Catholics in Canada in the late nineteenth century were generally supportive of Canadian imperialism as the Canadian Parliament had endorsed home rule for Ireland in 1882. Many notable French-Canadians like Prime Minister, Sir Wilfrid Laurier, who had himself accepted a knighthood in 1897, were also broadly supportive of imperialism, though careful at the same time to refrain from offending the more ardent Quebec Nationalists.

19 *Lisburn Gazette*, 21 January 1904. The identical advertisement appeared in several newspapers.

20 Some of these posters can be viewed online at the Canadian Pacific Archives website: www.cpheritage.com (accessed 23 September 2011).

21 Wells (1981: 242) points out that while *The Times* had a circulation of about 35,000 around the turn of the twentieth century, the *Daily Mail* had a circulation of approximately one million and was therefore quite influential with its regular coverage on emigration. The success of the Canadian advertising campaign in the competition for British migrants was reported in the Australian press in 1912 (Pope, 1968: 181).

22 See the discussion of emigration from Canada in the period from 1851 to 1956 in the *Canada Year Book 1957–1958* (pp. 158–60).

23 By 1930, the Canadian-born population resident in the United States had reached a high point at 1,278,512 and by 1950, the Canadian-born were the second largest group (994,562) of foreign-born in the United States. However, the overall proportion resident in the USA relative to the total Canadian-born population had been in decline since the turn of the twentieth century when 25 per cent of the Canadian-born were resident in the USA, by 1930, 15.8 per cent and by 1950, 8.3 per cent (*Canada Year Book*, 1957–1958: 159, 163). See also Akenson (2000: 125–6) for discussion of migration over the Canada/US border.

24 The Irish-born comprised 5.4 per cent of total immigration to Canada during the 1920s with a small number arriving every year via the United States. Canadian immigration data for that decade does not distinguish between the Northern and Southern Irish cohorts as Northern Ireland was recorded as a 'country of birth' only from 1930. However, Board of Trade emigration figures for Northern Ireland for the 1920s would suggest that the large majority of Irish arriving in Canada came from the North.

25 *Historical statistics of Canada*, Series A297–326: Country of birth of other British-born and the foreign-born population, census dates, 1871 to 1971, at (www.statcan.gc.ca/pub/11-516-x/sectiona/4147436-eng.htm#4). Northern and Southern

Irish-born are not differentiated in the Canadian census until 1951; the British-born figure here includes only England, Wales, Scotland and lesser isles.

26 Unless otherwise indicated, Canadian immigration data is from the *Canada Year Book* (1940–1967). No data is provided by country of birth for the year 1941. Statistics and articles about Canadian war brides have been brought together on the website: www.canadianwarbrides.com/intro.asp (accessed 25 July 2011).

27 *Historical Statistics of Canada*, Series A297–326: Country of birth of other British-born and the foreign-born population, census dates, 1871 to 1971. There is a troubling discrepancy in the number of both Irish-born groups arriving in the 1950s (total = 48,917) and the resident census counts of 1961 which showed an increase of only 13,682 of the total Irish-born population (representing only 28 per cent of the inflow). It seems unlikely that rates for death and return migration of Irish-born or perhaps even their onward migration to the United States during the decade could account for the whereabouts of 72 per cent of the Irish immigrant flow. In 1971, the Canadian census recorded 38,490 Irish-born residents from independent Ireland, an increase more in line with the immigration estimates for that group during the 1960s. However, from the Canadian census of 1971, country of birth data of 'British' immigrants was provided at the UK level only so it was no longer possible to distinguish the NI-born.

28 This rough estimate has been calculated by combining totals for UK immigrants by country of birth 1960–1965 reported in the *Canada Year Book* (total = 130,950) and British emigration figures for country of next residence 1966–1969 (201,900), as reported in Mitchell (1988: 84), giving a total of 332,850. The calculation is necessary because Canada discontinued the practice of recording immigrants by country of birth and ethnic origin from 1966 (Richmond and Rao, 1976: 188) and Mitchell's figures are available beginning only in 1964. Both data sets overlap for the years 1964–1965, however, and it is clear that Mitchell's British emigration figures tend to be higher than the Canadian immigration data for country of birth by 3–4,000 per annum (as Mitchell's estimates also include non-British nationals formerly resident in the UK). Using country of last residence immigration figures for 1960–1965 (UK = 140,797) in the *Canada Year Book* combined with Mitchell's British emigration estimates for 1966–1969 provides a higher estimate of 342,697 (this figure would include non-British nationals in both Canadian and British data sets, including Canadians returning from Britain).

29 Figures from the *Canada Year Book*, 1960–1967.

30 The office of Canadian Immigration Services was located at 65A Chichester Street in central Belfast ('Assisted emigration to Canada, new scheme announced', *The Times*, 1 February 1951).

31 The Board of Trade statistics record that 29,143 Northern Ireland emigrants went to Canada in the five years 1925–1929. It is therefore likely that Northern Ireland emigrants may have formed as much as 70 per cent of the total Irish cohort (67,951) that arrived in Canada during the 1920s.

32 The total number of migrants leaving Canada (1941–1951) was 378,918. In

addition to the departing British and Irish migrants, 60.6 per cent were Canadian-born; 12.7 per cent American-born, and 6.2 per cent from other countries.

33 In June 2002, the point system was updated with more emphasis placed on flexible skills, rather than attempting to match specific current needs in a constantly fluctuating job market (Li, 2003: 26).

34 The average annual immigration for 1965–1970 was 182,000 which declined to 167,000 for 1971–1975 due to a deteriorating economic climate which saw annual immigration targets lowered from 175,000 in 1970 to 50,000 in 1975. In 1968, immigrants from the UK and Europe (calculated on country of last residence) accounted for 68 per cent of Canadian immigration; by 1975 their proportion had already declined to 39 per cent, and it continued downwards to 27 per cent in 1989, while over roughly the same period African, Caribbean and Asian immigrants had increased from less than 15 per cent to around 37 per cent (Richmond and Rao, 1976: 186–9; Richmond, 1990: 160). By 2009, out of a total immigration of just over 252,000, 15.4 per cent were from Europe (including the UK) while 69.6 per cent came from countries in Asia and Africa (based on country of birth). The British proportion fluctuated from 18.4 per cent in 1968 down to 11.7 per cent in 1971, back up to 14.7 per cent in 1981, and thereafter to decline sharply reaching a low point in 2002 at 1.7 per cent, increasing slightly in recent years to just over 3 per cent (2007–2009) (Richmond and Rao, 1976: 188–9; Milan, 2011: 9–10).

35 Canada has four categories of admission for immigrants: 1) economic (includes skilled workers and business immigrants); 2) family class (spouses, children, grandparents of Canadian residents); 3) refugees; and 4) other immigrants (usually admitted on humanitarian grounds) (Milan, 2011: 3). In some years, however, more Canadians have moved to Britain than the reverse. From 2000 to 2004, for example approximately 8,500 Canadians per year relocated to Britain while only 5,200 British emigrants moved to Canada (Michalowski and Tran, 2008: 33).

36 The British Consulate in Ottawa was unable to provide an estimate of the NI-born resident in Canada. However, Courtney (2000: 288, Table 15.1) estimated total Irish-born in Canada at 42,000 in 1991, which given the 28,000 ROI-born listed in the census, would imply only 14,000 NI-born.

37 Ethnic origins: 2006 census counts for Canada provinces and territories – 20% sample data [table] (Ottawa: Statistics Canada, 2007); DETINI, 'Foster promotes tourism in Canada' [press release], 14 March 2011, at: www.northernireland.gov. uk/index/media-centre/news-departments/news-deti/news-deti-march-archive-2011/ news-deti-140311-foster-promotes-tourism.htm (accessed 27 February 2012).

38 Canada's census of 2011 did not include questions on birthplace or ethnic origin. See: www12.statcan.gc.ca/census-recensement/2011/ref/about-apropos/questions_ guides-eng.cfm (accessed 27 December 2012).

39 Paul Dunne, 'Welcome to the Irish', *Montreal Gazette*, 1 September 2011. Many of the young Irish arrive as part of an international work experience initiative which allows them to work in Canada for a year and in some cases, these special visas may be extended. The Ireland–Canada Chamber of Commerce, Toronto Branch has

recently (2011) produced an immigrants' guide which is available to download from their website (www.icccto.com/). The Irish in Toronto Facebook group and Irish in Canada Twitter group which can be accessed from the Irish Association of Toronto website (www.meetup.com/irish-society-toronto) are helpful in providing assistance to new or intending Irish immigrants.

[40] Unemployment rates for Northern Ireland have been recorded in the *Ulster Year Book* as 24.2 per cent (1925) and 23.3 per cent (1926); with slightly lower estimates provided by Mitchell (1988: 124–6) as 22.8 (1925) and 21.1 (1926).

[41] Leo Browne was interviewed by the author in Ottawa on 19 August 1994 during the course of PhD research in the Ottawa Valley which was later published (Trew, 2009b).

[42] Details of ship passage in this chapter have been sourced in the Board of Trade passenger records (1890–1960) from the National Archives Kew, at: www.findmypast.co.uk

[43] Canadian immigration records for the years 1925–1935 from the Library and Archives Canada website at: www.collectionscanada.gc.ca/databases/immigration-1925/ (accessed 2 August 2011).

[44] Leo was able to avail of the new passage rates to Canada for agricultural and domestic workers that had come into effect at the beginning of 1926: fares to Halifax, St John, New Brunswick, and Quebec amounted to three pounds; those onward to Winnipeg, Manitoba at five pounds ten shillings; and nine pounds to Vancouver ('Emigration to Canada: new passage rates effective today', *The Times*, London, 1 January 1926: 9).

[45] A significant part of the business of Morgan's, like so many other large department stores in Canada and the United States, was conducted by catalogue mail order to supply rural and remote areas. Leo's job involved the preparation of these order boxes for shipping. By my reckoning Leo and my grandmother, Roseena, whose story is in Chapter 3, would have been working at Morgan's at the same time and as both were new immigrants from Northern Ireland, it seems likely that they would have met.

[46] 'Assisted emigration to Canada, new scheme announced', *The Times*, London, 1 February 1951: 3.

[47] Substantial improvements to education were made through the Education Act Northern Ireland (1947), including the provision of secondary education in the state school system, increased funding to Catholic schools and the increased availability of grants to make third-level education more accessible to those from less privileged backgrounds. In addition, the Northern Ireland Government encouraged the expansion of technical and commercial education (including courses open to young women) ('The educational system in Northern Ireland', *Ulster Year Book 1953*: xvii–xxviii).

[48] See Bonesteel (2008) for a history of the governance of Inuit affairs.

[49] The Deh Cho Bridge crossing the Mackenzie River at Fort Providence was opened on 1 December 2012, providing a year round road link to southern Canada

for the first time.

50 Robert W. Service (1874–1958) was a Scottish poet who came to Canada in the mid-1890s, eventually moving up to the Yukon Territory in the first decade of the twentieth century. His famous narrative poem, 'The Shooting of Dan McGrew' published in *Songs of a Sourdough* (Toronto, 1907), depicted a saloon brawl with fatal consequences.

51 Canada's immigration regulations were subsequently changed in 1972, no longer allowing visitors or foreign students to apply for Canadian immigration while in Canada (Richmond and Rao, 1976: 186).

52 For the decade 1956–1965, Richmond (1968: 264) calculated that of the British labour force migrants that immigrated to Canada, 19 per cent returned to Britain. Studies were also conducted of the return of British migrants from Australia (Appleyard, 1962a, 1962b; and Richardson, 1968).

53 For example, in 1972 a new regulation was introduced requiring applicants for Canadian immigration to apply from outside the country. Thus, visitors like Craig, and those on temporary employment permits or visas could no longer apply for immigrant status while in Canada. All of these regulations introduced in the 1960s and 1970s were incorporated into the Immigration Act (1976). With increasing international competition for highly skilled migrants, however, the Canadian Government in 2005 announced an in-stream application process for some foreign workers and PhD students enrolled in Canadian universities, and in 2012 announced further measures to facilitate application for permanent residency for temporary workers and foreign postgraduate students already in Canada (King and Newbold, 2008: 98; footnote 64 below).

54 Similarly, Ita McCrory, a secretary employed at murdered solicitor Rosemary Nelson's firm in William Street, Lurgan, gave testimony to the Nelson Inquiry concerning an occasion in the early 1990s when they were not notified of a bomb alert on the street, while others were evacuated (Rosemary Nelson Inquiry, 9 May 2008), from the Committee on the Administration of Justice (CAJ), at: www.caj.org.uk/files/2011/10/07/Day_17.pdf

55 Cas is referring to the ten-point maximum awarded for the occupation demand criterion in the immigration selection grid used at the time of their interview. Points were also awarded for other criteria (e.g., age, education, language, work experience, arranged employment, etc.). See Li (2003: 41) for a description of the grid and the changes to the point system over time.

56 Hiram Walker founded his original whisky distillery in Detroit in 1858, but relocated it across the river to Windsor, Ontario several years later because of problems with prohibition. It is known for the brand Canadian Club whisky.

57 The Ulster Workers' Council (UWC) strike took place from 14 to 28 May 1974. It was supported by Unionists and Loyalists opposed to the Sunningdale Agreement (signed December 1973) which would have seen power-sharing with Nationalists in a new devolved Northern Ireland Executive and Assembly at Stormont with some involvement of the Southern Irish Government. The strike led to the collapse of the

new Assembly in May 1974 and the reimposition of direct rule from Westminster. See the Conflict Archive on the Internet (CAIN) which provides a bibliography and many full-text documents concerning the strike http://cain.ulst.ac.uk/events/uwc/soc.htm (accessed 6 January 2013).

58 Sudbury is a mining centre especially noted for its deposits of nickel sulphide mined by Inco and Falconbridge who were the major employers in the area during the 1970s. The recession of the early 1980s severely affected minerals and sparked huge lay-offs in the mining industry throughout Canada, badly affecting Sudbury in particular.

59 The CAIN archive provides a detailed chronology year by year of the conflict at: http://cain.ulst.ac.uk/othelem/chron/.htm

60 The bomb at McGurk's Bar caused the building to collapse. Fifteen Catholic civilians were killed, including Mrs McGurk and her daughter, and seventeen others were injured. It was the worst single event of the Troubles in terms of the number of casualties until the Omagh bomb in August 1998. Now attributed to the UVF, responsibility for the McGurk bomb was originally claimed by a group calling themselves 'Empire Loyalists', but was blamed on the IRA by John Taylor, then Minster of State for Home Affairs in the Northern Ireland Parliament. Robert Campbell is the only person to have been convicted for the bombing (1978), however, there has been much controversy over the original investigation in which collusion was alleged between the RUC and Loyalist paramilitaries. In July 2010, a controversial report into the McGurk's atrocity by the Northern Ireland Police Ombudsman, Al Hutchinson, concluded that there was no evidence of collusion, causing such a public outcry that the report had to be withdrawn. A new report was issued in February 2011 though Hutchinson was eventually forced to resign, effective January 2012. See the new report, *The bombing of McGurk's Bar, Belfast: Relating to the complaint by the relatives of the victims of the bombing of McGurk's Bar, Belfast on 4 December 1971*, at: (www.policeombudsman.org/modules/investigation_reports/index.cfm/reportId/231); and other documents relating to the incident from the Pat Finucane Centre at: www.patfinucanecentre.org/ (accessed 6 January 2013).

61 The Service, Office and Retail Workers' Union of Canada was founded in 1972 and disbanded in 1986. It was established as a predominantly female union to represent primarily office, restaurant, retail and bank workers and during its lifetime had a reputation for being tough, uncompromising and radical (Rooney, 1978).

62 The Canadian social insurance number (known as SIN) is akin to the National Insurance number in the UK, and is legally required to register with an employer.

63 Data is from the Longitudinal Survey of Immigrants to Canada (LSIC), a sample cohort of the immigrants that arrived in 2000–2001. A series of interviews was conducted with them over their first four years in Canada to monitor their experiences and perceptions of settlement, adaptation and integration to Canada. See Hawthorne's Introduction and other articles in the special issue of the journal *Canadian Issues* (spring 2007) devoted to the topic of foreign credential recognition.

64 The Foreign Credentials Referral Office (FCRO) was established in May 2007

within the Ministry of Citizenship and Immigration and in November 2009 launched the *Pan-Canadian Framework for the Assessment and Recognition of Foreign Qualifications*; a fifty million dollar investment with the cooperation of Canadian federal, provincial and territorial Governments, which identified fourteen occupations for priority processing. In addition, the new *Federal Internship for Newcomers* Programme run by the FCRO assists qualified immigrants to obtain Canadian work experience (Citizenship and Immigration Canada, 2011: 11, 17). See the FCRO website at: www.credentials.gc.ca/ (accessed 30 November 2011). In August 2012, the Ministry announced further modifications to the immigration point system which will take effect from 2013. More emphasis will be placed on language skills, younger age and 'adaptability' criteria which facilitates immigration for individuals already on work permits or studying in Canada, via the *Canadian Experience Class* scheme. Unlike the recent ill-considered Coalition Government initiatives to cap student migration and ensure their departure from Britain after graduation, in the global competition for skilled labour Canada is cognisant of the need to attract talented postgraduate students from abroad and retain them after graduation by facilitating permanent residency. These recent policy initiatives have improved Canada's ranking to third position (after Sweden and Portugal) according to the *Migrant Integration Policy Index* of thirty-one countries (www.mipex.eu). See the news releases of Citizenship and Immigration Canada, 'Revised federal Skilled Worker Programme unveiled' and 'A review of the past 12 months and beyond at Citizenship and Immigration Canada', 17 and 24 August 2012, at: www.cic.gc.ca/english/department/media/releases/2012/ and also 'Special report: Government overhauls economic immigration' Aug. 2012, at: www.cicnews.com/2012/08/special-report-government-overhauls-economic -immigration (all accessed 29 August 2012).

[65] Hathiyani interviewed taxi drivers in Toronto from six different countries all of whom had university degrees. His informants also reported that foreign names on job applications were another means of screening out racial and ethnic minorities. Reitz et al.'s review (2009) of religious and racial integration in Canada is noteworthy in demonstrating that racial discrimination rather than religion (regardless of degree of religiosity) was the key factor affecting the integration of visible minorities. Blacks, especially males, still face the most discrimination in employment in Canada in spite of the large majority being of Christian denomination. Thus, they support the conclusion of the Bouchard–Taylor Commission that the 'problem' concerning the integration of religious minorities has been largely media generated (Bouchard and Taylor, 2008: 721).

[66] Note that the unemployment rate (males twenty-five to fifty-four) peaked in 1992 at 10.7% falling very slowly to 5.7% by 2000 (Frenette and Morissette, 2005: 235).

[67] As good health is a criterion of entry to Canada and medical certification is required, the assumption is that immigrants were in good health at the time of their arrival.

[68] The link between migration, underemployment and downward social mobility, and poor mental health has been found in studies of immigrants in several developed

countries, sometimes extending into the second generation (Das-Munshi et al., 2012).

69 For example, in 2005, recent immigrant males with a university degree earned only 48 cents on average for every dollar earned by a Canadian-born male graduate, and 29.8 per cent of recent immigrant male graduates worked at jobs that required no more than secondary education; a figure more than twice the rate for the Canadian-born cohort (Frenette et al., 2008: 23).

70 The 2006 Canadian census recorded that 6.2 per cent of foreign workers (non-permanent residents) were from the UK and the ROI and almost 30 per cent of all non-permanent residents, like Richard, had been in Canada for at least five years (Thomas, 2010: 37, 39).

71 For information about the club see their website at: www.markhamirishrugby.com/ (accessed 24 January 2013). Munster rugby, especially strong in the Limerick region and popular among all classes, would be an exception to the traditionally middle-class dominance of the sport elsewhere in Ireland.

72 *The Canadian Outdoorsman* is the title of a popular magazine in Canada which sponsors an annual Canadian outdoorsman competition. *The Red Green Show* created by comedian Steve Smith (CBC, 1991–2006), was a well-loved spoof of the Canadian outdoorsman character inspired by *The Red Fisher Show* (CTV, 1968–1989). One of the most famous spoofs of the outdoorsman character was Mr Canoehead, a crime fighting superhero outdoorsman whose aluminium canoe had become welded to his head when struck by lightning while portaging in Algonquin Park. It was the creation of the Canadian comedy troupe, The Frantics, who had popular radio and television programmes on the CBC during the 1980s.

73 Term often used to describe Canada since it was used in, William Kilbourn (ed.) *Canada: A Guide to the Peaceable Kingdom* (Toronto: Macmillan, 1970) and notably employed the following year by Northrop Frye who described an aspect of the Canadian literary tradition as 'the quest for the peaceable kingdom' in, *The Bush Garden: Essays on the Canadian Imagination* (Toronto: Anansi, 1971) p. 249. See also Judy M. Torrance's discussion of this concept in, *Public Violence in Canada: 1867–1982* (Kingston: McGill-Queen's UP, 1986), pp. 100–106. According to the *Global Peace Index*, 2011, Canada is ranked 8th most peaceful out of 153 countries, in which comparative rankings are: Ireland (11th); United Kingdom (26th); and the United States (82nd). See: www.visionofhumanity.org/info-center/global-peace-index-2011/ (accessed 27 February 2012). It also ranks among the top four countries (averages 2nd place) according to the OECD (thirty-four countries) Better Life Index (based on 2008 data). See: http://oecdbetterlifeindex.org/#/11111111111 (accessed 27 February 2012).

74 This is evident in the titles of many books about Canada: Stephen Leacock, *Afternoons in Utopia: Tales of the New Time* (Toronto: Macmillan, 1932); William Johnson, *A Canadian Myth: Quebec, Between Canada and the Illusion of Utopia* (Montreal: R. Davies, 1994); Ishrad Manji, *Risking Utopia: On the edge of a New Democracy* (Vancouver: Douglas and McIntyre, 1997); Joseph Heath, *The Efficient Society: Why Canada is as Close to Utopia as it Gets* (Toronto: Viking, 2001); and

Michael Adams, *Unlikely Utopia: The Surprising Triumph of Canadian Multiculturalism* (Toronto: Penguin Canada, 2008).

75 Lester B. Pearson (1897–1972), was Minister of the Department of External Affairs from 1948 to 1957 in the Liberal Government of Louis St-Laurent and later Prime Minister of Canada, 1963–1968.

76 Canada has had a mediation role in the Northern Ireland Peace Process through retired Canadian General, John de Chastelain. Retired Canadian Supreme Court Justice, Peter Cory, chaired the Cory Collusion Inquiry which was established as an outcome of the Weston Park Agreement between the British and Irish Governments (July 2001) to investigate collusion between security forces and paramilitaries in six notorious murders in Northern Ireland. Judge Cory's reports were presented to the Irish and British Governments in October 2003 and are available from the Pat Finucane Centre: www.patfinucanecentre.org/ (accessed 16 July 2011). For discussion of Canadian unity issues, see McRoberts (1997); and Trew (2002).

77 Bruce Cockburn (born 1945) is a well-known Canadian singer-songwriter, whose song *If I Had a Rocket Launcher* (released 1984), was a hit in Canada and is still popular among political activists internationally. It was inspired by his visit to Central America in 1983 as a representative of Oxfam, where he witnessed first-hand the plight of Guatemalan and Nicaraguan refugees.

78 Clayoquot Sound is the body of water and its watershed located on the west coast of Vancouver Island, British Columbia.

79 Macmillan Bloedel Ltd versus Simpson [1994] B.C.J. No. 1913 (British Columbia Supreme Court). The injunction was appealed unsuccessfully to the Supreme Court of Canada, see MacMillan Bloedel Ltd. versus Simpson [1996] 2 S.C.R. 1048.

80 Claire Culhane (1918–1996) was a well-known Canadian peace activist and humanitarian who after spending five months in Vietnam in 1967–1968 as an aid worker, became an anti-war activist, especially against what she saw as the complicity of the Canadian Government in that war. See her collection in the online archive, *Peace and War in the 20th Century*, hosted by McMaster University at: http://pw20c. mcmaster.ca/ (accessed 1 August 2011). Sheila's description of her imprisonment is reminiscent of the demands of Republican prisoners in the H-Blocks of the Maze Prison who after being refused special category (i.e., political) status refused to wear prison uniforms and began the blanket protests (i.e., the wearing of blankets or bed sheets) in 1976 that eventually led to the Hunger strikes in 1980–1981.

81 The Clayoquot Sound UNESCO Biosphere Reserve is administered by the Clayoquot Biosphere Trust. Based on Nuu-chah-nulth First Nations 'living' philosophies, their aim is to achieve a sustainable diversified 'conservation economy' in which logging, fishing, hunting is carefully controlled (http://clayoquotbiosphere.org/ accessed 1 August 2011).

82 Critiques of multiculturalism have noted tensions between philosophy and the social sciences and some have argued that multicultural policies are in retreat especially in Europe (Joppke, 2004).

83 The *Migrant Policy Integration Index* found that among thirty-one countries surveyed

in 2010, Canada ranked only eighteenth for political participation, principally because immigrants prior to naturalisation do not have the right to vote or to stand in local elections as they do in eighteen EU member states, nor can they contribute to policy due to the lack of immigrant consultative bodies (www.mipex.eu/), accessed 27 December 2012.

84 While Bríd felt that she lost her perceived ethnic status with the increasing influx of visible minority immigration since the 1980s, a study of post-war Irish migrants in Winnipeg, Manitoba reported that they only became 'ethnic' with the introduction of official multiculturalism in 1971 when funding became available for ethnic organisations. In their discourse, Irish identity in Canada was denoted by multiple levels of belonging along a spectrum from 'Irish-born' to 'Canadian-born with some Irish heritage' (Clary-Lemon, 2010: 20).

85 Wilkes and Corrigall-Brown (2011) examined attitudes to immigration in Canada over time and found that from 1987 to 1996, approximately 70 per cent found immigration levels too high, but this had declined to less than 50 per cent by 2001 and in 2008 to 34 per cent. However, they noted that in Canada there is a very strong link between economic conditions (which have been generally good since the mid-1990s) and attitudes towards immigration and that there has been an ideological shift towards increasing acceptance of immigration, possibly due to cohort replacement (each new generation more accepting of immigration) and that general education levels are also rising. Winter (2011), however, has cogently argued that increasing acceptance of multiculturalism policy in Canada has largely occurred since the Quebec referendum on independence – sovereignty (30 October 1995). As the ethnic minority vote was largely on the 'no' side, ethnic minorities were lauded in English Canada as having 'saved' the country since the referendum was narrowly defeated with 50.6 per cent voting no and 49.4 per cent voting yes.

86 For information about Ireland Park, see (www.irelandparkfoundation.com/). The Ireland Fund of Canada supports a large number of causes and it has over many years maintained a special interest in integrated education (www.irlfunds org/canada/). The Ireland Canada Business Association (ICBA) and the many branches of the Ireland Canada Chamber of Commerce encourage trade between the two countries. Academic links are promoted by the Ireland Canada University Foundation (www.icuf.ie/) and many Irish universities have active alumni groups in Canada, for example, Queen's University Belfast alumni hold an annual dinner in Toronto. The Canada–Ireland Inter-Parliamentary Friendship Group, established in 1998, promotes links between parliamentarians (MPs, TDs and senators) in both countries and there are also many political organisations in Canada that support a united Ireland cause – note the Irish Unity Pledge campaign (www.Irishunity-pledge.com). Cultural organisations, such as Comhaltas Ceoltoirí Eireann and an Commissiún Rincí Gaelacha (Irish Dancing Commission), have branches in Canada (www.irishdancingcanada.com/) and there are several Irish theatre groups active in Canadian cities as well as many local Irish societies (e.g., www.irishsocietyncr.com/). The Gaelic Athletic Association (GAA) is active in Canada (www.canada.gaa.ie/); the

Ulster Provincial Council currently twinned with Canada GAA to provide development support. Rugby is popular among men and women and several cities host 'Irish' rugby clubs, for example, Toronto/Markham, Montreal and Ottawa (www. montrealirish.com/site/) and (ottawairishrugby.teampages.com/).

[87] Torrance (1986; 103) has described this 'mediocrity' as a consequence of the 'peaceable kingdom' philosophy; that the desire on the part of politicians for 'conciliation, moderation and quiet diplomacy' to settle disputes has not only resulted in dull politics but has 'encouraged governments [in Canada] to clothe themselves in excessive secrecy'.

[88] A reference to the two rival families in Shakepeare's *Romeo and Juliet*.

Notes to Chapter 7: Return Migration

[1] There are several estimates concerning the emigration and return flows from Europe in the nineteenth and early twentieth centuries. According to Russell King (1993: 20), fifty-five to sixty million people left Europe between 1820 and 1940; thirty-eight million went to the United States; and approximately ten million emigrants returned to Europe from North America between 1870 and 1940 (King, 2000: 29). In the period from 1815 to 1930, Dudley Baines (1995: 7–8) has estimated that between fifty-two to sixty million people left Europe; thirty-three million of them to the United States and that approximately one-quarter of them returned to Europe (Baines, 1995: 39). Mark Wyman (2005: 16) has suggested that fifty-two million people left Europe between 1824 and 1924 and that at least one-third of them returned to their homelands permanently. In another estimate Wyman (1993: 16) suggested that twenty-three million emigrated from Europe to the United States between 1870 and 1930 and between one-quarter to one-third of them returned home permanently. The variety of estimates demonstrates that comparisons are difficult as the data sets differ in the temporal or geographic frames. There are also inherent pitfalls, as noted by J. D. Gould (1980), in the employment of immigration statistics for calculating return flows since attempts by governments on both sides of the Atlantic to record outflow or return have been sketchy at best. The alien outflow data recorded by the United States Department of Immigration from 1908 to 1923 is perhaps the most comprehensive data set of this type in existence. From this source it is recorded that of 9,949,740 immigrants arriving in the United States (USA) during this period, 3,078,403 departed; 88 per cent of them European (Wyman, 1993: 9). Return flows were not evenly distributed among the ethnic groups with some such as the Bulgarian/Serbian/Montenegrin (89%); Greeks (46%); and southern Italians (60%) returning in greater numbers, while others such as the Scottish (13%); Irish (11%); and Jews (5%) had much lower repatriation rates. Thomas Archdeacon (1983: 139) reports a repatriation figure for the Irish during the same period as 8.9 per cent.

[2] See also John Jackson's supplement on Ireland (1967) to Reverdy's Report.

[3] Fairly comprehensive bibliographies of return migration literature and methods are

included in Gmelch (1980); Russell (1978, 1986, 2000); Morawska (1991); and Wyman (1993).

4 There is a large and growing literature in the British, Irish and European contexts; most important in terms of this study are: Appleyard (1962a, 1962b); Barrett and Goggin (2010); Barrett and O'Connell (2001); Barrett and Trace (1998); Barrett et al. (2002); Bovenkerk (1973); Chamberlain (1997); Corcoran (2003a, 2003b); Dunnigan (2007); Foeken (1980); Ghosh (2000); Gmelch (1983, 1986); Gmelch and Delaney (1979); Hammerton and Thomson (2005); Harper (2005); Long and Oxfeld (2004); McGrath (1991); Ní Laoire (2007, 2008a, 2008b, 2011); Punch and Finneran (1999); Ralph (2009); Richardson (1968); Richmond (1966, 1967, 1968); Schrier (1958); 'T Hart (1985); Thomson (1999, 2003, 2005); Tsuda (2009); and Wyman (1993).

5 There is a growing literature in refugee studies about the difficulties of repatriation programmes (Black, 2002; Black and Gent, 2006; Blitz et al., 2005; Huttunen, 2005; Koser, 2007b; Malkki, 1995; Serrano, 2008, etc.).

6 Larry sailed on board the steamship *Saxonia* of the Cunard Line which departed Liverpool on 28 October 1954, bound for Montreal.

7 The bombs exploded on 23 March 1972 and were attributed to the IRA. In March 1974 an incendiary bomb targeted the local shopping centre and on 16 March 1975 RUC officer Mildred Harrison was killed in a bomb explosion attributed to the UVF at the Ormeau Arms pub as she walked by on foot patrol. Bombs were also set in the main street in 1992 and 1993, and most recently (4 August 2010) an unexploded bomb targeted a policeman who lived in a quiet housing estate in the town. During the Troubles, eight people were killed in Bangor.

8 Abercorn Restaurant on Castle Lane in central Belfast bombed on Saturday 4 March 1972. Two people were killed, 130 injured and several severely maimed.

9 Belfast 21 July 1972; exploded twenty-two bombs which, in the space of seventy-five minutes killed nine people and seriously injured approximately 130 others, (http://cain.ulst.ac.uk/events/bfriday/) accessed 29 December 2012.

10 The association of the west of Ireland with Irish culture, identity and Irish nationalism that is a feature of the poetry of Patrick Pearse (1916) and is romantically portrayed in Hollywood films such as *The Quiet Man* (director John Ford, 1952), had a great influence on views of Ireland from abroad. There is an extensive literature on the topic but see Gibbons (1984) and Nash (1993). Edmondson (2000), however, reminds us that the view of the rural west as the well-spring of tradition belies the future orientation of real communities in the region.

11 In 2011, 93.4 per cent of people born and living in Northern Ireland had never resided elsewhere (NI census 2011: Table KS801NI: Usual residents born in Northern Ireland who have resided elsewhere).

12 Issues concerning the schooling of children of mixed marriage parents have also been found in other studies (Leonard, 2009; Muldoon et al., 2007).

13 Grosse Ile and Irish Memorial National Historic Site at: www.pc.gc.ca/eng/lhn-nhs/qc/grosseile/index.aspx (accessed 29 December 2012).

14 In the most recent Westminster election of 6 May 2010, North Down retained the only Unionist seat in Northern Ireland with Lady Sylvia Hermon gaining a massive 63.3 per cent of the vote running as an independent Unionist. According to the 2001 census, the community background of the North Down constituency is approximately 82 per cent Protestant, though with regard to the census question on religion, almost 25 per cent (the highest in Northern Ireland) claimed either 'no religion' or 'none stated'. Election statistics for Northern Ireland at: www.ark.ac.uk/elections/ (accessed 29 December 2012).

15 See specifically the chapter on North Down (McKay, 2005: 13–51).

16 NILT 2008, at: www.ark.ac.uk/nilt/datasets/ (accessed 28 February 2012). Unionist and Loyalist displays represent the vast majority (Bryan et al., 2010: 34).

17 See McDermott (2011: Chapter 3) for a summary of strategic initiatives and legislation aimed at developing an equality and human rights based policy framework for Northern Ireland. In a study of the Muslim community in Northern Ireland, Marranci (2003) found that the use of English was promoted over Arabic, not only as a *lingua franca* for Muslims of different national and language groups, but also as a symbol of integration to distance the community from association with the Republican/Palestinian and Loyalist/Israeli alignments in Middle Eastern politics.

18 NI census 2011, Table KS801NI: Usual residents born in Northern Ireland who have resided elsewhere.

19 This is administered by the Ministry of Housing and Urban Renewal through an amendment to the Capital Assistance Scheme. The experiences of returnees facilitated by the Safe-Home Programme have been documented by Fran Browner in *Coming Home* (2008). See www.safehomeireland.com/ (accessed 29 December 2012).

20 For information about the Aisling Project, see (www.aisling.org.uk/drupal/node/8). The Crosscare Migrant Project (formerly Emigrant Advice), run by the Dublin Archdiocese provides advice to returnees and new immigrants to Ireland (www.migrantproject.ie/). The Irish Government between 2004 and 2011 spent over ninety-three million Euros to fund over 200 organisations in twenty countries that assist Irish emigrants through its Emigrant Support Programme administered by the Irish Abroad Unit of the Ministry of Foreign Affairs and Trade. Almost sixty-eight million Euros of this has gone to organisations in Britain. Tánaiste and Minister of Foreign Affairs, Eamonn Gilmore, announced funding of over eleven and a half million Euros for this programme in 2012 (Dail Eireann Debates, Vol. 758, No. 6 [14862/12], 15 March 2012), at: http://debates.oireachtas.ie/dail/2012/03/15/00008.asp (all sites accessed 29 December 2012).

21 Due to the need for anonymity, all identifying information about this interviewee has been withheld.

Notes to Postscript

[1] Roland Barthes' *punctum*: a detail in a photograph, often a personal object, that serves as a point of memory, see discussion in Hirsch (2012: 61–3).

[2] The title of a BBC NI *Spotlight* programme first broadcast 31 January 2012. See Chapter 2, footnote 14.

Bibliography

Official Publications

Northern Ireland

Cabinet Papers of the Stormont Administration, 1921–1972

Census for Northern Ireland, 1926–2011

Dept. of Employment and Learning (DELNI); School leavers' survey; higher education enrolment

Dept. of Education (DENI): School census

Dept. of Enterprise, Trade and Investment (DETINI): Labour Force Survey, employment data

Northern Ireland Statistics and Research Agency:
Annual population estimates, migration estimates

Northern Ireland Passenger Survey

Parliamentary debates, 1921–1972
http://stormontpapers.ahds.ac.uk/stormontpapers/index.html

Registrar General annual reports, 1922–2011

Ulster Year Book, 1922–1983

Great Britain

Census for Great Britain, 1841

Census for England and Wales, 1921–2011

Census for Scotland, 1921–2011

Dept. of Work and Pensions: Employment and pensions data

House of Commons Parliamentary Papers

Home Office: Accession monitoring reports, immigration and asylum statistics

International Passenger Survey

Office of National Statistics: Migration quarterly reports, population estimates

Ireland

Census of Population, 1851, 1911 and 1926–2011

Central Statistics Office: Migration quarterly reports, annual population estimates

Dáil Éireann. Debates

Canada

Canada Year Book, 1890–2010
Census for Canada, 1851–1852, 1861 and 1871–2011
Citizenship and Immigration Canada: Migration and population reports
Ontario, Legislative Assembly. Debates (Hansard)
Statistics Canada: Migration and population reports

Australian Bureau of Statistics

Census of population, 2001 and 2006

New Zealand

Census of population, 2001 and 2006

United Nations

Statistics Division, 1998. Recommendations on international migration statistics, Revision 1
International data on migration, refugees and asylum seekers

Other Publications

Abbott, John, G. S. Mount and M. J. Mulloy. 2000. *The History of Fort St. Joseph*. Toronto: The Dundurn Group.

Abbotts, Joanne, Rory Williams, Graeme Ford, Kate Hunt and Patrick West. 1997. Morbidity and Irish Catholic Descent in Britain: An Ethnic and Religious Minority 150 years on. *Social Science and Medicine* 45 (1): 3–14.

——, Rory Williams, Graeme Ford, Kate Hunt and Patrick West. 1999a. Morbidity and Irish Catholic Descent in Britain: Relating Health Disadvantage to Behaviour. *Ethnicity and Health* 4 (4): 221–30.

——, Rory Williams and G. Davey–Smith. 1999b. Association of Medical, Physiological, Behavioural and Socio-Economic Factors with Elevated Mortality in Men of Irish Heritage in West Scotland. *Journal of Public Health Medicine* 21 (1): 46–54.

——, Rory Williams and Graeme Ford. 2001. Morbidity and Irish Catholic Descent in Britain: Relating Health Disadvantage to Socio-Economic Position. *Social Science and Medicine* 52: 999–1005.

Adams, Michael. 2008. *Unlikely Utopia: The Surprising Triumph of Canadian Multiculturalism*. Toronto: Penguin Canada.

Adelstein, A. M., M. G. Marmot, G. Dean and J. S. Bradshaw. 1986. Comparison of Mortality of Irish Immigrants in England with that of Irish and British Nationals. *Irish Medical Journal* 79: 185–9.

Ahmed, Sara. 2004. *The Cultural Politics of Emotion*. Edinburgh: Edinburgh University Press.

Akenson, Donald H. 1993. *The Irish Diaspora: A Primer.* Toronto: P. D. Meany.

———. 2000. Irish Migration to North America, 1800–1920, in *The Irish Diaspora*, edited by A. Bielenberg, pp. 111–38. Essex: Pearson Education.

Alea, Nicole. 2010. The Prevalence and Quality of Silent, Socially Silent, and Disclosed Autobiographical Memories Across Adulthood. *Memory* 18 (2): 142–58.

Anderson, Benedict. 1991. *Imagined Communities: Reflections on the Origin and Spread of Nationalism.* Rev. edn. London: Verso.

Anderson, James and Ian Shuttleworth. 1994. Sectarian Readings of Sectarianism: Interpreting the Northern Ireland Census. *Irish Review* 16: 74–93.

——— and Ian Shuttleworth. 1998. Sectarian Demography, Territoriality and Political Development in Northern Ireland. *Political Geography* 17 (2): 187–208.

Anderson, Kay and Susan Smith. 2001. Emotional Geographies. *Transactions of the Institute of British Geographers* 26: 7–10.

Anwar, Muhammad. 1979. *The Myth of Return: Pakistanis in Britain.* London: Heineman.

Appleyard, R. T. 1962a. Determinants of Return Migration: A Socio-Economic Study of UK Migrants who Returned from Australia. *The Economic Record* 38 (83): 352–68.

———. 1962b. The Return Movement of United Kingdom Migrants from Australia. *Population Studies* 15 (3): 214–25.

Archdeacon, Thomas. 1983. *Becoming American: An Ethnic History.* New York: The Free Press.

Ashe, Fidelma. 2007. Gendering Ethno-Nationalist Conflict in Northern Ireland: A Comparative Analysis of Nationalist Women's Political Protests. *Ethnic and Racial Studies* 30 (5): 766–86.

Aspinall, P. J. 2002. Suicide Amongst Irish Migrants in Britain: A Review of the Identity and Integration Hypothesis. *International Journal of Social Psychiatry* 48 (4): 290–304.

Aughey, Arthur. 1989. *Under Siege: Unionism and the Anglo-Irish Agreement.* Belfast: Blackstaff Press.

———. 2007. *The Politics of Englishness.* Manchester: Manchester University Press.

Aunger, Edmund. 1975. Religion and Occupational Class in Northern Ireland. *The Economic and Social Review* 7 (1): 1–18.

Austin, David. 2010. Narratives of Power: Historical Mythologies in Contemporary Québec and Canada. *Race and Class* 52 (1): 19–32.

Bade, Klaus J. 2003. *Migration in European History.* Oxford: Blackwell Publishing.

Bailey, P. H. and Stephen Tilley. 2002. Storytelling and the Interpretation of Meaning in Qualitative Research. *Journal of Advanced Nursing* 38 (6): 574–83.

Baillie, Sandra M. 2008. *Presbyterians in Ireland: Identity in the Twenty-First Century.* Basingstoke: Palgrave.

Baines, Dudley. 1995. *Emigration from Europe, 1815–1930.* Cambridge: Cambridge University Press.

Balarajan, R. 1995. Ethnicity and Variations in the Nation's Health. *Health Trends* 271: 114–19.

Baraniuk, Carol and Linda Hagan. 2007. Ireland's Hidden Diaspora? Finding a Place for the Ulster-Scots in Ireland's National Tale, in *Rethinking Diasporas: Hidden Narratives and Imagined Borders*, edited by A. Ní Eigeartaigh, K. Howard and D. Getty, pp. 70–7. Newcastle: Cambridge Scholars Publishing.

Barber, Marilyn. 1991. *Immigrant Domestic Servants in Canada, Canada's Ethnic Groups.* Ottawa: Canadian Historical Association.

——. 2005. Hearing Women's Voices: Female Migration to Canada in the Early Twentieth Century. *Oral History* 33 (1): 68–76.

Bardon, Jonathan and Stephen Conlin. 1985. *Belfast: 1000 Years.* Belfast: The Blackstaff Press.

Barnier, Amanda and John Sutton. 2008. From Individual to Collective Memory: Theoretical and Empirical Perspectives. *Memory* 16 (3): 177–82.

Barrett, Alan and Jean Goggin. 2010. Returning to the Question of a Wage Premium for Returning Migrants. ESRI Working Paper No. 337.

—— and Paul O'Connell. 2001. Is There a Wage Premium for Returning Irish Migrants? *Economic and Social Review* 32 (1): 1–22.

—— and Fergal Trace. 1998. Who is Coming Back? The Educational Profile of Returning Migrants in the 1990s. *Irish Banking Review* (summer): 38–51.

——, John FitzGerald and Brian Nolan. 2002. Earnings Inequality, Returns to Education and Immigration Into Ireland. *Labour Economics* 9 (5): 665–80.

Barritt, Denis P. and Charles F. Carter. 1962. *The Northern Ireland Problem: A Study in Group Relations.* Oxford: Oxford University Press.

Bauman, Richard. 1984. *Verbal Art as Performance.* Prospect Heights, ILL.: Waveland Press.

Beak, T. W. 1958. *We Came to Canada.* 2nd rev. edn. Montreal: Burton's Bookshop.

Bechhofer, Frank and David McCrone. 2007. Being British: A Crisis of Identity? *Political Quarterly* 78 (2): 251–60.

—— and David McCrone. 2010. Choosing National Identity. *Sociological Research Online* 15 (3): 13. Available at: www.socresonline.org.uk/15/3/3.html (accessed: 1 January 2012).

Belchem, John. 2007. *Irish, Catholic and Scouse: The History of the Liverpool Irish, 1800–1939.* Liverpool: Liverpool University Press.

Bell, John, Anne Caughey, Ulf Hansson and Agnieszka Martynowicz. 2009. *'Easy Life, Great People, Bad Weather': A Report on the Experiences of Migrant Workers in Northern Ireland.* Belfast: Institute for Conflict Research.

——, Ulf Hansson and Nick McCaffery. 2010. *'The Troubles Aren't History Yet': Young People's Understanding of the Past.* Belfast: Community Relations Council.

BenEzer, Gadi. 2002. *The Ethiopian Jewish Exodus: Narratives of the Migration Journey to Israel, 1977–1985.* London: Routledge.

Benmayor, Rina and Andor Skotnes. 1994. Some Reflections on Migration and Identity, in *Migration and identity*, edited by R. Benmayor and A. Skotnes, pp. 1–18. Oxford: Oxford University Press.

Bernard, André. 2008. Immigrants in the Hinterlands. *Perspectives (Statistics Canada)* January: 5–14.

Berry, John W. 2006. Mutual Attitudes Among Immigrants and Ethnocultural Groups in Canada. *International Journal of Intercultural Relations* 30: 719–34.

Bew, Paul, Henry Patterson and Paul Teague. 1997. *Between War and Peace: The Political Future of Northern Ireland.* London: Lawrence and Wishart.

Bibby, R. W. 1990. *Mosaic Madness: The Poverty and Potential of Life in Canada.* Toronto: Stoddart.

Bielenberg, Andy (ed.). 2000. *The Irish Diaspora.* Essex: Pearson Education.

Bissoondath, Neil. 1994. *Selling Illusions: The Cult of Multiculturalism in Canada.* Toronto: Penguin Books.

Black, Richard. 2002. Conceptions of 'Home' and the Political Geography of Refugee Repatriation: Between Assumption and Contested Reality in Bosnia-Herzegovina. *Applied Geography* 22 (2): 123–38.

—— and Saskia Gent. 2006. Sustainable Return in Post–Conflict Contexts. *International Migration* 44 (3): 15–38.

Blakely, Brian L. 1988. The Society for the Oversea Settlement of British Women and the Problems of Empire Settlement, 1917–1936. *Albion* 20 (3): 421–44.

Blethen, H. Tyler and Curtis W. Wood (eds). 1997. *Ulster and North America: Transatlantic Perspectives on the Scotch-Irish.* Tuscaloosa: University of Alabama Press.

Blitz, Brad K., Rosemary Sales and Lisa Marzano. 2005. Non-Voluntary Return? The Politics of Return to Afghanistan. *Political Studies* 53 (1): 182–200.

Boal, Frederick W. 2006. Big Processes, Little People: The Population of Metropolitan Belfast 1901–2001, in *Enduring City: Belfast in the Twentieth Century*, edited by F. W. Boal and S. A. Royle, pp. 57–83. Belfast: Blackstaff Press.

——, John A. Campbell and David N. Livingstone. 1991. The Protestant Mosaic: A Majority of Minorities, in *The Northern Ireland Question: Myth and Reality*, edited by P. J. Roche and B. Barton, pp. 99–129. Aldershot: Avebury.

Bonesteel, Sarah. 2008. *Canada's Relationship with Inuit: A History of Policy and Program Development.* Ottawa: Indian and Northern Affairs Canada.

Bouchard, Gerard and Charles Taylor. 2008. *Consultation Commission on Accommodation Practices Related to Cultural Difference* [Bouchard–Taylor Commission]. Quebec: Government of Quebec.

Bovenkerk, Frank. 1973. On the Causes of Irish Emigration. *Sociologia Ruralis* 13 (4–5): 263–75.

Bowen, Kurt. 1983. *Protestants in a Catholic State: Ireland's Privileged Minority.* Montreal: McGill–Queen's University Press.

Boyd, Andrew. 1969. *Holy War in Belfast.* Tralee: Anvil Books.

Boyd, Monica. 2002. Educational Attainments of Immigrant Offspring: Success or Segmented Assimilation? *International Migration Review* 36 (4): 1037–60.

—— and Michael Vickers. 2000. 100 Years of Immigration in Canada. *Canadian Social Trends*, (autumn): 2–12.

Boyle, Joseph F. 1977. Educational Attainment, Occupation, Achievement and Religion in Northern Ireland. *The Economic and Social Review* 8 (2): 79–100.

Boyle, Joseph W. 1962–1963. The Belfast Protestant Association and the Independent Orange Order, 1901–10. *Irish Historical Studies* 13: 117–52.

Boyle, Kevin. 1968. The Irish Immigrant in Britain. *Northern Ireland Legal Quarterly* 19 (4): 418–45.

Bracken, Patrick J. and Patrick O'Sullivan. 2001. The Invisibility of Irish Migrants in British Health Research. *Irish Studies Review* 9 (1): 41–51.

——, Liam Greenslade, B. Griffin and M. Smyth. 1998. Mental Health and Ethnicity: The Irish Dimension. *British Journal of Psychiatry* 172 (2): 103–5.

Bradley, John. 1999. The History of Economic Development in Ireland, North and South, in *Ireland North and South: Perspectives From the Social Sciences*, edited by A. F. Heath, R. Breen and C. T. Whelan, pp. 35–68. Oxford: Oxford University Press.

Brah, Avtar. 1996. *Cartographies of Diaspora*. London: Routledge.

Braidwood, John. 1964. Ulster and Elizabethan English, in *Ulster Dialects: An Introductory Symposium*, edited by G. Brendan Adams, pp. 5–110. Cultra: Ulster Folk and Transport Museum.

Brennan, Niamh. 1997. A Political Minefield: Southern Loyalists, the Irish Grants Committee and the British Government, 1922–1931. *Irish Historical Studies* 30 (119): 406–19.

Brettell, Caroline. 1979. Emigrar Para Voltar: A Portuguese Ideology of Return Migration. *Papers in Anthropology* 20 (1): 1–20.

Brewer, John D. 2004. Continuity and Change in Contemporary Ulster Protestantism. *The Sociological Review* 52 (2): 265–83.

Bridge, Carl and Kent Fedorowich. 2003. Mapping the British World, in *The British World: Diaspora, Culture and Identity*, edited by C. Bridge and K. Fedorowich, pp.1–15. London: Frank Cass.

British Oversea Settlement Delegation to Canada. 1924. *Report to the Secretary of State for the Colonies, President of the Oversea Settlement Committee, from the Delegation Appointed to Obtain Information Regarding the System of Child Migration and Settlement in Canada* [Bondfield Report]. London: HMSO, cmd. 2285.

Brown, Roger and James Kulik. 1977. Flashbulb Memories. *Cognition* 5 (1): 73–99.

Browner, Fran. 2008. *Coming Home*. Mulranny, County Mayo: Safe-Home Programme Ireland.

Brubaker, Rogers. 2005. The 'Diaspora' Diaspora. *Journal of Ethnic and Migration Studies* 28 (1): 1–19.

Bryan, Dominic, Clifford Stevenson, John Gillespie and John Bell. 2010. *Public Displays of Flags and Emblems in Northern Ireland Survey 2006–2009* [report]. Belfast: Institute of Irish Studies, Queen's University Belfast.

Bryson, Anna. 2007. 'Whatever You Say, Say Nothing': Researching Memory and Identity in Mid–Ulster, 1945–1969. *Oral History* 35 (2): 45–56.

Buckner, Phillip. 2008. The Creation of the Dominion of Canada, 1860–1901, in *Canada and the British Empire*, edited by P. Buckner, pp. 66–86. Oxford: Oxford University Press.

Bueltmann, Tanja, David Gleeson and Don MacRaild (eds). 2012. *Locating the English Diaspora, 1500–2010*. Liverpool: Liverpool University Press.

Bull, Peter. 2006. Shifting Patterns of Social Identity in Northern Ireland. *The Psychologist*

19 (1): 40–43.

Burke, A. W. 1976. Attempted Suicide Among Irish-born Population in Birmingham. *British Journal of Psychiatry* 128: 534–7.

Burrell, Kathy. 2006. *Moving Lives: Narratives of Nation and Migration Among Europeans in Post-War Britain*. Aldershot: Ashgate.

Butler, David. 1995. *The Trouble with Reporting Northern Ireland: The British State, the Broadcast Media and Nonfictional Representation of the Conflict*. Aldershot: Avebury.

Butler, David and Joseph Ruane. 2009. Identity, Difference and Community in Southern Irish Protestantism: The Protestants of West Cork. *National Identities* 11 (1): 73–86.

Byrne, Joseph. 2004. *Byrne's Dictionary of Irish Local History*. Cork: Mercier Press.

Cairns, Ed. 1982. Intergroup Conflict in Northern Ireland, in *Social Identity and Intergroup Relations*, edited by H. Tajfel, pp. 277–97. London: Cambridge University Press.

—— and Christopher Alan Lewis. 1999. Collective Memories, Political Violence and Mental Health in Northern Ireland. *British Journal of Psychology* 90 (1): 25–33.

—— and John Mallett. 2003. Who are the Victims? Self–Assessed Victimhood and the Northern Irish Conflict. *NIO Research and Statistical Series, Report No. 7*. Belfast: Northern Ireland Office Statistics and Research Branch.

—— and Micheál D. Roe. 2003. Introduction: Why Memories in Conflict? in *The Role of Memory in Ethnic Conflict*, edited by E. Cairns and M. D. Roe, pp. 3–8. Basingstoke: Palgrave Macmillan.

Callaghan, Marie Hammond. 2002. Surveying Politics of Peace, Gender, Conflict and Identity in Northern Ireland: The Case of the Derry Peace Women in 1972. *Women's Studies International Forum* 25 (1): 33–49.

Cameron Commission. 1969. *Disturbances in Northern Ireland: Report of the Commission Appointed by the Governor of Northern Ireland*. Chairman: The Honourable Lord Cameron, D. S. C. Belfast: HSMO, cmd. 532.

Canadian Council on Social Development (CCSD). 2007. *Populations Vulnerable to Poverty: Urban Poverty in Canada, 2000*. Ottawa: Canadian Council on Social Development, at: www.ccsd.ca/pubs/2007/upp/vulnerable_populations.pdf (accessed 8 January 2012).

Cannadine, David. 2001. *Ornamentalism: How The British Saw Their Empire*. London: Allen Lane, Penguin Press.

Carey, Hilary M. 2011. *God's Empire: Religion and Colonialism in the British World, c. 1801–1908*. Cambridge: Cambridge University Press.

Carrier, N. H. and James R. Jeffery. 1953. *External Migration: A Study of the Available Statistics, 1815–1950*. London: HMSO.

Carter, Sarah. 1999. Infamous Proposal: Prairie Indians and Soldier Settlement After World War I. *Manitoba History* 37: 9–21.

Cassidy, Clare and Karen Trew. 1998. Identities in Northern Ireland: A Multidimensional Approach. *Journal of Social Issues* 54 (4): 725–40.

Castles, Stephen. 2010. Understanding Global Migration: A Social Transformation Perspective. *Journal of Ethnic and Migration Studies* 36 (10): 1565–86.

Cavalli, Alessandro. 2004. Generations and Value Orientations. *Social Compass* 51 (2): 155–68.

Cavanaugh, Catherine and Jeremy Mouat (eds). 1996. *Making Western Canada: Essays on European Colonization and Settlement.* Toronto: Garamond.

Cavell, Janice. 2006. The Imperial Race and the Immigration Sieve: The Canadian Debate on Assisted British Migration and Empire Settlement, 1900–30. *Journal of Imperial and Commonwealth History* 34 (3): 345–67.

Cerase, Francesco P. 1974. Migration and Social Change: Expectation and Reality: A Case Study of Return Migration from the United States to Southern Italy. *International Migration Review* 8: 245–62.

Chamberlain, Mary. 1997. *Narratives of Exile and Return.* New York: St Martin's.

——. 2009. Diasporic Memories: Community, Individuality, and Creativity – a Life Stories Perspective. *Oral History Review* 36 (2): 177–87.

—— and Selma Leydesdorff. 2004. Transnational Families: Memories and Narratives. *Global Networks* 4 (3): 227–41.

Chan, Susanna. 2006. 'God's Little Acre' and 'Belfast Chinatown': Cultural Politics and Agencies of Anti-Racist Spatial Inscription. *Translocations: The Irish Migration, Race and Social Transformation Review* 1 (1): 56–75.

Chiba, Yuko. 2010. Educational Integration in a Divided Society: Lived Experiences of Settled Immigrants in Northern Ireland. *Translocations: The Irish Migration, Race and Social Transformation Review* 6 (2): 20p.

Chilton, Lisa. 2007. *Agents of Empire: British Female Migration to Canada and Australia, 1860s–1930.* Toronto: University of Toronto Press.

Citizenship and Immigration Canada. 2011. *Building Canada's Prosperity: Government of Canada Progress Report 2010: Foreign Credential Recognition.* Ottawa: Minister of Public Works and Government Services Canada.

Clary-Lemon, Jennifer. 2010. 'We're Not Ethnic, We're Irish!': Oral Histories and the Discursive Construction of Immigrant Identity. *Discourse and Society* 21 (1): 5–25.

Clifford, James. 1994. Diasporas. *Cultural Anthropology* 9 (3): 302–38.

Clucas, Marie. 2009. The Irish Health Disadvantage in England: Contribution of Structure and Identity Components of Irish Ethnicity. *Ethnicity and Health* 14 (6): 553–73.

Coakley, John. 2007. National Identity in Northern Ireland: Stability or Change? *Nations and Nationalism* 13 (4): 573–97.

Coats, R. H. 1931. Canada, in *International Migrations, Vol. 2: Interpretations*, edited by W. F. Willcox, pp. 123–42. New York: National Bureau of Economic Research.

Cochrane, Feargal. 2007. Irish–America, the End of the IRA's Armed Struggle and the Utility of 'Soft Power'. *Journal of Peace Research* 44 (2): 215–31.

Cochrane, Raymond. 1977. Mental Illness in Immigrants to England and Wales: An Analysis of Mental Hospital Admissions, 1971. *Social Psychiatry* 12: 25–35.

—— and S. Bal. 1989. Mental Hospital Admission Rates of Immigrants to England: A Comparison of 1971 and 1981. *Social Psychiatry and Psychiatric Epidemiology* 24: 2–11.

—— and Mary Stopes–Roe. 1979. Psychological Disturbance in Ireland, in England and in Irish Emigrants to England: A Comparative Study. *Economic and Social Review* 10 (4): 301–20.

Cohen, Robin. 1997. *Global Diasporas*. Seattle, WA: University of Washington Press.

Cohen, Ronald L. 2002. Silencing Objections: Social Constructions of Indifference. *Journal of Human Rights* 1 (2): 187–206.

Combat Poverty Agency. 2005. *All Over the Place: People Displaced To and From the Southern Border Counties as a Result of the Conflict, 1969–1994: Research Report*. Monaghan: Area Development Management and Combat Poverty Agency.

Commission on Emigration and Other Population Problems (Ireland). 1948–54, 1956. *Reports*. Dublin: Government Stationery Office.

Community Relations Commission (CRC). 1971. *Flight: A Report on Population Movement in Belfast During August, 1971*. Belfast: Community Relations Commission Research Unit.

Compton, Paul A. 1976. Religious Affiliation and Demographic Viability in Northern Ireland. *Transactions of the Institute of British Geographers*, new ser., 1 (4): 433–52.

———. 1978. *Northern Ireland: A Census Atlas*. Dublin: Gill and Macmillan.

———. 1985. An Evaluation of the Changing Religious Composition of the Population of Northern Ireland. *The Economic and Social Review* 16 (3): 201–24.

———. 1989. The Changing Religious Demography of Northern Ireland: Some Political Implications. *Studies: An Irish Quarterly Review* 78 (312): 393–402.

———. 1991a. Demography: The 1980s in Perspective. *Studies: An Irish Quarterly Review* 80 (318): 157–68.

———. 1991b. Employment Differentials in Northern Ireland and Job Discrimination: A Critique, in *The Northern Ireland Question: Myth and Reality*, edited by P. J. Roche and B. Barton, pp. 40–76. Aldershot: Avebury.

———. 1992. Migration Trends for Northern Ireland: Links with Great Britain, in *Migration Processes and Patterns, Vol. 2: Population Redistribution in the United Kingdom*, edited by J. Stillwell, P. Rees and P. Boden, pp. 81–99. London: Belhaven Press.

———. 1995. *Demographic Review Northern Ireland 1995*. Belfast: Northern Ireland Economic Development Office.

——— and John Power. 1991. Migration from Northern Ireland: A Survey of New Year Travellers as a Means of Identifying Emigrants. *Regional Studies* 25: 1–11.

Connerton, Paul. 2008. Seven Types of Forgetting. *Memory Studies* 1 (1): 59–71.

Connolly, Tracey. 2000. Emigration from Ireland to Britain During the Second World War, in *The Irish Diaspora*, edited by A. Bielenberg, pp. 51–64. Essex: Pearson Education.

Constantine, Stephen. 1990. Introduction: Empire Migration and Imperial Harmony, in *Emigrants and Empire: British Settlement in the Dominions Between the Wars*, edited by S. Constantine, pp. 1–21. Manchester: Manchester University Press.

———. 1991. Empire Migration and Social Reform 1880–1950, in *Migrants, Emigrants and Immigrants: A Social History of Migration*, edited by C. G. Pooley and I. D. Whyte, pp. 62–83. London: Routledge.

——. 1998. Waving Goodbye? Australia, Assisted Passages, and the Empire and Commonwealth Settlement Acts, 1945–72. *Journal of Imperial and Commonwealth History* 26 (2): 176–95.

——. 2003. British Emigration to the Empire–Commonwealth Since 1880: From Overseas Settlement to Diaspora? *Journal of Imperial and Commonwealth History* 31 (2): 16–35.

Conway, Martin A. 1995. *Flashbulb Memories*. Hove: Lawrence Erlbaum Associates.

——. 1996. Autobiographical Knowledge and Autobiographical Memories, in *Remembering Our Past: Studies in Autobiographical Memory*, edited by D. C. Rubin, pp. 67–93. Cambridge: Cambridge University Press.

—— and Shamsul Haque. 1999. Overshadowing the Reminiscence Bump: Memories of a Struggle for Independence. *Journal of Adult Development* 6 (1): 45–59.

—— and Christopher W. Pleydell–Pearce. 2000. The Construction of Autobiographical Memories in the Self-Memory System. *Psychological Review* 107 (2): 261–88.

Cooper, David. 2009. *The Musical Traditions of Northern Ireland and its Diaspora*. Aldershot: Ashgate.

Corak, Miles. 2011. Age at Immigration and the Educational Outcomes of Children. Ottawa: Statistics Canada, No. 11F0019M – No. 336.

Corcoran, Mary P. 2003a. Global Cosmopolites: Issues of Self-Identity and Collective Identity Among the Transnational Irish Elite. *Études Irlandaises* 28 (2): 135–50.

——. 2003b. The Process of Migration and the Reinvention of Self: The Experiences of Returning Irish Emigrants, in *New Directions in Irish–American History*, edited by K. Kenny, pp. 302–18. Madison: University of Wisconsin Press.

Corcoran, Terry. 1989. Tracking Emigration Flows, in *Emigration, Employment and Enterprise*, edited by J. Mulholland and D. Keogh, pp. 29–33. Dublin: Hibernian University Press.

Cormack, Robert, Anthony Gallagher and R. D. Osborne. 1997. Higher Education Participation in Northern Ireland. *Higher Education Quarterly* 51 (1): 68–85.

Corrigan, Karen P. 1999. Language Contact and Language Shift in County Armagh, 1178–1659. *Ulster Folklife* 45: 54–69.

Courtney, Damien. 2000. A Quantification of Irish Migration with Particular Reference on the 1980s and 1990s, in *The Irish Diaspora*, edited by A. Bielenberg, pp. 287–316. Essex: Pearson Education.

Cowley, Ultan. 2001. *The Men Who Built Britain: A History of the Irish Navvy*. Dublin: Wolfhound Press.

Crawford, Heather K. 2010. *Outside the Glow: Protestants and Irishness in Independent Ireland*. Dublin: University College Dublin Press.

Curtis, Liz. 1984a. *Ireland and the Propaganda War: The British Media and the 'Battle for Hearts and Minds'*. London: Pluto Press.

——. 1984b. *Nothing But the Same Old Story: The Roots of Anti–Irish Racism in Britain*. London: Information on Ireland.

Curtis, L. P. 1968. *Anglo–Saxons and Celts: A Study of Anti–Irish Prejudice in Victorian England*. New York: New York University Press.

Cwerner, Saulo B. 2001. The Times of Migration. *Journal of Ethnic and Migration Studies* 27 (1): 7–36.

Daly, Mary E. 2001. Irish Citizenship Since 1922. *Irish Historical Studies* 32 (127): 377–407.

——. 2006. *The Slow Failure: Population Decline and Independent Ireland, 1920–1973.* Madison: University of Wisconsin Press.

Das-Munshi, J., G. Leavey, S. A. Stansfeld and M. J. Prince. 2012. Migration, Social Mobility and Common Mental Disorders: Critical Review of the Literature and Meta-Analysis. *Ethnicity and Health* 17 (1–2): 17–53.

Dawson, Graham. 2007. *Making Peace with the Past? Memory, Trauma and the Irish Troubles.* Manchester: Manchester University Press.

Dean, Jennifer Asanin and Kathi Wilson. 2009. 'Education? It is Irrelevant to My Job Now. It Makes Me Very Depressed …': Exploring the Health Impacts of Under/ Unemployment Among Highly Skilled Recent Immigrants in Canada. *Ethnicity and Health* 14 (2): 185–204.

Delaney, Enda. 1998. The Churches and Irish Emigration to Britain, 1921–60. *Archivium Hibernicum* 52: 98–114.

——. 2000. *Demography, State and Society: Irish Migration to Britain, 1921–1971.* Liverpool: Liverpool University Press.

——. 2002. *Irish Emigration Since 1921.* [Dundalk]: Economic and Social History Society of Ireland.

——. 2005. Transnationalism, Networks and Emigration from Post-War Ireland. *Immigrants and Minorities*, 23 (2/3): 425–46.

——. 2007. *The Irish in Post-War Britain.* Oxford: Oxford University Press.

——. 2011. Directions in Historiography: Our Island Story? Towards a Transnational History of Late Modern Ireland. *Irish Historical Studies* 37 (148): 599–621.

——, Kevin Kenny and Donald MacRaild. 2006. Symposium: Perspectives on the Irish Diaspora. *Irish Economic and Social History* 33: 35–58.

DeMartini, Joseph R. 1985. Change Agents and Generational Relationships: A Re-Evaluation of Mannheim's Problem of Generations. *Social Forces* 64 (1): 1–16.

Dempsey, G. T. 1999. The American Role in the Northern Ireland Peace Process. *Irish Political Studies* 14 (1): 104–17.

Denial of North–East Ulster. 1912. *The Irish Review (Dublin)* 2 (17): 228–34.

de Nie, Michael. 2004. *The Eternal Paddy: Irish Identity and the British Press, 1798–1882.* Madison: University of Wisconsin Press.

Department of Enterprise, Trade and Investment (DETINI). 2005. *An Economic Vision for Northern Ireland.* Belfast: DETINI.

Devine, Frances, Tom Baum, Niamh Hearns and Adrian Devine. 2007. Cultural Diversity in Hospitality Work: The Northern Ireland Experience. *International Journal of Human Resource Management* 18 (2): 333–49.

DeVoretz, Don J. 2006. The Education, Immigration and Emigration of Canada's Highly Skilled Workers in the 21st Century, in *Working Paper Series; No. 6–16.* Vancouver: Research on Immigration and Integration in the Metropolis.

Dixon, Paul. 2006. Performing the Northern Ireland Peace Process on the World Stage. *Political Science Quarterly* 121 (1): 61–91.

Doherty, Paul and Michael A. Poole. 2002. Religion as an Indicator of Ethnicity in Northern Ireland: An Alternative Perspective. *Irish Geography* 35 (1): 75–89.

Dominions Royal Commission. 1917. *Fifth Interim Report of the Royal Commission on the Natural Resources, Trade, and Legislation of Certain Portions of His Majesty's Dominions.* London: HMSO, cd. 8457.

Dooley, Brian. 2004. *Choosing the Green? Second Generation Irish and the Cause of Ireland.* Belfast: Beyond the Pale Publishers.

Dooley, Terence. 1996. Protestant Migration From the Free State to Northern Ireland, 1920–25: A Private Census for Co. Fermanagh. *Clogher Record* 15 (3): 87–132.

———. 2000. *Plight of the Monaghan Protestants, 1912–26.* Dublin: Irish Academic Press.

Douglas, R. M. 2002. Anglo–Saxons and Attacotti: The Racialization of Irishness in Britain Between the World Wars. *Ethnic and Racial Studies* 25 (1): 40–63.

Dowler, Lorraine. 1998. 'And They Think I'm Just a Nice Old Lady': Women and War in Belfast, Northern Ireland. *Gender, Place and Culture* 5 (2): 159–76.

Dowling, Martin. 1999. *Tenant Right and Agrarian Society in Ulster, 1600–1870.* Dublin: Irish Academic Press.

Doyle, David. N. 1989. The Irish in Australia and the United States: Some Comparisons, 1800–1939. *Irish Economic and Social History* 16: 73–94.

———. 1994. Small differences? The Study of the Irish in the United States and Britain [review article]. *Irish Historical Studies* 29: 114–19.

Drudy, P. J. 1986. Migration Between Ireland and Britain Since Independence, in *Ireland and Britain Since 1922*, edited by P. J. Drudy, pp. 107–23. Cambridge: Cambridge University Press.

Dunn, Seamus and Valerie Morgan. 1994. *Protestant Alienation in Northern Ireland – a Preliminary Survey.* Coleraine: Centre for the Study of Conflict, University of Ulster.

Dunnigan, Diane. 2007. *A South Roscommon Emigrant: Emigration and Return, 1890–1920*, Maynooth Studies in Local History. Dublin: Four Courts Press.

Dustmann, Christian and Yoram Weiss. 2007. Return Migration: Theory and Empirical Evidence from the UK. *British Journal of Industrial Relations* 45 (2): 236–56.

Earner-Byrne, Lindsey. 2003. The Boat to England: An Analysis of the Official Reactions to the Emigration of Single Expectant Irishwomen to Britain, 1922–1972. *Irish Economic and Social History* 30: 52–70.

Edmondson, Ricca. 2000. Rural Temporal Practices: Future Time in Connemara. *Time and Society* 9 (2/3): 269–88.

Edmunds, June and Bryan S. Taylor. 2005. Global Generations: Social Change in the Twentieth Century. *British Journal of Sociology* 56 (4): 559–77.

Elliott, Bruce S. 1988. *Irish Migrants in the Canadas: A New Approach.* Kingston: McGill-Queen's University Press.

Elliott, Marianne. 2000. *The Catholics of Ulster.* London: Allen Lane, Penguin Press.

———. 2002. Religion and Identity in Northern Ireland, in *The Long Road to Peace in Northern Ireland: Peace Lectures From the Institute of Irish Studies at Liverpool*

University, edited by M. Elliott, pp. 169–85. Liverpool: Liverpool University Press.

——. 2009. *When God Took Sides: Religion and Identity in Ireland – Unfinished History.* Oxford: Oxford University Press.

Elliott, Sydney. 1999. The Northern Ireland Electoral System: A Vehicle for Disputation, in *The Northern Ireland Question: Nationalism, Unionism and Partition*, edited by P. J. Roche and B. Barton, pp. 122–38. Aldershot: Ashgate.

English, Richard. 2011. Is There an English Nationalism? London: IPPR.

Equality Commission Northern Ireland (ECNI). 2001. *Racial Equality in Education: A Good Practice Guide.* Belfast: ECNI.

——. 2003. *Racial Equality in Health and Social Care.* Belfast: ECNI.

——. 2007. *Assessing the Impact of Section 75 of the Northern Ireland Act 1998 on Individuals.* Auckland: Reeves Associates.

Erikson, E. H. 1959. *Identity and the Life Cycle.* New York: International Universities Press.

——. 1963. *Childhood and Society.* 2nd edn. New York: Norton.

Errington, Elizabeth Jane. 2008. British Migration and British America, 1783–1867, in *Canada and the British Empire*, edited by P. Buckner, pp. 140–59. Oxford: Oxford University Press.

Fahey, Tony, B. C. Hayes and R. Sinnott. 2005. *Conflict and Consensus: A Study of Values and Attitudes in the Republic of Ireland and Northern Ireland.* Dublin: Institute of Public Administration.

Fairweather, Eileen, Roisin McDonough and Melanie McFadyean. 1984. *Only the Rivers Run Free, Northern Ireland: The Women's War.* London: Pluto Press.

Fang, Tony and John S. Heywood. 2010. Immigration, Ethnic Wage Differentials and Output Pay in Canada. *British Journal of Industrial Relations* 48 (1): 109–30.

Fanning, Charles (ed.). 2000. *New Perspectives on the Irish Diaspora.* Carbondale: Southern Illinois University Press.

Farrell, Michael. 1980. *Northern Ireland: The Orange State.* 2nd edn. London: Pluto Press.

Farrington, Christopher and Graham Walker. 2009. Ideological Content and Institutional Frameworks: Unionist Identities in Northern Ireland and Scotland. *Irish Studies Review* 17 (2): 135–52.

Fay, Marie–Therese, Mike Morrissey and Marie Smyth. 2001. *The Cost of the Troubles Study: Report on the Northern Ireland Survey: The Experience and Impact of the Troubles.* 2nd edn. Londonderry: INCORE.

Fedorowich, Kent. 1995. *Unfit for Heroes: Reconstruction and Soldier Settlement in the Empire Between the Wars.* Manchester: Manchester University Press.

——. 1996. The Problems of Disbandment: The Royal Irish Constabulary and Imperial Migration, 1919–29. *Irish Historical Studies* 30 (117): 88–110.

——. 1999. Reconstruction and Resettlement: The Politicization of Irish Migration to Australia and Canada, 1919–29. *English Historical Review* 114 (459): 1143–78.

Fegan, Gillian and David Marshall. 2008. *Long–Term International Migration Estimates for Northern Ireland (2006–2007).* Belfast: NISRA.

Feinstein, C. H. 1972. *National Income, Expenditure, and Output of the United Kingdom,*

1855–1965. Cambridge: Cambridge University Press.

Fenton, Steve. 2007. Indifference Towards National Identity: What Young Adults Think About Being English and British. *Nations and Nationalism* 13 (2): 221–39.

Ferriter, Diarmaid. 2009. *Occasions of Sin: Sex and Society in Modern Ireland*. London: Profile Books.

Finch, Tim, Holly Andrew and Maria Latorre. 2010. *Global Brit: Making the Most of the British Diaspora*. London: Institute for Public Policy Research.

——, Maria Latorre, Naomi Pollard and Jill Rutter. 2009. *Shall We Stay or Shall We Go? Remigration Trends Among Britain's Immigrants*. Executive Summary. London: Institute for Public Policy Research.

Fine, Ellen. 1988. The Absent Memory: The Act of Writing in Post-Holocaust French Literature, in *Writing and the Holocaust*, edited by B. Lang, pp. 41–57. New York: Holmes and Meier.

Finlay, Andrew. 2001. Defeatism and Northern Protestant 'Identity'. *Global Review of Ethnopolitics* 1 (2): 3–20.

Fisher, Lettice Ilbert. 1925. Canada and British Immigration. *Contemporary Review* 128 (July/December): 601–605.

Fitzgerald, Joseph M. 1988. Vivid Memories and the Reminiscence Phenomenon: The Role of a Self-Narrative. *Human Development* 31: 261–73.

Fitzgerald, Patrick. 1992. 'Like Crickets to the Crevice of a Brew-House': Poor Irish Migrants in England, 1560–1640, in *Patterns of Migration*, edited by P. O'Sullivan, pp. 13–35. London: Leicester University Press.

——. 2006. Mapping the Ulster Diaspora 1607–1960. *Familia* 22: 1–17.

—— and Brian Lambkin. 2008. *Migration in Irish History, 1607–2007*. Basingstoke: Palgrave Macmillan.

Fitzpatrick, David. 1989. 'A Curious Middle Place': The Irish in Britain, 1871–1921, in *The Irish in Britain, 1815–1939*, edited by R. Swift and S. Gilley, pp. 10–59. Savage, MD: Barnes and Noble Books.

——. 1994. *Oceans of Consolation: Personal Accounts of Irish Migration to Australia*. Cork: Cork University Press.

——. 1996. Emigration, 1871–1921, in *A New History of Ireland, Vol.6: Ireland Under the Union, II*, edited by W. E. Vaughan, pp. 606–52. Oxford: Clarendon Press.

——. 1998. *The Two Irelands, 1912–1939*. Oxford: Oxford University Press.

Fivush, Robyn. 2008. Remembering and Reminiscing: How Individual Lives are Constructed in Family Narratives. *Memory Studies* 1 (1): 49–58.

——. 2010. Speaking Silence: The Social Construction of Silence in Autobiographical and Cultural Narratives. *Memory* 18 (2): 88–98.

——, Jennifer G. Bohanek and Marshall Duke. 2008. The Intergenerational Self: Subjective Perspective and Family History, in *Self Continuity: Individual and Collective Perspectives*, edited by F. Sani, pp. 131–43. Mahwah, NJ: Lawrence Erlbaum Associates.

Flackes, W. D. 1983. *Northern Ireland: A Political Directory, 1968–83*. London: Ariel Books/BBC.

Foeken, Dick. 1980. Return Migration to a Marginal Area in North–Western Ireland.

Tidjschrift voor Economische en Sociale Geografie 71 (2): 114–20.

Ford, Robert, James R. Tilley and Anthony F. Heath. 2011. Land of My Fathers? Economic Development, Ethnic Division and Ethnic National Identity in 32 Countries. *Sociological Research Online* 16 (4): 13 at: www.socresonline.org.uk/16/4/8.html (accessed 1 January 2012).

Forsythe, Frank P. and Vani K. Borooah. 1992. The Nature of Migration Between Northern Ireland and Great Britain: A Preliminary Analysis Based on the Labour Force Surveys, 1986–88. *The Economic and Social Review* 23 (2): 105–27.

Frenette, Marc and René Morissette. 2005. Will They Ever Converge? Earnings of Immigrant and Canadian-Born Workers Over the Last Two Decades. *International Migration Review* 39 (1): 228–57.

——, Feng Hou, René Morissette, Ted Wannell and Maryanne Webber. 2008. Earnings and Incomes of Canadians Over the Past Quarter Century: 2006 Census. Ottawa: Statistics Canada, No. 97–563–X.

Fresco, Nadine. 1984. Remembering the Unknown. *International Review of Psycho-Analysis* 11: 417–27.

Fries, Christopher J. and Paul Gingrich. 2010. A 'Great' Large Family: Understandings of Multiculturalism Among Newcomers to Canada. *Refuge* 27 (1): 36–49.

Froggatt, Peter. 1965. The census in Ireland of 1813–15. *Irish Historical Studies* 14 (55): 227–35.

Frye, Northrop. 1971. *The Bush Garden: Essays on the Canadian Imagination.* Toronto: Anansi Press.

Gaffikin, Frank and Mike Morrissey. 1990. *Northern Ireland: The Thatcher Years.* London: Zed Books.

Gallagher, Michael. 1995. How Many Nations are There in Ireland? *Ethnic and Racial Studies* 18 (4): 715–39.

Ganga, Deianira. 2006. Reinventing the Myth of Return: Older Italians in Nottingham, in *Histories and Memories: Migrants and Their History in Britain,* edited by K. Burrell and P. Panayi, pp. 114–30 and 280–83. London: Tauris Academic Studies.

Ganiel, Gladys. 2006. Ulster Says Maybe: The Restructuring of Evangelical Politics in Northern Ireland. *Irish Political Studies* 22 (2): 137–55.

Gardiner, David. 2008. *Whatever You Say, Say Nothing: A Report on the Views and Experiences of Border Protestants for the Church of Ireland Diocese of Clogher.* Clogher: Hard Gospel Project, Church of Ireland Diocese of Clogher.

Garrett, Paul Michael. 2000. The Abnormal Flight: The Migration and Repatriation of Irish Unmarried Mothers. *Social History* 25 (3): 330–43.

Garside, W. R. 1990. *British Unemployment, 1919–1939: A Study in Public Policy.* Cambridge: Cambridge University Press.

Geoghegan, Peter. 2010. *A Difficult Difference: Race, Religion and the New Northern Ireland.* Dublin: Irish Academic Press.

Geraghty, Teresa, Celine McStravick and Stephanie Mitchell. 2010. *New to Northern Ireland: A Study of the Issues Faced by Migrant, Asylum Seeking and Refugee Children in Northern Ireland.* London: National Children's Bureau.

Ghosh, Bimal (ed.). 2000. *Return Migration: Journey of Hope or Despair?* Geneva: International Organization for Migration and the United Nations.

Gibbons, Luke. 1984. Synge, Country and Western: The Myth of the West in Irish and American Culture, in *Culture and Ideology in Ireland,* edited by C. Curtin, M. Kelly and L. O'Dowd, pp. 1–19. Galway: UCG Press.

Gibbs, Julie. 2010. *Financial Inclusion Amongst New Migrants in Northern Ireland.* London: Information Centre about Asylum and Refugees.

Giddens, Anthony. 1991. *Modernity and Self-Identity: Self and Society in the Late Modern Age.* Cambridge: Polity Press.

Gilley, Sheridan. 2009. English Catholic Attitudes to Irish Catholics. *Immigrants and Minorities* 27 (2/3): 226–47.

Gilligan, Chris, Paul Hainsworth and Aidan McGarry. 2011. Fractures, Foreigners and Fitting In: Exploring Attitudes Towards Immigration and Integration in 'Post-Conflict' Northern Ireland. *Ethnopolitics* 10 (2): 253–69.

Gilroy, Paul. 1993. *The Black Atlantic.* Cambridge, Mass.: Harvard University Press.

Gmelch, George. 1980. Return Migration. *Annual Review of Anthropology* 9: 135–59.

——. 1983. Who Returns and Why? Return Migration Behaviour in Two North Atlantic Societies. *Human Organization* 42 (1): 46–54.

——. 1986. The Adjustment of Return Migrants to the West of Ireland, in *Return Migration and Regional Economic Problems*, edited by R. King, pp. 152–70. London: Croom Helm.

—— and Lawrence Delaney. 1979. Irish Return Migration: The Sociodemographic Characteristics of Return Emigrants. *Papers in Anthropology* 20: 155–66.

Goodall, H. L. 2005. Narrative Inheritance: A Nuclear Family with Toxic Secrets. *Qualitative Inquiry* 11 (4): 492–513.

Gothard, Janice. 1990. 'The Healthy Wholesome British Domestic Girl': Single Female Migration and the Empire Settlement Act, 1922–1930, in *Emigrants and Empire: British Dettlement in the dominions Between the Wars,* edited by S. Constantine, pp. 72–95. Manchester: Manchester University Press.

Gould, J. D. 1980. European Inter-Continental Emigration: The Road Home: Return Migration From the U.S.A. *Journal of European Economic History* 9 (1): 41–111.

Gould, Michael and Heather Skinner. 2007. Branding on Ambiguity? Place Branding Without a National Identity: Marketing Northern Ireland as a Post-Conflict Society in the USA. *Place Branding and Public Diplomacy* 3 (1): 100–113.

Gray, Ann Marie and Goretti Horgan. 2009. *Figuring It Out: Looking Behind the Social Statistics in Northern Ireland.* Belfast: ARK.

Gray, Breda. 2000. Gendering the Irish Diaspora: Questions of Enrichment, Hybridization and Return. *Women's Studies International Forum* 23 (2): 167–85.

——. 2002a. 'Breaking the Silence' – Questions of Staying and Going in 1950s Ireland. *Irish Journal of Psychology* 23 (3/4): 158–83.

——. 2002b. The Irish Diaspora: Globalised Belonging(s). *Irish Journal of Sociology* 11 (2): 123–44.

——. 2002c. 'Whitely Scripts' and Irish Women's Racialized Belonging(s) in England.

European Journal of Cultural Studies 5 (3): 257–75.

——. 2004. *Women and the Irish Diaspora*. London: Routledge.

——. 2006a. Migrant Integration Policy: A Nationalist Fantasy of Management and Control? *Translocations: The Irish Migration, Race and Social Transformation Review* 1(1): 121–41.

——. 2006b. Redefining the Nation Through Economic Growth and Migration: Changing Rationalities of Governance in the Republic of Ireland? *Mobilities* 1 (3): 353–72.

——. 2007. Breaking the Silence: Emigration, Gender and the Making of Irish Cultural Memory, in *Modern Irish Autobiography: Self, Nation and Society*, edited by L. Harte, pp. 111–31. Basingstoke: Palgrave.

——. 2008. Putting Emotion and Reflexivity to Work in Researching Migration. *Sociology* 42 (5): 935–52.

——. 2009. Migration, Life Narratives, Memory and Subjectivity: Reflections on an Archival Project on Irish Migration. *Migration Letters* 6 (2): 109–17.

Greenslade, Liam. 1991. White Skins, White Masks; Psychological Distress Among the Irish in Britain, in *The Irish in the New Communities* edited by P. O'Sullivan, pp. 201–25. Leicester: Leicester University Press.

——. 1994. Caoineann an Lon Dubh: Towards an Irish Dimension in 'Ethnic' Health. *Irish Studies Review* 8: 2–5.

——. 1997. The Blackbird Calls in Grief: Colonialism, Health and Identity Among Irish Immigrants in Britain, in *Location and Dislocation in Contemporary Irish Society: Emigration and Irish Identities*, edited by J. Mac Laughlin, pp. 36–60. Cork: Cork University Press.

——, Maggie Pearson and Moss Madden. 1991. *Irish Migrants in Britain: Socio-Economic and Demographic Conditions, Occasional Papers in Irish Studies; No. 3*. Liverpool: Institute of Irish Studies, University of Liverpool.

——, Maggie Pearson and Moss Madden. 1995. A Good Man's Fault: Alcohol and Irish People at Home and Abroad. *Alcohol Alcoholism* 30 (4): 407–17.

——, Moss Madden and Maggie Pearson. 1997. From Visible to Invisible: The 'Problem' of the Health of Irish People in Britain, in *Migrants, Minorities and Health: Historical and Contemporary Studies*, edited by L. Marks and M. Worboys, pp. 147–77. London: Routledge.

Greer, James. 1883. *Three Wee Ulster Lassies or, News From Our Irish Cousins*. London: Cassell and Co.

Gregg, Robert. 1985. *The Scotch–Irish Dialect Boundaries in the Province of Ulster*. Port Credit, Ontario: Canadian Federation for the Humanities.

Griffin, Patrick. 2001. *The People With No Name: Ireland's Ulster Scots, America's Scots Irish, and the Creation of a British Atlantic World, 1689–1764*. Princeton, NJ: Princeton University Press.

Grinberg, León and Rebeca Grinberg. 1989. *Psychoanalytic Perspectives on Migration and Exile*. New Haven, CT: Yale University Press.

Guelke, Adrian. 1996. The United States, Irish Americans and the Northern Ireland Peace

Process. *International Affairs* 72 (3): 521–36.

——. 2008. Israeli Flags Flying Alongside Belfast's Apartheid Walls: A New Era of Comparisons and Connections, in *The Failure of the Middle East Peace Process*, edited by G. Ben-Porat, pp. 19–38. Basingstoke: Palgrave Macmillan.

Hagerstrand, Torsten. 1973. The Domain of Human Geography, in *Directions in Geography*, edited by R. J. Chorley, pp. 67–87. London: Methuen.

Halfacree, Keith. 2004. A Utopian Imagination in Migration's Terra Incognita? Acknowledging the Non-Economic Worlds of Migration Decision-Making. *Population, Space and Place* 10 (3): 239–53.

Halpin, Brendan. 2000. Who are the Irish in Britain? Evidence from Large-Scale Surveys, in *The Irish Diaspora*, edited by A. Bielenberg, pp. 89–107. Essex: Pearson Education.

Hamber, Brandon. 2006. Flying Flags of Fear: The Role of Fear in the Process of Political Transition. *Journal of Human Rights* 5 (1): 127–42.

Hamilton, Paula and Linda Shopes. 2008. Introduction: Building Partnerships Between Oral History and Memory Studies, in *Oral History and Public Memories*, edited by P. Hamilton and L. Shopes, pp. vii–xvii. Philadelphia: Temple University Press.

Hammack, Phillip L. 2008. Narrative and the Cultural Psychology of Identity. *Personality and Social Psychology Review* 12 (3): 222–47.

Hammerton, A. James and Alistair Thomson. 2005. 'Ten Pound Poms' – Australia's Invisible Migrants: A Life History of British Postwar Emigration to Australia. Manchester: Manchester University Press.

Hancock, W. K. 1937 (reprinted 1964). *Survey of British Commonwealth Affairs, Vol. 1: Problems of Nationality, 1918–1936*. Oxford: Oxford University Press.

——. 1942 (reprinted 1964). *Survey of British Commonwealth Affairs, Vol. 2: Problems of Economic Policy, 1918–1939*. London: Oxford University Press.

Hanna, Charles A. 1902. *The Scotch-Irish or the Scot in North Britain, North Ireland, and North America*. New York; London: G. P. Putnam's Sons; The Knickerbocker Press.

Harbinson, Timothy. 2010. Narratives of Belonging: Identity, Place and Belonging in the Lives of Northern Irish, Middle Class Returned Migrants from the Protestant Community. Unpublished M.Sc. Thesis, Centre for Human Ecology, Strathclyde University.

Harding, S. and R. Balarajan. 1996. Patterns of Mortality in Second Generation Irish Living in England and Wales: Longitudinal Study. *British Medical Journal* 312 (7043): 1389–92.

—— and R. Balarajan. 2001. Patterns of Mortality in Third Generation Irish Living in England and Wales: Longitudinal Study. *British Medical Journal* 322 (7284): 466–7.

—— and R. Maxwell. 1997. Differences in Mortality of Migrants, in *Health Inequalities – Decennial Supplement*, edited by F. Drever and M. Whitehead, pp. 108–21. London: ONS.

Harkness, D. A. E. 1931. Irish Emigration, in *International Migrations, Vol. 2: Interpretations*, edited by W. F. Willcox, pp. 261–82. New York: National Bureau of Economic Research.

Harmon, Colin and Ian Walker. 2000. Education and Earnings in Northern Ireland.

Belfast: Department of Higher and Further Education, Training and Employment.

Harper, Marjory (ed.). 2005. *Emigrant Homecomings: The Return Movement of Emigrants 1600–2000*. Manchester: Manchester University Press.

——. 2008. Rhetoric and Reality: British Migration to Canada, 1867–1967, in *Canada and the British Empire*, edited by P. Buckner, pp. 160–80. Oxford: Oxford University Press.

Harper, Marjory and Stephen Constantine. 2010. *Migration and Empire*. Oxford: Oxford University Press.

Harris, Ruth-Ann. 1990. Seasonal Migration Between Ireland and England Prior to the Famine. *Canadian Papers in Rural History* 7: 363–86.

Harrison, Henry. 1939. *Ulster and the British Empire, 1939: Help or Hindrance?* London: Robert Hale.

Harrison, L. and R. Carr-Hill. 1992. *Alcohol and Disadvantage Among the Irish in Britain*. London: Federation of Irish Societies.

Harvey, David. 1990. Between Space and Time: Reflections on the Geographical Imagination. *Annals of the Association of American Geographers* 80: 418–34.

Haskey, J. 1996. Mortality Among Second Generation Irish in England and Wales. *British Medical Journal* 312: 1373–4.

Hathiyani, Abdulhamid. 2007. Professional Immigrants on the Road to Driving Taxis. *Our Diverse Cities* 4 (autumn): 128–33.

Hawthorne, Lesleyanne. 2007. Foreign Credential Recognition and Assessment: An Introduction. *Canadian Issues* (spring): 3–13.

Hayes, Bernadette C. and Ian McAllister. 2004. Protestant Disillusionment With the Northern Ireland Peace Agreement. *Irish Journal of Sociology* 13 (1): 109–25.

Hazleton, William. 2000. Encouragement From the Sidelines: Clinton's Role in the Good Friday Agreement. *Irish Studies in International Affairs* 11: 103–19.

Heath, Anthony F. and James R. Tilley. 2005. British National Identity and Attitudes Towards Immigration. *International Journal on Multicultural Societies* 7 (2): 119–32.

—— and James R. Tilley. 2007. The Decline of British National Pride. *British Journal of Sociology* 58 (4): 661–78.

Heath, Joseph. 2001. *The Efficient Society: Why Canada Is As Close To Utopia As It Gets*. Toronto: Viking.

Heenan, Deirdre and Derek Birrell. 2011. *Social Work in Northern Ireland: Conflict and Change*. Bristol: Policy Press.

Herson, John. 2006. Family History and Memory in Irish Immigrant Families, in *Histories and Memories: Migrants and Their History in Britain*, edited by K. Burrell and P. Panayi, pp. 210–33. London: Tauris Academic Studies.

Heslinga, M. W. 1979. *The Irish Border as a Cultural Divide: A Contribution to the Study of Regionalism in the British Isles*. 3rd edn. Assen: Van Gorcum.

Heuston, R. F. V. 1950. British Nationality and Irish Citizenship. *International Affairs* 26 (1): 77–90.

Hickman, Mary J. 1995. *Religion, Class and Identity: The State, the Catholic Church and the Education of the Irish in Britain*. Aldershot: Avebury.

——. 1996a. Incorporating and Denationalising the Irish in England: The Role of the Catholic Church, in *Religion and Identity*, The Irish World-Wide, Vol. 5, edited by P. O'Sullivan, pp. 196–216. Leicester: Leicester University Press.

——. 1996b. *The Irish Community in Britain: Myth or Reality? Irish Studies Centre Occasional Papers Series; No. 8*. London: University of North London Press.

——. 1998. Reconstructing Deconstructing 'race': British Political Discourses About the Irish in Britain. *Ethnic and Racial Studies* 21 (2): 288–307.

——. 1999. Alternative Historiographies of the Irish in Britain: A Critique of the Segregation/Assimilation Model, in *The Irish in Victorian Britain: The Local Dimension*, edited by R. Swift and S. Gilley, pp. 236–53. Dublin: Four Courts Press.

——. 2002. 'Locating' the Irish Diaspora. *Irish Journal of Sociology,* 11 (2): 8–26.

——. 2005. Migration and Diasporas, in *The Cambridge Companion to Modern Irish Culture,* edited by J. Cleary and C. Connolly, pp. 117–36. Cambridge: Cambridge University Press.

——. 2007. Immigration and Monocultural (Re)imaginings in Ireland and Britain. *Translocations,* 2(1): 12–25.

——. 2011. Census Ethnic Categories and Second-Generation Identities: A Study of the Irish in England and Wales. *Journal of Ethnic and Migration Studies* 37 (1): 79–97.

—— and Bronwen Walter. 1997. *Discrimination and the Irish Community in Britain: A Report of Research Undertaken for the Commission for Racial Equality.* London: CRE.

——, Helen Crowley and Nicola Mai. 2008. *Immigration and Social Cohesion in the UK: The Rhythms and Realities of Everyday Life.* London: London Metropolitan University with the Joseph Rowntree Foundation.

——, Sarah Morgan and Bronwen Walter. 2001. *Second-Generation Irish People in Britain: A Demographic, Socio-Economic and Health Profile.* London: Irish Studies Centre, University of North London.

——, Sarah Morgan, Bronwen Walter and Joseph Bradley. 2005. The Limitations of Whiteness and the Boundaries of Englishness: Second-Generation Irish Identifications and Positionings in Multiethnic Britain. *Ethnicities* 5 (2): 160–82.

Hiebert, Daniel, Nadine Schuurman and Heather Smith. 2007. Multiculturalism 'on the Ground': The Social Geography of Immigrant and Visible Minority Populations in Montreal, Toronto, and Vancouver, Projected to 2017. RIIM *Working Paper Series; No. 7–12*. Vancouver: Metropolis British Columbia, Centre of Excellence for Research on Immigration and Diversity.

Hill, Andrew and Andrew White. 2008. The Flying of Israeli Flags in Northern Ireland. *Identities: Global Studies in Culture and Power* 15 (1): 31–50.

Hill, C. Bruce. 1948. New Homemakers for Canada. *The Rotarian*, March, 20–22.

Hillyard, Patrick 1993. *Suspect Community: People's Experiences of the Prevention of Terrorism Acts in Britain.* London: Pluto Press.

Hirsch, Marianne. 1997. *Family Frames: Photography, Narrative, and Postmemory.* Cambridge: Harvard University Press.

——. 2012. *The Generation of Postmemory: Writing and Visual Culture After the Holocaust.* New York: Columbia University Press.

Hirschman, Albert O. 1970. *Exit, Voice and Loyalty: Responses to Decline in Firms, Organizations and States.* Cambridge, MA: Harvard University Press.

Hoare, Anthony and Mark Corver. 2010. The Regional Geography of New Young Graduate Labour in the UK. *Regional Studies* 44 (4): 477–94.

Hoerder, Dirk. 2002. *Cultures in Contact: World Migrations in the Second Millennium.* Durham, NC: Duke University Press.

Holmes, Alison and Martin A. Conway. 1999. Generation Identity and the Reminiscence Bump: Memory for Public and Private Events. *Journal of Adult Development* 6 (1): 21–34.

Hornsby–Smith, Michael P. 1987. *Roman Catholics in England: Studies in Social Structure Since the Second World War.* Cambridge: Cambridge University Press.

—— and Angela Dale. 1988. The Assimilation of Irish Immigrants in England. *British Journal of Sociology* 39 (4): 519–44.

Houle, René and Grant Schellenberg. 2010. New Immigrants' Assessments of Their Life in Canada. Ottawa: Statistics Canada, No. 11F0019M – No. 322.

—— and Lahouaria Yssaad. 2010. Recognition of Newcomers' Foreign Credentials and Work Experience. *Perspectives (Statistics Canada),* (September): 18–33.

Houston, Cecil J. and William J. Smyth. 1980. *The Sash Canada Wore: A Historical Geography of the Orange Order in Canada.* Toronto: University of Toronto Press.

Houston, Cecil J. and William J. Smyth. 2007. The Faded Sash: The Decline of the Orange Order in Canada, 1920–2005, in *The Orange Order in Canada,* edited by D. A. Wilson, pp. 146–91. Dublin: Four Courts Press.

Howe, Stephen. 2000. *Ireland and Empire: Colonial Legacies in Irish History and Culture.* Oxford: Oxford University Press.

Hughes, Joanne and Caitlin Donnelly. 2003. Community Relations in Northern Ireland: A Shift in Attitudes? *Journal of Ethnic and Migration Studies* 29 (4): 643–61.

——, Andrea Campbell, Miles Hewstone and Ed Cairns. 2007. Segregation in Northern Ireland: Implications for Community Relations Policy. *Policy Studies* 28 (1): 35–53.

Hull, Eleanor. 1918. The Black Pig of Kiltrustan. *Folklore* 29 (3): 226–37.

Hume, David. 2005. *Far From the Green Fields of Erin: Ulster Emigrants and Their Stories.* Newtownards, County Down: Colourpoint Books.

——. 2011. *Eagle's Wing: The Journey of the Ulster Scots and Scotch-Irish.* Newtownards, County Down: Colourpoint Books.

Huttunen, Laura. 2005. 'Home' and Ethnicity in the Context of War: Hesitant Diasporas of Bosnian Refugees. *European Journal of Cultural Studies,* 8 (2): 177–95.

Hyam, Ronald. 2006. *Britain's Declining Empire: The Road to Decolonisation, 1918–1968.* Cambridge: Cambridge University Press.

——. 2010. *Understanding the British Empire.* Cambridge: Cambridge University Press.

Irish Boundary Commission. 1969. *Report of the Irish Boundary Commission, 1925,* edited by G. Hand. Shannon: Irish University Press.

Isles, K. S. and Norman Cuthbert. 1957. *An Economic Survey of Northern Ireland.* Belfast: HMSO.

Jackson, Alvin. 1996. Irish Unionists and the Empire, 1880–1960: Classes and Masses, in *'An Irish empire'? Aspects of Ireland and the British Empire*, edited by K. Jeffery, pp. 123–48. Manchester: Manchester University Press.

Jackson, Harold. 1979. *The Two Irelands: The Problem of the Double Minority – a Dual Study of Inter-Group Tensions*. 2nd edn. London: Minority Rights Group.

Jackson, John A. 1963. *The Irish in Britain*. London: Routledge and Kegan Paul.

———. 1967. Ireland, in: *Emigrant Workers Returning to Their Home Country: Supplement to the Final Report*, pp. 101–18. Athens: OECD Publications.

Jansari, Ashok and Alan J. Parkin. 1996. Things That go Bump in Your Life: Explaining the Reminiscence Bump in Autobiographical Memory. *Psychology and Aging* 11 (1): 85–91.

Jarman, Neil. 2005. Changing Patterns and Future Planning: Migration and Northern Ireland, in *ICR Working Paper No. 1*. Belfast: Institute for Conflict Research.

———. 2006. Diversity, Economy and Policy: New Patterns of Migration to Northern Ireland. *Shared Space* 2: 45–61.

——— and Jonny Byrne. 2007. *New Migrants and Belfast: An Overview of the Demographic Context, Social Issues and Trends*. Belfast: Institute for Conflict Research.

——— and Agnieszka Martynowicz. 2009. *New Migration, Equality and Integration: Issues and Challenges for Northern Ireland*. Belfast: Equality Commission for Northern Ireland.

Jeffery, Keith. 2006. Crown, Communication and the Colonial Post: Stamps, the Monarchy and the British Empire. *Journal of Imperial and Commonwealth History* 34 (1): 45–70.

———. 2008. Distance and Proximity in Service to the Empire: Ulster and New Zealand Between the Wars. *Journal of Imperial and Commonwealth History* 36 (3): 453–72.

Jenkins, William. 2002–2003. Patrolmen and Peelers: Immigration, Urban Culture, and 'the Irish Police' in Canada and the United States. *Canadian Journal of Irish Studies* 28 (2) and 29 (1): 10–28.

———. 2003. Between the Lodge and the Meeting-House: Mapping Irish Protestant Identities and Social Worlds in Late Victorian Toronto. *Social and Cultural Geography* 4 (1): 75–98.

———. 2005. Deconstructing Diasporas: Networks and Identities Among the Irish in Buffalo and Toronto, 1870–1910. *Immigrants and Minorities* 23 (2/3): 359–98.

Jensen, Bernard Eric. 2009. Usable Pasts: Comparing Approaches to Popular and Public History, in *People and Their Pasts: Public History Today*, edited by P. Ashton and H. Kean, pp. 42–56. Basingstoke: Palgrave Macmillan.

Johnson, D. S. and Liam Kennedy. 2003. The Two Economies in Ireland in the Twentieth Century, in *New History of Ireland, Vol. 7: 1921–1984*, edited by J. R. Hill, pp. 452–86. Oxford: Oxford University Press.

Johnson, William. 1994. *A Canadian Myth: Quebec, Between Canada and the Illusion of Utopia*. Montreal: R. Davies Pub.

Johnston, H. J. M. 1972. *British Emigration Policy 1815–1830: 'Shovelling Out Paupers.'* Oxford: Oxford University Press.

Jones, Greta. 2012. A Mysterious Discrimination: Irish Medical Emigration to the United

States in the 1950s. *Social History of Medicine* 25 (1): 139–56.

Jones, Richard C. 2003. Multinational Investment and Return Migration in Ireland in the 1990s: A County-Level Analysis. *Irish Geography* 36 (2): 153–69.

Joppke, Christian. 2004. The Retreat of Multiculturalism in the Liberal State: Theory and Policy. *British Journal of Sociology* 55 (2): 237–57.

Joyce, P. W. 2000 [1879]. *Old Celtic Romances*. London: Wordsworth Editions in association with The Folklore Society.

Kaiser, Susana. 2005. *Postmemories of Terror: A New Generation Copes with the Legacy of the 'Dirty War'*. Basingstoke: Palgrave Macmillan.

Kallen, Jeffrey. 1999. Irish English and the Ulster Scots Controversy. *Ulster Folklife* 45: 70–85.

Kansteiner, Wulf. 2002. Finding Meaning in Memory: A Methodological Critique of Collective Memory Studies. *History and Theory* 41: 179–97.

Kaufmann, Eric. 2007. The Orange Order in Ontario, Newfoundland, Scotland and Northern Ireland: A Macro-Social Analysis, in *The Orange Order in Canada*, edited by D. A. Wilson, pp. 42–68. Dublin: Four Courts Press.

—— and Oded Haklai. 2008. Dominant Ethnicity: From Minority to Majority. *Nations and Nationalism* 14 (4): 743–67.

Kazemipur, Abdolmohammed and Shiva S. Halli. 2001. Immigrants and 'New Poverty': The Case of Canada. *International Migration Review* 39 (4): 1129–56.

Kelleher, D. and S. Hillier. 1996. The Health of the Irish in England, in *Researching Cultural Differences in Health*, edited by D. Kelleher and S. Hillier, pp. 237–48. London: Routledge.

Kells, Mary. 1995. 'I'm Myself and Nobody Else': Gender and Ethnicity Among Young Middle-Class Irish Women in London, in *Irish Women and Irish Migration*, edited by P. O'Sullivan, pp. 201–34. London: Leicester University Press.

Kempny, Marta. 2011. Interpretative Repertoire of Victimhood: Narrating Experiences of Discrimination and Ethnic Hatred Among Polish Migrants in Belfast. *Anthropological Journal of European Cultures* 20 (1): 132–51.

Kenna, G. B. [pseudonym for Father John Hassan]. 1997 [1922]. *Facts and Figures: Belfast Pogrom 1920–22*. Dublin: The O'Connell Publishing Company. New edn. edited by Thomas Donaldson and reprinted by the Donaldson Archives.

Kennedy, Billy. 2001. *The Making of America: How the Scots–Irish Shaped a Nation*. Belfast: Ambassador Publications.

Kennedy, Liam. 1994. *People and Population Change: A Comparative Study of Population Change in Northern Ireland and the Republic of Ireland*. Belfast: Co-Operation North.

——, Kerby A. Miller and Mark Graham. 1991. The Long Retreat: Protestants, Economy and Society, 1660–1926, in *Longford: Essays in County History*, edited by R. Gillespie and G. Moran, pp. 31–61. Dublin: Lilliput Press.

Kennedy, Michael. 2000. *Division and Consensus: The Politics of Cross-Border Relations in Ireland, 1925–1969*. Dublin: Institute of Public Administration.

Kennedy, Robert E. 1973. *The Irish: Emigration, Marriage, and Fertility*. Berkeley, CA: University of California Press.

Kenny, Kevin. 2003. Diaspora and Comparison: The Global Irish as a Case Study. *Journal of American History* 90 (1): 134–62.

Kiely, Richard, Frank Bechhofer and David McCrone. 2005. Birth, Blood and Belonging: Identity Claims in Post-Devolution Scotland. *The Sociological Review* 53 (1): 150–71.

Kilbourn, William (ed.). 1970. *Canada: A Guide to the Peaceable Kingdom*. Toronto: Macmillan.

King, Karen M. and Bruce K. Newbold. 2008. Return Immigration: The Chronic Migration of Canadian Immigrants, 1991, 1996 and 2001. *Population Space and Place* 14 (2): 85–100.

King, Russell. 1978. Return Migration: A Neglected Aspect of Population Geography. *Area* 10 (3): 175–82.

——. 1986. Return Migration and Regional Economic Development: An Overview, in *Return Migration and Regional Economic Problems*, edited by R. King, pp. 1–37. London: Croom Helm.

——. 1993. European International Migration 1945–90: A Statistical and Geographical Overview, in *Mass Migrations in Europe: The Legacy and the Future*, edited by R. King, pp. 19–39. London: Belhaven Press.

——. 2000. Generalizations From the History of Return Migration, in *Return Migration: Journey of Hope or Despair?* edited by B. Ghosh, pp. 7–55. Geneva: International Organization for Migration and the United Nations.

—— and Anastasia Christou. 2011. Of Counter-Diaspora and Reverse Transnationalism: Return Mobilities To and From the Ancestral Homeland. *Mobilities* 6 (4): 451–66.

——, Alan Strachan and Jill Mortimer. 1983. Return Migration: A Review of the Literature. *Discussion Paper in Geography, No. 19.* Oxford Polytechnic.

King, Thomas. 2003. *The Truth About Stories: A Native Narrative*. Toronto: House of Anansi Press.

King, William Lyon Mackenzie. 1908. *Report of the Royal Commission Appointed to Inquire Into the Methods by Which Oriental Labourers Have Been Induced to Come to Canada.* Ottawa: Government Printing Bureau.

Koser, Khalid. 2007a. International Migration: A Very Short Introduction. Oxford: Oxford University Press.

——. 2007b. Refugees, Transnationalism and the State. *Journal of Ethnic and Migration Studies* 33 (2): 233–54.

Kumar, Krishan. 2006. English and British National Identity. *History Compass* 4 (3): 428–47.

Kuznets, Simon and Ernest Rubin. 1954. *Immigration and the Foreign Born*. New York: National Bureau of Economic Research.

Kymlicka, Will. 1995. *Multicultural Citizenship: A Liberal Theory of Minority Rights*. Oxford: Oxford University Press.

—— 2010a. The Current State of Multiculturalism in Canada and Research Themes on Canadian Multiculturalism 2008–2010. Ottawa: Citizenship and Immigration Canada, Catalogue No. Ci96–112/2010E–PDF. Available at: http://www.cic.gc.ca/english/pdf/pub/multi–state.pdf (accessed 17 December 2011)

——. 2010b. Testing the Liberal Multiculturalist Hypothesis: Normative Theories and Social Science Evidence. *Canadian Journal of Political Science* 43 (2): 257–71.

Lambkin, Brian, Patrick Fitzgerald and Johanne Devlin Trew. 2013. Migration in Belfast History: Trajectories, Letters, Voices, in *Belfast: The Emerging City, 1850–1914*, edited by O. Purdue, pp. 235–69. Dublin: Irish Academic Press.

Latif, Nazia and Agnieszka Martynowicz. 2009. *Our Hidden Borders: The UK Border Agency's Powers of Detention.* Belfast: Northern Ireland Human Rights Commission.

Lawson, Victoria A. 2000. Arguments Within Geographies of Movement: The Theoretical Potential of Migrants' Stories. *Progress in Human Geography* 24 (2): 173–89.

Leacock, Stephen. 1932. *Afternoons in Utopia: Tales of the New Time.* Toronto: Macmillan of Canada.

Leavey, Gerard. 1999. Suicide and Irish Migrants in Britain: Identity and Integration. *International Review of Psychiatry* 11: 168–72.

——. 2001. Too Close for Comfort: Mental Illness and the Irish in Britain, in *Colonialism and Psychiatry*, edited by D. Bhugra and R. Littlewood, pp. 167–84. New Delhi: Oxford University Press.

——, Grania Clarke, Michael King and Roland Littlewood. 1997. Health Research on the Irish in Britain: Invisible and Excluded. *Psychiatric Bulletin* 21 (12): 739–40.

——, Linda Rosmovits, Louise Ryan and Michael King. 2007. Explanations of Depression Among Irish Migrants in Britain. *Social Science and Medicine* 65 (2): 231–44.

——, Sati Sembhi and Gill Livingston. 2004. Older Irish Migrants Living in London: Identity, Loss and Return. *Journal of Ethnic and Migration Studies* 30 (4): 763–79.

Lee, J. J. 1990. Emigration: A Contemporary Perspective, in *Migrations: The Irish at Home and Abroad*, edited by R. Kearney, pp. 33–44. Dublin: Wolfhound Press.

——. 2005. The Irish Diaspora in the Nineteenth Century, in *Nineteenth-Century Ireland*, edited by L. Geary and M. Kelleher, pp. 182–222. Dublin: University College Dublin Press.

Lennon, Mary, Marie McAdam and Joanne O'Brien. 1988. *Across the Water: Irish Women's Lives in Britain.* London: Virago Press.

Leonard, Madeleine. 2009. 'It's Better to Stick to Your Own Kind': Teenagers Views on Cross-Community Marriages in Northern Ireland. *Journal of Ethnic and Migration Studies* 35 (1): 97–113.

Leonard, Marion. 2005. Performing Identities: Music and Dance in the Irish Communities of Coventry and Liverpool. *Social and Cultural Geography* 6 (4): 515–29.

Levi, Primo. 1988. *The Drowned and the Saved.* London: Michael Joseph.

Leyburn, J. G. 1962. *The Scotch–Irish.* Chapel Hill, NC: University of North Carolina Press.

Li, Peter S. 2000. Earning Disparities Between Immigrants and Native-Born Canadians. *Canadian Review of Sociology and Anthropology* 37 (3): 289–311.

——. 2003. *Destination Canada: Immigration Debates and Issues.* Toronto: Oxford University Press.

Lobo, A. P. and J. J. Salvo. 1998. Resurgent Irish Immigration to the US in the 1980s and Early 1990s: A Socio-Demographic Profile. *International Migration* 36 (2): 257–80.

Loizos, Peter. 2007. Generations in Forced Migration: Towards Greater Clarity. *Journal of Refugee Studies* 20 (2): 193–209.

Long, Lynellyn D. and Ellen Oxfeld (eds). 2004. *Coming Home? Refugees, Migrants, and Those who Stayed Behind.* Philadelphia: University of Pennsylvania Press.

Loughlin, James. 1995. *Ulster Unionism and British National Identity Since 1885.* London: Pinter.

Lucassen, Jan and Leo Lucassen (eds). 1999. *Migration, Migration History, History: Old Paradigms and New Perspectives.* Bern: Peter Lang.

Lynch, Robert. 2003. The Northern IRA and the Early Years of Partition, 1920–22. PhD diss., University of Stirling.

Lyotard, Jean–François. 1989. Lessons in Paganism, in *The Lyotard Reader*, edited by A. Benjamin, pp. 122–54. Oxford: Basil Blackwell.

Ma, Xin. 2002. The First Ten Years in Canada: A Multi-Level Assessment of Behavioral and Emotional Problems of Immigrant Children. *Canadian Public Policy* 28 (3): 395–418.

Mac an Ghaill, Mairtin. 2000. The Irish in Britain: The Invisibility of Ethnicity and Anti-Irish Racism. *Journal of Ethnic and Migration Studies* 26 (1): 137–47.

———. 2001. British Critical Theorists: The Production of the Conceptual Invisibility of the Irish Diaspora. *Social Identities* 7 (2): 179–201.

Mac Éinrí, Piaras and Brian Lambkin. 2002. Whose Diaspora? Whose Migration? Whose Identity? Some Current Issues in Irish Migration Studies. *Irish Journal of Psychology*, 23(3–4): 127–57.

MacGinty, Roger. 1997. American Influences on the Northern Ireland Peace Process. *Journal of Conflict Studies* 17 (2): no pages at: http://journals.hil.unb.ca/index.php/JCS/article/view/11750/12522

MacIntyre, Alasdair. 1981. *After Virtue: A Study in Moral Theory.* London: Gerald Duckworth and Company.

MacRaild, Donald. 2002–2003. Wherever Orange is Worn: Orangeism and Irish Migration in the 19th and early 20th Centuries. *Canadian Journal of Irish Studies* 28 (2) and 29 (1): 98–116.

———. 2005a. *Faith, Fraternity and Fighting: The Orange Order and Irish Migrants in Northern England, c. 1850–1920.* Liverpool: Liverpool University Press.

———. 2005b. Networks, Communication and the Irish Protestant Diaspora in Northern England, c. 1860–1914. *Immigrants and Minorities* 23 (2/3): 311–37.

Mageean, Deirdre M. 1991. From Irish Countryside to American City: The Settlement and Mobility of Ulster Migrants in Philadelphia, in *Migrants, Emigrants and Immigrants: A Social History of Migration*, edited by C. G. Pooley and I. D. Whyte, pp. 42-61. London: Routledge.

Malcolm, Elizabeth. 1996. *Elderly Return Migration from Britain to Ireland.* Dublin: National Council for the Elderly.

Malkki, Liisa. 1992. National Geographic: The Rooting of Peoples and the Territorialization of National Identity Among Scholars and Refugees. *Cultural Anthropology* 7(1): 22–44.

———. 1995. *Purity and Exile: Violence, Memory, and National Cosmology Among Hutu Refugees in Tanzania*. Chicago: University of Chicago Press.

Mallett, Susan. 2004. Understanding Home: A Critical Review of the Literature. *The Sociological Review* 52(1): 62–89.

Malone, Mary. 2001. The Health Experience of Irish People in a North West London 'Community Saved'. *Community, Work and Family* 4 (2): 195–213.

—— and John P. Dooley. 2006. 'Dwelling in Displacement': Meanings of 'Community' and Sense of Community for Two Generations of Irish People Living in North-West London. *Community, Work and Family* 9 (1): 11–28.

Mancuso, Rebecca. 2010. 'Give Me a Canadian': Gender Identity and Training Hostels for British Domestics for Canada, 1927–30. *Journal of Imperial and Commonwealth History* 38 (4): 599–618.

Mandler, Peter. 2006. What is 'National Identity?' Definitions and Applications in Modern British Historiography. *Modern Intellectual History* 3 (2): 271–97.

Manji, Ishrad. 1997. *Risking Utopia: On the Edge of a New Democracy*. Vancouver: Douglas and McIntyre.

Mannheim, Karl. 1952 [1926]. The Problem of Generations, in *Essays on the Sociology of Knowledge*, pp. 286–320. London: Routledge.

Manning, Patrick. 2004. *Migration in World History*. London: Routledge.

Mansergh, Nicholas. 1968 [1958]. *Survey of British Commonwealth Affairs: Problems of War-Time Cooperation and Post-War Change, 1939–1952*. Reprint edn. London: Frank Cass.

Marmot, M. G., A. M. Adelstein and L. Bulusu. 1984. Immigrant Mortality in England and Wales, 1970–1978: Causes of Death by Country of Birth. *Studies on Medical and Population Subjects, No. 47*. London: HMSO.

Marranci, Gabriele. 2003. 'We Speak English': Language and Identity Processes in Northern Ireland's Muslim Community. *Ethnologies* 25 (2): 59–75.

Marshall, W. F. 1944. *Ulster Sails West*. Belfast: The Quota Press.

Martin, Irene. 2011. *In Search of Buchanan*. Letterkenny: Rosnashannagh Publishers.

Maume, Patrick. 2009. Trew, Arthur, in *Dictionary of Irish Biography: From the Earliest Times to 2002*, edited by J. McGuire and J. Quinn, Vol. 9, 488–9. Cambridge: Cambridge University Press for the Royal Irish Academy.

Maynard, Maria J., Michael Rosato, Alison Teyhan and Seeromanie Harding. 2012. Trends in Suicide Among Migrants in England and Wales, 1979–2003. *Ethnicity and Health* 17 (1/2): 135–40.

McAdams, Dan P. 1985. *Power, Intimacy, and the Life Story: Personological Inquiries Into Identity*. New York: Guilford Press.

———. 1993. *The Stories We Live By: Personal Myths and the Making of the Self*. New York: Morrow.

———. 2001. The Psychology of Life Stories. *Review of General Psychology* 5 (2): 100–122.

———. 2006. *The Redemptive Self: Stories Americans Live By*. Oxford: Oxford University Press.

McAuley, James W. 1996. Under an Orange Banner: Reflections on the Northern

Protestant Experiences of Emigration, in *The Irish World Wide: Religion and Identity*, edited by P. O'Sullivan, pp. 43–69. Leicester: Leicester University Press.

McBride, Ian. 1997. *The Siege of Derry in Ulster Protestant Mythology*. Dublin: Four Courts Press.

McCafferty, Kevin. 2003. Plural Verbal *–s* in Nineteenth-Century Ulster: Scots and English Influence on Ulster Dialects. *Ulster Folklife* 48: 62–86.

McCarthy, Angela. 2005. *Irish Migrants in New Zealand, 1840–1937*. Woodbridge: Boydell Press.

——. 2006. Ulster Protestant Letter Writers in New Zealand, in *Ulster–New Zealand Migration and Cultural Transfers*, edited by B. Patterson, pp. 71–84. Dublin: Four Courts Press.

——. 2007. *Personal Narratives of Irish and Scottish Migration, 1921–65: 'For Spirit and Adventure'*. Manchester: Manchester University Press.

McCourt, Frank. 1996. *Angela's Ashes: A Memoir*. London: HarperCollins.

McDowell, R. B. 1997. *Crisis and Decline: The Fate of the Southern Unionists*. Dublin: Lilliput Press.

McDermott, Philip. 2011. *Migrant Languages in the Public Space: A Case Study From Northern Ireland*. Berlin: Lit Verlag.

McGarry, John and Brendan O'Leary. 1995. *Explaining Northern Ireland: Broken Images*. London: Blackwell.

McGowan, Mark. 1999. *The Waning of the Green: Catholics, the Irish, and Identity in Toronto, 1887–1922*. Montreal: McGill-Queen's University Press.

McGrath, Fiona. 1991. The Economic, Social and Cultural Impact of Return Migration to Achill Island, in *Contemporary Irish Migration*, edited by R. King, pp. 55–69. Dublin: Geographical Society of Ireland.

McGree, Sheila T. and Victoria M. Esses. 1990. The Irish in Canada: A Demographic Study Based on the 1986 Census. *Canadian Journal of Irish Studies* 16 (1): 1–14.

McGregor, Pat, Róisín Thanki and Patricia McKee. 2002. Home and Away: Graduate Experience From a Regional Perspective. *Applied Economics* 34 (2): 219–30.

McIntyre, David W. 1999. The Strange Death of Dominion Status. *Journal of Imperial and Commonwealth History* 27 (2): 193–212.

McKay, Susan. 2005. *Ulster Protestants: An Unsettled People*. New updated edn. Belfast: Blackstaff.

McLean, Kate C., Monisha Pasupathi and Jennifer L. Pals. 2007. Selves Creating Stories Creating Selves: A Process Model of Self-Development. *Personality and Social Psychology Review* 11 (3): 262–78.

McNulty, Margaret. 2012. *Embracing Diversity: Information Update 2012*. Belfast: Embrace NI.

McQuaid, Ronald and Emma Hollywood. 2008. *Educational Migration and Non-Return in Northern Ireland*. Edinburgh: Employment Research Institute, Napier University.

McRoberts, Kenneth. 1997. *Misconceiving Canada: The Struggle for National Unity*. Oxford; Toronto: Oxford University Press.

Megaw, John. 1949. British Subjects and Eire Citizens. *Northern Ireland Legal Quarterly*

8 (3): 129–39.

Michalowski, Margaret and Kelly Tran. 2008. Canadians Abroad. *Canadian Social Trends*, March: 31–8.

Milan, Anne. 2011. Migration: International, 2009. Report on the Demographic Situation in Canada. Ottawa: Statistics Canada, No. 91–209–X.

Miller, David. 1994. *Don't Mention the War: Northern Ireland, Propaganda and the Media.* London: Pluto Press.

Miller, Kerby A. 1985. *Emigrants and Exiles: Ireland and the Irish Exodus to North America.* Oxford: Oxford University Press.

———. 2008. *Ireland and Irish America: Culture, Class, and Transatlantic Migration.* Dublin: Field Day; Keogh-Naughton Institute for Irish Studies, University of Notre Dame.

———, Arnold Schrier, Bruce D. Boling and David N. Doyle. 2003. *Irish Immigrants in the Land of Canaan: Letters and Memoirs From Colonial and Revolutionary America, 1675–1815.* Oxford: Oxford University Press.

Mitchell, Brian R. 1988. *British Historical Statistics.* Cambridge: Cambridge University Press.

———. 2007. *International Historical Statistics: Europe, 1750–2005.* 6th edn. Basingstoke: Palgrave Macmillan.

Mitchell, Claire. 2003. Protestant Identification and Political Change in Northern Ireland. *Ethnic and Racial Studies* 26 (4): 612–31.

———. 2006. *Religion, Identity, and Politics in Northern Ireland: Boundaries of Belonging and Belief.* Aldershot: Ashgate.

——— and James R. Tilley. 2004. The Moral Minority: Evangelical Protestants in Northern Ireland and Their Political Behaviour. *Political Studies* 52 (3): 585–602.

——— and Jennifer Todd. 2007. Between the Devil and the Deep Blue Sea: Nationality, Power and Symbolic Trade-Offs Among Evangelical Protestants in Contemporary Northern Ireland. *Nations and Nationalism* 13 (4): 637–55.

Mitchell, James. 2006. Undignified and Inefficient: Financial Relations Between London and Stormont. *Contemporary British History* 20 (1): 55–71.

Mjøset, Lars. 1992. *The Irish Economy in Comparative Institutional Perspective; Report No. 93.* Dublin: National Economic and Social Council.

Molavi, Afshin. 2002. *Persian Pilgrimages: Journeys Across Iran.* New York: Norton.

Moran, Gerald. 2004. *Sending Out Ireland's Poor: Assisted Emigration to North America From Nineteenth-Century Ireland.* Dublin: Four Courts Press.

Moran, James. 2010. *Irish Birmingham: A History.* Liverpool: Liverpool University Press.

Morgan, Craig, Monica Charalambides, Gerard Hutchinson and Robin M. Murray. 2010. Migration, Ethnicity, and Psychosis: Toward a Sociodevelopmental Model. *Schizophrenia Bulletin* 36 (4): 655–64.

Morgan, Sarah and Bronwen Walter. 2008. 'No, We Are Not Catholics': Intersections of Faith and Ethnicity Among the Second-Generation Protestant Irish in England, in *Irish Protestant Identities*, edited by M. Busteed, F. Neal and J. Tonge, pp, 171–84. Manchester: Manchester University Press.

Morawska, Ewa. 1991. Return Migrations: Theoretical and Research Agenda, in *A Century of European Migrations, 1830–1930*, edited by R. J. Vecoli and S. M. Sinke, pp. 277–92. Urbana: University of Illinois Press.

Morris, C. and Paul A. Compton. 1985. 1981 Census of Population in Northern Ireland. *Population Trends* 40: 16–20.

Morrison, Toni. 1987. *Beloved: A Novel.* London: Chatto and Windus.

Morrissey, Mike and Marie Smyth. 2002. *Northern Ireland After the Good Friday Agreement: Victims, Grievance and Blame.* London: Pluto Press.

Moxon-Browne, Edward. 1983. *Nation, Class and Creed in Northern Ireland.* Aldershot: Gower.

——. 1991. National Identity in Northern Ireland, in *Social Attitudes in Northern Ireland: The First Report*, edited by P. Stringer and G. Robinson, pp. 23–30. Belfast: Blackstaff Press.

Muldoon, Orla, Katharina Schmid and Ciara Downes. 2009. Political Violence and Psychological Well-Being: The Role of Social Identity. *Applied Psychology* 58 (1): 129–45.

——, Katharina Schmid, Ciara Downes, John Kremer and Karen Trew. 2005. *The Legacy of the Troubles: Experience of the Troubles, Mental Health and Social Attitudes: A Research Report.* Belfast: School of Psychology, Queen's University Belfast.

——, Karen Trew, Jennifer Todd, Nathalie Rougier and Katrina McLaughlin. 2007. Religious and National Identity After the Belfast Good Friday Agreement. *Political Psychology* 28 (1): 89–103.

Mulholland, Joe and Dermot Keogh (eds). 1989. *Emigration, Employment and Enterprise.* Cork: Hibernian University Press.

Mullen K., R. Williams and K. Hunt. 1996. Irish Descent, Religion and Alcohol and Tobacco Use. *Addiction* 91: 237–48.

Munck, Ronnie. 1993. *The Irish Economy: Results and Prospects.* London: Pluto Press.

Murray, Paul. 2011. *The Irish Boundary Commission and its Origins 1886–1925.* Dublin: University College Dublin Press.

Murtagh, Brendan. 2002. *The Politics of Territory: Policy and Segregation in Northern Ireland.* Basingstoke: Palgrave Macmillan.

Nafisi, Azar. 2004. *Reading Lolita in Tehran.* New York: Random House.

——. 2010. *Things I've Been Silent About: Memories of a Prodigal Daughter.* London: Windmill Books.

Nash, Catherine. 1993. Embodying the Nation: The West of Ireland Landscape and Irish Identity, in *Tourism in Ireland: A Critical Analysis*, edited by B. O'Connor and M. Cronin, pp. 86–112. Cork: Cork University Press.

——. 2008. *Of Irish Descent: Origin Stories, Genealogy and the Politics of Belonging.* Syracuse: Syracuse University Press.

National Economic and Social Council (NESC). 1991. *The Economic and Social Implications of Emigration. NESC Report No. 90.* Dublin: NESC.

Neisser, Ulric. 1982. Snapshots or Benchmarks? in *Memory Observed: Remembering in Natural Contexts*, edited by U. Neisser, pp. 43–8. San Francisco: W. H. Freeman.

Newbold, K. Bruce. 2001. Counting Migrants and Migrations: Comparing Lifetime and Fixed-Interval Return and Onward Migration. *Economic Geography* 77 (1): 23–39.

——. 2009. The Short-Term Health of Canada's New Immigrant Arrivals: Evidence From LSIC. *Ethnicity and Health* 14 (3): 315–36.

Newfoundland and Labrador (Government). 1970. *Historical Statistics of Newfoundland*. St. John's, NL: Government of Newfoundland and Labrador, Department of Finance.

Ní Laoire, Caitríona. 2002. Discourses of Nation Among Migrants From Northern Ireland: Irishness, Britishness and the Spaces In-Between. *Scottish Geographical Journal* 118 (3): 183–99.

——. 2007. The Green Green Grass of Home: Return Migration to Rural Ireland. *Journal of Rural Studies* 23 (3): 332–44.

——. 2008a. Complicating Host-Newcomer Dualisms: Irish Return Migrants as Home-Comers or Newcomers? *Translocations* 4 (1): 35–50.

——. 2008b. 'Settling back'? A Biographical and Life-Course Perspective on Ireland's Recent Return Migration. *Irish Geography* 41 (2): 195–210.

——. 2011. Narratives of 'Innocent Irish Childhoods': Return Migration and Intergenerational Family Dynamics. *Journal of Ethnic and Migration Studies* 37 (8): 1253–71.

Noakes, Lucy. 2012. Our Excess Girls. *BBC History Magazine* 13 (3): 24–7.

Nora, Pierre. 1984. *Les Lieux de Mémoire* (7 vols). Paris: Gallimard.

Northern Ireland Museums Council. 2005. *Our People, Our Times: A History of Northern Ireland's Diversity*. Belfast: NIMC.

Norton, Christopher. 2001. Creating Jobs, Manufacturing Unity: Ulster Unionism and Mass Unemployment, 1922–34. *Contemporary British History* 15 (2): 1–14.

O Connor, Fionnuala. 1993. *In Search of a State: Catholics in Northern Ireland*. Belfast: Blackstaff Press.

O'Connor, Kevin. 1972. *The Irish in Britain*. London: Sidgwick and Jackson.

O Connor, T. P. 1917. The Irish in Great Britain, in *Irish Heroes in the War*, edited by Felix Lavery, pp, 13–34. London: Everett and Co.

Ødegaard, Ø. 1932. Emigration and Insanity [Special Issue]. *Acta Psychiatrica Neurologica Scandinavia* Supplement (4): 1–206.

Odhiambo, Elly and Philip McDermott. 2010. *Voices From the Global South: A Research Report on Migration*. Belfast: Centre for Global Education.

Ó Dochartaigh, Niall. 2009. Reframing Online: Ulster Loyalists Imagine an American Audience. *Identities: Global Studies in Culture and Power* 16 (1): 102–27.

O'Dowd, Anne. 1991. *Spalpeens and Tattie Hokers: History and Folklore of the Irish Migratory Agricultural Worker in Ireland and Britain*. Dublin: Irish Academic Press.

Offer, John. 2006. *An Intellectual History of British Social Policy: Idealism Versus Non-Idealism*. Bristol: Policy Press.

OFMDFM. 2005. A Racial Equality Strategy for Northern Ireland: First Implementation Action Plan, 2005–2010. Belfast: OFMDFM.

——. 2006. A Shared Future: Policy and Strategic Framework for Good Relations in Northern Ireland. Belfast: OFMDFM.

———. 2010. Programme for Cohesion, Sharing and Integration: Consultation Document. Belfast: OFMDFM.

O'Grada, Cormac. 1997. *A Rocky Road: The Irish Economy Since the 1920s*. Manchester: Manchester University Press.

——— and Brendan Walsh. 1995. Fertility and Population in Ireland, North and South. *Population Studies* 49 (2): 259–79.

O'Halloran, Claire. 1987. *Partition and the Limits of Irish Nationalism*. Dublin: Gill and Macmillan.

O'Hearn, Denis. 2008. How Has Peace Changed the Northern Irish Political Economy? *Ethnopolitics* 7 (1): 101–18.

Ollerenshaw, Philip. 1996. Businessmen in Northern Ireland and the Imperial Connection, 1886–1939, in *'An Irish Empire?' Aspects of Ireland and the British Empire*, edited by K. Jeffery, pp. 169–190. Manchester: Manchester University Press.

———. 2007. War, Industrial Mobilisation and Society in Northern Ireland, 1939–1945. *Contemporary European History* 16 (2): 169–97.

Ó Murchú, Niall. 2005. Ethnic Politics and Labour Market Closure: Shipbuilding and Industrial Decline in Northern Ireland. *Ethnic and Racial Studies* 28 (5): 859–79.

Ong, Walter J. 1982. *Orality and Literacy: The Technologizing of the Word*. London: Routledge.

O'Reilly, D. and Stevenson, M. 2003. Mental Health in Northern Ireland: Have 'the Troubles' Made it Worse? *Journal of Epidemiology and Community Health* 57 (7): 488–92.

Ornstein, Michael. 2006. *Ethno-Racial Groups in Toronto, 1971–2001: A Demographic and Socio-Economic Profile*. Toronto: York University, Institute for Social Research.

Osborne, R. D. 2006. Access To and Participation in Higher Education in Northern Ireland. *Higher Education Quarterly* 60 (4): 333–48.

———, Robert Cormack, R. Miller and A. Williamson. 1987. Graduates: Geographical Mobility and Incomes, in *Education and Policy in Northern Ireland*, edited by R. D. Osborne, R. Cormack and R. Miller, pp. 231–44. Belfast: Policy Research Institute, Queen's University Belfast and University of Ulster.

———, Alayne Smith and Amanda Hayes. 2006. *Higher Education in Northern Ireland: A Report on Factors Associated with Participation and Migration*. Belfast: Office of the First Minister and Deputy First Minister [Northern Ireland].

Ostrovsky, Yuri. 2008. Earnings Inequality and Earnings Instability of Immigrants in Canada. Ottawa: Statistics Canada, No. 11F0019M – No. 309.

O'Sullivan, Patrick (ed.). 1992–1997. *The Irish Worldwide*. 6 vols. Leicester: Leicester University Press.

——— and Russell Murray. 2001. The Impact on Policy, and Implementation of Policy, of Recent Research Into the Needs of the Irish Community in England. Bradford: Irish Diaspora Research Unit, University of Bradford.

Oversea Settlement Board. 1938. *Report of the Oversea Settlement Board, May 1938*. London: HMSO, cmd. 5766.

Page Moch, Leslie. 2003. *Moving Europeans: Migration in Western Europe Since 1650*. 2nd edn. Bloomington: Indiana University Press. Original edition 1992.

Paisley, Ian. 1976. *America's Debt to Ulster*. Belfast: Martyrs Memorial Publications.

Palameta, Boris. 2007. Economic Integration of Immigrants' Children. *Perspectives on Labour and Income (Statistics Canada)* 8 (10): 1–16.

Parkhill, Trevor. 1997. Philadelphia Here I Come: A Study of the Letters of Ulster Immigrants in Pennsylvania, 1750–1875, in *Ulster and North America: Transatlantic Perspectives on the Scotch-Irish*, edited by H. T. Blethen and C. W. Wood, pp. 118–33. Tuscaloosa: University of Alabama Press.

———. 2005. Pre-Famine Protestant, Post-Famine Catholic: Do Emigrants' Letters Reflect the Stereotypes? in *Industry, Trade and People in Ireland, 1650–1950: Essays in Honour of W. H. Crawford*, edited by B. Collins, P. Ollerenshaw and T. Parkhill, pp. 154–72. Belfast: Ulster Historical Foundation.

Parkinson, Alan F. 2004. *Belfast's Unholy War: The Troubles of the 1920s*. Dublin: Four Courts Press.

Passerini, Luisa. 1992. Introduction, in *Memory and Totalitarianism*, edited by L. Passerini, pp. 1–19. Oxford: Oxford University Press.

———. 2003. Memories Between Silence and Oblivion, in *Contested Pasts: The Politics of Memory*, edited by K. Hodgkin and S. Radstone, pp. 238–54. London: Routledge.

Pasupathi, Monica, Kate C. McLean and Trisha Weeks. 2009. To Tell or Not To Tell: Disclosure and the Narrative Self. *Journal of Personality* 77 (1): 89–123.

Patterson, Brad, (ed.). 2006. *Ulster–New Zealand Migration and Cultural Transfers*. Dublin: Four Courts Press.

Pehrson, Samuel, Mirona A. Gheorghiu and Tomas Ireland. 2012. Cultural Threat and Anti-Immigrant Prejudice: The Case of Protestants in Northern Ireland. *Journal of Community and Applied Social Psychology* 22 (2): 111–24.

Pemberton, Simon and Jennifer Mason. 2007. Uncovering the 'Invisible' Minority: Irish Communities, Economic Inactivity and Welfare Policy in the United Kingdom. *European Planning Studies* 15 (10): 1439–59.

Pendakur, Krishna and Ravi Pendakur. 2004. Colour My World: Have Earnings Gaps for Canadian-born Ethnic Minorities Changed Over Time? *Canadian Public Policy* 28 (4): 489–512.

Pendakur, Ravi and Fernando Mata. 1999. Where do Immigrants Work? Tracking Industrial Location Propensities of 1960s Immigrants. *Working Paper Series No. 99–13*. Vancouver: Research on Immigration and Integration in the Metropolis.

Phillips, Jock. 2006. Who Were New Zealand's Ulster Immigrants? in *Ulster–New Zealand Migration and Cultural Transfers*, edited by B. Patterson, pp. 55–70. Dublin: Four Courts Press.

Phoenix, Eamonn. 1994. *Northern Nationalism: Nationalist Politics, Partition and the Catholic Minority in Northern Ireland, 1890–1940*. Belfast: Ulster Historical Foundation.

Picot, Garnett and Feng Hou. 2003. The Rise in Low-Income Rates Among Immigrants in Canada. Ottawa: Statistics Canada, No. 11F0019MIE – No. 198.

——— and Feng Hou. 2011. Preparing for Success in Canada and the United States:

The Determinants of Educational Attainment Among the Children of Immigrants. Ottawa: Statistics Canada, No. 11F0019M – No. 332.

——, Feng Hou and Simon Coulombe. 2007. Chronic Low Income and Low-Income Dynamics Among Recent Immigrants. Ottawa: Statistics Canada, No. 11F0019MIE – No. 294.

Pile, Steve. 2010. Emotions and Affect in Recent Human Geography. *Transactions of the Institute of British Geographers* 35: 5–20.

Pillemer, David B. 1998. *Momentous Events, Vivid Memories*. Cambridge, MA: Harvard University Press.

Plant, George F. 1951. *Oversea Settlement: Migration From the United Kingdom to the Dominions*. Oxford: Oxford University Press.

Pollock, Della. 2005. Introduction: Remembering, in *Remembering: Oral History Performance*, edited by D. Pollock, pp. 1–18. Basingstoke: Palgrave Macmillan.

Poole, Michael A. 1999. Religious Residential Segregation in Urban County Derry, 1831–1991: A Study of Variation in Space and Time, in *Derry and Londonderry: History and Society*, edited by G. O'Brien, pp. 557–72. Dublin: Geography Publications.

—— and Paul Doherty. 1996. *Ethnic Residential Segregation in Northern Ireland*. Coleraine: University of Ulster.

Pooley, Colin G. 2000. From Londonderry to London: Identity and Sense of Place for a Protestant Northern Irish Woman in the 1930s, in *The Great Famine and Beyond: Irish Migrants in Britain in the Nineteenth and Twentieth Centuries*, edited by D. M. MacRaild, pp. 189–213. Dublin: Irish Academic Press.

Pope, David. 1968. Empire Migration to Canada, Australia and New Zealand, 1910–1929. *Australian Economic Papers* 7 (11): 167–88.

Porritt, Edward. 1913. Grain-Growing and Canadian Expansion. *North American Review* 197: 203–12.

Portelli, Alessandro. 1981. The Peculiarities of Oral History. *History Workshop Journal*, 12(1): 96–107.

—— 2003. *The Order has Been Carried Out: History, Memory and Meaning of a Nazi Massacre in Rome*. Basingstoke: Palgrave Macmillan.

Portes, Alejandro. 2010. Migration and Social Change: Some Conceptual Reflections. *Journal of Ethnic and Migration Studies* 36 (10): 1537–63.

Punch, A. and C. Finneran. 1999. The Demographic and Socio-Economic Characteristics of Migrants, 1986–1996. *Journal of the Statistical and Social Inquiry Society of Ireland* 28 (1): 1–39.

Purvis, Dawn and the Working Group on Educational Disadvantage and the Protestant Working Class. 2011. *A Call to Action: Educational Disadvantage and the Protestant Working Class*. Belfast: WGEDPWC.

Raczymow, Henri. 1986. La Mémoire Trouée. *Pardès* 3: 177–82.

Raftery, J., D. R. Jones and M. Rosato. 1990. The Mortality of First and Second Generation Irish Immigrants in the UK. *Social Science and Medicine* 31: 577–84.

Ralph, David. 2009. 'Home is Where the Heart Is?' Understandings of 'Home' Among Irish-Born Return Migrants From the United States. *Irish Studies Review* 17 (2):

183–200.

Rankin, K. J. 2001. County Armagh and the Boundary Commission, in *Armagh History and Society: Interdisciplinary Essays on the History of an Irish County*, edited by A. J. Hughes and W. Nolan, pp. 947–89. Dublin: Geography Publications.

——. 2007. Deducing Rationales and Political Tactics in the Partitioning of Ireland, 1912–1925. *Political Geography* 26 (8): 909–33.

——. 2008. The Role of the Irish Boundary Commission in the Entrenchment of the Irish Border: From Tactical Panacea to Political Liability. *Journal of Historical Geography* 34 (3): 422–47.

——. 2009. The Search for Statutory Ulster. *History Ireland* 17 (3): 28–32.

Rapport, Nigel and Andrew Dawson. 1998. *Migrants of Identity: Perceptions of 'Home' in a World of Movement*. Oxford: Berg.

Rathbone, Clare J., Chris J. A. Moulin and Martin A. Conway. 2008. Self-Centered Memories: The Reminiscence Bump and the Self. *Memory and Cognition* 36 (8): 1403–14.

Ravenstein, E. G. 1885, 1889. The Laws of Migration. *Journal of the Royal Statistical Society* 48: 167–227; 52: 214–301.

Redington, F. M. and R. D. Clarke. 1951. The Papers of the Royal Commission on Population. *Journal of the Institute of Actuaries* 77: 81–97.

Redmond, Jennifer. 2008. 'Sinful Singleness?' Exploring the Discourses on Irish Single Women's Emigration to England, 1922–1948. *Women's History Review, 17*(3): 455–76.

Reese, Elaine and Robyn Fivush. 2008. The Development of Collective Remembering. *Memory* 16 (3): 201–12.

Refugee Action Group (RAG). 2007. *Forced to Flee: Frequently Asked Questions About Refugees and Asylum Seekers in Northern Ireland*. 3rd edn. Belfast: Refugee Action Group.

Reininghaus, Ulrich, K. J. Thomas, Helen L. Fisher, Gerard Hutchinson, Paul Fearon, Kevin Morgan, Paola Dazzan, Gillian A. Doody, Peter B. Jones, Robin M. Murray and Craig Morgan. 2010. Ethnic Identity, Perceptions of Disadvantage, and Psychosis: Findings From the AESOP Study. *Schizophrenia Research* 124: 43–8.

Reitz, Jeffrey G. and Rupa Banerjee. 2007. Racial Inequality, Social Cohesion, and Policy Issue in Canada, in *Belonging? Diversity, Recognition and Shared Citizenship in Canada: The State of the Art, Vol. 3*, edited by K. Banting, T. J. Courchene and F. L. Seidle, pp. 489–545. Montreal: Institute for Research on Public Policy.

——, Rupa Banerjee, Mai Phan and Jordan Thompson. 2009. Race, Religion, and the Social Integration of New Immigrant Minorities in Canada. *International Migration Review* 43 (4): 695–726.

Reverdy, J. C. 1967. *Emigrant Workers Returning to Their Home Country: Final Report* (International Management Seminar, Athens 18–21 October 1966), International Seminars 1966–4. Paris: Organisation for Economic Cooperation and Development (OECD).

Richards, Eric. 2004. *Britannia's Children: Emigration From England, Scotland, Wales and Ireland Since 1600*. London: Hambledon and London.

Richardson, Alan. 1968. A Shipboard Study of Some British-Born Immigrants Returning to the United Kingdom From Australia. *International Migration* 6 (4): 221–38.

Richmond, Anthony H. 1966. Demographic and Family Characteristics of British Immigrants Returning From Canada. *International Migration* 4 (1): 21–7.

———. 1967. *Post-War Immigrants in Canada*. Toronto: University of Toronto Press.

———. 1968. Return Migration From Canada to Britain. *Population Studies* 22 (2): 263–71.

———. 1990. Race Relations and Immigration: A Comparative Perspective. *International Journal of Comparative Sociology* 31 (3/4): 156–76.

——— and G. Lakshmana Rao. 1976. Recent Developments in Immigration to Canada and Australia: A Comparative Analysis. *International Journal of Comparative Sociology* 17 (3/4): 183–205.

Ricoeur, Paul. 2004. *Memory, History, Forgetting.* Translated by K. Blamey and D. Pellauer. Chicago: University of Chicago Press.

Robb, Nesca A. 1942. *An Ulsterwoman in England, 1924–1941.* Cambridge: Cambridge University Press.

Roche, Michael. 2011. World War One British Empire Discharged Soldier Settlement in Comparative Focus. *History Compass* 9 (1): 1–15.

Rodriguez, Marc S. (ed.). 2004. *Repositioning North American Migration History: New Directions in Modern Continental Migration, Citizenship, and Community.* Rochester, NY: University of Rochester Press.

——— and Anthony T. Grafton (eds). 2007. *Migration in History: Human Migration in Comparative Perspective.* Rochester, NY: University of Rochester Press.

Roe, Michael. 1995. *Australia, Britain, and Migration, 1915–1940: A Study of Desperate Hopes.* Cambridge: Cambridge University Press.

Rooney, Frances. 1978. SORWUC [The Service, Office and Retail Workers' Union of Canada]. *Canadian Woman Studies* 1 (2): 56–7.

Rose, Richard. 1971. *Governing Without Consensus: An Irish Perspective.* London: Faber and Faber.

Rosenzweig, Roy and David Thelen. 1998. *The Presence of the Past: Popular Uses of History in American Life.* New York: Columbia University Press.

Rothberg, Michael. 2009. *Multidirectional Memory: Remembering the Holocaust in the Age of Decolonization.* Stanford: Stanford University Press.

Rothon, Catherine, Anthony F. Heath and Laurence Lessard–Phillips. 2009. The Educational Attainments of the 'Second Generation': A Comparative Study of Britain, Canada, and the United States. *Teachers College Record* 111 (6): 1404–43.

Rowthorn, Bob and Naomi Wayne. 1988. *Northern Ireland: The Political Economy of Conflict.* Cambridge: Cambridge University Press.

Ruane, Joseph and David Butler. 2007. Southern Irish Protestants: An Example of De-Ethnicisation? *Nations and Nationalism* 13 (4): 619–35.

——— and Jennifer Todd. 1996. *The Dynamics of Conflict in Northern Ireland: Power, Conflict, and Emancipation.* Cambridge: Cambridge University Press.

Rubin, David C. 1996a. Introduction, in *Remembering Our Past: Studies in Autobiographical*

Memory, edited by D. C. Rubin, pp. 1–15. Cambridge: Cambridge University Press.

——. 1996b. *Reconstructing Our Past: An Overview of Autobiographical Memory.* Cambridge: Cambridge University Press.

Ryan, Liam. 1990. Irish Emigration to Britain Since World War II, in *Migrations: The Irish at Home and Abroad*, edited by R. Kearney, pp. 45–67. Dublin: Wolfhound Press.

Ryan, Louise. 2008. Navigating the Emotional Terrain of Families 'Here' and 'There': Women, Migration and the Management of Emotions. *Journal of Intercultural Studies* 29 (3): 299–313.

——, Gerard Leavey, Anne Golden, Robert Blizard and Michael King. 2006. Depression in Irish Migrants Living in London: Case-Control Study. *British Journal of Psychiatry* 188 (6): 560–66.

Safran, William. 1991. Diasporas in Modern Societies: Myths of Homeland and Return. *Diaspora*, 1(1): 83–99.

Sales, Rosemary. 1997. *Women Divided: Gender, Religion and Politics in Northern Ireland.* London: Routledge.

Samuel, Raphael. 1994. *Theatres of Memory, Vol. 1: Past and Present in Contemporary Culture.* London: Verso.

Sarna, Jonathan D. 1981. The Myth of No Return: Jewish Return Migration to Eastern Europe, 1881–1914. *American Jewish History* 71 (2): 256–68.

Scanlon, Karen, Seeromanie Harding, Kate Hunt, Mark Petticrew, Michael Rosato and Rory Williams. 2006. Potential Barriers to Prevention of Cancers and to Early Cancer Detection Among Irish People Living in Britain: A Qualitative Study. *Ethnicity and Health* 11 (3): 325–41.

Schama, Simon. 1995. *Landscape and Memory.* London: Harper Collins.

Schellenberg, Grant and Hélène Maheux. 2007. Immigrants' Perspectives on Their First Four Years in Canada: Highlights From Three Waves of the Longitudinal Survey of Immigrants to Canada. *Canadian Social Trends*, (April): 2–34.

Schneider, Jens and Maurice Crul. 2010. New Insights Into Assimilation and Integration Theory: Introduction to the Special Issue. *Ethnic and Racial Studies* 33 (7): 1143–8.

Schole, Robert and Robert Kellogg. 1966. *The Nature of Narrative.* Oxford: Oxford University Press.

Schrauf, Robert W. and Lesa Hoffman. 2007. The Effects of Revisionism on Remembered Emotion: The Valence of Older, Voluntary Immigrants' Pre-Migration Autobiographical Memories. *Applied Cognitive Psychology* 21: 895–913.

—— and David C. Rubin. 1998. Bilingual Autobiographical Memory in Older Adult Immigrants: A Test of Cognitive Explanations of the Reminiscence Bump and the Linguistic Encoding of Memories. *Journal of Memory and Language* 39: 437–57.

—— and David C. Rubin. 2001. Effects of Voluntary Immigration on the Distribution of Autobiographical Memory Over the Lifespan. *Applied Cognitive Psychology* 15 (supplement): s75–s88.

Schrier, Arnold. 1958. *Ireland and the American Migration, 1850–1900.* Minneapolis: University of Minnesota Press.

Schubotz, Dirk. 2008. Is There a Protestant Brain Drain From Northern Ireland? *Shared Space* 6: 5–19.

Schultz, John A. 1990. 'Leaven for the Lump': Canada and Empire Settlement, 1918–1939, in *Emigrants and Empire: British Settlement in the Dominions Between the Wars*, edited by S. Constantine, pp. 150–73. Manchester: Manchester University Press.

Senior, Hereward. 1966. *Orangeism in Ireland and Britain, 1795–1836*. Toronto: The Ryerson Press.

———. 1972. *Orangeism: The Canadian Phase*. Toronto: McGraw-Hill Ryerson.

Serrano, Immaculada. 2008. Understanding the Dynamics of Return: The Importance of Microfoundations. *Refuge* 25 (1): 27–34.

Service, Robert W. 1907. *Songs of a Sourdough*. Toronto: William Briggs.

Sexton, J. J. 2003. Emigration and Immigration in the Twentieth Century: An Overview, in *A New History of Ireland, Vol. 7: Ireland, 1921–84*, edited by J. R. Hill, pp. 796–825. Oxford: Oxford University Press.

——— and Richard O'Leary. 1996. Factors Affecting Population Decline in Minority Religious Communities in the Republic of Ireland, in *Building Trust in Ireland: Studies Commissioned by the Forum for Peace and Reconciliation*, pp. 255–332. Belfast: Blackstaff Press.

Sheffer, Gabriel. 2003. *Diaspora Politics*. Cambridge: Cambridge University Press.

Shirlow, Peter, Brian Graham, Amanda McMullan, Brendan Murtagh, Gillian Robinson and Neil Southern. 2005. *Population Change and Social Inclusion Study, Derry/Londonderry*. Derry/Londonderry: St. Columb's Park House.

——— and Brendan Murtagh. 2006. *Belfast: Segregation, Violence and the City*. London: Pluto Press.

Shuttleworth, Ian and Anne E. Green. 2009. Spatial Mobility, Workers and Jobs: Perspectives From the Northern Ireland Experience. *Regional Studies* 43 (8): 1105–15.

——— and Chris Lloyd. 2006. Are Northern Ireland's Two Communities Dividing? Evidence From the Census of Population 1971–2001. *Shared Space* 2: 5–14.

Simpson, John. 1983. Economic Development: Cause or Effect in the Northern Irish Conflict, in *Northern Ireland: The Background to the Conflict*, edited by J. Darby, pp. 79–109. Belfast: Appletree Press.

Smith, G. N., J. Boydell, R. M. Murray, S. Flynn, K. McKay, M. Sherwood and W. G. Honer. 2006. The Incidence of Schizophrenia in European Immigrants to Canada. *Schizophrenia Research* 87 (1/3): 205–11.

Smith, James P. and Duncan Thomas. 2003. Remembrance of Things Past: Test-Retest Reliability of Retrospective Migration Histories. *Journal of the Royal Statistical Society* 166 (1): 23–49.

Smyth, Seamus. 2007. In Defence of Ulster: The Visit of Sir Basil Brooke to North America. *Canadian Journal of Irish Studies* 33 (2): 10–18.

Snow, C. E. 1931. Emigration From Great Britain, in *International Migrations, Vol. 2: Interpretations*, edited by W. F. Willcox, pp. 239–60. New York: National Bureau of Economic Research.

Soja, Edward W. 1989. *Postmodern Geographies: The Reassertion of Space in Critical Social*

Theory. London: Verso.

Sorohan, Sean. 2012. *Irish London During the Troubles*. Dublin: Irish Academic Press.

Southern, Neil. 2005. Ian Paisley and Evangelical Democratic Unionists: An analysis of the role of Evangelical Protestantism Within the Democratic Unionist Party. *Irish Political Studies* 20 (2): 127–45.

———. 2007. Protestant Alienation in Northern Ireland: A Political, Cultural and Geographical Examination. *Journal of Ethnic and Migration Studies* 33 (1): 159–80.

Southworth, Joanna R. 2005. 'Religion' in the 2001 Census for England and Wales. *Population Space and Place* 11 (2): 75–88.

Soysal, Y. N. 2000. Citizenship and Identity: Living in Diasporas in Post-War Europe? *Ethnic and Racial Studies* 23(1): 1–15.

Spender, Edward Harold. 1925. Will the Empire Hold Together? *Contemporary Review* 127: 409–16.

Spicer, Keith (ed.). 1991. *Citizen's Forum on Canada's Future: Report to the People and Government of Canada* [Spicer Commission]. Ottawa: Supply and Services Canada.

Spiers, E. M. 1996. Army Organisation and Society in the Nineteenth Century, in *A Military History of Ireland*, edited by Thomas Bartlett and Keith Jeffery, pp. 335–57. Cambridge: Cambridge University Press.

Sriskandarajah, Dhananjayan and Catherine Drew. 2006. *Brits Abroad: Mapping the Scale and Nature of British Emigration*. London: Institute for Public Policy Research.

Staudinger, Ursula M. 2001. Life Reflection: A Social-Cognitive Analysis of Life Review. *Review of General Psychology* 5(2): 148–60.

Stevenson, Clifford, Susan Condor and Jackie Abell. 2007. The Majority–Minority Conundrum in Northern Ireland: An Orange Order Perspective. *Political Psychology* 28 (1): 105–25.

Stevenson, J. A. 1923. The Latest Canadian Census. *Edinburgh Review* 237 (484): 340–53.

Stewart, A. T. Q. 1977. *The Narrow Ground: Aspects of Ulster, 1609–1969*. London: Faber.

Stillwell, J., P. Rees and P. Boden. 1992. Internal Migration Trends: An Overview, in *Migration Processes and Patterns, Vol. 2: Population Redistribution in the United Kingdom*, edited by J. Stillwell, P. Rees and P. Boden, pp. 28–55. London: Bellhaven Press.

Storhaug, Hans. 2003. European Return Migration: Numbers, Reasons and Consequences. *AEMI Journal* 1: 69–77.

Stout, Matthew. 1996. The Geography and Implications of Post-Famine Population Decline in Baltyboys, County Wicklow, in *Fearful Realities: New Perspectives on the Famine*, edited by Chris Morash and Robert Hayes, pp. 15–34. Dublin: Irish Academic Press.

Swaffer, Spencer. 1947. Operation 'New Horizon': Ontario Government's Scheme of Air Immigration From Britain. *Flight*, 6 November, pp. 532–3.

Swift, Roger. 2009. Identifying the Irish in Victorian Britain: Recent Trends in Historiography. *Immigrants and Minorities* 27 (2/3): 134–51.

Tajfel, Henri. 1981. *Human Groups and Social Categories: Studies in Social Psychology*. Cambridge: Cambridge University Press.

Task Force on Emigrants (Ireland). 2002. *Ireland and the Irish Abroad: Report of the Task Force on Policy Regarding Emigrants to the Minister for Foreign Affairs Mr Brian Cowen, TD, Dublin.*

Taylor, Charles. 1992. The Politics of Recognition, in *Multiculturalism and 'The Politics of Recognition'*, edited by A. Gutmann, pp. 25–73. Princeton: Princeton University Press.

——. 1996. Deep Diversity and the Future of Canada. *Transactions of the Royal Society of Canada*, 6th Series (7): 29–35.

Tennant, Lorraine M. 1988. Ulster Emigration 1851–1914. MPhil. Thesis, Faculty of Humanities, University of Ulster, Coleraine.

Tennant, Victoria. 2000. *Sanctuary in a Cell: The Detention of Asylum Seekers in Northern Ireland.* Belfast: Law Centre NI.

Terchek, Ronald J. 1984. Options to Stress: Emigration and Militancy in Northern Ireland. *Social Indicators Research* 15 (4): 369–87.

'T Hart, Marjolein. 1985. Irish Return Migration in the Nineteenth Century. *Tidjschrift voor Economische en Sociale Geografie* 76 (3): 223–31.

Thomas, Derek. 2010. Foreign Nationals Working Temporarily in Canada. *Canadian Social Trends* (8 June): 34–48.

Thomsen, Dorthe Kirkegaard. 2009. There is More to Life Stories than Memories. *Memory* 17 (4): 445–57.

—— and Dorthe Berntsen. 2008. The Cultural Life Script and Life Story Chapters Contribute to the Reminiscence Bump. *Memory* 16 (4): 420–36.

Thomson, Alistair. 1999. Moving Stories: Oral History and Migration Studies. *Oral History* 27 (1): 24–37.

——. 2003. 'I live on My Memories': British Return Migrants and the Possession of the Past. *Oral History* 31 (2): 55–65.

——. 2005. 'My Wayward Heart': Homesickness, Longing and the Return of British Post-War Immigrants From Australia, in *Emigrant Homecomings: The Return Movement of Emigrants 1600–2000*, edited by M. Harper, pp. 105–30. Manchester: Manchester University Press.

——. 2007. Four Paradigm Transformations in Oral History. *Oral History Review* 34 (1): 49–70.

Threlfall, Emily. 2003. *Sanctuary in a Cell Update: The Detention of Asylum Seekers in Northern Ireland: A Progress Report.* Belfast: Law Centre NI.

Tilki, Mary. 1994. Ethnic Irish Older People. *British Journal of Nursing* 3 (17): 909–13.

——, Eddie Mulligan, Ellen Pratt, Ellen Halley and Eileen Taylor. 2010. Older Irish People with Dementia in England. *Advances in Mental Health* 9 (3): 221–32.

——, Louise Ryan, Alessio D'Angelo and Rosemary Sales. 2009. *The Forgotten Irish: Report of a Research Project Commissioned by The Ireland Fund of Great Britain.* London: Social Policy Research Centre, Middlesex University.

Todd, Jennifer. 2007. Introduction: National Identity in Transition? Moving Out of Conflict in Northern Ireland. *Nations and Nationalism* 13 (4): 565–71.

——, Theresa O'Keefe, Nathalie Rougier and Lorenzo Cañás Bottos. 2006. Fluid or Frozen? Choice and Change in Ethno-National Identification in Contemporary

Northern Ireland. *Nationalism and Ethnic Politics* 12 (3/4): 323–46.

——, Nathalie Rougier, Theresa O'Keefe and Lorenzo Cañás Bottos. 2009. Does Being Protestant Matter? Protestants, Minorities and the Remaking of Ethno-Religious Identity After the Good Friday Agreement. *National Identities* 11 (1): 87–99.

Tolia–Kelly, Divya P. 2006. A Journey Through the Material Geographies of Diaspora Cultures: Four Modes of Environmental Memory, in *Histories and Memories: Migrants and their History in Britain*, edited by K. Burrell and P. Panayi, pp. 149–70. London: Tauris Academic Studies.

Torrance, Judy M. 1986. *Public Violence in Canada: 1867–1982*. Kingston: McGill-Queen's University Press.

Tötölyan, Khachig. 1996. Rethinking Diaspora(s): Stateless Power in the Transnational Moment. *Diaspora* 5 (1): 3–36.

Trew, J. D. 2002. Conflicting Visions: Don Messer, Liberal Nationalism and the Canadian Unity Debate. *International Journal of Canadian Studies* 26: 41–58.

——. 2005a. Challenging Utopia: Irish Migrant Narratives of Canada. *Canadian Journal of Irish Studies* 27 (2): 108–16.

——. 2005b. The Forgotten Irish? Contested Sites and Narratives of Nation in Newfoundland. *Ethnologies* 27 (2): 43–77.

——. 2007. Negotiating Identity and Belonging: Migration Narratives of Protestants From Northern Ireland. *Immigrants and Minorities* 25 (1): 22–48.

——. 2009a. Migration in Childhood and its Impact on National Identity Construction Among Migrants from Northern Ireland. *Irish Studies Review* 17 (3): 297–314.

——. 2009b. *Place, Culture and Community: The Irish Heritage of the Ottawa Valley*. Newcastle: CSP.

——. 2010. Reluctant Diasporas of Northern Ireland: Migrant Narratives of Home, Conflict, Difference. *Journal of Ethnic and Migration Studies* 36 (4): 541–60.

Tsuda, Takeyuki, 2009. Introduction: Diasporic Return and Migration Studies, in *Diasporic Homecomings: Ethnic Return Migration in Comparative Perspective*, edited by T. Tsuda, pp. 1–18. Palo Alto: Stanford University Press.

Ulster Historical Foundation. 2007. *Fifty Years of the Ulster Historical Foundation 1956–2006*. Belfast: Ulster Historical Foundation.

Vallely, Fintan. 2008. *Tuned Out: Traditional Music and Identity in Northern Ireland*. Cork: Cork University Press.

van Rijswijk, Wendy, Nick Hopkins and Hannah Johnston. 2009. The Role of Social Categorization and Identity Threat in the Perception of Migrants. *Journal of Community and Applied Social Psychology* 19 (6): 515–20.

Vann, Barry Aron. 2008. *In Search of Ulster-Scots Land: The Birth and Geotheological Imagings of a Transatlantic People, 1603–1703*. Columbia: University of South Carolina Press.

Vaughan, W. E. and A. J. Fitzpatrick. 1978. *Irish Historical Statistics: Population, 1821–1971*. Dublin: Royal Irish Academy.

Vertovec, Steven. 2009. *Transnationalism*. London: Routledge.

Walker, Brian. 2007. 'The Lost Tribes of Ireland': Diversity, Identity and Loss Among the Irish Diaspora. *Irish Studies Review* 15 (3): 267–82.

Wallace, Martin. 1971. *Northern Ireland: 50 Years of Self-Government*. Newton Abbott: David and Charles.

Walls, Patricia. 1996. *Researching Irish Mental Health: Issues and Evidence, a Study of the Mental Health of the Irish Community in Haringey*. London: Muintearas.

——. 2005. *Still Leaving: Recent, Vulnerable Irish Emigrants to the UK: Profile, Experiences and Pre-Departure Solutions*. Dublin: Emigrant Advice Bureau.

—— and Rory Williams. 2003. Sectarianism at Work: Accounts of Employment Discrimination Against Irish Catholics in Scotland. *Ethnic and Racial Studies* 26 (4): 632–61.

Walsh, Brendan. 1974. Expectations, Information and Human Migration: Specifying an Econometric Model of Irish Migration to Britain. *Journal of Regional Science* 14 (1): 107–20.

Walsh, James J. and Fergus P. McGrath. 2000. Identity, Coping Style and Health Behaviour Amongst First-Generation Irish Immigrants to England. *Psychology and Health* 15: 467–82.

Walter, Bronwen. 1988. *Irish Women in London*. London: London Strategic Policy Unit.

——. 1998. Challenging the Black/White Binary: The Need for an Irish Category in the 2001 Census. *Patterns of Prejudice* 32 (2): 73–86.

——. 2001. *Outsiders Inside: Whiteness, Place and Irish Women*. London: Routledge.

——. 2004. Invisible Irishness: Second-Generation Identities in Britain. *AEMI Journal* 2: 185–93.

——. 2008a. From 'Flood' to 'Trickle': Irish Migration to Britain 1987–2006. *Irish Geography* 41 (2): 181–94.

——. 2008b. Voices in Other Ears: 'Accents' and Identities of the First- and Second-Generation Irish in England, in *Neo-Colonial Mentalities in Contemporary Europe? Language and Discourse in the Construction of Identities*, edited by G. Rings and A. Ife, pp. 174–82. Newcastle: CSP.

——. 2011. Whiteness and Diasporic Irishness: Nation, Gender and Class. *Journal of Ethnic and Migration Studies* 37 (9): 1295–312.

——, Sarah Morgan, Mary J. Hickman and Joseph Bradley. 2002. Family Stories, Public Silence: Irish Identity Construction Among the Second Generation in England. *Scottish Geographical Journal* 118 (3): 201–17.

Walters, Johanna L. 2009. Immigration, Transnationalism and 'Flexible Citizenship' in Canada: Ong's Thesis Ten Years On. *Tidjschrift voor Economische en Sociale Geografie* 100 (5): 635–45.

Webb, James H. 2004. *Born Fighting: How the Scots-Irish Shaped America*. New York: Broadway Books.

Wellings, Ben. 2007. Rump Britain: Englishness and Britishness, 1992–2001. *National Identities* 9 (4): 395–412.

Wells, Ronald A. 1981. The Voice of Empire: The *Daily Mail* and British Emigration to North America. *Historian* 43 (2): 240–57.

——. 1991. *Ulster Migration to America: Letters From Three Irish Families*. New York:

Peter Lang.

Whelan, B. J. and J. G. Hughes. 1976. *A Survey of Returned and Intending Emigrants in Ireland*. Dublin: ESRI.

White, Ian. 2012. A Brief History of the Census in Ireland/Northern Ireland, in *Registrar General Report for Northern Ireland 2011*, pp. 35–68. Belfast: NISRA.

White, Richard. 1998. *Remembering Ahanagran: Storytelling in a Family's Past*. New York: Hill and Wang.

Whyte, John H. 1990. *Interpreting Northern Ireland*. Oxford: Clarendon Press.

Wild, S. and P. McKeigue. 1997. Cross-Sectional Analysis of Mortality by Country of Birth in England and Wales. *British Medical Journal* 314: 705–10.

Wilkes, Rima and Catherine Corrigall-Brown. 2011. Explaining Time Trends in Public Opinion: Attitudes Towards Immigration and Immigrants. *International Journal of Comparative Sociology* 52 (1/2): 79–99.

Willcox, Walter F. 1929. *International Migrations, Vol. 1: Statistics*. New York: National Bureau of Economic Research.

Williams, Fiona. 1987. The Black Pig and Linear Earthworks. *Emania: Bulletin of the Navan Research Group* 3 (August): 12–19.

Williams, Rory. 1992. The Health of the Irish in Britain, in *The Politics of Race and Health*, edited by W. Ahmad, pp. 81–103. Bradford: Race Relations Unit.

—— and Russell Ecob. 1999. Regional Mortality and the Irish in Britain: Findings From the ONS Longitudinal Study. *Sociology of Health and Illness* 21: 344–67.

Wilson, Andrew J. 1995. *Irish–America and the Ulster Conflict, 1968–1995*. Washington: Catholic University of America Press.

——. 1997. From the Beltway to Belfast: The Clinton Administration, Sinn Féin, and the Northern Ireland Peace Process. *New Hibernia Review* 1 (3): 23–39.

——. 2000. The Billy Boys Meet Slick Willy: The Ulster Unionist Party and the American Dimension to the Northern Ireland Peace Process, 1994–1999. *Irish Studies in International Affairs* 11: 121–36.

Wilson, David A. (ed.). 2007. *The Orange Order in Canada*. Dublin: Four Courts Press.

—— and Mark G. Spencer (eds). 2006. *Ulster Presbyterians in the Atlantic World: Religion, Politics and Identity*. Dublin: Four Courts Press.

Wilson, Robin. 2010. *Distant Voices, Shaken Lives: Human Stories of Immigration Detention From Northern Ireland*. Belfast: Refugee Action Group.

Winter, Elke. 2011. 'Immigrants Don't Ask for Self-Government': How Multiculturalism is (De)Legitimized in Multinational Societies. *Ethnopolitics* 10 (2): 187–204.

Woodburn, James B. 1914. *The Ulster Scot: His History and Religion*. London: H. R. Allenson.

Woods, Vincent. 1998. At the Black Pig's Dyke [play], in *Far From the Land*, edited by J. Fairleigh. London: Methuen.

Wyman, Mark. 1993. *Round-Trip to America: The Immigrants Return to Europe, 1880–1930*. Ithaca: Cornell University Press.

——. 2005. Emigrants Returning: The Evolution of a Tradition, in *Emigrant Homecomings: The Return Movement of Emigrants 1600–2000*, edited by M. Harper, pp. 16–31.

Manchester: Manchester University Press.

Wyn Jones, Richard, Guy Lodge, Ailsa Henderson and Daniel Wincott. 2012. *The Dog That Finally Barked: England as an Emerging Political Community*. London: IPPR.

List of Interviews

VMR no.	Interviewee name (may be pseudonym)	Location of interview	Interview date
VMR–001	Angela	Omagh	09/07/04 and 05/01/05
VMR–002	Eamonn	Dublin	15–16/07/04
VMR–003	Sean	Omagh	09/08/04
VMR–004	Ellen	Ballyshannon, Co. Donegal	13/08/04
VMR–005	Eilish	Derry	16/08/04
VMR–006	Ena	Derry	16/08/04
VMR–007	Mark	Burtonport, Co. Donegal	17/08/04
VMR–008	William	Gortin, Co. Tyrone	07/09/04
VMR–009	Anthony	Ballyshannon, Co. Donegal	14/09/04
VMR–010	Sharon	Cookstown, Co. Tyrone	16/09/04
VMR–011	Alex	Whitehead, Co. Antrim	30/09/04
VMR–012	Ken	Omagh	05/10/04
VMR–013	Rose	Gortin, Co. Tyrone	12/10/04
VMR–014	Don	Omagh	18/10/04
VMR–015	Stephen	Belfast	22/10/04
VMR–016	Christine	Belfast	22/10/04
VMR–017	Seamus	Strabane, Co. Tyrone	02/11/04
VMR–018	Roy	Belfast	12/11/04
VMR–019	Bríd	Belfast	13/11/04
VMR–020	Patrick	Gortin, Co. Tyrone	20/11/04
VMR–021	David	Omagh	06/12/04
VMR–022	Gary	Omagh	07/12/04
VMR–023	Kathleen	Manorhamilton, Co. Leitrim	06/01/05
VMR–024	Ciaran	Omagh	27/01/05
VMR–025	Freddie	Ballymoney, Co. Antrim	02/02/05
VMR–026	Mona	Monaghan	15/02/05
VMR–027	Niall	Newcastle, Co. Down	16/02/05
VMR–028	Nick	Omagh	01/03/05

VMR no.	Interviewee name (may be pseudonym)	Location of interview	Interview date
VMR–029	Alan	Belfast	09/03/05
VMR–030	Marie	Omagh	16/03/05
VMR–031	Julia	Co. Fermanagh	29/03/05
VMR–032	Victor	Co. Fermanagh	21/04/05
VMR–033	Fergal	Omagh	01/04/05
VMR–034	Susan	Belfast	07/04/05
VMR–035	Stewart	Derry	12/04/05
VMR–036	Una	Larne, Co. Antrim	18/04/05
VMR–037	Teresa	South Down	19/04/05
VMR–038	Denis	Belfast	19/04/05
VMR–039	Jim	Carrickfergus, Co. Antrim	25/04/05
VMR–040	Elizabeth	Carrickfergus, Co. Antrim	25/04/05
VMR–041	Eugene	Belfast	26/04/05
VMR–042	Deirdre	Strabane, Co. Tyrone	19/05/05
VMR–043	Harry	Armagh	30/06/05
VMR–044	Brendan	Omagh	18/01/06
VMR–045	Robert	Kilkeel, Co. Down	28/05/06
VMR–046	Michael	Bangor, Co. Down	11/07/06
VMR–047	Barry	Liverpool	11/07/06
VMR–048	Sam	Liverpool	12/07/06
VMR–049	Paula	Liverpool	12/07/06
VMR–050	Jane	Liverpool	13/07/06
VMR–051	Andrew	Liverpool	13/07/06
VMR–052	Laura	Liverpool	13/07/06
VMR–053	Steve	Liverpool	14/07/06
VMR–054	Brian	Liverpool	14/07/06
VMR–055	Shane	Liverpool	14/07/06
VMR–056	Orla	Liverpool	15/07/06
VMR–057	Liz	Holywood, Co. Down	07/08/06
VMR–058	Siobhan	Omagh	14/08/06
VMR–059	Bill	Toronto	13/09/06
VMR–060	Stan	Toronto	14/09/06
VMR–061	John	Toronto	15/09/06
VMR–062	Michael	Toronto	15/09/06

VMR no.	Interviewee name (may be pseudonym)	Location of interview	Interview date
VMR–063	Kevin	Toronto	15/09/06
VMR–064	Craig	Toronto	16/09/06
VMR–065	Pamela	Toronto	17/09/06
VMR–066	Susannah	Kitchener, Ontario	18/09/06
VMR–067	Larry	Guelph, Ontario	19/09/06
VMR–068	Martin, Cas and Colette	Windsor, Ontario	20/09/06
VMR–069	Eve	Toronto	21/09/06
VMR–070	Margaret	Toronto	22/09/06
VMR–071	Herb and Edith	Toronto	23/09/06
VMR–072	Richard	Toronto	24/09/06
VMR–073	Fergus	Belleville, Ontario	25/09/06
VMR–074	Heather	Ottawa	28/09/06
VMR–075	Jack and Shirley	Ottawa	29/09/06
VMR–076	Terry	London	13/02/07
VMR–077	David	London	13/02/07
VMR–078	Aimie	Colchester, Essex	14/02/07
VMR–079	Eileen	London	14/02/07
VMR–080	Imelda and Lily	London	15/02/07
VMR–081	Rosemary	London	16/02/07
VMR–082	Gary	London	16/02/07
VMR–083	Mary	West Sussex	17/02/07
VMR–084	Chris	Ballynahinch, Co. Down	07/03/07
VMR–085	Sheila	Denman Island, B.C.	28/03/07
VMR–086	Peter	Omagh	27/04/07
VMR–087	Pat	Belfast	23/11/07
VMR–088	Agniezska	Omagh	03/06/10

Index

Printed and bound by CPI Group (UK) Ltd, Croydon, CR0 4YY

13/04/2025

14656573-0007